AP English Literature & Composition For Dummies®

Cheat Sheet

What to Bring on Exam Day

The College Board has more security precautions than you could ever imagine. The CIA could learn from it! Your AP proctor will limit what you can bring into the test room. Specifically, you're allowed the following items:

- ❑ Sharpened #2 pencils with good erasers for the multiple-choice scan sheet
- ❑ Pens with dark blue or black ink
- ❑ Your school or home-schooling code number and a photo ID
- ❑ A watch that doesn't beep, burp, ring, or give you the answers
- ❑ The SSD Accommodation letter, if you're allowed accommodations for special needs
- ❑ Your mind (Whatever you do, don't forget this one!)

Useful Literary Terms for the Exam

These terms are useful when you write about literature:

Conflict: The struggle or fight in a literary work (may be external or internal)

Diction: Word choice

Dynamic and static characters: Dynamic characters change, but static characters don't

Enjambment: Ending a line of poetry without a punctuation mark so that the reader continues to the next line

Metaphor: An implied comparison

Meter: The rhythm created by a pattern of stressed and unstressed syllables in a poem

Narrator: The character who tells the story in a prose work

Personification: Giving human qualities to a nonhuman entity

Protagonist: The most important character

Rhyme: Matching sounds at the end of a line or within a line

Simile: A comparison using "like" or "as"

Speaker: The I/me/my voice in a poem

Stanza: A unit of a poem

Syntax: The grammatical relationship between parts of a sentence

Tone: The attitude of the author or a character within a literary work

Poetry Analysis Questions to Consider

In the best poetry, meaning and style work together. And high-scoring AP poetry essays explain the connection between the two. Also, don't forget that many of the multiple-choice questions ask about the relationship between style and meaning. Here's what to look for when you're reading a poem on the AP English exam or anywhere else:

- ✔ **How does the poem sound?** Does it have a regular beat or a rhythmic pattern? Do you hear rhymes? Are any words linked by similar sounds? Do the sounds emphasize certain ideas and downplay others? Can you imagine an emotion or a quality tied to the sound — innocence, complexity, sadness, jubilation?

- ✔ **How does the poem look?** Is it divided into stanzas or presented as a whole? Where do the lines break? What about the margins? Does the appearance of the poem reflect divisions of the main idea of the poem? What's connected or disconnected by the line and stanza breaks?

- ✔ **What setting, story, or situation is in the poem?** What details has the poet included or omitted? What words convey the content? Is the vocabulary simple or

sophisticated? How about the sentences? Do you see complicated or easy sentence structure? How do word choice and sentence structure reinforce the ideas in the poem? Are any characters present?

- ✔ **How imaginative or literal is the language in the poem?** If the poet employs figures of speech, do they relate to the themes of the poem? If they clash, why did the poet create a contrast?

- ✔ **What's the tone?** Can you imagine hearing the poet read the poem? What attitude does the poet have? Does the attitude differ from that of any characters in the poem? Why is the distance there?

For Dummies: Bestselling Book Series for Beginners

AP English Literature & Composition For Dummies®

Cheat Sheet

AP Multiple-Choice Plan of Attack

Follow these tips when you're answering AP multiple-choice questions:

- ✔ Read and annotate the passage.
- ✔ Determine what the questions are asking.
- ✔ Do the easy questions first.
- ✔ Eliminate wrong choices, and guess if you have two or three possible answers.
- ✔ Skip questions that completely stump you.

Checklist for Fantastic AP Essays

If you want to score high on the AP essays, be sure to do the following when you're writing them:

- ❑ Answer the question.
- ❑ State a thesis.
- ❑ Include evidence from the literary work.
- ❑ Create a logical structure.
- ❑ Display good grammar and a polished writing style.

Outline for Your Open-Ended Essay

Use this form to keep track of your reading, especially works that you may want to write about for the open-ended essay. (See Chapter 14 for more information on the open-ended essay.)

Title:

Author:

Date of Publication or Writing:

Main Characters:

Setting:

Important Plot Points:

Themes and Symbols:

Important Quotations:

For Dummies: Bestselling Book Series for Beginners

AP English Literature & Composition

FOR DUMMIES®

by Geraldine Woods

WILEY

Wiley Publishing, Inc.

AP English Literature & Composition For Dummies®

Published by
Wiley Publishing, Inc.
111 River St.
Hoboken, NJ 07030-5774
www.wiley.com

Copyright © 2008 by Wiley Publishing, Inc., Indianapolis, Indiana

Published simultaneously in Canada

For general information on our other products and services, please contact our Customer Care Department within the U.S. at 800-762-2974, outside the U.S. at 317-572-3993, or fax 317-572-4002.

For technical support, please visit www.wiley.com/techsupport.

Wiley also publishes its books in a variety of electronic formats. Some content that appears in print may not be available in electronic books.

Library of Congress Control Number: 2007942001

ISBN: 978-0-470-19425-6

Manufactured in the United States of America

10 9 8 7 6 5 4 3 2 1

WILEY

About the Author

Geraldine Woods has taught and tutored every level of English from 5th grade through AP for the past three decades. She's the author of more than 40 books, including numerous books published by Wiley: *English Grammar For Dummies, English Grammar Workbook For Dummies, Research Papers For Dummies, College Admissions Essays For Dummies, SAT I For Dummies*, and *Punctuation: Simplified and Applied.*

Dedication

To Paul, whom I've always known and am still getting to know.

Author's Acknowledgments

I offer sincere thanks to these poets, playwrights, and novelists, who spin words into beauty: John Allman, Dana Crum, Dave Johnson, Hettie Jones, and Abigail Wender. I also acknowledge a debt of gratitude to the wonderful students who graciously allowed me to print their essays in this book: Emily Gerard, Jessica A. Moldovan, Sophia Shapiro, and Peter Weinberg. I appreciate the unfailing help and good humor of Kristin DeMint, Stacy Kennedy, Joyce Pepple, and Jessica Smith of Wiley Publishing, as well as my technical reviewer, David P. Wetta of York Community High School in Elmhurst, IL. Finally, thanks are due to my supportive and wise agent, Lisa Queen of Queen Literary.

Publisher's Acknowledgments

We're proud of this book; please send us your comments through our Dummies online registration form located at www.dummies.com/register/.

Some of the people who helped bring this book to market include the following:

Acquisitions, Editorial, and Media Development

Project Editor: Kristin DeMint

Acquisitions Editor: Stacy Kennedy

Copy Editor: Jessica Smith

Editorial Program Coordinator: Erin Calligan Mooney

Technical Editor: David P. Wetta

Editorial Manager: Michelle Hacker

Editorial Assistants: Joe Niesen, Leeann Harney

Cover Photos: © Getty Images

Cartoons: Rich Tennant (www.the5thwave.com)

Composition Services

Project Coordinator: Lynsey Osborn

Layout and Graphics: Claudia Bell, Stacie Brooks, Carrie A. Cesavice, Brooke Graczyk, Stephanie D. Jumper, Christine Williams

Proofreaders: John Greenough, Evelyn W. Still

Indexer: Potomac Indexing LLC

Publishing and Editorial for Consumer Dummies

Diane Graves Steele, Vice President and Publisher, Consumer Dummies

Joyce Pepple, Acquisitions Director, Consumer Dummies

Kristin A. Cocks, Product Development Director, Consumer Dummies

Michael Spring, Vice President and Publisher, Travel

Kelly Regan, Editorial Director, Travel

Publishing for Technology Dummies

Andy Cummings, Vice President and Publisher, Dummies Technology/General User

Composition Services

Gerry Fahey, Vice President of Production Services

Debbie Stailey, Director of Composition Services

Contents at a Glance

Table of Contents

Introduction

*A*P English Literature & Composition For Dummies prepares you for — you guessed it — the AP Literature and Composition Exam (not to be confused with the AP English *Language* and Composition exam, which covers all-purpose, general writing on current events, personal experience, and culture). This exam is a product of the College Board, a not-for-profit outfit based in Princeton, New Jersey. The College Board is the group of educators and educational institutions that administers the SAT, the PSAT/NMSQT, and other laugh-a-minute hurdles that you face before entering college. "AP" stands for "advanced placement," which means that anyone passing the exam has demonstrated college-level achievement before actually entering an ivy-covered building. In other words, the AP label is for serious brainwork.

Did I scare you? Calm down. AP material is tough, but it's also teachable. You don't have to be a natural-born literary genius to score well on the AP English exam. You just have to scrape the rust off your thinking cap and do some of the exercises in this book. In fact, you don't even have to go through all the exercises. (You'll still have some time to download some music and chat with your friends.) After you get acquainted with the AP exam format and brush up on your reading and writing skills, you can score big on the AP English Literature and Composition exam.

Most people taking an AP exam spend a year in an AP course, probably in a real classroom but increasingly in virtual, online courses. However, you can take the exam even if you've never taken an official AP course — the test is available to all those willing to glue themselves to uncomfortable chairs, spit out answers, and pay the exam fee. Homeschoolers and people resuming their education after time away from school (welcome back!) can also take the AP English Literature and Composition exam.

AP English courses are generally souped-up versions of regular junior or senior English classes, with extra reading and writing assignments and perhaps tougher grading standards. Again, not to worry. With *AP English Literature & Composition For Dummies* you can prepare for both the course and the exam because most assignments and tests in the AP English course closely resemble the work you have to do on the AP English exam.

If you're a fairly good English student — and if you aren't, this book will help you sharpen your skills — you'll find that the AP English Literature and Composition exam isn't much more difficult than the tests you've faced in English class before. In fact, in some ways it may even be easier than the exams you're used to. All AP exams are designed by experts with tons of time to check the clarity of every question — not by the average classroom teacher who has to create essay and multiple choice questions while doing the wash, finding a renewable caffeine source, and walking the dog. Oh, and did I mention that classroom teachers have to correct the tests and homework they gave last week too, even as they spin out new questions? No wonder so many English tests are punctuated by announcements such as "In section four, choice D should read "Homer's *Odyssey*," not "Homer's Simpson." The AP English Literature and Composition exam taxes your brain, but at least it's fair and accurate.

About This Book

After a quick overview of the exam and a crash course on timelines and strategies for test preparation, this book hits each of the *genres* (types) of literature covered on the exam. Within each genre, I review the basic elements and tell you what to look for when you're reading. I also show you how to keep track of what you found — important events, characters, themes, and elements of style. To improve your literary skills — and grades! — even more, I detail the easiest strategies for writing an essay about poetry, prose, and dramatic works.

I also explain the general format of the most common multiple-choice questions for each genre. I give you a step-by-step method for approaching each type of multiple-choice question and supply examples and explanations. Next I tackle the essays you may have to write on a literary text from each genre. I help you decode the *prompt* — the English-teacher term for the essay question you have to answer — and show you how to gather evidence and formulate a thesis. After you've figured out how to approach multiple-choice and essay questions, I hit you with a practice chapter complete with answers and explanations. I also throw in chapters on two types of AP questions that require special approaches: the paired-passages essay and the open-ended essay. Finally, I offer two complete AP English tests, complete with answers, explanations, and scoring guides, so you can see how you're doing.

Conventions Used in This Book

In this book, I used the Auto-Parts Distributors Convention and the Flat-Earth Society Convention to road-test the practice exams. No, not really. The conventions I used are fairly simple to grasp:

- When I tell you about a Web site, I use `monofont` to indicate the address.
- **Bold** text highlights key words in bulleted lists and the action parts of numbered steps.
- Anytime I define a term, I set that term in *italics*. Literary terminology isn't as prominent on the AP as it used to be, but some words still appear, and you should know them.

What You're Not To Read

As an English teacher I find it almost impossible to restrict anyone's reading. But as a human being who often needs 25 hours in a day, even without time for little luxuries such as eating and sleeping, I understand that you may skip some things in this book. So if you need to skip anything, jump over the sidebars. They contain interesting information, but you certainly don't need them in order to pass the test.

Foolish Assumptions

Years ago I taught a great kid named Ralph. Ralph, though only ten at the time, was smart, creative, and skeptical. "Oh yeah? Show me!" was his basic attitude toward life. When I wrote this book, I imagined Ralph, only older and wiser. These are the assumptions that I made about Ralph and about you, the reader:

✔ You plan to take the AP English Literature and Composition exam within a year, and you want to be prepared.

✔ Even if you're enrolled in an AP English course, you'd like a little extra practice or a chance to refresh your reading comprehension and writing skills with this book.

✔ You have a life, so you have no time for longwinded, meaningless explanations.

✔ You have already read a lot of high-quality literature in your English classes, and you've done some writing about these works.

✔ You have a reasonable grasp of English grammar.

How This Book Is Organized

To help you navigate through this book quickly and easily, I organized similar chapters into parts — seven of them. Here's a quick description of each.

Part I: Hamlet Hits the Answer Grid: An Overview of the AP Lit Exam and Prep

You don't want to walk into the AP English Literature and Composition exam and say the equivalent of "Hi, my name is Fred and you are . . . ?" The exam should be an old friend, with no surprises in store. This part explains everything: what the test looks like, how much time you have, even how to sign up. I also tell you how to get ready no matter how much time you have before the exam. And for you "I-work-only-under-pressure" types, I describe the best way to spend the last weeks and the night before the exam. Finally, I give you some tips on getting the most out of your English class. A good score on the AP exam is valuable, but so is a high grade in your English course!

Part II: Poetry in Motion

I happen to have thousands of favorite poems, but I recognize that not every reader is as nuts about verse as I am. Whether you like poetry or not, in this part I help you decode a poem, dig for deeper meanings, and recognize elements of poetic style. I show you how to ace multiple-choice poetry questions and how to compose a great essay on a poetry selection. Then I give you tons of practice questions, all with answers and explanations.

Part III: Getting the Story from Prose and Drama

The AP English exam throws bits of novels, memoirs, essays, and plays at you and then asks you to figure out what's what. So you won't feel as if you're being thrown to the wolves, I tell you what kind of prose and drama passages you may meet on the exam and what sorts of questions to expect. Then I take you through every type of passage, explain the best approach to each one, and give you practice, practice, and then, for a change of pace, more practice.

Part IV: Paired Passages and the Open-Ended Essay

Okay, I admit it: These two types of questions are together in this part because they don't fit anywhere else. They're too weird, so I put them here so they can be weird together and find happiness at last. *Paired passages* are two literary selections placed side by side in the same question. You may have to write a compare/contrast essay about the duo. The *open-ended essay* gives you some elbow room; you get to choose a work to write about. This part provides tips, strategies, and all kinds of helpful information about this fairly important chunk of the test, along with sample questions and answers.

Part V: Dress Rehearsal: Practice Exams

Here you hit the big time — two full-length AP English Literature and Composition exams. These tests aren't from the College Board, which understandably is sitting on the rights to its own material. I wrote these tests, but they're close enough to the official exam to prepare you well for test day, which surprisingly isn't a national holiday. Each exam is accompanied by a chapter of answers, explanations, and scoring guides.

Part VI: The Part of Tens

This wouldn't be a *For Dummies* book without a part of tens. In this part, I explain the ten ways to kill your essay score and the ten ways to improve your English skills without studying. Even though these chapters are short, sweet, and to the point, they're chock-full of useful information.

Part VII: Appendixes

Which literary works should you choose for the open-ended essay? Which ones reward you with great stories, amazingly beautiful writing, and incredible originality? Check out Appendix A to find out. Nervous about your grammar skills? Check out Appendix B for a lightning-fast review.

Icons Used in This Book

No, I didn't design these cute little drawings myself, but I love them all the same. In this book you find four icons, each of which functions like a tap on the shoulder, alerting you to an important point. Here's what they mean.

You can't learn to ride a bike unless you actually have a bike. Similarly, you can't learn to answer questions or to recognize elements of literature unless you see some examples. This icon alerts you to a sample question that resembles those on the actual exam.

The souvenir you take home is sometimes the best part of vacation. This icon identifies the most essential ideas — the ones you want to "take home" and make a part of your life.

Want to make your life easier when you study AP English and take the exam? I thought so. Check out this icon for a little grease to smooth the path to success.

Heading for a cliff? This icon tells you how to swerve and avoid a fall in your score.

Where to Go From Here

In writing this book, I cover all the bases — poetry, fiction and nonfiction prose, and drama. I provide practice in both multiple-choice and essay questions. But you don't have to touch every base in order to hit a homerun on the AP English exam. So don't feel like you have to read chapters that contain info you already know. Think about your skills as an English student, and then follow the table of contents to find guidance and practice for your weakest points. For instance, if you aren't sure what the test is like, check out Part I. If you need more poetry experience, turn to Part II. Or, if everything's a blur and you aren't sure where to begin, try Practice Exam 1 in Chapter 16. Score it with help from Chapter 17, analyze your performance, and then hit the sections that address the topics that you didn't know. And remember: No matter what, June inevitably follows May, and the test *will* be over someday.

Part I

Hamlet Hits the Answer Grid: An Overview of the AP Lit Exam and Prep

The 5th Wave   By Rich Tennant

"Oh, Will — such passion, such pathos, such despair and redemption. I've never read a more moving grocery list."

In this part . . .

Get ready to read this part like a racer. In Chapter 1, you're in the starting block, scanning the track, checking out what's where, and sneaking a glance at the trophy awaiting you at the finish line. In other words, Chapter 1 tells you everything you need to know about the AP English Literature and Composition exam — what the test is like, how to sign up, and whether you should take an AP English Literature class. Chapter 2 is all about time and is aimed at both marathoners and sprinters. It explains how to hone your skills in reading and writing if you have a few months or more to prepare for the AP exam, if you're reading this book only a week or so before the exam, or even (gulp!) the night before. Chapter 3 addresses overall fitness. I tell you how to get the most out of your English class, whether it carries the AP designation or not. The strategies in Chapter 3 will improve your grades, both on your report card and on the AP exam.

Chapter 1

Flying Over the AP Lit Exam: An Overview

● ●

In This Chapter

▶ Surveying the important details of the test

▶ Exploring possible questions

▶ Understanding how the test is scored

▶ Taking care of the practical aspects of the exam

● ●

*I*t started in kindergarten, right? Someone pushed a pencil into your chubby little hand and said, "This is a test." All of a sudden you weren't allowed to talk to your friends, ask a handy grownup for help, or play with that interesting new purple crayon. You left the land where learning was fun and entered Test Land. And you're still in it! But now the stakes feel higher, especially for the AP, which comes with its own shrink-wrap, barcode labels, student packs, and color-coded sections. The only thing that remains the same is that you still aren't allowed to talk, ask for most types of help, or play with a cool new crayon.

Regardless of your situation, while you're in AP English Exam Land you need a map. And you're in luck because in this chapter, I give you just that. I tell you what to expect — what the test looks like, how long it takes, how to sign up, what it covers, and all sorts of un-fun but useful things.

The Content and Structure of the Exam

When you walk into the test room on a lovely day in May, what kind of questions will you face? Briefly, the College Board hits you with two sections, one for multiple-choice and one for essays. Check out this chart for more details:

Section	Time Allowed	Number of Questions	Details about the Questions
Multiple-choice	1 hour	About 55, give or take a couple	Five potential answers to each question; you interpret five or six pieces of literature that are printed on the exam; selections include poems, maybe a dramatic scene or a slice of memoir, and one or two excerpts from novels
Essays	2 hours	3	Two essay questions are based on a piece of literature (a poem, a passage from a play or novel, and so on) that's provided on the exam; the third is an open-ended essay based on a work of literary quality that you choose

What to expect if you take an AP English class

Every teacher of AP English has a certain degree of freedom in the design of the course. This is a very good idea, too. In my experience, getting English teachers to agree on something is a little harder than herding cats. Though AP English Literature classes vary, some things remain the same:

✔ **An AP English Literature course must, according to College Board rules, throw college-level work at you.** In other words, the course material has to be difficult.

✔ **The College Board doesn't mandate a particular reading list, but it does ask that students read a wide variety of literature in the AP class.** By the time you finish your course, the College Board wants you to have read something from every genre and every time period from the 16th century through the present day. Both British and American writers must be on the reading list as well as some translated works. (You don't have to read *everything* in your AP year; you just have to read it sometime.)

✔ **All the material is supposed to be of good literary quality, which means writing that rewards close**
reading. If you read a work once and you get it all, it isn't AP material. However, if you find something new to think about every time you read a particular work, you've witnessed literary quality. (For more detail on determining whether a work is of good literary quality, flip to Chapter 14.)

✔ **Expect the amount of reading to equal or surpass the amount you read in an honors English class.** Ten or 12 full-length works and a good fistful of poetry is what you should expect.

✔ **Some AP English teachers start you off with homework for the summer.** You may have to read a couple of books or write something to hand in on the first day of school. Oh, joy!

✔ **Expect to write a lot.** In fact, expect to write everything from informal journal entries to polished essays.

✔ **The grading may be tougher in an AP class than in a regular, non–AP English section.** Evaluation of your work in an AP course is more stringent because teachers apply college-level standards.

Literary selections on the exam may include anything from Tudor times (16th century) onwards. The selections will most likely be American or British, though works from other English-speaking countries may pop up as well. Literature translated into English from another language is also fair game. One-third to slightly less than half of the literature is usually poetry.

In addition to the time it takes for you to complete the exam, tack on 45 minutes to an hour for getting settled, listening to directions, taking a break, and having your paper collected at the end. Expect to be at the test center for about four hours. (I recommend that you get there 30 to 45 minutes early just to make sure you're registered on time and aren't flustered as the test begins.) When all is said and done, add about two weeks for screaming, "It's over!"

Taking a Closer Look at Typical AP Exam Questions

Hamlet asks, "To be or not to be?" That's probably the most famous question ever asked, but you won't find it on the AP English Literature and Composition exam. After all, who could possibly know the right answer? But you will find questions — lots of them! — when you sit down on AP exam day. This section gathers the usual suspects, the question types that appear year after year, so you can make their acquaintance and ace the test.

The multiple-choice section

The multiple-choice questions, at their easiest, are standard reading comprehension queries. At their most difficult, however, these questions are downright torturous. The exam writers ask you to shoehorn your interpretation of the literary work into one of five choices, none of which may be worded exactly the way you perceive the poem or passage. Somewhere in the middle (in terms of difficulty) are questions that address how the piece is written or the way in which the writing technique and meaning work together. The following sections go over the most common types of multiple-choice questions. For more information on these questions, check out Chapters 6 (poetry) and 11 (prose and drama).

Vocabulary-in-context

The AP English selections are tough, and many times they come with tough vocabulary. Or they may come with common vocabulary that has an obscure meaning. For example, you may see a question like this one:

In the context of line 34, "fall" means

(A) autumn

(B) slip

(C) hit the deck

(D) attachment of fake hair

(E) loss of respect or approval

The tricky part here is deciding which meaning appears in line 34, because all of the answers may be definitions of "fall." Yes, even choice (D). Look it up if you don't believe me!

Literal meaning

To see whether you can decode complex writing, the exam writers ask you what happened on the simplest, literal level. However, because the exam is supposed to be difficult (and because great writers often employ complex sentences), you may have to untangle complicated *syntax,* the literary term for how the sentence is put together in order to unearth a simple fact. Here's a type of question you may come across from this category:

The actions of the shopkeeper include all of the following EXCEPT

(A) faking celebrity autographs

(B) inserting spinach leaves between chapters 28 and 29 of his rival's autobiography

(C) charging a "shipping and handling" fee to customers in the store

(D) playing annoyingly soft versions of hard-rock classics

(E) hiring an indie band to promote his store

All you have to do to answer this sort of question is figure out what's being asked (in this case, the answer that does *not* appear), and then you simply have to go back to the passage and check the facts. However, decoding the passage may turn your hair gray. For help with reading comprehension, turn to Chapter 5 (for poetry) or 9 (for prose and drama).

Tone and diction

Wow, do the exam writers love tone! I don't know why they're so stuck on this topic, but they are. You have to determine whether the passage sounds sad, argumentative, sarcastic, or ironic. Tone often depends partly on *diction,* or word choice (formal, colloquial, and so on). Check out this example:

The tone of the passage may best be characterized as

(A) nostalgic

(B) ironic

(C) descriptive

(D) speculative

(E) respectful

As you're reading a passage, hear it in your head and think about the author's language to get a head start on tone. Put those factors together with meaning, and you've got a winner.

Inference and attitude

Inference questions ask you to extend beyond what's stated in the selection. They force you to take the next logical step. You also may be asked to figure out the attitude of the author or of a character or speaker toward a certain topic or issue, based on the clues in the selection. Here's what an inference question might look like:

The shopkeeper is never arrested most likely because

(A) the cop is involved in the spinach incident

(B) the cop has a deep-seated fear of spinach

(C) the shopkeeper's humble assistant has super powers

(D) everyone in the village loves spinach leaves

(E) the shopkeeper becomes a superhero, stops time, and removes the evidence

Okay, I played around a little here, but I know you get the point. You have to leap beyond the passage into the territory of probability, using the content of the passage as your guide.

Figurative language

Things aren't always what they seem in literary works. After all, just to make things interesting and to add meaning, authors often employ figurative language. For instance, symbols, metaphors, and similes show up all over the place (including on the AP English exam). Check out this sample question:

The spinach leaves in line 12 may symbolize

(A) the shopkeeper's love of nature

(B) the rival's lack of muscle tone

(C) an unhealthy attachment to vegetables

(D) death

(E) the gap between appearance and reality

I threw in choices (D) and (E) because those themes appear nearly everywhere in literature. However, when you answer this sort of question, be sure to focus on the element of figurative language (the symbol, metaphor, or simile, for example) that they're asking about — not just on the piece in general.

Form, structure, and style

Don't expect a ton of multiple-choice questions filled with literary terms describing form, structure, and style. Even though literary terms still appear here and there on the exam, they seem to be falling out of favor in recent years. However, you'll definitely see questions that address *how* the piece is written. Even though you may not see a question about literary terms, it never hurts to be prepared. Take a look at this example:

The style of the fourth paragraph differs from that of the first three paragraphs in that it is

(A) descriptive, not metaphorical

(B) argumentative, not descriptive

(C) symbolic, not literal

(D) analytical, not metaphorical

(E) expository, not analytical

Even without the fancy literary vocabulary, these kinds of questions can be tough because you have only a couple of minutes to examine a paragraph or two and figure out which terms apply. To answer this type of question, look at the section of text that the question focuses on and try out the most likely candidates for Answer of the Year. See what fits the text.

The essay section

On the essay portion of the AP English exam, the College Board tests your skills, not your ability to recall information. The questions are designed to determine whether you know how to analyze a literary work and write about it, not to see whether you can name four Romantic poets. Nor do you have to memorize dates or know the names and characteristics of literary movements. In fact, you aren't expected to have any factual stuff stored in your memory except some literary terms. And even then, you don't need to know many of them. You do, however, need to prove that you can do the following:

- ✔ **Relate the way a piece is written to its meaning and its effect on the audience.** Even though they aren't as common in the multiple-choice section of the exam, form, structure, and style questions are frequent fliers on the essay portion. For instance, you may see questions that ask you to comment on the poetic devices that the author employs or to discuss the way in which one element of fiction (setting or characterization, perhaps) contributes to the effect of the piece as a whole.

- ✔ **Provide evidence for your assertions.** Support for your claims is a key element of the essay. When you write the first two essays, you're expected to quote directly from the literary selections provided. You can't easily quote when you write the open-ended essay (unless you have a *very* good memory), but you do need to use details from the work that you're discussing.

The essay questions have what are called *prompts*. These prompts provide a central idea that your essay must address in the context of the literary selection provided or the literary work you've chosen for the open-ended question. You've probably seen prompts in every English class you've ever taken. Here are a few examples: "Discuss the role of friendship in . . .";

"Discuss loyalty to family or country conflicts with personal morality in . . ."; "Discuss the role of figurative language in . . ."; We English teachers manufacture prompts even when we're sleeping. (Kinda creepy, huh?)

The open-ended essay has a prompt and then a list of suggested works. You can choose one of those works to write about, or you can substitute something of similar quality. Just remember that on the AP English exam, "quality" is *not* your call. The College Board graders decide. Your best bet is to play it safe and choose a work that you studied in school. You can write a winning Pulitzer Prize essay on your favorite Spiderman comic some other time. Check out Chapter 14 for more tips on choosing works for the open-ended essay.

One weird breed of AP English essay is the paired selection. Not every exam has one of these paired essay questions, but many do. The pairs may be two poems, two prose pieces, or one of each genre. They address the same subject or consider the same themes. The prompt asks you to compare and contrast the works. Nervous? Don't be. Turn to Chapter 15 for help.

All Things Score-Related

When you finish the AP English exam, your job is over, but the scoring gnomes of the College Board are just getting started. The multiple-choice sheets are bundled up and sent through a scanner, and the essays are sent to hotels where they drink margaritas and eat macadamia nuts from the minibar. Okay, I'm kidding about the margaritas and the macadamia nuts, but not about the hotels. Here's how it works: The College Board hires platoons of high school and college English teachers and sends them, as well as the essays, to hotels. For one fun-filled week, the teachers read and grade all those essays while ingesting vast amounts of caffeine. You knew you wanted to be an English teacher, didn't you?

Multiple-choice scoring

During multiple-choice scoring, all those darkened ovals made with No. 2 pencil lead flash through a scanning machine, and then out pops a number, which is determined this way:

- The multiple-choice counts as 45 percent of your final score.
- Each correct multiple-choice answer receives one point. Questions left blank receive no points.
- Every wrong multiple-choice answer deducts ¼ point. Therefore, it's best to guess only if you can eliminate a couple of choices.
- The raw multiple-choice score is converted with a complicated formula that varies slightly from test to test. The College Board has platoons of statisticians who create this formula based on the average number of students who chose the correct answer.

Most students panic a little the first time they try their hand at an AP multiple-choice section. Even excellent readers who can crack a poem at first glance find the multiple-choice questions difficult. Not to worry: Simply practice with this book and you won't have that initial panic on exam day.

Also, calm your nerves with this information: You can get quite a few multiple-choice questions wrong (10 or even a few more) and still score a five overall, which is the highest score you can get on the exam. Furthermore, the College Board expects that most students will leave some questions blank. After all, the exams have approximately 55 multiple-choice questions, to be answered in 60 minutes. Plus you have to read the selections. Not surprisingly, time is an issue. But remember that it's an issue for *everyone* taking the test, and the scoring allows for that fact.

Essay scoring

Scoring is always a touchy subject. In fact, fights sometimes break out about which multiple-choice answer is better. Luckily, those fights take place secretly in the College Board head-quarters while the exam is being written. Essay fights, on the other hand, occur in public while the tests are being reviewed.

Here's some background on the essay scoring process: The College Board runs workshops on essay scoring for all the teachers hired to slap numbers on your brilliant writing. At those workshops, teachers are given sample student essays to grade as well as a set of very specific standards for grading. Then the fun begins! After they've graded their sample essays, the teachers have to compare the scores that they awarded with the official College Board scores. You probably can't even imagine how passionate people get about one point! (Seriously, English teachers — and I include myself — need to get a life.) After four or five rounds, most graders see what the College Board is looking for, and the room begins to calm down.

Here's the lowdown on essay scoring:

- ✔ **Each essay is given a grade from 0–9.** Nine is the highest score, but anything in the 7-and-up range deserves a pat on the back.

- ✔ **You'll almost always receive at least one point on an essay, just for trying.** The only way to get a zero is to leave the essay blank or to ignore the prompt and write something completely different from what the question is actually asking.

- ✔ **The scoring is holistic.** In other words, the grader doesn't award 10 percent for good writing, 25 percent for evidence, 17 percent for originality, and so on. Instead, the graders simply go through the whole thing once (okay, maybe twice) and select a score they feel is appropriate. Because you can't attend a workshop on grading — and believe me, watching grass grow is more fun — in this book I've created grids to help you arrive at a realistic number. The grids appear in Chapters 17 and 19.

- ✔ **The graders consider the depth of your analysis and the amount and relevance of the evidence that you've provided to back up your ideas.** Basically, they want to see that you can read beyond the literal level and that you can make and support a case for your interpretation.

  The graders also look at the quality of your writing. I hate to admit this fact, but grammar and spelling count only if the errors seriously impede the reader from understanding what the writer is trying to convey. The graders are much more interested in writing style — whether your work reads fluently and shows a command of the language.

- ✔ **You can get by in the essay section without using official lit-speak.** All you really need to do is to analyze the material in regular, everyday language. However, your graders are English teachers, and their hearts beat a little faster when they see terms such as *assonance, protagonist,* and so forth. Throw them in if you're confident they make sense and connect to a significant point about the literature; leave them out if they don't.

  Steer clear of the "laundry list" approach to literary terminology. In other words, don't just work your way through five or six terms, saying that they do or do not appear in the selection. Also, don't define the terms. Your graders are English teachers, so they know what a simile is. Both of these practices waste time and result in lower scores.

- ✔ **Each essay gets two readings by two different graders. Each grader assigns a number. The two essay grades are averaged, and averages that end in 0.5 are rounded up.** If the numbers are more than two apart (one reader awards a 5 and the other awards an 8, for example), a College Board expert steps in to render a final judgment. Essays good enough to receive a 9 — the highest grade possible — are cause for celebration and comments, such as "you have to read this one" and "here's the next Shakespeare." In fact, the other graders usually pause to read the essay worthy of a 9 — even though they've already read a zillion other essays and are propping their eyelids open with toothpicks.

The envelope, please! Your final score

The multiple-choice and essay scores meet for a drink and . . . sorry, I got carried away with the romance of it all. The scores from each part of the test are weighted so that the multiple-choice counts for 45 percent of your final score and the essays for 55 percent.

Then the statisticians use complicated formulas to convert the multiple-choice and essay scores into a number from 1–5. (I've supplied a version of this formula, adapted to the practice exams in this book, in Chapters 17 and 19.) These numbers, according to the College Board, mean the following:

> 5 = extremely well qualified (equivalent to an A in a college course)
>
> 4 = well qualified (in the B range in a college course)
>
> 3 = qualified (a C in a college course)
>
> 2 = possibly qualified (a D in a college course)
>
> 1 = no recommendation (a failing grade)

As you can probably figure out, colleges don't give you credit for a 1 or a 2. Even a score of 3 is iffy — some colleges are okay with it, and others aren't. Some colleges award credit for entry-level courses to those who scored four or five, and others bump you to a higher-level course if you're in that winning category. If you're unsure about your prospective school's requirements, ask its admissions office.

Receiving your score

The minute I take a test I want to know how I've done, and I assume you feel the same way. When you take the AP English exam, you have to wait a bit. The exam graders need time to plow through your superlative literary essays. They don't need too long, though. You take the test in May, and in July the College Board mails your grade to you, to your high school, and to the college of your choice. The first college report is free; if you want more than one, you have to pay a fee. That fee is currently $15 — or $25 if you're in a huge hurry and want expedited service. You can also get your grade over the phone at the beginning of July for a steep $8 a call.

Here are some important tips to keep in mind:

✔ If you had a headache, a breakup, or a crackup on the day of the exam, you can ask the College Board to cancel your score, in which case it disappears forever. (Go to www.collegeboard.com for instructions on how to cancel a score. Or, speak with your school's AP coordinator.) You have to make your request by mid-June, and you never get to see your score. You don't pay for score cancellation, but you aren't reimbursed for your exam fee either.

✔ If you want to withhold a score from a particular college, you pay about $10. Withheld scores still go to your high school and to you, just not to a college. However, they don't disappear; your score can be sent to a college later if you change your mind — and, of course, if you pay $15.

✔ You can take any AP exam more than once, though you have to wait an entire year to do so because they're given only in May. Both scores will be reported to your school and to the college(s) you've selected. If your first score was pretty bad (say a 2), you may want to withhold that score from prospective colleges.

For a fee (what else is new?) you can get your essay answer booklet back to review with a teacher or tutor before you try the AP again. The booklet will have no teacher comments on it, just a score. The deadline for this service is mid-September, and the cost is currently $7.

Check out the College Board Web site (www.collegeboard.com) or call 888-225-5427 for information, score reports, cancellations, and so forth.

Dealing with the Practical Stuff

If you're taking an AP English course, your teacher will probably tell you everything you need to do in order to sign up for the exam. However, if you're home schooled or not in an AP class (or if your English teacher has inhaled a little too much chalk dust), this section will help you. Here I explain the practical aspects of the test, including registering, getting score reports, fee waivers, accommodations for special needs, and so on. Because the AP exam has stranger procedures than a super-secret spy agency, I also explain candidate packs, seals, shrink wraps, and other annoying stuff so you won't be surprised on test day.

Signing up

In the winter of the academic year in which you plan to take the exam, pick up a College Board student bulletin. The College Board issues these pamphlets to give you the date of the test, registration materials, deadlines, and information on fees. You can get the student bulletin from your school's AP Coordinator (who may be identified by the worried look and hurried stride of someone who has way too much to do). In many schools, the AP Coordinator is a college or guidance counselor. If you aren't sure who has the student bulletins, check with the principal or with your English teacher.

You can also find AP information, including a downloadable student bulletin, on the College Board's Web site, www.collegeboard.com/apstudents. You can't sign up on line, but you can find out where and how to register for the test. No Internet access? Not to worry. Call the College Board at 888-225-5427 for registration information. As long as you're on the Web site, take a look at the practice exams and sample questions the test-writers provide.

AP exams aren't cheap; currently you have to plunk down $83 for one test. You pay in advance to the AP Coordinator at your school. You may also face extra fees if you want extra score reports. (See the section "Receiving your score" earlier in this chapter for more details on these extra fees.)

If the test fee is a stretch for your wallet, ask the AP Coordinator about reduced fees. In general, the price drops to $53 for those in financial need. Sometimes the federal or state government provides additional funds to defray the cost of the test.

If you aren't currently attending a high school (you're returning after time away or you're home-schooled), call the College Board AP Services no later than the end of February (888-225-5427). They will put you in touch with the nearest AP Coordinator. Be sure to contact the coordinator as soon as possible, and no later than mid-March. Tell the coordinator that you want to take the AP English Literature and Composition exam, and notify him or her of whether you have any special accommodations (more on accommodations later in this chapter). The coordinator will give you a list of schools offering the AP English exam and will order an exam for you. The coordinator will also collect your fee and give you a code number, which is different from the general number used by students attending the school where the test is given. Be sure to bring a government-issued photo ID (passport, driver's license, or a similar official document) and your code number with you on test day. (See the yellow tear-out card at the front of this book for a list of items to bring along on the big day.)

Being mindful of important deadlines

You can't be late for a couple of very important dates in connection with the AP English exam and still be sure that you have everything you need — permission to take the exam, accommodation (if allowed), and so forth. Here are the basics:

- ✔ **Early February:** If you need accommodations on the exam (extra time, Braille or large-type text, and so forth) and you haven't yet been certified, need a change in certification, or have changed schools, now is the time to submit documentation to the College Board.

- ✔ **Late February:** If you need accommodations and have been certified by your school already, you still have to check that the correct forms have been sent to the College Board. Ask your guidance counselor, principal, or AP coordinator whether the correct forms have been mailed.

- ✔ **Early March:** If you're a home-schooler or a student in a school that doesn't offer the AP program, you must contact the College Board for the name and phone number of an AP Coordinator who can arrange the exam for you. Also, all test takers need to get a government-issued photo ID. If you don't have one, get one now.

- ✔ **Beginning of April:** If you're enrolled in an AP English Lit course and you don't need accommodations, check with your teacher for the time and place of the exam. Find out when the fee is due and determine which school official will collect it.

I can't supply exact dates because they vary slightly from year to year. Check out www.collegeboard.com/apstudents for more information. No Internet connection? Call 888-225-5427 for details.

Showing up: What to expect on test day

On test day, expect to have a nervous breakdown. Just kidding! If you've spent some quality time with this book, you should be in great shape to do well on the exam. Here's what to expect.

Upon arrival

When you arrive at the test center, your teacher or a *proctor* (an adult who monitors the test) will direct you to the correct room. You'll be asked to leave everything in a locker or storage area except for what you actually need for the test. (Check out the yellow tear-out sheet at the beginning of this book for permitted items.) Usually exam-takers are asked to wait outside the testing room until the proctor is ready. Then you rush inside. Oops! I mean you calmly, confidently stroll into the room. Allow about a half hour before the official start time of the test for pre-exam visits to the restroom, locker room, padded room, and so forth.

In the classroom, before the exam

After you're in the room, you have to be quiet. No last minute whispers about Emily Dickinson, the Beatles, or the party next week. Any hint of cheating and you're gone, so be careful to maintain silence and to limit your field of vision to the proctor, your watch, and the ceiling.

Before the exam begins, the proctor gives you a *student pack.* The student pack, also known as the *candidate pack,* has bar-coded, self-stick labels that identify you and your test materials. If you're taking more than one AP exam, the proctor will take the student pack at the end of every exam except the last, at which point you can take it home and frame it. Okay, well, actually you use the ID number on that pack to get your scores over the phone. Don't throw it away until you know how you did.

The proctor also distributes answer sheets. At this point, you have to take an ID label from your student pack and stick it on the answer sheet. Then you answer some easy questions, such as your name, address, and so forth. (Some schools take care of these tasks ahead of time, just to save test-day energy for the things that count. Others sweat you through it right before the exam.)

At this time, the proctor will also distribute the exam, which is wrapped in clear plastic, and he or she will read some legal notices. What these legal notices basically mean is that when you open the plastic package you accept the College Board's right to investigate if it thinks you or anyone you know on this planet has cheated. You also give the College Board the right to use your answers for any purpose it wants. No one will recite your essay on *American Idol,* but your work may be used in one of the College Board's publications as, perhaps, a sample to train graders.

You're getting closer to being ready to begin the exam, but you aren't quite there yet. You still need to copy the name of the test and the form number (it's on the test booklet) onto your answer sheet. You also have to read the legal stuff on the front and back covers of your exam and then sign your name, indicating that you accept the terms. By accepting these terms, you agree not to cheat, not to talk about the multiple-choice questions *ever* (they reuse some), and not to divulge the essay questions for a few days.

During the exam

After you finish the multiple-choice section, you seal the question booklet with little stickers that are in your student pack. The proctor then collects the question booklets and answer sheets, and you get a ten-minute break (during which you're pretty much in solitary confinement, though you can sprint for a bathroom if necessary). You aren't allowed phone calls or conversation about the questions.

During the second part of the exam, you return and open the next plastic-wrapped package. This pack contains a green question sheet and a pink answer sheet. Now you get to listen to all the legal stuff again, write your name and stick a few more bar-coded labels on the booklets, and then compose your essays. Two hours later, you hand in the whole thing and begin to breathe again. You're done!

Life happens: What to do if you can't take the exam

If you wind up sick on test day, chances are good that nothing terrible will happen if you can't take the exam. If you have the sniffles or a once-in-a-lifetime chance to play in the state championship softball game, simply tell your AP Coordinator. He or she will arrange for an exam during the makeup week, which is the first week following the usual AP period — in other words, around the third week in May. If you're out for more than that (you couldn't make bail, fell terribly ill, or got stranded on an island with polar bears and mysterious hatches), you're out of luck. You have to wait until next year, and you have to pay the fee all over again.

Before you give up, however, check with your AP Coordinator. He or she may be able to arrange a last-minute accommodation (perhaps extra time for someone with a sprained wrist) that will save the day.

Dealing with special needs

Students with special needs can take the AP English exam, and many do. Depending on your situation, you may be entitled to extra time, a computer (for those with *dysgraphia,* which is an impairment that causes you not to be able to write), large-type or Braille exams, a reader for the questions, or a writer to take down your answers.

If you need accommodations, the AP Coordinator in your high school should take care of everything; home-schoolers or those not enrolled in a school that has an AP program can get help from the AP Coordinator in their area. (See the earlier section, "Signing up," for more information on finding an AP Coordinator.) The College Board's Services for Students with Disabilities Office is another good resource. Contact the office at 609-771-7137 (TTY 609-882-4118). You can also e-mail the office at ssd@collegeboard.org. Or, check the Web site for more information (www.collegeboard.com/ssd/student/index.html).

The school has to fill out and submit a "Services for Students with Disabilities Eligibility" form, affectionately known as the SSDE. In general, after the College Board has certified you as needing accommodations on one of its exams (the SAT, for example), you're certified for all. However, if anything changes — your address, your school, your physical or mental ability — you need a new form.

The school has to do the work here, but you're the one who's ultimately responsible for making sure that the SSDE is in proper shape, in the proper hands, at the proper time. The deadlines are in February or March before the exam, with the earlier date for students who are being certified for the first time and the later date for those who have been through the ordeal before. Check with your AP Coordinator well before that time to be sure everything's in order and to find out the exact dates.

Chapter 2

"The Readiness Is All": Preparing for the Exam

In This Chapter
▶ Creating a schedule for test preparation
▶ Making good use of your time during the exam

*W*illiam Shakespeare was a pretty smart guy. Consider, for example, the quotation in the title of this chapter, a comment Hamlet makes when warned about a potentially fatal fencing match. The AP English Literature and Composition exam has never, as far as I know, done anything worse than provoke a few migraines and some nervous stomachs. Nevertheless, as old Will wrote, "The readiness is all."

This chapter is all about scheduling. It provides a countdown for the "I'm still in kindergarten but I've got a retirement plan" types as well as for those who scratch their heads and ask, "Oh, the test is tomorrow? Really?"

Many roads lead to Rome, according to the old saying, and many plans take you straight to a five — the top score — on the AP exam. The schedule that I lay out in this chapter is just a starting point. AP exams are given in early May; the date varies slightly from year to year. Look at a calendar to find out when the exam is, and then look at *your* calendar. See where you jump in. After you pick a spot — say, "September Preceding the Exam" — read all the sections after that one for helpful suggestions taking you all the way to the morning of the exam. Because the theme of this chapter is "it's all in the timing," I also throw in a section showing you how to hit warp speed on the AP exam without sacrificing quality.

You can prepare for and take the AP English exam even if you aren't in an AP English class. Chances are your English or language arts class is laying a strong foundation of reading and writing skills. If it isn't and you still want to take the exam, fill the gap with some help from Chapter 3, which explains how to strengthen reading comprehension and essay writing. Chapter 3 can also help you with some of the many tasks that I suggest in this chapter, such as planning your summer reading, annotating the texts that you read, starting a reading notebook, and working on your vocabulary. Take the time to peruse Chapter 3 when you're tackling these helpful tasks.

When it comes to test preparation, one size doesn't fit all. Tailor the schedule to fit your learning style, your strengths and weaknesses, and your own particular daily grind.

Exam Minus One Year

Just so you know: Everyone who's beginning AP exam prep at the last minute *hates* you. But don't pay them any mind. Instead, congratulate yourself. You're in great shape if you have a whole year to prepare for the AP English Literature and Composition exam. Here's what you need to do now:

- ✔ Confer with your English teacher or with a guidance counselor about whether you should sign up for an AP English Literature course. (See Chapter 1 for more information about these courses.)

- ✔ Plan some quality summer reading. (Appendix A has a list of great works of literature.)

- ✔ Annotate the books you read and begin keeping a reader's notebook.

- ✔ Work on improving your vocabulary so that you're prepared to decode the difficult reading passages on the exam. I'm talking about regular words that people actually use, not the terminology that English teachers throw around. Learning those words is helpful too, but those terms aren't crucial to the AP exam.

- ✔ Gather and file corrected papers and notes from your most recent English classes. When you have a moment — okay, a nanosecond, given your busy schedule — look through the file and assess your work. You may discover areas to work on — thesis statements or evidence, for example. Focus your energy on improving those skills.

I know you're a paragon of organization, but I have one more task for you: Have some fun! The summer's a good time to get a head start on academics, but it's also a good time. Period. End of story. Take advantage of it.

September Preceding the Exam

Because you're starting your AP preparations post–Labor Day, you obviously can't take on any summer reading (see the preceding section). But you still have a ton of time for some great pre-exam preparation. Here are the most important tasks you should take care of right now:

- ✔ If you haven't done so already, work on your vocabulary. The literature you read in AP English classes and on the exam is filled with tough vocabulary, so increasing your fund of words is a good strategy. You can also pick up some literary terminology, though those words play a minimal role on the exam.

- ✔ Annotate the literary works you read, and continue or start a reader's notebook.

- ✔ Start or add to a file of your writing assignments and tests from current and previous English classes. From time to time browse through the file to see where your strengths and weaknesses lie. This file also helps you remember details about works you've read — a plus for the open-ended AP essay that allows you to choose what to write about.

- ✔ Keep a notebook or computer file of important points from the teacher and from student discussions in your current English class.

- ✔ Read one critical essay about every major work that you're currently studying in English class, preferably just after you've completed the class-unit on the work. Don't let the critics' views overpower your own interpretation. As you read a critical essay, argue with "the expert" and assert your own ideas. Your own response, if you can support it with evidence from the text, is valid.

Taking up speed-reading

When I was in high school, the dumbest thing I had on my schedule (or so I thought at the time) was a three-week course in speed-reading. Decades later I understand that the ability to read fast is one of the best things I ever learned. Why? Because no matter how hard I try, I can't seem to break the space-time continuum and squeeze five extra hours into the day. Without speed-reading, I'd never be able to get through all those student papers, not to mention the boring faculty memos that clutter my inbox.

With a minimum of effort you can read more quickly as well. Think of yourself as an athlete, with your sport being reading. When athletes are preparing for a race, they build stamina by logging a certain number of miles. Similarly, you "log miles" simply by reading a lot. But runners also do wind-sprints when they train — short bursts of the fastest pace they can manage. A reading wind-sprint occurs when, for a few minutes, you consciously zoom as quickly as possible down the page, without passing the point where the words become meaningless. If you do one literary wind-sprint per day, after a few weeks your reading speed will increase. Fast reading is a great advantage on the AP exam because time is very tight. Besides, after the AP exam, you can go to college and sprint through your homework, leaving you much more time for . . . well, I'll let you fill in *that* blank.

The first half of the school year can short-circuit fairly easily. After all you're still figuring out what each teacher wants from you — and that's always a stressful task. (How do you determine the teacher's non-negotiables? Read his or her handouts and listen to the assignments. Note key words such as "must include" or "will not be accepted if.") If you're a senior, you're also probably obsessing over college applications. Take a deep breath each morning, face the mirror, and say, "All I can do is my best." That attitude is good for your blood pressure and also for your grades. You can't prepare for the AP English exam or do anything else properly if you're sizzling with tension.

January Preceding the Exam

January through March is a calmer portion of the academic year. By now you know your teachers, and you probably have the lunch-table politics under control. And at last, seniors have sent in all those angst-laden envelopes stuffed with college applications. Now you can focus on enjoying yourself a little while you prepare for the AP exam (and don't forget that I said *a little*).

Once the New Year's champagne goes flat, though, the AP test seems a lot more real; at this point, you have a bit more than four months until the exam. Now's the time to buckle down and do some serious exam prep, including the following:

- ✔ Start or continue with the steps listed in the earlier section, "September Preceding the Exam."

- ✔ Set aside 30–45 minutes each week to read a chapter in Parts II through IV of this book. If you're unfamiliar with the exam format, turn to Chapter 1.

- ✔ Go through your tests, quizzes, and papers from your current and previous English classes. Study the teachers' comments and note where you lost points. Doing so helps you figure out which skills you need to improve, and then you can carefully review the chapters in this book that explain those points.

- ✔ If you aren't sure what you need, take the practice exam in Chapter 16 and score it with Chapter 17. Analyze your weaknesses and hit the corresponding chapters in this book.

March Preceding the Exam

Spring break is a great time to catch up — with your social life and with AP test prep. As you near exam day, you can probably glimpse the light at the end of the tunnel. Don't worry: It isn't a train! You still have about two months to ready yourself for the exam; schedule an hour or so a day of "AP" time and enjoy the rest. Here are some tasks you need to stay on top of during this month:

✔ Start on or continue with the steps that I list in the previous sections.

✔ If you haven't already done so, take the practice exam in Chapter 16 and score it with Chapter 17. Go over any topics that tripped you up.

✔ Select and answer practice questions from the chapters addressing areas that worry you (poetry, perhaps, or the open-ended essay).

✔ Seek out the help of a friendly English teacher (that's all of us!) who can read one of your practice essays and point out where you need to improve. Zoom through the table of contents or the index to find sections in this book that address your weak spots.

Two Weeks before the Exam

All you long-rangers (those who started preparing a couple of months ago) can now lighten up. Try not to brag about your foresight to anyone who's beginning exam preparations at this point. They'll put toads in your locker or find some other way to express the overwhelming envy that they feel.

On the other hand, if you're parachuting in at this point, you're in damage-control mode because 14 days for AP prep isn't a lot. Drop everything from your social and academic life that isn't crucial. I don't mean for you to skip your brother's wedding or the history paper that's required to pass the course. But you should probably decline that tempting invitation to your grandmother's Ultimate Frisbee tournament. And it would help to ease up on the trips to the mall or the paintball arena. You need to replace all this extra time with the following tasks:

✔ Review your class notes and papers on works you read in junior- or senior-level English classes and skim through your reader's notebook. The goal is to prepare four that are suitable for the open-ended essay. (Chapter 14 explains how to choose works and what you should know about each one.)

✔ Take the practice exam in either Chapter 16 or Chapter 18. For early birds, this is your second round. For panic-planners, this is round one. You can score the exams with Chapter 17 (for the exam in Chapter 16) or Chapter 19 (for the exam in Chapter 18).

✔ After taking the practice exam, make a list of things you have to watch out for. For example, if you know that your essays seldom include enough support for your ideas, put "evidence" on your "watch out" list. The simple act of writing this list will focus your energy and help you remember what you need to do on exam day.

✔ Check out the later section "General Strategies for Saving Time on the Exam" for last minute reminders on cramming four hours' worth of thought into a three-hour test period.

✔ Log on to www.collegeboard.com, register (it's free!), and click on the AP English Literature and Composition section. There you see recent essay questions and sample responses.

- Locate everything you need for the exam, including a supply of No. 2 pencils, pens with dark blue or black ink, photo identification, and an accommodation letter for special needs. (I explain how to qualify for accommodations in Chapter 1.) Store everything in one place.

- Determine how you will travel to the exam — school bus, family car, taxi, dog sled.

- If you're taking the exam in a place that you aren't familiar with, consider making a trip to map out the route from your home to the test site. Nothing is worse than getting lost on exam day (except maybe if you allot too little time for the journey to the testing center!).

Life being what it is, no matter how closely you follow the preceding suggestions, last-minute disasters still occur. Be ready for them! For instance, find an alternate route to the test site just in case the Highway Construction Authority decides that AP morning is a great time to tear up asphalt on your primary route. And be sure that the dog, cat, piranha, or other household pet can't get to your exam gear. (Can't you just picture yourself explaining that the shredded driver's license really *is* your own, even though half the photo is now inside Fido's belly?)

The Night before the Exam

If you just opened this book for the first time, go to Chapter 1 immediately. Read about the format of the exam, and then turn to Chapter 16 or Chapter 18 for a practice exam. Don't do all the questions. Instead, hit the multiple-choice questions for one selection and check your answers (in either Chapter 17 or Chapter 19). Then write one essay from either practice exam and read the sample answers and criteria for grading. After grading your answers, make a "watch out" list that includes the errors that show up most frequently, as well as the correct answers. Then go on to the following list of tasks.

If you've been preparing for a while, you're almost home free. You just need to take care of a few more last-minute tasks:

- Read your "watch out" list and then stop studying. Anything you do now will only make you more nervous.

- Do something that's relaxing but not too strenuous. An hour or two of television, a chat with a friend (who isn't taking the exam), or an easy game of basketball are all good activities. Cleaning out the attic, partying all night, and playing high-stakes poker aren't the best choices.

- After making sure that you have everything you need for the exam packed and ready, (see the preceding section for a list) and after unearthing your car keys or rechecking your travel arrangements, go to bed early. Set your alarm clock so that you won't have to rush in the morning. Sweet dreams!

Zero Hour: The Morning of the Test

Hamlet says, "If it be now, 'tis not to come." Although William Shakespeare himself never took an AP exam, he obviously understood that one advantage of facing something horrible (and three hours of testing certainly places the AP test in that category) is that at least you can stop agonizing about it. On exam day morning, check out these tips for gliding smoothly through your day:

- Get up early enough so that you don't have to rush.

- Wear comfortable clothing. Layers are a good idea because you never know how warm or cool the test room will be.

✔ Leave anything that you can't bring into the test at home or in the car, which is pretty much everything not required in the exam room, including electronic devices, beverages, papers, and books. (And make sure that you bring everything you need! See the earlier section, "Two Weeks before the Exam" and Chapter 1 for details.)

✔ Eat a real breakfast, even if you usually (gasp!) skip this all-important meal. Go heavy on the protein (eggs, cheese, tofu, meat, and the like). Avoid sugary stuff, such as doughnuts, pastries, and pancakes, because sugar gives you a spike of energy and then a huge drop — which will likely be right around the middle of the exam.

✔ If you have time, skim your notes on the four works that you may write about for the open-ended essay. (Check out Chapter 14 for details on selecting and preparing those works.)

✔ To avoid nerves as much as possible, resolve to avoid fellow exam sufferers when you arrive at the testing site. If you're carpooling, make a strong effort to talk about baseball, who should have won *American Idol,* and any other non-test-related topics. Any discussion of the exam at this point will only rev up your nervous system, which is probably in high gear already.

✔ When you walk into the test room, choose a seat (if you're allowed) with a good view of the clock. However, if someone's coughing, sniffling, burping, or otherwise making annoying sounds, be sure to head for the other side of the room. Distractions will not help you now.

✔ After you're in your exam seat, indulge in a little desk yoga. Raise and lower your shoulders a couple of times. Wiggle your feet. With your eyes closed, roll your neck in a circle. Breathe deeply and feel your tension melt away. Tell yourself that you're ready, you're set, and it's time to produce your best test results *ever.*

Tucked into the legalese at the beginning of the test is the rule that you will not discuss the multiple-choice questions at any time — during the exam, of course, but during the breaks and even after the exam is over. Nor may you divulge the essay topics for a specified period (usually a few days). The College Board is serious about security, and you should be too. If you blab, the College Board may cancel your score.

General Strategies for Saving Time on the Exam

I've placed exam-strategy instructions throughout this book near relevant topics. For example, I show you how to approach the poetry multiple-choice questions in Chapter 6, which is devoted to that sort of question. But for now, here's a lightning round of general strategy points about saving time when it counts the most, during the exam itself.

Zooming through multiple-choice questions

The multiple-choice section asks you to read five or six passages or poems and answer approximately 55 questions in 60 minutes. You don't have to be a mathematician to figure out that you need to hurry! Fortunately, a few time-saving techniques go a long way. For example, be sure to do the following:

✔ **Maximize your point total by concentrating on the genre that you know the most about.** For instance, tackle the poetry questions if that's your thing or the drama set if you're a theater fan. *Remember:* You don't have to do the questions in order! Concentrating on what you do well increases the odds of answering correctly.

✔ **If you read a passage that totally confuses you, skip the whole question set, regardless of genre.** The torturers (oops, I mean the exam writers) don't expect you to answer every question. You can receive a five on the AP English exam without completing all the multiple-choice questions (because you don't lose points for unanswered questions). You can always go back to that passage if time permits. If you skip a question, circle it in the test booklet so you can quickly locate it later.

Especially when you skip questions, be sure that you record your answers in the correct answer bubbles. Remember that if you omit a question — but not a row of answers — every succeeding answer will be wrong. (Makes your stomach flip-flop just contemplating that possibility, doesn't it?) To avoid this nightmare, I recommend saying — with your internal, noiseless voice — something like "I'm answering question 2, and this is answer-slot 2" as you darken each oval.

✔ **While reading a poem or passage, use the margin to jot down a word or two, noting what's going on at that spot in the selection.** However, don't write too much. Write just enough to orient yourself when it's time to answer the questions. Check out Figure 2-1 for a sample of these notes.

✔ **Mark a slash through the obvious wrong answers in the test booklet right away.** By doing so, you allow yourself to concentrate on the two or three answers that *may* be correct.

Speed-writing the essays

So many words, so little time. On the AP English exam, you have two measly hours to write three essays. It doesn't sound like much, does it? But when you think about it, you're really probably used to this pace. Sure, when you write a paper for English class the teacher may give you a week or so to write, but we all know that the time period soon evaporates when you subtract band practice, calculus homework, the cross-country meet, your Grandma Ethel's 80th birthday party, and all your other obligations. Thus you may have already mastered a method for gathering your thoughts, putting them in order, and writing them down in the shortest amount of time possible. If not, here's a good way to divide the 40 minutes recommended for each essay. Just remember that the best essays come from planning, writing, and revising.

The planning stage: The first 5 to 10 minutes

When beginning an AP essay, instinct probably tells you to grab your pen and begin writing immediately. Bad idea. You should prepare for a couple of minutes first. To do so, follow these steps:

1. **Read the prompt carefully.**

   Prompts — the two- or three-sentence questions that you have to answer by writing an essay — seem perfect for skim-reading, particularly when you're under time pressure. But that definitely isn't the case! Here's why: I can't tell you how many great essays I've read that reveal an understanding of the literary work, a good grasp of writing technique, and a complete misreading of the question. Sadly, this situation is the only one (other than turning in a completely blank sheet of paper) that merits a zero on the AP exam. Your classroom teacher knows and loves you and therefore may give you some credit for an essay that ignores the question. But not the exam graders! Instead of sprinting through a prompt, slow down.

Alice was beginning to get <u>very tired</u> of sitting by her sister on the bank, and of having nothing to do: once or twice she had peeped into the book her sister was reading, but it had no pictures or conversations in it, ëand what ï the use of a book,' thought Alice 'without pictures or conversation?'

A. reads

So she was considering in her own mind (as well as she could, for the hot day made her feel <u>very sleepy and stupid</u>), whether the pleasure of making a daisy-chain would be worth the trouble of getting up and picking the daisies, when suddenly a White Rabbit with pink eyes ran close by her.

sees Rabbit

There was nothing so *very* remarkable in that; <u>nor did Alice think it so *very* much out of the way</u> to hear the Rabbit say to itself, 'Oh dear! Oh dear! I shall be late!' (when she thought it over afterwards, it occurred to her that she ought to have wondered at this, but at the time it all seemed quite natural); but when the Rabbit actually *took a watch out of its waistcoat-pocket*, and looked at it, and then hurried on, Alice started to her feet, for it flashed across her mind that <u>she had never before seen a rabbit</u> with either a waistcoat-pocket, or a watch to take out of it, and burning with curiosity, she ran across the field after it, and fortunately was just in time to see it pop down a large rabbit-hole under the hedge.

In another moment down went Alice after it, <u>never once considering</u> how in the world she was to get out again.

A. follows W.R.

The rabbit-hole went straight on like a tunnel for some way, and then dipped suddenly down, so suddenly that Alice <u>had not a moment to think</u> about stopping herself before she found herself falling down a very deep well.

Either the well was very deep, or she fell very slowly, for she had plenty of time as she went down to look about her and to wonder what was going to happen next. First, she tried to look down and make out what she was coming to, but it was too dark to see anything, then she looked at the sides of the well, and noticed that they were filled with cupboards and book-shelves; here and there she saw maps and pictures hung upon pegs. She took down a jar from one of the shelves as she passed; it was labelled 'ORANGE MARMALADE', but to <u>her great disappointment it was empty</u>: she did not like to drop the jar for fear of killing somebody, so managed to put it into one of the cupboards as she fell past it.

fall

jar

'Well!' thought Alice to herself, 'after such a fall as this, I shall think nothing of tumbling down stairs! <u>How brave they'll all think</u> me at home! Why, I wouldn't say anything about it, even if I fell off the top of the house!' (Which was very likely true.)

Down, down, down. Would the fall *never* come to an end! 'I wonder how many miles I've fallen by this time?' she said aloud. 'I must be getting somewhere near the centre of the earth. Let me see: that would be four thousand miles down, I think —' (for, you see, Alice had <u>learnt several things</u> of this sort in her lessons in the schoolroom, and though this was not a *very* good opportunity for showing off her knowledge, as there was no one to listen to her, still it was good practice to say it over) '— yes, that's about the right distance — but then I wonder what Latitude or Longitude I've got to?' (Alice <u>had no idea</u> what Latitude was, or Longitude either, but <u>thought they were nice grand words</u> to say.)

A's thoughts

Figure 2-1:
An annotated literary passage.

2. Read the literary work, or think about it, with the question in mind.

You may be working from a poem or a prose or drama passage provided on the exam. (Two of the three essays on the AP exam fall into this category). If so, read the literary selection, underlining anything that seems relevant to the prompt and noting your ideas in the margin. (Figure 2-1 is an example of an annotated selection.) If you're working from memory (as you do in the third, open-ended essay on the AP exam), jot down everything that comes to mind when you think of the question. Go through your notes for a minute or so until you know what you want to write.

3. Create a thesis statement and locate evidence.

A *thesis* is the main idea of your essay. It's the statement you'll prove with evidence from the literary work you're writing about. AP thesis statements work from the prompt, adding the original idea that "answers" the question posed by the prompt. (Chapter 3 explains in detail how to create a thesis statement.) Once you know what you're proving, go back to the literary selection and select portions that support the case you're going to make.

4. Group your notes into subtopics.

When you're grouping "like" things together, don't rewrite anything; you have no time to waste! Instead, simply draw circles around similar ideas or connect them with arrows. Take a peek at Figure 2-2 for an example of notes that have been grouped into subtopics. The question for this grouping concerns the characterization of the title character of Lewis Carroll's *Alice in Wonderland*. The selection on which these notes are based is shown in Figure 2-1.

5. Place the subtopics in order.

Sometimes the order of your subtopics doesn't matter. But other times you'll find that one subtopic may lead to another in a logical progression. Again, don't waste time writing a formal outline. Instead, just label your groupings #1, #2, #3, and so on. Check out Figure 2-2 for an example.

Chapter 3 can help guide you through each of these steps in further detail, so be sure to give it a read through before you take the exam.

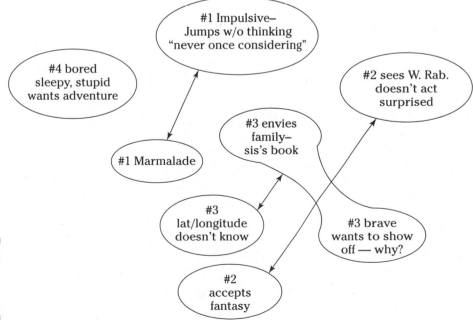

Figure 2-2:
An example of subtopic groupings.

Fleshing out your ideas in complete sentences: The next 25 to 28 minutes

Now, of course, you write the essay. Introduce the thesis and your supporting points in one or two sentences. Next take each supporting point in turn, inserting evidence that makes an airtight case for your ideas. Hop right along from one brilliant idea to another. Because you have little time, you want to make every word count. Don't waste time repeating yourself or making general statements that have nothing to do with the point that you're trying to make. Also, be sure that your final product is legible. No matter how brilliant you are, if the graders need an electron microscope to decode your handwriting, you're at a disadvantage. (Chapter 3 goes into detail on essay structure, topic sentences, and all sorts of things you need to know about writing an essay.)

When you're preparing to write, you can save time by abbreviating character's names (*A* for "Alice," for example) and by using shorthand (*w/o* for "without" or *&* for "and"). However, when you're actually writing an essay in the AP exam booklet, be sure to stay away from abbreviations or other shortcuts. Especially avoid IM-speak (and I mean avoid it like the plague). It isn't that exam graders (a.k.a. English teachers) are in the dark ages in terms of technology. It's more that they loathe sentences such as "BTW, she 8 early." They much prefer "By the way, she ate early."

Reviewing and polishing: The last 2 to 3 minutes

If you're good at math (or maybe even if you're awful at it), you've probably figured out by now that approximately 10 minutes of the recommended 40-minute essay is *not* devoted to writing. Yup. So you need to reread the essay quickly, fixing spelling and other errors and tucking in the last-minute ideas with a neat caret (^). All in all, you just want to polish it up so that it shines bright for the exam graders.

Polishing, you say? Isn't it enough that you got the thing on the paper? Actually, under exam conditions it probably is enough. But if you have even two minutes to reread what you wrote, you can catch some glaring errors that mar the essay. Look for spelling and grammar mistakes, omitted words (especially when you move from one page to the next), and missing punctuation or capital letters. If you think of an extra, amazingly insightful idea that will improve your essay, try to squeeze it in too. I guarantee you that the final product will be better if you take the time to spruce it up. (Chapter 3 provides some tips for effective polishing, and Appendix B provides a whirlwind tour through Grammarland.)

Unless you're allowed to type the essay on a computer as an accommodation for a special need, you can't easily insert an extra word or sentence into your written essay. And, although essay-graders are fairly good at deciphering bad handwriting, even they can't grade what they can't read. If you insert a word, be sure to do so *neatly*. Write the inserted word(s) above the line, and insert a caret (^) under the line, indicating where the extra material should go.

Chapter 3

Getting the Most Out of English Class

· ·

In This Chapter

▶ Improving your reading comprehension

▶ Taking better notes in class

▶ Researching and reading literary criticism

▶ Developing a larger vocabulary

▶ Mastering the essay-writing process

▶ Polishing your writing skills

· ·

*W*hen my son returned from his first semester at college, he went on and on about his wonderful English teacher. "He wants us to call him 'Hank,'" my son said. After a couple of minutes I asked whether "Hank" wore a flannel shirt or an old suit jacket with patches on the elbows. Surprised, my son replied, "Flannel shirt." How did I know? Because I've spent a lot of time in English classes.

You've probably spent enough time in English classes to recognize the basic teacher wardrobe too. In fact, you're probably enrolled in one right now. And whether your English class has the designation "AP" attached to its name or not, you're still preparing for the AP English Literature and Composition exam. What you learn in the class is important not only when you take the exam but also when you receive a grade.

This chapter explains how to make better use of the information you learn and how to do so more efficiently with a few simple techniques for note taking and reading comprehension. I also throw in some tips on vocabulary-building and speed-reading techniques, and I explain where to find good literary essays as supplements to your reading and as models for your writing. Finally, I outline an effective method for writing a literary essay, a task you face in class as well as on the AP exam.

Preparing for Class, Solo-Style: Working on Reading Comprehension

When I close up shop for the night and toss my books into the corner (or *fling* them if it's been a bad day), I almost always read another book purely for relaxation. I'm aware of the contradiction, but here's the thing: I love great literature. When I dive into a well-written book, I lose myself and my world. (Okay, I admit it. Sometimes I watch junk television. Come on, I'm not perfect.)

I hope you love the books you're reading for English class, but even if you don't, you can get more out of them — and maybe even like them better — if you approach them properly. Plus, reading with the techniques that I explain in this section helps you score well when the AP exam comes around.

Beach books — the kind you pick up for a page-turning, mind-numbing experience — are wonderful because they require no effort at all. Quality literature, on the other hand, asks you to invest some brainpower, and then it rewards you tenfold by stimulating your thoughts and emotions. Don't bother with the techniques in this section if you're reading feather-weight stuff. And don't even *consider* writing about beach books on the AP exam. For help distinguishing AP from non–AP exam material, turn to Chapter 14.

Decoding and interpreting literature

Let's say that your mission (and you have to choose to accept it or get an F for missing homework) is to read Chapter 38 of *Great Assigned Novel*. How should you proceed? By reading Chapter 38? Yes — and no. Of course you have to read the chapter, but a quick once-over isn't enough. You have to crack open the chapter like a walnut shell and digest the good stuff inside. The same is true if your homework is to read poetry. In this section, I take you through some techniques for solo work, also known as homework reading.

Curl up with the book you have to read for homework (or the one you're reading just because you want to). Because reading literature is intertwined with writing, also take out a pen or a highlighter. Don't write in the book unless you own it, of course. If you're reading a library or a school-owned text, confine your comments to a notebook instead. Or, if you find typing easier than writing by hand, power up your computer.

I prefer to take notes on a computer, but I don't like to read with my laptop on my lap. Here's my solution: I keep a pad of sticky notes nearby. When I come to a section that I want to write more than a few words about, I slap a sticky note on that spot. When I finish reading, I turn to the sticky note and type my thoughts. The sticky notes can be reused, too. That way you save some money and the planet at the same time.

Grasping content

Your simplest task when you're reading is to figure out what's happening. Specifically, you should do the following:

✔ **As you're reading, keep a "reader's notebook" containing thoughts and information about the works you read.** I said "notebook," but if you're more comfortable at the computer, keep a "reader's file." Every time you read, use the reader's notebook or file to record what's going through your head. Jot down plot points (for a novel, play, or story) and important ideas (for any type of literature). Take note of symbols and conflicts. Reflect on the writer's style. Argue with the author or copy out passages that you love. Review your reader's notebook before the AP English exam and whenever you have a class assignment and need a writing idea. Check out Figure 3-1 for a sample from a reader's notebook. Can you spot some potential essay topics? The treatment of an outsider comes to my mind as well as the symbolism of the conch.

Figure 3-4 later in this chapter contains a form that shows you how to record key facts about a literary work. It resembles a page from a reader's notebook, but it's just a skeleton. If you're really pressed for time, this form may substitute for a reader's notebook. However, if you can find the extra minutes to create a true reader's notebook, I highly suggest that you do so.

✔ **Take notes that help you create a skeletal outline of the chapter.** This technique is called *annotation*, and it's illustrated in Figure 3-2. Don't write too much. If you own the book, jot down a couple of words in the margin that summarize the content of each part. For example, you might write: "party scene," "Gregor wakes up," "boss visits," and so forth. If you're reading a poem, you may not find a narrative. Nevertheless, you should still note a couple of key points in the margin ("lover's description" or "compass comparison," for example). If you don't own the book that you're reading, list the page or line number and content summary in your reader's notebook ("line 12: lover's description" or "p. 21: compass symbol," for example).

✔ **If you're confused at any point, highlight or underline the difficult section or make a note of the page in your reader's notebook.** It may also be helpful to put a couple of question marks to indicate that you're puzzled. After all, by the time you finish reading you may forget why you highlighted or underlined the text! Go back to that section later, and try to decipher it with the context you've gleaned from the rest of the chapter. If you're still at sea, ask the teacher or do a little research. (You can read more on researching in "Hearing Out the Critics: Reading Literary Essays" later in this chapter.)

✔ **If you come to a word that you don't know, underline it or write it in your notebook and keep going.** Don't stop reading unless that one unknown word greatly hinders your reading. Later you can use a dictionary to check the definition, or you can ask a handy adult for help. (I explain this vocabulary-building technique in more detail later in this chapter.)

The dictionary built into your word processing program is too limited for serious literature. Instead, consult a printed dictionary, such as *Webster's New World Dictionary*, or turn to a good online source, such as www.answers.com or the dictionaries of the Internet Public Library (www.ipl.org).

Figure 3-1:
A sample
from a
reader's
notebook.

Lord of the Flies by William Golding

I just read the scene where Ralph meets Piggy for the first time. Piggy's really smart, but he's annoying. He's the one who says that they can use the conch to call a meeting. The conch seems important — maybe it's a sign of unity? But Piggy says, "My auntie wouldn't let me blow [the conch] on account of my asthma." Piggy's always sick, and he wouldn't be much fun to hang out with. Piggy is outside the group. Maybe that's why he can't blow on the conch, because the conch is a symbol of the group getting together, and Piggy is excluded as much as possible from the group. Ralph tolerates Piggy, but when Jack and the choir boys arrive, Ralph says, "His real name's Piggy." He sells out Piggy to get on Jack's good side. Now that they have a common enemy, Ralph and Jack are united. Poor Piggy — "even the tiniest child" joined in the laughter. Piggy's used to this treatment; he 'bowed his head' when they laughed. Piggy protests, but in the end he can't do anything, and Ralph just tells him that "Piggy" is better than "Fatty."

Figures 3-2 and 3-3 are examples of annotated texts. In Figure 3-2, which shows an excerpt from Jane Austen's *Pride and Prejudice,* notice that two vocabulary words, *reverie* and *conjecture,* are underlined. An asterisk and a question accompany a puzzling statement from Elizabeth ("Mr. Darcy is all politeness."). Marginal notes keep track of what's going on ("Miss B. disses E," for example). As you see, abbreviations are fine, and you don't have to be formal. I use "dis" as shorthand for "disrespects," just as my students do. (Who said English teachers weren't hip?)

In Figure 3-3, showing an excerpt from John Keats's "Ode on a Grecian Urn," *sensual* and *unwearié*d are questioned, the first for vocabulary and the second because of the accent. (In case you're curious, the accent is there to add an extra syllable, keeping the rhythm uniform.) Another annotation in this sample asks why the "love" is "more happy." Other marginal notes summarize ideas (for example, "unheard = better" and "talks to lover under tree").

"My dear Miss Eliza, why are you not dancing? Mr. Darcy, you must allow me to present this young lady to you as a very desirable partner. You cannot refuse to dance, I am sure when so much beauty is before you." And, taking her hand, he would have given it to Mr. Darcy who, though extremely surprised, was not unwilling to receive it, when she instantly drew back, and said with some discomposure to Sir William: *[WM. Lucas tells D. to dance w/ E.]*

"Indeed, sir, I have not the least intention of dancing. I entreat you not to suppose that I moved this way in order to beg for a partner."

[D's manners] Mr. Darcy, with grave propriety, requested to be allowed the honour of her hand, but in vain. Elizabeth was determined; nor did Sir William at all shake her purpose by his attempt at persuasion.

"You excel so much in the dance, Miss Eliza, that it is cruel to deny me the happiness of seeing you; and though this gentleman dislikes the amusement in general, he can have no objection, I am sure, to oblige us for one half–hour."

[Why does she turn him down?] ✳ "Mr. Darcy is all politeness," said Elizabeth, smiling.

"He is, indeed; but, considering the inducement, my dear Eliza, we cannot wonder at his complaisance — for who would object to such a partner?"

[Lucas thinks he knows how E. feels] "I can guess the subject of your reverie." **? ? ?**

"I should imagine not."

"You are considering how insupportable it would be to pass many evenings in this manner — in such society; and indeed I am quite of your opinion. I was never more annoyed! The insipidity, and yet the noise — the nothingness, and yet the self–importance of all those people! What would I give to hear your strictures on them!" *[Miss B disses E.]*

? ? ? "Your conjecture is totally wrong, I assure you. My mind was more agreeably engaged. I have been meditating on the very great pleasure which a pair of fine eyes in the face of a pretty woman can bestow." *[D. praises E.]*

Figure 3-2: An example of an annotated prose excerpt.

Heard melodies are sweet, but those <u>unheard</u>

Are sweeter; therefore, ye soft pipes, play on;   *unheard = better*

? ? ?

Not to the <u>sensual</u> ear, but, more endear'd,

Pipe to the <u>spirit ditties of no tone:</u>

talks to lover under tree   Fair youth, beneath the trees, thou canst not leave

Thy song, nor ever can those trees be bare;

<u>Bold Lover, never, never canst thou kiss,</u>   *frozen in time*

Though winning near the goal — yet, do not grieve;

<u>She cannot fade,</u> though thou hast not thy bliss,

For ever wilt thou love, and she be fair!

Ah, happy, happy boughs! that cannot shed

Your leaves, nor ever bid the Spring adieu;   *trees always green*

And, happy melodist, <u>unwearièd</u>. *? ? ?*

For ever piping songs for ever new;

Why? <u>More happy love!</u> more happy, happy love!

Figure 3-3:
An example of an annotated poem.

Excavating the subtext

In great literature, all the action is below the surface. Therefore, it's time to dig a little deeper and explore the *subtext,* the ideas that fall beyond the literal, "this-is-what-happened" level. Here's a map to guide you while you're underground in Literature Land:

✔ **As you read, think about the themes.** *Themes* are those ideas that the author's exploring. For example, in *Moby-Dick* Herman Melville isn't simply describing a whale hunt. He's pondering the nature of obsession, the drive to succeed at one particular task regardless of the cost. Here's another example: In *Antigone,* Sophocles tells the story of one woman's refusal to obey the law. But Antigone's defiance is the platform for Sophocles' consideration of the nature of power and the conflict between religion and the state, among other themes.

When you finish reading, slip on the author's shoes and walk a couple of steps. Can you figure out what ideas the author is grappling with? Jot down a few notes on the possible themes.

✔ **Underline or highlight any sentence or phrase that intrigues you, even if you don't know why, and then take a moment to free-associate about a keyword or about the whole thing.** When free-associating, write down what comes to mind when you see these words or sentences. Don't censor yourself. Just record everything that pops into your head. These random notes sometimes reveal themes or *symbols,* elements in the story or poem that represent more than themselves. If the book isn't yours, don't deface it! Instead, write the page numbers in your reader's notebook or use a sticky note.

Free association is especially productive when you're reading poetry. After all, poets seldom come right at you. They "tell all the Truth but tell it slant," as the great American writer Emily Dickinson put it. Free association is often the fastest way into a poem. (Check out Part II for more tips on decoding poetry.)

Go back over Figures 3-2 and 3-3 to see how themes are noted. In Figure 3-2, for example, the notation "D.'s manners" relates to the theme of appearance as a substitute for reality. The statement "Lucas thinks he knows how E. feels" relates to assumptions. Figure 3-3 contains the phrase "frozen in time," which is an important theme of the poem.

Recognizing style

Every writer has a style, even if it's a bad one. When you're reading good stuff, you should check out *how* something is written. In fine literature, style works hand in hand with meaning, quietly pushing the reader to a particular reaction. If you pay attention to style, as a bonus, you pick up some writing techniques to apply to your own work. Here's how you can get better acquainted with style:

✔ **Pay close attention to language.** Zero in on any word or phrase that catches your eye. These words and phrases may catch your eye because they're different or, conversely, because they're typical of the work. Why did the author choose that word or phrase? Would the effect be different if the author had substituted another?

✔ **Reread your notes and take a moment to consider *structure*, (how the piece is organized).** Does the structure relate to the meaning or affect the way the reader perceives the work? Why did the writer choose a particular structure?

For example, Mary Shelley's *Frankenstein* has a "frame" around the main plot, which is the creation of the "monster." The book begins and ends with a desperate man telling his story after having been rescued from an icy sea. The entire middle section of the novel *is* that man's story. The narrator of the "frame" echoes the desperation of the creature brought to life by Dr. Frankenstein. Therefore, before the creature enters the story, the reader is prepared.

✔ **Consider sentence length and the amount of space or emphasis given to various events or ideas.** Ask yourself why one event is emphasized and another is downplayed.

For instance, in *To the Lighthouse* Virginia Woolf places many important events in brackets. A major character's death is reported in one bracketed sentence, but a simple walk through town consumes ten pages. This style reinforces Woolf's belief in the importance of everyday life and the limitations of human perception of time.

✔ **Think about how the writer employs various elements of fiction.** Does the author use a lot of dialogue or a ton of description? How do these elements change the way you perceive the work?

✔ **Look for figurative language, which is the term for imaginative, non-literal expression.** Examples of figurative language include metaphors, similes, personification, and symbolism. (Check out Chapter 4 for more on these devices.) What effect does figurative language have on the meaning of the work or on the reader's reaction?

✔ **In a poem, notice how the lines appear on the page and how the words sound.** If you happen to be alone, read the poem aloud. (If you're in the library or in a crowd, hear it in your inner voice.) Examine the poetic techniques that the poet employs to achieve a certain sound or form.

These tasks sound like a lot of work, but they represent a change, not a huge addition, to the way you read. The few extra minutes they subtract from your life add a great deal of information to your head. Try them and see!

Taking Notes in Class

Consider this situation: You're in the middle of a heated discussion about a poem in class, and then the teacher throws out a probing question. Half a dozen students weigh in with their opinions. The comments zing around the room until the period is over. That's when you look down at your notebook; it's completely empty. Have you been there and done that?

How about this scenario: The teacher asks you to open to a page of James Joyce's *A Portrait of the Artist as a Young Man*. She then begins to talk about the symbols tucked into each sentence. She's excited about the literature, so she's talking fast. You scribble word after word in your notebook, but at the end of the period you have 15 pages of notes, none of which make much sense. I'm guessing you've been in this situation too.

Okay, maybe I'm exaggerating a little, but most students have trouble with notetaking. They write too much or too little, or they write just the right amount in such a disorganized fashion that the information isn't accessible. Yet as you know, it's crucial to extract the important points of each literature lesson and to record those points clearly.

The next time you're discussing a work of literature or are studying it on your own, try these strategies to make your notetaking more effective:

✔ **Dedicate one notebook or loose-leaf section of your binder to English notes and nothing but English notes.** Once every week or so, photocopy your handwritten notes and store them away from your notebook or binder. Then if you lose one copy, you won't come up empty when a test or a paper deadline looms. Having everything in one place allows for quick and efficient review of important points.

If you prefer computers, create a file called "English notes." Save the file, and don't forget to back it up every day. Computer crashes are the 21st century edition of "the dog ate my homework." In other words, your teacher will *not* be happy to hear that you need a deadline extension because something's wrong with your computer's hard drive.

✔ **Concentrate only on identifying the most important ideas, not on everything the teacher says.** Don't try to write down everything — even if you're a speed-writer. A word-for-word transcript is a waste of time and energy. If the teacher is lecturing, he or she may emphasize certain words or write a phrase or two on the board. Copy those words into your notebook. Then record a few of the comments that the teacher makes about those words or phrases.

During a lecture or a discussion class, most people aren't fast enough to catch every important point. Therefore, when you're taking notes on paper, always leave a large margin. During your next free moment, dig into your memory bank or consult a friend and add what you missed. (Computer files, of course, are infinitely expandable.)

✔ **Whenever the teacher says something that puzzles you, ask for clarification.** The best sort of learning is interactive for the same reason that makes playing a video game more fun than watching one. You need to be involved in order to engage your brain fully. When you get an answer, record the main idea and leave extra blank space. Later, fill in the details.

✔ **Don't ignore other students. If someone brings up a point that really makes you think, write the key words, just as you do when the teacher is speaking.** However, be sure to listen to the teacher's response. For instance, if you hear "interesting point, but . . ." you need to qualify the student's comment and not accept it as wholly on target. On the other hand, pay special attention to remarks greeted by "great point" or "excellent idea."

✔ **To wring the most literary knowledge out of your English class, find a study-buddy who's willing to read your notebook while you read his or hers.** Each of you can then add the notes that you missed the first time around. A short follow-up to class discussion with a study-buddy goes a long way toward increasing your knowledge of English literature. Two heads are always better than one!

Good notetaking doesn't just help you study for tests. It also helps you with your class essays. You probably have a hefty number of writing assignments to complete if you're at the AP level, and those assignments will be easier if you keep good notes. The notes provide factual information for your essays. Also, if the assignment requires you to come up with your own topic, your notes may be a goldmine of ideas.

Reading the Extra Mile: Beyond Course Assignments

You're probably already reading a pile of assigned texts that's several inches thick, so it's pretty daring of me to suggest that you read even more. Consider this section a lit-lover's "dare-to-dream" moment, because I'm going to propose that you find a couple of poems a week or one book a month that you read just for fun. Fun? *Fun?* I can hear your teeth grinding. But the fact is that if you pick something you like, reading it actually will be fun. And if you choose something you like that's also of good literary quality, you can prepare for the AP English exam without grinding even one tooth. (Chapter 14 includes standards for determining "good literary quality," and Appendix A gives you a list of great works that you can consider reading.)

After all that fun, keep the literary work fresh in your mind by recording a few facts about the work. You can use a form for all of your readings. Check out Figure 3-4 for a completed sample form on *Lord of the Flies.* You can fill out such a form for each extra poem or book you read. They'll serve as a sort of deposit slip for your memory bank. (A blank form, suitable for photocopying, is on the back of the yellow tear-out card at the front of this book.) As the AP exam nears, go through the forms and select a few works that you would feel comfortable writing about in the open-ended essay. Review those forms extra carefully. (Chapter 14 tells you everything you need to know about the open-ended essay.)

Title Lord of the Flies
Author William Golding
Date of Publication or Writing post–World War II

Main Characters
Ralph – leader of the "civilized" group on the island
Jack – leader of the hunters, turns on Ralph and Piggy
Piggy – fat, unpopular, smart, attaches himself to Ralph
Simon – oddball who sees what's going on
Samneric – twins, Sam and Eric, who are always together
Roger – a follower of Jack
"Littluns" – young kids, think monsters are on island

Setting
Uninhabited island, wartime - modern times

Important Plot Points
Evacuation plane crashes, no adults survive. Boys marooned. Ralph becomes
leader. Piggy finds conch shell. Jack leads hunters but lets signal fire go out.
"Littluns" convince everyone there's a monster. Hunt for monster. "Tribes"
split. Simon discovers the monster is a dead Parachutist. Jack's tribe kills
Piggy and hunts Ralph. Adult arrives to rescue the boys.

Themes and Symbols
Violence of human beings – innate. Civilization v. savagery. Loss of innocence.
Fear of the unknown.
Symbols = conch, fire, Piggy's glasses, pig's head.

Important Quotations
"There was a space around Henry . . . into which he dare not throw."
"Maybe it's [the monster] only us" – Simon.
"Ralph wept for the end of innocence, the darkness of man's heart, and for the
fall through the air of a true, wise friend called Piggy."

Figure 3-4: A completed sample of a form to keep track of important points in various works.

Hearing Out the Critics: Reading Literary Essays

Despite your best efforts, you may still be confused by what you're reading for an AP English class. The works of some of the very best writers, I have to admit, aren't particularly easy to figure out the first time you encounter them. I also have to admit that not every teacher is crystal clear all the time. And even if you have your own interpretation of a work, you may want to compare your thoughts to those of a literary scholar. Therefore, you should read some critical essays, also known as "literary criticism," on those works that you study.

Using criticism correctly, as a supplement to your reading

Literary criticism is essentially the printed version of the lectures or arguments you hear in English class. Studying literary criticism is most helpful *after* you've finished reading the work itself. Why? If you read the critics first, your response to the author's words is blunted by someone else's reaction. Your chance to see the work from a different angle may be lost.

Needless to say, you should never consider reading *about* the literary work as a substitute for reading the work itself. Yes, plot summaries and interpretations exist on the Internet, in bookstores, and in libraries. But these tools have their place, and that place is *following* your completely thoughtful reading of the literature. Use these summaries and character lists to help you remember or to clarify confusing points. See literary criticism as an aid, a supplement to your own thoughts.

Guess what? Reading literary essays has an added benefit: A quality piece of writing may serve as a model for your own work. Of course, some critics are better than others, both in interpreting and writing about literature. But if you turn to a good source, you can probably pick up some pointers. In fact, a bit of the critic's style may rub off on your own prose. At the very least, you'll know what you're aiming for.

After you read a literary essay, compare the author's ideas to your own. Do you agree with everything he or she says? If not, why not? Don't give up on your own ideas too quickly. If you hang out in the literary criticism world for a while, you discover that even the most learned scholars fight with each other over the meaning of a line or over an entire work. Join the battle by testing your ideas against theirs.

With all this talk of using other people's work as a guide, let me throw out this warning: Plagiarism is one of the worst offenses in the academic world (and, well, it's pretty bad in the real world too). The word is derived from a Latin word for "kidnapping." Literally, plagiarism is kidnapping someone's brainchild. I'm not exaggerating. When you're writing a paper for English class and you consult literary criticism in books or on the Internet, you *must* credit the source if you use his or her idea. Otherwise you're in big trouble, and you should be. If you're writing from memory — in a situation such as the AP exam — you probably won't remember where you found a particular idea. The graders understand this fact and therefore don't expect you to cite literary criticism. If you quote from a literary work provided on the exam, however, they do want to see quotation marks and line numbers. I explain how to cite works in Chapter 7 (poetry) and Chapter 12 (prose), both of which deal with writing essays.

Finding well-written criticism

After you're convinced of the importance of studying literary criticism, the next issue you have to tackle is where to find the best criticism. (Hint: You won't find it in the communal try-on room of your local clothing store. That's where you hear criticism regarding whether that purple-and-orange-striped bikini is *really* a good idea.) Try these sources:

✔ **The "800" numbers of the Dewey Decimal System:** This classification system is used by nearly every library, so check the catalog in your school or public library. The search term is the title or author of the work. You may find a whole book devoted to the work that you're reading, or you may stumble across a book of essays on various works.

✔ **Electronic databases:** Some libraries subscribe to electronic databases to expand their reference collection without building a bricks-and-mortar extension to the building. A professional in the field generally screens the material before it's accepted into the electronic databases. Some good literary criticism can be found in the following electronic sources:

- *Columbia Granger's World of Poetry*

- *JStor*

- *Literature Resource Center*

- *ProQuest Learning*

- *Twayne's Authors Series*

✔ **Critical editions:** Some literary works are published in "critical editions," which include a literary work and a sampling of the most famous critical essays about the work. The introduction or afterword of a literary text, which isn't necessarily an official literary essay, may also be a valuable source of ideas.

✔ **The Internet:** The Internet has some fine sites for literary criticism. Check out the Internet Public Library at www.ipl.org. The stuff on the IPL site isn't perfect, but much of it has passed muster after being reviewed by reputable scholars. If you don't find what you're looking for there, you can also try an all-purpose search engine, such as Google. With the "advanced search" function, enter the title and author of the work and the exact phrase "full text." You may turn up some fine critical essays that way.

The minute you hit the Internet, you open yourself up to a million authors, some of whom are wonderful scholars and some of whom are teens posting their homework essays. I'm not trying to disparage the young folk, but they aren't exactly the experts you need. Always look at the Web address (the URL), and take a moment to evaluate what you're reading. If someone's discussing "Mac Beth" and his wife, "Mrs. Beth," you're in the wrong place. A good rule is to stay with sites that are sponsored by universities. *Tip:* To identify a university-sponsored site, look for "edu" in the Web address.

If you run across any trouble with these literary criticism sources or you aren't finding what you're looking for, be sure to consult your friendly librarian. They always love a good research challenge and would be glad to help.

Building Vocabulary for Fun and Profit

Have you ever watched babies learn to talk? The little guys toddle around, pointing at everything they see, asking the large creatures that supply food, diapers, and hugs to teach them vocabulary lessons. And babies are so cute that anyone nearby immediately begins to coo, "*Tree*. That's a *tree*. Do you like the *tree*? Say hello to the *tree*," and a bunch of silly sentences like that.

Vocabulary building was simple in those days. It's simple now, too, but different. You already know the words you need to survive everyday life. Now you just have to learn the ones that help you survive standardized tests. Granted, the AP English exam doesn't include an official "vocabulary section." However, a few "vocabulary-in-context" questions pop up in the multiple-choice section. (Flip to Chapter 1 for a sample "vocabulary-in-context" question.) A strong vocabulary helps you understand the literary passages provided on the exam and gives you a fund of words to pick from when you're writing essays. Pretty good payoff for a wee bit of effort.

Happily, vocabulary building doesn't have to be a big production. Just tweak the way you read and, if you're willing, add a bit of vocabulary study. At that point, the fund of words you know will increase rapidly. Try these steps:

1. **Underline or list unfamiliar words.**

   If you're a reasonably good reader, you probably skip over words you don't know when you're engrossed in a book. You do so because you're looking for the main idea, and you can usually grasp the meaning even if one or two words are strangers to you. Not a bad technique, but a better way exists. Read with a pen and underline unfamiliar words (if you own the book). You can also note them on scrap paper, indicating the page on which you found them. Unless you're completely at sea, don't stop reading when you find a word that puzzles you.

2. **When you're finished reading, write one of your unfamiliar words on an index card, including the sentence or phrase in which the word appeared.**

   The context is crucial. Human beings don't learn particularly well from lists. If you can picture where you found a word and recreate its context, you have a much better chance of remembering it.

3. **Jot down the meaning of the word on the other side of the index card.**

   Be sure to select the definition of the word that fits the context of the sentence. You can use a dictionary to figure out the appropriate meaning. If someone's around who might know the meaning (a teacher or a parent, perhaps), just ask. Their definitions are just as good.

   When you look up a word in the dictionary, you may find 20 or more meanings. Be sure to select the definition that makes sense, given the meaning of the sentence or paragraph in which the word appears. Otherwise your effort will be wasted.

4. **Once a week, go through your index cards.**

   Read each word and the sentence you found it in. Try to remember the meaning. If you can't, turn the card over and check the definition.

5. **Add to your index-card dictionary whenever you hear an unfamiliar word.**

   I learn new words all the time from television, radio, and movies. (Not all of them are AP material, and some aren't even printable in a family-friendly book. However, as an English teacher, I'm always happy to expand my vocabulary.) If you hear an unfamiliar word in the media or in class — any class, not just English — put it in your index-card dictionary.

Hate index cards? Have handwriting that looks like a chicken walked through an ink puddle and then onto your paper? No problem. You can do the vocabulary exercise described in the preceding list on your PDA or on your computer. You obviously can't put the meaning on the other side of the card, because, well, you don't have a card. However, you *can* number the words and sentences. Number the definitions too, and place them at the bottom of the file. When you go through your vocabulary file, quiz yourself. Then scroll down to check the meaning.

The method described in this section may not be enough if vocabulary is really an issue for you. In that case you may want to devote even more time to a systematic study. I recommend *Vocabulary For Dummies* by Laurie Rozakis (Wiley, 2002).

Words have definitions, which are easy to find and memorize, but they also have *connotations,* or extra baggage of attitude and emotion that they carry around. For example, "slender" and "emaciated" have similar dictionary meanings, but they have very different connotations. Dieting to become *slender* is okay; moving on toward *emaciated* means you need a doctor's attention. Don't throw a new vocabulary word into your AP essays (or into your conversation, for that matter) until you're sure of the word's connotation. You pick up connotations from context; every time you hear the word, note how it's used.

Honing Your Essay-Writing Skills

AP essay writers usually are tripped up by four tasks:

- ✔ Getting all the words on the page before the time's up
- ✔ Deciding what to write
- ✔ Constructing a sturdy framework to hold your ideas
- ✔ Writing with a mature style (what English teachers like to call a "command of language")

In case you're wondering whether the AP English exam has anything to do with real life, I'm here to tell you that when I write a book, four things are difficult for me: getting all the words to my editor before deadline, deciding what to write, creating a suitable structure, and writing with style. The AP English exam certainly has a lot to do with *my* real life.

In Chapter 2, I explain how to gather your thoughts and quickly put them on paper when you're under time pressure. This situation occurs during the school year when you're writing an essay in one class period or when essays are part of the tests that your English teacher assigns you once a month or so. And of course, you have to produce three full-length essays in two hours on the AP English exam. No pressure there.

In this section I tackle the other three issues — content, style, and structure — for essays and English papers. *Note:* This section addresses essay-writing in general. For more detailed suggestions about a specific *genre,* or type of literature, turn to Chapter 7 (poetry essays) or Chapter 12 (prose and drama essays).

Deciding what to write

By the time you're old enough to even think about taking the AP English exam, you've probably penned a zillion essays and papers. And I'm guessing that at least once in all that writing you've hit the Wall. The Wall is tall, wide, and strong. It has question marks painted all over it. Hence its official name: Writer's Block. If your home address is on Writer's Block, you've got lots of company. However, you also have a way to move out. This section serves as your moving van.

Writing assignments in English class may be sorted into two barrels:

- ✔ **Assignments written in response to a specific question about a literary work.** These assignments are pretty straightforward (and sometimes downright stuffy!). The works you may be asked to write about include poems, novels, stories, nonfiction works, or plays.

- ✔ **Essays you write when the teacher gives you more freedom.** In this category, the teacher may say the equivalent of "write anything you want," or he or she may place some limits (for example, "Write anything you want about *A Tale of Two Cities*" or "Analyze how a character faces a moral dilemma in a literary work of your choice.").

Surprisingly, both barrels require you to make some decisions — even the first one. For instance, if you have a question *and* an assigned literary work, you still have to decode the question and figure out what point you want to make, which is the *thesis* of your essay. If you're working on an open-ended assignment, the possibilities are infinite, and so obviously you have to make some decisions to narrow them down.

When deciding what to write, you need a plan. Follow these steps:

1. **Decipher what the prompt, or question, requires.**

2. **Narrow your focus.**

3. **Create a thesis statement.**

4. **Gather evidence from the literary work to support your ideas and arrange them as subtopics under your thesis.**

I explain each of these steps in the following sections. For specific instructions on selecting evidence from literary works of each genre, turn to Chapter 7 (for poetry) and Chapter 12 (for prose and drama).

On the AP English Lit exam, you always work from a specific question, but sometimes you're given a passage or a poem to read, and sometimes you're allowed to choose the literary work. The information in the following sections helps you with both situations.

Scalpel, please! Dissecting an essay prompt

Half the battle in writing an essay in response to a specific question is figuring out what the exam writers want from you. *Prompts,* the two- or three-sentence questions about literary works, tell you what to do. (You may have some counter-suggestions for the College Board or your teacher, but it's probably better to keep them to yourself.) This section helps you deal with the prompt, the all-important first step in writing a great AP-quality essay.

Follow these steps when dissecting your prompt:

1. **Read the prompt carefully.**

   I can hear you now! You're saying, "What does she think I'm going to do, write the essay without reading the question?" But surprisingly, quite a few students read only part of the prompt or slide over it too quickly for real understanding. Needless to say, the resulting essay is a mess (and perhaps earns you nothing but a zero). Hence, I repeat: Read the prompt.

2. **Underline important words.**

   "The" doesn't count. Look for literary terms (setting, metaphors, conflict, and so on). Also check for the specific detail(s) you're supposed to focus on — character, plot point, theme, or whatever.

3. **Restate the question.**

   Reduce the query to its simplest terms, as if a child were asking it. However, don't bother writing the restated question; just hear it in your head.

4. **Write a couple of words to remind yourself of the focus.**

   Don't spend a lot of time on this step. Even if you're working at home, theoretically without a time limit (you've decided to forgo eating, sleeping, and math in order to maximize your English grade), you should keep written notes short and to the point. Besides, you want to practice for the AP exam!

Time for some examples of this technique in action:

Prompt: After reading the following poem, explain in a well-organized essay how the poet's <u>imagery</u> conveys the <u>complex attitude</u> of the <u>speaker</u> toward her <u>home</u>.

Restated prompt: How does the speaker feel about her home? What do I see, hear, smell, etc. in the poem that tells me how the speaker feels?

Notes: attitude of spkr → home, imagery

Now try another prompt:

> **Prompt:** In a well-organized essay, explain the <u>literary techniques</u> Eleanor Howard uses to <u>contrast</u> two stages of <u>Oliver's</u> life, <u>youth and old age</u>, in her novel *Against the Tide*.

> **Restated prompt:** What's the difference between Oliver's youth and old age? What literary techniques show the difference?

> **Notes:** O's youth/old age, lit tech → show difference

Narrowing your focus when you don't have a prompt

If you're allowed to write anything you want, an ocean of possibilities swamps you. You have to turn that ocean into a small stream — one that's easy to manage. In other words, you have to narrow your focus. This section explains how to do so, by following these steps.

- ✔ **Ask yourself what you *don't* know about the text.** Yes, I know this tactic runs counter to your instinct to go with something you're sure of. But writing is a form of thinking that may help you discover something about the work. If you start with a puzzle and note some possible interpretations, you generally come up with more original and creative ideas than a canned, "here's-what-we-said-in-class" essay.

- ✔ **Try a brain dump.** For ten minutes or so, take everything in your head relating to the assignment and pour it into your reader's notebook. Don't worry about paragraphs, spelling, or grammar. Just pour. When you're finished, reread what you wrote. You probably have one or two ideas to work with. Now take another ten minutes to "brain dump" about those possible ideas. Reread your writing. Chances are by now you have a topic and some subtopics as well.

- ✔ **Create a web of ideas.** If you're a visual person, forget about the lines on the paper. Jot down the ideas in random spots on a sheet of paper. Next, connect those that seem to belong together by enclosing them in a circle, square, or geometric figure of your choice. Or use little lines and arrows to connect things. Don't censor yourself, but do try to stay on topic. After everything that comes to mind is on paper, you should have at least one possible writing topic and several possible subtopics.

Creating a thesis statement

After you've decided what to write about — Iago's jealousy, the identity of the "secret sharer" in Joseph Conrad's story by the same name, the figurative language of Gregory Corso's poem "Marriage," for example — you're almost at the starting line. But before you write the essay, you still have to create a thesis statement and choose subtopics.

The *thesis* is the idea that you're going to prove, and it's written as one sentence. If you're working from a prompt, a good thesis may be a simple restatement of the question, with an added bit of originality from you. If the prompt asks you how the figurative language conveys the speaker's attitude toward art, for instance, your thesis may be something like "The figurative language in William Shakespeare's "Sonnet 107" reveals the speaker's belief that art confers immortality." The only new idea in this thesis statement is "art confers immortality."

If you don't have a prompt, you may have to dig through your notes a little until one idea takes over. Look for an idea that can be discussed. In other words, make sure it has room for analysis. *Warning:* Beware of creating a thesis statement that relies only on plot summary or stays on the surface of the literary work that you're writing about. For example, imagine that you're supposed to write about fate in Sophocles' masterpiece, *Oedipus the King,* and you come up with this thesis: "Oedipus meets his fate because he attempts to avoid it." Yes, this statement is true, but it doesn't leave you much to say beyond recounting Oedipus's flight from his adoptive parents in Corinth and his subsequent, fated interactions with his biological parents.

Also steer clear of thesis statements that are too broad or that contain too many ideas. You don't want to be in a situation where you have too much to prove. For example, a thesis statement that declares "Oedipus suffers the worst fate in literature" involves a comparison between Oedipus and every other character ever written. (I can't even begin to calculate how long the essay would be!) Here's another clunker: "Oedipus fights with Tiresias because Oedipus doesn't like the prophecy, but he fights with all the other characters too, such as Jocasta, Creon, and Laius, though he does get along fairly well with the chorus." Again, you would have to write all day to support that thesis. And even if you do take the time to write all day, the essay will lack focus because the thesis is all over the place.

The following are some examples of good thesis statements:

> In Edwidge Danticat's story, "A Wall of Fire Rising," the balloon symbolizes Guy's unattainable goals.

> Prospero, the main character in Shakespeare's play *The Tempest,* must forgo his magical powers in order to reestablish normal human relationships.

> Homer's *Odyssey* establishes a higher standard of loyalty for Penelope than for Odysseus.

Choosing subtopics

After your thesis statement is in place, zero in on *subtopics,* the supporting points or divisions of the main idea that you're discussing in the essay. The number and nature of the subtopics depend on the question, so I can't give you an all-purpose formula. However, do look for logical divisions, or "baskets" into which you sort ideas. For example, if you're writing an essay about diction, rhyme, and meter in a poem, you may have three baskets — one for each of those poetic techniques.

Lots of people think that three subtopics — no more and no less — are mandatory. This mythical requirement probably exists because a fine, sturdy structure for an essay is the five-paragraph plan, which includes an introduction, a conclusion, and three body paragraphs. You've probably been writing this sort of essay since elementary school. If what you want to say in your AP essay breaks down into three subtopics, great. But don't shoehorn four good subtopics or expand two great subtopics into three. Let the content determine the number of subtopics, not the reverse.

It's tempting to throw in a great but irrelevant idea just because it's, well, a great idea. Resist that temptation. Your essay will turn out better if the subtopics support your thesis. After all, you may love tuna salad and chocolate chip cookies, but I doubt that you'd appreciate tuna mixed with chocolate chips.

Construction zone: Building the essay

I currently live next to a construction site, and though I'm not enjoying the mess, I am interested in the process. The builders' first (and I imagine most crucial) job was to create a sturdy framework. You face the same challenge in writing an essay. The only difference is in the materials that each of you use. My neighborhood builders construct with bricks and steel; you work with an introduction, body paragraphs, and a conclusion. I explain these three literary building blocks in the following sections.

Introduction

In order to introduce the topic of introductions, I want to present three for your consideration. Here's the first one:

> Mr. or Ms. Essay Grader, may I present Famous Poet and offspring, "Great Poem"?

Oops. Not the introduction you need. You're in a literature exam, not a ballroom. Now take a look at this one:

> Poetry is a fine art, and everyone loves to read poems that deal with important issues. Poets approach issues from unique points of view. In "Great Poem" by Famous Poet, several important issues surface. One of these issues is . . .

Nope. Still not the introduction you need. As a matter of fact, the essay grader probably gave up by the end of the second sentence. The introduction should focus on the literary work you're discussing, not on literature in general. Here's one last example:

> In Sylvia Plath's poem "Tulips," the speaker contrasts the red, vibrant flowers with the stark whiteness of a hospital room. The imagery in the poem emphasizes the speaker's fragility.

Okay, third time's the charm. This last example introduction contains all the essentials: the name of the author, the title of the work, and the issues the essay will address (imagery and the speaker's condition). Notice how short this example is. I broke off after two and a half sentences, but you can see how the stage is set for a full-scale analysis of the poem's imagery and the speaker's mental and physical health.

Here are a couple of points to remember about introductions:

- ✔ In an essay that needs to be written in 40 minutes, such as those on the AP exam, get to the point quickly and concisely. Think *short, specific,* and *focused.* If time isn't a problem, you can throw in some fancy flourishes, such as an intriguing lead sentence or a quotation.

- ✔ The title of a novel or a play is underlined (if you're writing by hand) or italicized (if you're typing). The title of a poem usually appears in quotation marks, unless the poem is book-length (such as Homer's *Odyssey*).

- ✔ Avoid passive voice. For instance, refer to "Shakespeare's *Macbeth*," not "*Macbeth* written by William Shakespeare."

- ✔ Talk about the literary work, not the essay. In other words, you don't need to explain that "in this essay I will. . . ." As the sneaker advertisement says, "Just do it."

Body paragraphs

The body paragraphs are the meat of your essay. This is where you get the job done, actually answering the question. When planning out your body paragraphs, remember that you should devote one paragraph to each subtopic.

A *topic sentence* is the instant-message-length summary of a paragraph; it's the statement that orients the reader to the content. Think of the topic sentence as the kind of umbrella you want to carry in a rainstorm. It has to be large enough to cover everything, but not so huge that you knock out someone's eye. You can place a topic sentence anywhere in the paragraph, but the easiest spot is at the beginning. Here are a few examples:

> *The conflict between Guy and his wife is evident when they discuss their son's future.* (This sentence begins a paragraph analyzing a conversation about whether to place the son on the list for a factory job.)

> *Pronoun choices also emphasize the universality of the experience of "Diving into the Wreck."* (The paragraph cites the pronouns, which are embedded in lines such as "I am she I am he.")

> *Many allusions to Thomas Jefferson further emphasize the irony of slavery.* (This topic sentence starts off a paragraph about Jefferson and slavery in the context of a memoir.)

The best essay writers knit body paragraphs together into a seamless whole by inserting transitions. However, the AP exam doesn't allow time for elegance; your goal is a simple transition that gets the job done. Think about the subtopic in the preceding paragraph and the subtopic in the paragraph that you're about to write. Build a short, logical bridge between the two. (The later section "Writing with Flair: How to Take Your Prose Up a Notch" tackles transitions in more detail.)

After the topic sentence is in place, insert evidence and analysis. I discuss evidence and analysis for each genre in Chapter 7 (poetry) and Chapter 12 (prose and drama).

Throughout your essay (in the introduction, the body, and the conclusion), write in present tense. For example, the speaker *is,* not *was,* in the hospital. The only time you move into past tense is when you're talking about a narrative (a literary work that tells a story). In that case, you need to set one event before another, saying something like "The bell tower fell, and the townspeople are collecting funds to restore it."

Conclusion

Even though the conclusion is the cherry on top of the ice cream sundae, you may not have a lot of time to formulate one if you're writing under exam conditions. In fact, on the actual AP exam you may not get to the conclusion at all. Don't worry; you can still do well if your essay stops abruptly. If you *do* have a moment, however, you can impress the exam grader with a short but powerful conclusion.

When you're writing a conclusion, here's what to do and what to avoid:

- **Do** show what the reader gets from the literary work. In an essay about Chinua Achebe's *Things Fall Apart,* you may state that the reader sees the ignorance of the colonial administration.

- **Do** emphasize the significance of the point you've made. If you wrote about the role of the gods in *Antigone,* for instance, you might end with a statement about the inevitable conflict between human and divine law.

- **Do** end with a quotation. This tactic's a zinger if you do it right. In an essay about the power of art expressed in a Shakespearean sonnet, you may conclude like this: "Shakespeare's figurative language expresses the transience of human life, in contrast to art. The sonnet ends with a reference to the poem itself: 'So long lives this, / And this gives life to thee.'"

- **Don't** repeat what you've already said. You're writing a conclusion, not a summary.

- **Don't** say, "In conclusion . . ." If you have to tell the reader that the paragraph is the conclusion, you haven't been clear enough.

- **Don't** refer to the essay, saying, "In this essay I have proved that. . . ." Every English teacher I know *hates* that sentence.

Writing with Flair: How to Take Your Prose Up a Notch

Anyone who sees the contents of my closet knows that I am *not* the most style-conscious person on the planet (even though I live in Manhattan, one of the fashion centers of the country). However, I am very focused on writing style, and you should be also. Don't forget that your writing style develops as you read attentively. The section "Recognizing Style" earlier in this chapter explains the best techniques for reading as a writer. Special attention to these techniques will improve your style.

The easiest way to make writing more difficult for yourself is to aim for perfection. You want a flawless piece of prose, but nobody starts at perfection. You have to work toward it. Give yourself the freedom to write imperfectly, but leave time to fix your mistakes and add some extra, late-but-brilliant ideas. If you tell yourself that you're working on a rough draft that you can edit, you'll likely end up closer to perfection.

Choosing specific statements over general claims

A good rule to remember is that specific statements form the basis of your essay. Of course, you may insert some general statements into an essay, but the ratio between specific and general in your writing should resemble a nicely prepared steak dinner, with the specifics being the steak and generalities the seasoning. Make sure you serve up enough specifics to satisfy your reader.

Consider the following examples, drawn from an essay about Zora Neale Hurston's novel *Their Eyes Were Watching God.*

Bad general statement: Janie's many exciting adventures help her to mature.

Why this statement is bad: Janie, the main character, does have an interesting life, but this statement about her is boring! In fact, I nearly fell asleep writing it. Besides, "many exciting adventures" may be applied to thousands of literary characters. You want something that's specific to Janie.

Better general statement: Janie's three husbands, her flight with Teacake from respectability, the flood that nearly drowns them, the rabid dog, and Janie's shooting Teacake are all steps in Janie's journey to maturity.

Why this statement is better: This statement isn't one-size-fits-all. Unlike the general sentence about "many exciting adventures," this one gets to the episodes that the writer will discuss in his or her essay.

Expressing yourself clearly

The essay every teacher hates to grade is the one written by someone who spits out lofty vocabulary left and right. To put this point another way: Don't write sentences such as "The interaction between filial personages led to Roger's ultimate lack of approbation." The only way to respond to that sort of sentence is to skip over it and hope the essay improves. The ideas are fine, but the style is so pretentious that readers flee for their lives.

New words enter your working vocabulary gradually. First you recognize them in someone else's writing. After you've "dated" a new word for a while, you're ready to bring it home to meet the parents and insert it into your own writing. Be patient, though. Don't plop a word that you've just learned into an essay. If you do, you may wind up using it inaccurately.

Another enemy of clarity is overly complicated sentence structure. Check out the following:

Bad sentence structure: On that day it was this perusal of the night sky, which was only a morsel that had been strewn onto Henry's path by his twin brother after a long day in the windowless cubicle that was his life that led to his aspiration to become an astronomer.

Why this structure is bad: Do I have to explain? Do you have *any* idea what that thing calling itself a sentence is actually saying? If so, please report to Stockholm for the Nobel Prize in Understanding Bad Writing.

Better sentence structure: One day, after Henry had spent a few years of work in a windowless office cubicle, his twin brother insisted that they go to the park. The night sky inspired Henry to study astronomy.

Why this structure is better: The preceding sentence may not earn you a trip to Sweden to pick up the Nobel Prize for Literature, but at least the reader can decode it. Here's the bottom line: You don't want to sound like a two-year-old, but you do want to write intelligible prose.

Proceeding logically

Hopping around may be fun on the playground, but it's deadly in an essay — your essay reader is traveling with you from one idea to the next. Don't skip around unnecessarily, moving the reader from London to Topeka and back to Britain.

To help yourself proceed logically through your essay, spend a few minutes gathering ideas before you write. After you know what you want to say, put the ideas in logical order. And don't forget to employ transitions to guide your reader smoothly from one thought to the next. (For more details, check out the earlier section "Honing Your Essay-Writing Skills.")

Suppose you're writing about Franz Kafka's masterpiece, *The Metamorphosis,* which is the story of a man named Gregor Samsa who wakes up one day and discovers that he has turned into a giant bug. (And you think your morning is bad when the coffeemaker breaks!) Suppose you include in your essay one paragraph that describes the way that Gregor's father takes advantage of his son and another paragraph regarding the harshness of Gregor's employer. The transition may be something like the italicized sentence in this excerpt:

> Mr. Samsa lives off Gregor's income and does not attempt to find work himself until forced to do so by Gregor's metamorphosis. After Gregor changes, Mr. Samsa beats Gregor with a stick and confines him to a bedroom.
>
> *The parents are not the only characters who exploit Gregor.* Despite Gregor's unblemished record, the chief clerk comes to Gregor's house to complain that Gregor missed the early train and soon accuses Gregor of financial impropriety.

Notice that the transition sentence nods toward the discussion of Gregor's father in the preceding paragraph. The phrase "not the only characters" sets the stage for the next idea, the discussion of Gregor's employer.

Spicing up your writing with variety

Little kids like to hear the same story over and over, read in exactly the same way, just before bedtime. Why? Because monotony leads to sleep. Think about that fact when you write an AP essay. Do you really want to buy a ticket to the Land of Nod for your exam grader? Keep in mind that exam graders get the equivalent of a half-price ticket. After all, they're already tired from reading a few hundred essays when they open your pink AP answer booklet. The same warning applies to essays written for your English teacher. Do us all a favor and spice up your writing by

- Avoiding repetition
- Varying sentence length and structure

Here are a few examples:

> **Bad statement:** Telemachus matures and grows up as he searches for his father, Odysseus.

> **Why this statement is bad:** Pardon my snoring. A dictionary writer may certainly find a tiny distinction between "matures" and "grows up," but in this sentence they refer to the same process.

> **Better statement:** Telemachus matures as he searches for his father, Odysseus.

> **Why this statement is better:** This statement gets straight to the point without repetition. The bottom line here: Say it once and move on.

> **Bad statement:** Penelope remains faithful to her absent husband. Penelope never gives in to the suitors. Penelope tells her suitors why she cannot marry. Penelope must weave a shroud first. Penelope fools the suitors by unraveling her weaving each night.

> **Why this statement is bad:** Five sentences in a row begin with "Penelope." Each is of a similar length (around seven words) and has the same structure (subject-verb). Time to kick it up, as the television chef says.

> **Better statement:** Faithful to her absent husband, Penelope resists the suitors. After telling them that she cannot marry until the shroud is completed, she unravels her weaving each night.

> **Why this statement is better:** The choppiness is gone, and the two sentences have different patterns.

Part II
Poetry in Motion

The 5th Wave By Rich Tennant

"This next poem is called, 'Never Try to Milk a Bull.'"

In this part . . .

What's it to you? Poetry, I mean. Do you think of it as "Ooh, I get to read all this great stuff and maybe change everything I think about life?" Or is your response something more like "if that's what they mean, why don't poets just say it?" Regardless of which category you fall into — and I'm planted firmly in the first one — Part II holds something for you. Chapters 4 and 5 refresh your memory of poetry basics and provide a can opener so you can extract the meaning of a poem and appreciate the techniques poets use to convey that meaning. Chapter 6 enters multiple-choice territory, surveying common types of questions and explaining the best approach to each. Chapters 7 and 8 let you practice both multiple-choice and essay questions on poetry.

Chapter 4

Sorting Out Poetic Devices

. . . .

In This Chapter

▶ Understanding the literary terms used in poetry

▶ Appreciating how sound and form influence poetry

. . . .

American novelist Ernest Hemingway was once asked why it took him so long to write just a few pages. The hard part, said Hemingway, is "getting the words right." Poets spend even more time than novelists on "the hard part," mostly because a poem's word choice can add, subtract, or change meaning. And so can word order, punctuation, capitalization, the appearance of the words on the page, the sound of the poem, figurative language, and other similar elements. In this chapter, I review some of the poetic techniques that poets employ to carry meaning to their audiences. On the AP English Literature and Composition exam, you'll likely be asked about poetic elements in the multiple-choice section. Skill in recognizing these elements and their effect on the poem can also improve your essay on a poetry selection.

Your Link to a Poem's World: Imagery

The five senses — sight, smell, hearing, touch, and taste — connect human beings to the real world. In a poem, sensory details, or *imagery,* may link readers to the imaginary world created by the poet. For example, Samuel Taylor Coleridge's poem "The Rime of the Ancient Mariner" takes you into a fantastic, perfect for a dark-and-spooky-night situation. How fantastic? Death plays dice in one stanza, and dead seamen sail a ship in another. (And you thought the dead pirates' tale started with Johnny Depp!) The sensory details of this poem take you into the Ancient Mariner's world. Here are a couple of samples:

Sight:

> "*Her* lips were red, *her* looks were free,
>
> Her locks were yellow as gold.
>
> Her skin was as white as leprosy."

Taste and hearing:

> "With throats unslaked, with black lips baked,
>
> We could nor laugh nor wail;
>
> Through utter drought all dumb we stood!
>
> I bit my arm, I sucked the blood,
>
> And cried, A sail! a sail!"

Touch:

> "I closed my lids, and kept them close,
>
> And the balls like pulses beat,
>
> For the sky and the sea, and the sea and the sky
>
> Lay like a load on my weary eye . . ."

Smell:

> ". . . the rotting deck
>
> The cold sweat melted from their limbs,
>
> Nor rot nor reek did they . . ."

Poets have an unlimited number of sensory details to choose from when they're writing. The key consideration for you, then, is to determine *why* the poet has selected or left out particular details. Consider both of these categories when you're analyzing a poem. Figure out the overall impression created by the details included. Imagine additional, missing details. How would that extra information change the effect of the poem?

Expressing Creativity with Figurative Language

A very large portion of the official poet's toolkit is devoted to *figurative language,* the overall term for *figures of speech.* Figurative language, in the English-teacher world, refers to language that leaves the literal and hits the realm of imagination. My own theory, which I can't prove, is that figurative language is attractive to poets because they have only words to express the ideas that reside in the preverbal level. The only way out of this paradoxical situation is imagination, the lifeblood of figurative language. When you're reading a poem, pay special attention to the figures of speech explained here.

Similes and metaphors

Similes and metaphors probably first showed up in your English class years ago. They're elementary, in both academia and real life, because people use them every day to express comparisons. *Similes* are explicit comparisons using "like" or "as," and *metaphors* are implied comparisons without "like" or "as." Sometimes these comparisons are clichéd ("pretty as a picture" or "life is not a bowl of cherries"), but in quality poems they're creative and original. Here are some examples:

Similes:

> "We harden like trees, and like rivers are cold." (from "The Lover" by Lady Mary Wortley Montague)

> "Like a fawn from the arrow, startled and wild, / A woman swept by us, bearing a child . . ." (from "Eliza Harris" by Frances E. W. Harper)

> "He watches from his mountain walls, / And like a thunderbolt he falls." (from "The Eagle" by Alfred, Lord Tennyson)

What do you call an extraordinarily clever metaphor?

Metaphors place two things (or people) together, letting one describe the other. When metaphors stretch into really strange and clever territory and compare two things that are seemingly very dissimilar, they're called *conceits*. This sort of conceit has nothing to do with snobbery but a lot to do with ingenuity and complex meaning. Two of my favorite conceits are in John Donne's poem "A Valediction Forbidding Mourning." The speaker in the poem is going on a journey that will take him away from his beloved for a long time. He tells her not to worry about losing his love, which he compares to gold that has been "to airy thinness beat." It will endure hammering by stretching, but it will not break. (All the ladies can sigh and swoon now.) He also compares himself and his lover to a compass, the mathematical device that draws circles. His lover is the "fixed foot" that "in the center sit[s]. / Yet when the other far doth roam, / It leans and hearkens after it." How clever!

Metaphors:

"*A mother's love!* deep grows / That plant of Heaven . . ." (from "Lines Suggested on Reading 'An Appeal to Christian Women of the South' by A.E. Grimke" by Ada, Sarah L. Forten)

". . . these boughs which shake against the cold, / Bare ruined choirs, where late the sweet birds sang." (from Sonnet 73 by William Shakespeare)

"Thy rights are empire. . . ." (from "The Rights of Women" by Anna Laetitia Barbauld)

When you encounter a simile or a metaphor and want to find out what it's supposed to mean, examine the comparison. (Visualizing may help. For more on this technique, check out Chapter 5.) Ask yourself what the comparison brings to the poem. For example, Barbauld's metaphor (the last example in the previous list) compares women's rights to an empire. Empires are usually large (bigger than countries) and powerful. Because they can be aggressive, they must be defended. These ideas are folded into the poem by the metaphor, enriching the statement the poet makes about women.

Personification, apostrophe, synecdoche

Turning people into things and things into people is a poet's right. So is raising the dead, or at least talking to them. (Wouldn't you love to have such power? You do. Just write a poem.) Several figures of speech come from these poetic powers, including the following:

- ✔ *Personification,* a specialized type of metaphor in which you ascribe human traits to nonhuman objects or ideas
- ✔ *Apostrophe,* which addresses an idea, an object, or a dead or absent person
- ✔ *Synecdoche,* which refers to a part as if it were the whole (or vice versa)

Here are some examples of each:

Personification:

". . . but Patience to prevent / That murmur, soon replies. . . ." (from "When I Consider How My Light Is Spent," by John Milton)

"The river glideth at his own sweet will . . ." (from "Composed upon Westminster Bridge, September 3, 1802," by William Wordsworth)

"Because I could not stop for Death / He kindly stopped for me—" (from an untitled poem by Emily Dickinson)

Apostrophe:

"*Imagination!* who can sing thy force?" (from "On Imagination" by Phyllis Wheatley)

"With how sad steps, Oh Moon, thou climb'st the skies . . ." (from *Astrophil and Stella* by Sir Philip Sidney)

"O wild West Wind, thou breath of Autumn's being . . ." (from "Ode to the West Wind" by Percy Bysshe Shelley)

Synecdoche:

"Till hearts shall relax their tension, / And careworn brows forget." (from "Son for the People" by Frances E. W. Harper)

". . . I should have been a pair of ragged claws / Scuttling across the floors of silent seas." (from "The Love Song of J. Alfred Prufrock" by T.S. Eliot)

"Friends, Romans, countrymen! Lend me your ears." (from *Julius Caesar* by William Shakespeare)

Do some arithmetic when you encounter these three figures of speech. Think about what each adds or subtracts. If an object or a quality is personified, you relate to it on a more emotional (or dare I say *personal*?) level. Thus feelings are added. If the part substitutes for the whole, some humanity is subtracted. For instance, when "all hands are on deck," the sailors cease to be individuals and are reduced to their capacity to work.

Discovering Symbolism, Irony, and Allusion

American writer Dorothy Parker, famous for her cutting wit, wrote about receiving "one perfect rose" in her poem of the same name. Ever practical, Parker mused that a better present would be "one perfect limousine." The rose, of course, symbolizes romantic love. In real life or in poetry, a *symbol* represents more than itself.

A *metaphor* is usually a one-liner, a single comparison in a poem. Kick it up a notch and you have an *extended metaphor* — a comparison that's explored in detail in perhaps an entire stanza. In comparison, a *symbol* takes imaginative comparisons to the max, weaving extra meaning into the entire work. The symbol may be a place (the setting), an object, or an action.

Irony is easy to recognize but difficult to define. You're in ironic territory when a dog bumps into the dogcatcher, knocks him into a cage, and slams the door shut with a wagging tail. You're also in ironic territory when someone says the opposite of what he or she means. For example, had Dorothy Parker been an ardent conservationist, the kind of person who would rather walk 20 miles rather than burn carbon fuel, her comment about the limousine would be ironic. Irony can be *situational* (the dog/dogcatcher example above) or *verbal* (the Parker comment).

Allusion is a reference to something outside the literary work that brings everything associated with the allusion (literary, historic, biographical, and cultural) into the work. In his poem "Marriage," Gregory Corso alludes to "Flash Gordon," a character from a sci-fi space adventure. The allusion reinforces the idea that the speaker is entering unexplored territory (married life).

Here are some examples of these three literary terms.

Symbolism and irony:

"A Poison Tree" by William Blake

(01) I was angry with my friend:

 I told my wrath, my wrath did end.

 I was angry with my foe:

 I told it not, my wrath did grow.

(05) And I waterd it in fears,

 Night & morning with my tears;

 And I sunnéd it with smiles,

 And with soft deceitful wiles.

 And it grew both day and night,

(10) Till it bore an apple bright.

 And my foe beheld it shine,

 And he knew that it was mine,

 And into my garden stole,

 When the night had veild the pole;

(15) In the morning glad I see

 My foe outstretchd beneath the tree.

William Blake's short poem packs as much of a wallop as the apple (line 10), which is symbolic of the hidden wrath or anger that grows and grows in the speaker until it kills the enemy who eats it. The tree (line 16) is also a symbol, representing the slow process by which anger turns to vengeance and violence.

Not all symbols are as obvious as Blakes's apple and tree or Dorothy Parker's rose. When you're symbol-hunting, *free-association* is often the best technique to use. (Turn to Chapter 5 for more information on this technique.)

Blake's poem is also heavy with irony. The foe eats the apple because he knew that it was the speaker's (line 12). Therefore the foe's attempt to hurt the speaker (by stealing his apple) results, ironically, in death.

Allusion:

 And that one talent which is death to hide

 Lodged with me useless, though my soul more bent

 To serve therewith my Maker, and present

 My true account, lest he returning chide . . .

The preceding lines from John Milton's poem, "When I Consider How My Light Is Spent," allude to a story in the Bible's New Testament in which a servant is given a "talent" (a coin) by his master. Rather than making use of the gift, the servant buries it. When the master returns, he scolds the servant and banishes him "into outer darkness." The biblical allusion brings the idea of divine punishment and human accountability into the poem, which is the speaker's tortured reflection on how he uses his own poetic talent.

Talking the Talk: Understanding Diction and Tone

Excuse me, dearest reader. I humbly entreat you to eschew the latest news about Britney, Brangelina, and Paris and instead to devote your attention to diction and tone. Your failure to attend to this matter may result in irreparable harm. Do I sound funny talking like that? Maybe this will sound a bit more commonplace: Listen up! Drop the gossip magazine, turn off your PDA, and get with the diction/tone program! Or else . . .

Why do these two comments sound different? Let me count the ways. The words come from two separate planets. The first comment resides in formal territory, and the second comment lives on the streets. Put the two side by side and you see contrasting *diction*, or the vocabulary with which a writer expresses himself or herself.

I bet you were still in your cradle when you first understood *tone*, which is the way an author communicates a feeling or attitude toward the subject he or she is writing about. For example, in speaking terms, a sympathetic tone, as in "Oh, did you skin your knee? Poor baby!" can be distinguished from "Take out the garbage now!" without any formal lessons. Tone in writing is a little more difficult to determine, of course, because you can't hear the author's words as the author intended them to be read. Instead, you have to pick up clues from the text.

AP English Lit exam writers love to ask about tone, so be sure to get a good handle on it. To determine tone in poetry (or in other writing), you have to consider diction and *syntax,* the grammatical structure of the sentence. You also have to consider which details are included and which are left out. A little common sense helps as well. For instance, if the author is listing reasons and answering likely objections in advance, the tone is argumentative or persuasive. If the poet goes on and on about the snowy, picture-perfect holidays of childhood, nostalgia is a good bet.

Here's a poetic fragment written by John Keats entitled "This Living Hand":

(01)   This living hand, now warm and capable

Of earnest grasping, would, if it were cold

And in the icy silence of the tomb,

So haunt thy days and chill thy dreaming nights

(05)   That thou wouldst wish thine own heart dry of blood

So in my veins red life might stream again.

And thou be conscience-calmed — see here it is —

I hold it towards you.

To figure out the tone of "This Living Hand," you don't have to know that these were probably the last lines of poetry that Keats wrote before his death at age 26. Nor do you need to know that Keats was aware that he was dying. Take away those biographical facts, and you still see that this poetic fragment is both mournful and realistic in tone. The words are straightforward. For instance, the "icy silence" (line 3) contrasts with "red life" (line 6). The first five lines are almost brutal: This hand would "haunt" and "chill" (line 4) you. Line 7 is a command. This poet isn't turning away in sentimentality. He's facing death, and he's making the reader face it also, as he stretches out his still "living hand" — "I hold it towards you" (line 8).

When you're determining tone, "hear" the poem in your head. Put yourself in the author's shoes and imagine what he or she feels. Examine the language closely, and bring your own experience to the poem.

Adding Meaning with Sound

The earliest poetry was an auditory experience only — no one wrote anything down, possibly because no one could. Interestingly, lots of modern poetry isn't written down either, as anyone who's attended a poetry slam knows. However, sound matters in poetry regardless of whether written text is involved. Sometimes it matters a little and sometimes a lot.

Poets, like songwriters, manipulate sound in several ways. They play with rhythm and rhyme, with patterns and pattern breaks, and with a few established forms. Tune your ears to "extra sharp" and consider the elements of sound that are discussed in the following sections.

Rhyme

I imagine that the tendency to rhyme is hardwired into human brains. Rhyme is probably the first element you notice when you hear poetry, and it's also the element that little kids invariably insert into the first poems they write. In the earliest, nonwritten poetry, rhyme probably helped the poet or performer remember the poem. And even now, you can probably recall song lyrics more easily than a nonrhymed poem. The most obvious rhymes occur at the end of a line, but repetitive sounds may occur inside lines also.

End-of-line rhymes

End-of-line rhymes do some neat things. For instance, they create patterns, they tie particular lines together, and they separate some thoughts from others. You can name a *rhyme scheme* (a rhyme pattern) with letters of the alphabet. The first sound is "a," the second "b," and so forth. Here's an example of one popular rhyme scheme:

    a b b a a b b a a b b a c c

How would you expect the units of meaning to break down? How about three groups of four, with a pair of lines for the final punch, like this:

    a b b a   a b b a   a b b a   cc

The previous rhyme scheme belongs to an English sonnet. (I explain sonnets in more detail later in the chapter.) It works together with meaning. The first four lines present an idea. The second and third sets of lines elaborate on the idea. The last two lines, or *couplet,* present the logical conclusion, an extension of the idea, or the moral of the story. In Shakespeare's "Sonnet 73," for example, the poet presents three different images of aging — winter, sunset, and a dying fire. The couplet hits hard: You love more intensely what you're about to lose.

Poets have created thousands of standard rhyme schemes and about a million variations on those standards. Therefore, when you're analyzing a poem, don't get hung up on the rhyme scheme if you have letters all over the place — something resembling abcdbeccghij, for example. That's too weird to matter much. But if you see a simple pattern, check to see how meaning and rhyme scheme relate to each other.

Internal rhymes

Sound patterns that don't occur at the end of lines are also important. Look for repetition of vowels, which is called *assonance,* or consonants, which is called *alliteration*). If you hear repetition, examine the linked words for meaning.

Take a look at the following poem, "To Lucasta, Going to the Wars," by Richard Lovelace, a 17th-century poet:

(01)　Tell me not, Sweet, I am unkind,

　　　That from the nunnery

　　　Of thy chaste breast and quiet mind,

　　　To war and arms I fly.

(05)　True, a new mistress now I chase,

　　　The first foe in the field;

　　　And with a stronger faith embrace

　　　A sword, a horse, a shield.

　　　Yet this inconstancy is such

(10)　As you too shall adore;

　　　I could not love thee, dear, so much,

　　　Loved I not honor more.

Check out the long "I" sounds: Besides the actual word "I," which appears in several spots, you have "unkind" (line 1), "quiet mind" (line 3), and "fly" (line 4). These words, linked together, imply that the speaker is going to "fly" (escape) perhaps from "quiet," which is in the "mind" more than in reality. The speaker also worries about being thought "unkind." Now for the consonants: Search for the letter F and you turn up "fly" (line 4), "first foe" and "field" (line 6), and "faith" (line 7). Here's the meaning behind all this: The escape and the battle with the enemy is a matter of faith.

Rhythm (meter)

In poetry, *rhythm*, also known as *meter,* comes from two factors: how long a poem's lines are and where the *accents* occur in a line. By accents, I don't mean the tendency of New Yorkers to refer to pasta's favorite mate as "spaghetti source." Instead, what I mean is that English words have accented, or stressed, syllables. The word "syllable," for example, is really three sounds, with the first sound being the strongest, written in all capital letters here: SILL ah bull. If you say, "sill AH bull," no one will understand you. (Well, they'll at least think you talk funny.)

By manipulating line length and stressed and unstressed syllables, poets create patterns. The most important element of a pattern isn't its regularity, although the regularity can convey important thematic meaning as well as imply harmony or unity. It's the pattern breaks that truly matter.

To understand this effect, think of the children's game, Duck Duck Goose, in which one child walks around a circle of kids, tapping each on the head and saying "duck" over and over, finally declaring one of the children "goose." The "goose" has to get up and chase the child around the circle, racing for the empty spot. The word "goose" breaks the pattern and initiates a response. Pattern breaks in poetry do the same thing.

Read aloud the following poem, "She Dwelt Among the Untrodden Ways," by William Wordsworth:

(01)　　She dwelt among the untrodden ways

　　　　Beside the springs of Dove.

　　　　A Maid whom there were none to praise

　　　　And very few to love;

(05)   A violet by a mossy stone

    Half hidden from the eye!

—Fair as a star, when only one

    Is shining in the sky.

She lived unknown, and few could know

(10)   When Lucy ceased to be;

But she is in her grave, and, oh,

    The difference to me!

The lines in the preceding poem have a heartbeat sound: da DUM, da DUM, da DUM. Consider line 2, rewritten here with the stressed syllables capitalized:

be SIDE the SPRINGS of DOVE

Hear the pattern? Now consider line 1, which has the break underlined here:

she DWELT a MONG the un TROD en WAYS

The break here emphasizes "untrodden." Other spots in this poem where the rhythm breaks are at the words "violet" (line 5), "Half" (line 6), and "Fair" (line 7). All the qualities of Lucy are emphasized with these breaks: she's pretty, not usually noticed (if the path is untrodden, people aren't around), and mortal (flowers, such as violets, don't last long). The "Half" break is interesting: Not many people notice her, but the speaker does, so before her death she was only "Half hidden."

Poets sometimes cheat a little when they're creating a rhythm. If they need an extra syllable, for example, they add an accent, which of course stresses that letter. In "A Poison Tree," shown earlier in this chapter, Blake wrote "sunnéd" because he wanted two syllables, not the single syllable that he would have had with "sunned." In the same way, an apostrophe (the punctuation mark that creates contractions) cuts out a syllable if the pattern demands a shorter sound.

Because the literary world thrives on terminology, way too many names have been given to various rhythms. You've probably heard of some, including *iambic pentameter,* the heartbeat sound (da DUM) repeated five times per line. Sonnets and Shakespearean plays are written in this rhythm. Another popular term is *blank verse,* which is unrhymed iambic pentameter. I could add another 20 pages and give you a migraine by listing and explaining all the terms that apply to rhythm, but I won't. If you really want to know what a *trochee* is, check out a poetry textbook. On the actual AP exam, you can score a five without knowing all that literary vocabulary. The important thing is to know that rhythms exist and affect the reader's perception of the poem.

Examining Form: Line Breaks, Stanzas, and Enjambment

How does the poem look on the page? Where do the lines and stanzas break? The answers to these questions partly expose the *form* of a poem. Other elements of poetic technique also contribute to form, such as rhythm and rhyme (discussed earlier in the chapter). Some poetic forms are standard; these standard forms, such as ballads and epics, have names and more requirements than an Ivy League college. You don't need to know a lot about these standard forms for the AP English Lit exam, so in this section I take you through only the basic forms you may encounter.

You can impress the exam grader no end if you *correctly* identify the form of a poem that you're writing about. If you aren't sure, however, don't take a chance. You don't want a grader shouting, "Hey, everybody! This guy thinks that 42-line poem is a haiku!" Even if you can't name a particular form, you should consider the appearance of the poem and the line and stanza breaks. Seeing how those elements relate to meaning takes you a step closer to a great AP essay and to a higher score on the multiple-choice questions.

Appearance on the page

Poets in the old days before computers had to cross out and rewrite every time they changed a line break. Today, poets get to play endlessly with the end of a line, the end of a stanza, and the right and left margins.

Line breaks

Where a line breaks is a very big deal. Unconsciously, the reader sees a pause, which may or may not be reinforced by a punctuation mark. Zoom your eyes over these two selections, each from a separate poem:

> There is a lady sweet and kind,
>
> Was never face so pleased my mind;
>
> I did but see her passing by,
>
> And yet I love her till I die.

> The time is come, I must depart
>
>   from thee, oh famous city;
>
> I never yet to rue my smart,
>
>   did find that thou had'st pity.

The first selection, which is an excerpt from an anonymous, early-17th-century poem, has a punctuation mark at the end of each line. This punctuation creates a double-whammy: The end of the line signals the reader to stop and so does the punctuation. Each line comes across as a forceful unit. You can almost imagine someone making a case: "Your honor, There is a lady sweet and kind." (Slap on witness stand.) "Was never face so pleased my mind." (Slap.) "I did but see her passing by." (Stronger slap.) "And yet I love her till I die." (Triple-strength slap.)

Now check out the second selection. No punctuation mark appears at the end of the first line. The line break ends with the word "depart," which means "leave." However, "depart" also brings thoughts of death (the "dearly departed," as the saying goes). The line break says stop, and the reader thinks, at least subconsciously, "I must depart — I must die." But because there's no punctuation, the reader continues: "I must depart / from thee, oh famous city." Now instead of death, the reader imagines the idea of a physical journey away from a "famous city" or perhaps a permanent move.

The title of this poem, by the way, is "A Communication Which the Author Had to London, Before She Made Her Will." The author is Isabella Whitney, who in fact *was* leaving London to escape mounting debts. The title shows you that the punctuation-free first line wasn't an accident. The poet actually wanted to bring up the idea of death. For those of you who are addicted to literary terminology (perhaps you should join a support group), a line break without punctuation, with the thought continuing into the next line or stanza, is called *enjambment*.

Stanza breaks

Stanzas, grouped lines in a poem, are analogous to paragraphs in a piece of prose or to verses in a song. Stanzas may contain complete, separate thoughts. A stanza may also connect to another stanza in the same way that a line may run into the next if no punctuation stops the reader. However, a stanza break gives an extra forceful message, a kind of giant stop sign. When that stop sign is contradicted by a line that runs on, the poet has probably tucked a double meaning into the poem, much like the use of "depart" in Whitney's poem.

Lines, of course, may be cut to create a regular pattern — a particular number of syllables or a certain rhyme scheme. Ditto for stanzas, only now you're looking at a particular number of lines instead of syllables. When you're reading a poem, notice where the lines and stanzas break and, most importantly, *why* the lines and stanzas break where they do.

Margins

The well-dressed poem, conscious of its appearance, also has to manage its margins. The simplest poems are flush left, with the right margin determined by the logical line break. Consider this excerpt from "To the Right Honourable William" by Phyllis Wheatley:

> I, young in life, by seeming cruel fate
>
> Was snatch'd from *Afric's* fancy'd happy seat:
>
> What pangs excruciating must molest,
>
> What sorrows labour in my parent's breast?

Poets will often play with margins also, indenting lines to focus extra attention on them or to separate them from the preceding or following lines, as in this excerpt from "In Memorium A. H. H." by Alfred, Lord Tennyson:

> What are thou then? I cannot guess;
>
>   But though I seem in star and flower
>
>   To feel thee some diffusive power,
>
> I do not therefore love thee less.

Notice that the first and last lines of this stanza make one complete thought: What are you? I can't guess, but that doesn't mean I love you less. The second and third lines are also a unit of thought: I feel something, some power, when I see a star or a flower. As you see from the title, this poem is written in memory of "A. H. H." Hence the stanza is a meditation on death and the speaker's relationship to the dead person. The margins reinforce the separation of the two ideas that the stanza contains.

Margins can get even more creative. Lawrence Ferlinghetti's poem "Constantly Risking Absurdity," for example, compares the poet's art to a circus performer's balancing on a high wire. Some lines are flush left, some are flush right, and some are in the middle. Visually, the poem appears to teeter-totter, striving for balance. That appearance matches the meaning of the poem.

Some poets take special effects to the max and mold their words into a visual pattern. John Hollander has a great poem shaped like a swan and another that resembles a key. The French writer Apollonaire sends words about rain streaking in vertical columns down the page. You probably won't find any of these *shape poems* on the AP English Lit exam; the exam writers avoid controversy, and shape poems are sometimes seen as gimmicks. They are, however, lots of fun. After you've finished your exam, take a look at some shape poems and write one yourself.

Standard forms

The AP English Literature and Composition exam won't plop a lot of questions about standard forms in the multiple-choice portion of the test. And the literary selection you write about in the first or second essays may or may not be an easily recognizable form. Because you don't need to know much about these standard forms, and because so many are out there that a thorough discussion of the topic would make this book so thick that only a fork-lift could pick it up, I'll stick to the basics.

Here's a list of the few poetry forms that you should keep in mind:

✔ **Ballads:** A *ballad* sounds like a song, and for very good reason: Lots of ballads were originally sung, and a good ballad is musical even without an accompanying orchestra. Ballads have regular rhythm and rhyme, four- or five-line stanzas, and lots of repetition. They generally tell a story, complete with characters, dialogue, and description. Many ballads have been passed down orally from generation to generation, and you often see several versions of one ballad. My highly subjective list of great ballads includes "Sir Patrick Spens," "Bang the Drum Slowly," and "The Streets of Laredo."

✔ **Epics:** An *epic* is a long poem — book length! — that tells a story, usually about a hero or heroine. Homer's *Odyssey* is an epic, as is *Omeros*, which is Derek Walcott's modern take on the *Odyssey*. An epic generally has regular rhythm and may have rhyme as well.

✔ **Odes:** An *ode* praises or contemplates a person, an object, or a quality. Unlike some standard forms, the form of an ode isn't governed by a ton of rules. Many odes have three stanzas, but some have two and some have four (or even more). An ode is serious and formal. Think of an ode as the poetic equivalent of an essay. Read "Ode on a Grecian Urn" by John Keats and "Ode to the West Wind" by Percy Bysshe Shelley for two fine examples of this form.

✔ **Sonnets:** A *sonnet* is a 14-line poem that has, in my mind, the tightest set of rules in Poetry Land. I once asked a poet who was visiting my class why anyone would want to be bound by the sonnet form. Her answer? She said that when her feelings were out of control, the only way she could express them was by keeping them in a secure cage, and the sonnet form was the strongest cage she could find.

Apart from the 14-line rule, sonnets must be written in iambic pentameter (which I explain earlier in the chapter). Sonnets also have to follow a definite rhyme scheme. To make things even more complicated, the divisions created by the rhyme scheme have to relate to the content. Here are a couple types of sonnets you might come across:

 • The *English sonnet* distinguishes three sets of four lines (four lines is a *quatrain* in lit-speak) and one *couplet* (pair of lines). The rhyme scheme may be abab cdcd efef gg or abba abba abba cc or another variation. In this sonnet, the first 12 lines generally set out an idea that is restated three ways. The couplet is the "moral of the story" or the logical conclusion.

 • The *Italian sonnet* has a set of eight lines (an *octave*) and a set of six (a *sestet*). In this type of sonnet, you may find a question or a problem in the octave and a solution in the sestet.

Shakespeare wrote more than a hundred amazing sonnets. You may also enjoy the sonnets of Elizabeth Barrett Browning and some modern sonnets by Claude McKay and William Butler Yeats.

✔ **Free verse:** As opposed to blank verse, which I mention in the "Rhythm (meter)" section earlier in this chapter, *free verse* has no set structure at all. Lots of modern poets write in free verse, no doubt sighing with relief as they do so. Anything goes in this form!

Chapter 5

Unraveling Poetic Meaning

In This Chapter

▶ Identifying the literal and deeper meanings of a poem

▶ Using context and point of view to understand a poem

▶ Connecting your own experience to a poem

According to a famous but possibly untrue story, poet Robert Browning was once stopped by a poetry-groupie (yes, they exist) and asked to explain a line from one of his poems. After thinking for a few minutes, Browning supposedly said that when the line was written, only God and Robert Browning understood what it meant. "And now, Madam," continued Browning, "only God knows."

I doubt you'll have to puzzle through anything as difficult as Browning's poem when you take the AP English Literature and Composition exam. However, you will have to read some complicated works and nail both the literal and the deeper meanings. And don't forget that poetry accounts for anywhere from one third to one half of the exam. Poems appear in both the multiple-choice and the essay sections of the test. In this chapter, I refresh your memory of the basics of poetry, explaining how to approach a poem and how to identify and appreciate poetic techniques. I also take you on a test-drive of these techniques using some terrific poems.

Decoding Literal Meaning

The comment that most often makes me grind my teeth (and it's made so frequently that I'm chewing with little more than stubs) is "Poetry means whatever you think it means." I'll unclench my jaw long enough to explain why this statement is *not* true.

Yes, you interpret a poem, and yes, you bring your own experience to bear on the text. And yes, poets work from such a deep, intuitive level that sometimes even they don't know what themes and ideas they're tucking into their poems. But the poem *does* have a text, and that text isn't infinite. You can't, for example, turn "Mary Had a Little Lamb" into a poem about the horrors of war. Therefore, before you dive into interpretation (covered later in this chapter), you have to decode the *literal meaning* of the poem — what the poem actually says. The exam-writers are wise to this point, and quite a few multiple-choice questions examine your decoding skills.

Discovering poetic meaning with a simple set of steps

Chances are the first time you read a poem, you sense at least some of what the poet is trying to convey. You may know right away, for example, that the poem is about war and its tragic effects or about love and its tragic effects. However, if you stop after that first reading, you miss most of the good stuff. Quality poetry packs a lot of meaning into a relatively small space. To discover what's really there on the literal level, you have to read the poem a couple of times — not passively, but interactively. To do so, try these steps:

1. **Zero in on unfamiliar words.**

   To a poet, words are the perfect pail and shovel in the world's best sandbox. Some poets delight in finding words that hardly anyone ever uses. Others specialize in the most obscure definition of a common word. On the first read-through, underline any word that you don't understand. If you aren't operating under test security conditions, haul out a good dictionary or turn to a quality online source to check the definitions of the words that you've underlined. If you're taking an AP exam, dictionaries aren't allowed. In this situation, you have to work from context. Check out the later section "Considering Context and Point of View" for strategies that help you answer "vocabulary-in-context" questions.

   When dictionaries are off-limits and a word totally stumps you, don't give up on the poem. You may still be able to understand the main idea and get most or all of the multiple-choice answers right. If the poem appears in the essay portion of the exam, you probably have tons to write about, even without knowing one or two puzzling words.

2. **Examine punctuation.**

   Punctuation helps you untangle one sentence from another. Look for periods, question marks, or exclamation points that mark the end of a sentence. Also check for semi-colons, colons, commas, dashes, and parentheses. A semicolon continues a sentence and tells you that the words before the semicolon belong to one unit of thought and the words after the semicolon belong to another unit. Whatever the semicolon connects is closely related. A colon may precede an explanation, or it may introduce a list. Commas and parentheses set off words that should be grouped together.

   Poets are rebels, and they don't always feel bound by the usual rules of punctuation (or spelling, capitalization, the tax code, or anything else for that matter). When you check punctuation, keep in mind that the poet may be bending or breaking rules. If so, ask *why* he or she is breaking the rules, because chances are the change is intended to make a point.

3. **Check syntax.**

   Syntax is the English-teacher term for the way a sentence is put together grammatically. Poets often fiddle with the usual subject-verb order, so you may need to rearrange words or phrases in order to grasp what's going on. Start by asking yourself which ideas belong together. Then focus on the *verb*, the word that expresses action or state of being. To determine the subject, ask who or what is doing the action or exists in that state of being. Next, restate the subject-verb pair and ask "what?" The answer, if you get one, is a *complement*.

   You don't need to memorize grammatical terms. What's important is that once you have the subject-verb-complement (or subject-verb, if there is no complement), you've established the foundation of the sentence. Now turn to descriptive words or phrases. Ask "where," "how," "what kind," and similar questions to sort out what's describing what.

4. **Paraphrase the poem.**

   If you haven't done so already, read the poem a second time. Don't forget the title! It adds meaning also. After you've reread the poem, restate it in your own words. This activity is called *paraphrasing.*

5. **Identify the people in the poem.**

   If you have time, one more reading may be in order — unless, of course, you're 100 percent sure that you've grasped everything already. During this third reading, find out who's who. Also check on the *speaker,* or the "I" in the poem. (Remember, however, that not every poem has a speaker.) What can you determine about the identity of the speaker? Can you find any other people in the poem? What do you know about those folks?

Poets often write from personal experience, but they reserve the right to invent characters, even when they're using *first person* (the "I, me, my" form). In other words, don't confuse the poet with the speaker.

6. Identify the setting and situation.

Not all poems have a distinct setting, but some do. To get a thorough understanding of the poem, as you read, ask "where," "when," and "what's going on."

Applying the steps to a classic poem

Now that you know what steps to take, it's time to see them in action. For starters, read the following poem, "To Lucasta, Going to the Wars" by Richard Lovelace, a 17th-century poet:

(01) Tell me not, Sweet, I am unkind,

That from the nunnery

Of thy chaste breast and quiet mind,

To war and arms I fly.

(05) True, a new mistress now I chase,

The first foe in the field;

And with a stronger faith embrace

A sword, a horse, a shield.

Yet this inconstancy is such

(10) As you too shall adore;

I could not love thee, dear, so much,

Loved I not honor more.

To analyze this poem, apply the steps I gave you earlier. Here's a quick rundown of what to do:

1. Glance through the poem, searching for words that are new to you.

Some words that might be new to you include "inconstancy" (disloyalty), "nunnery" (a place where nuns live), or "chaste" (pure). Now that you know the vocabulary in the poem, you can proceed to Step 2.

2. Review punctuation and the breakup of text.

You can see that each *stanza,* or grouping of lines in a poem, is one complete sentence. Now you know that you're looking for a complete, separate thought in each stanza. The semicolons in the second and third stanzas subdivide each of those complete thoughts into two smaller units. To decode the poem, examine each separate thought in turn.

3. Consider the syntax in the poem.

Line 1, for example, is fairly conventional. The verb is "tell" and the subject is an implied "you" because the sentence is giving a command. The only word in a strange spot is "not," but you can easily see that "tell me not" is the equivalent of "don't tell me."

After line 1, the syntax is more unusual but still accessible. Simply look for the next verb, which is "fly" (line 4). The subject is "I." Now you have a base ("I fly") to hang the other words on. Where do I fly? "To war and arms" (line 4). From where? "I fly from the nunnery / Of thy chaste breast and quiet mind." Now you've cracked the first stanza, except for the word "That" (line 2). You may expect it to belong to the first line, which would then read "Tell me not, Sweet, that I am unkind." However, the comma after "unkind" hints at a break. So, "That" belongs to lines 2–4, where it means "because."

The first line of the second stanza contains the verb "chase," which is easily paired with the subject "I." So what is the "I" chasing? A new mistress. The next verb in this stanza is "embrace," but no subject leaps into view. Reread the stanza. Who's going to embrace? The only possibility is the "I" of line 5. What does the "I" embrace? A sword, a horse, a shield. (I hope the speaker has unusually long arms.) The only words left to figure out in this stanza are in the phrase "the first foe in the field." The semicolon tells you that lines 5 and 6 are lumped together, so the first foe in the field must be the speaker's new mistress.

In the third stanza, the first subject-verb combo is "you shall adore." What shall "you" adore? Inconstancy. Why? The clue here is "such," which means you should expect a description or a qualifier for the meaning of inconstancy. Bringing it all home, the last two lines explain the meaning of "such." Start with the subject-verb combo in line 11: "I could not love." (Grammatically speaking, "not" isn't part of the verb, but don't quibble. It belongs with the verb to make the meaning clear.) The second verb, "loved," is missing a subject, but the "I" stretches to cover this verb too. The tricky word in the last line is "not," which isn't in its usual spot before the verb. Unscramble the order and add some implied words, and you see that the last line means "if I didn't love."

4. **Bring everything together and paraphrase the poem.**

   Paraphrased, the poem says something like this:

   - **Stanza 1:** Don't tell me, sweetheart, that I am unkind because I am going away from the nunnery of your pure breast and quiet mind. I am going to war.

   - **Stanza 2:** True, I have a new mistress to chase now. The new mistress is the first enemy I find in the field of battle. I am embracing a sword, a horse, and a shield with a stronger faith.

   - **Stanza 3:** However, you will appreciate my disloyalty because of what motivates it. I could not love you the way I do if I didn't love honor more.

5. **Find out who's present in the poem.**

   The speaker is a man who's leaving the one he loves in order to go to war. The other person in the poem is "Lucasta," whose name appears only in the title.

6. **Determine any facts about the setting and situation.**

   The poem doesn't tell you much about the situation. You never find out which wars he's going to, where Lucasta lives, or how she reacts to her lover's comments. But in this situation, it's okay because you already know the basic, literal meaning of "To Lucasta, Going to the Wars."

Not many poems yield their literal meaning on one reading. Look over the poem two or three times until you're sure you know what the poem says. Don't give up if a portion of the poem is unclear. You may be able to answer most exam questions even if you haven't nailed every single idea.

Unearthing Deeper Meanings in Poetry

The "poem" in the average greeting card may be touching in its sentiment. It may sound pretty, and it will certainly look nice. However, I doubt that a greeting-card poem has anything below its surface. What you see is what you get. The sort of poetry you encounter on the AP exam, on the other hand, has a secret life. Poets work at least partly from their subconscious, reaching into that magic spot that's also home to dreams. Like dreams, poems may contain symbols, odd juxtapositions, and strange images. And, like dreams, a poem won't yield its deeper meaning until you give up logic and allow yourself to make some intuitive leaps from one idea to another.

Don't be dismayed. Unearthing the deeper meaning of a poem isn't a nightmare. A couple of simple techniques, which I explain in the following sections, serve as ladders to take you down the hatch.

Some techniques work better than others, depending on the poem that you're reading. Go with whichever technique is most productive. And if you hit a dead end, try a different approach.

Checking connotations and double meanings

Emotions, ideas, and attitudes latch onto words. If these qualities influence how the word is understood, you're talking about *connotation*. For instance, many people over 65 years old call themselves "seniors" rather than "old" because for them "old" has negative connotations — a sense of being irrelevant, physically impaired, or over the hill. (I'm not 65 yet, but when I get there, I plan to use the term "experienced.") To make your life even more miserable, connotations may change over time. What was once a compliment or a neutral remark may now have a negative connotation. For example, "gossip" originally meant a gathering of women. The connotation was positive, in the sense of females helping each other (through childbirth, for example.) Nowadays, "gossip" carries another meaning, as in *I heard that he said that she liked* . . . well, you know what I mean.

The easiest way to see what a connotation brings to the poem is to substitute other words with the same definition or denotation. If the line reads, "this old pair," think how the effect would be different if it were "these two senior citizens."

Double meanings are important, also. The poem "To Lucasta, Going to Wars" that's discussed earlier in the chapter contains the word "arms." Literally, the speaker is talking about armaments (bows and arrows, swords, spit balls, water balloons, or whatever else they fought with back then). However, "Lucasta" also has arms, and presumably she has used them to hug her lover.

Applying free association

In my work as an English teacher, I probably do more with *free association* — a technique borrowed from Freud, where random thoughts are linked and analyzed — than the average psychoanalyst. Free association can tear down writer's block (see Chapter 3) and can help your reading by uncovering meaning in all sorts of writing. To that end, it's especially helpful when you're reading poetry. Here's how it works:

1. **Select a couple of important words from the poem.**

   You know a word is important if it shows up several times, if it surprises you, or if it occupies a key position (close to the beginning or the end of a line). On a piece of scrap paper or in the margin of the test booklet, write the words you've chosen. Leave some room around each.

2. **Concentrate on the word and write down the ideas that pop into your mind.**

   When jotting down your ideas, don't bother with sentences or punctuation. Keep your comments short; write just enough to remind you of the thought.

3. **Reread what you've written.**

   Do any of the ideas relate to the poem? If so, they become part of the meaning.

Figure 5-1 is an example of a free association to the word "honor" from "To Lucasta, Going to the Wars." Here are some of the words that I jotted down around the word "honor," along with the reasons why:

- ✔ **"Male and female roles":** I wrote this because way back when Lovelace wrote this poem, honor had different implications for men and women. I wrote "virtue" to represent the association of honor with Lucasta's purity and virginity, because in Lovelace's time much emphasis was placed on a woman's virginal state. Therefore "honor" in line 12 relates to the words "nunnery" (line 2) and "chaste" (line 3). These ideas contrast with "inconstancy" (line 9).

- ✔ **"Religion":** When jotting down "religion," I thought about the many religious rules that govern sexuality. That idea led me to write "sex," which relates to the word "breast" (line 3). However, in the poem "breast" is paired with "chaste," so the implication is that the speaker has sought comfort with Lucasta, not sex.

- ✔ **"Active/passive" and "defend honor":** When associated with men, honor links with fighting because traditionally — and certainly in Lovelace's era — it fell to the men to defend their honor and the honor of their loved ones by fighting or "going to wars," (which is obviously a phrase found in the title of the poem). This association led me to think about how men took action to uphold their honor, in contrast to women, who were to refrain from action; that is, they were obligated to remain virginal. Thus in this poem, the speaker is going to war, and Lucasta is supposed to understand his actions and remain pure, presumably waiting for him.

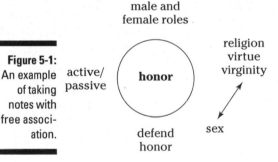

Figure 5-1:
An example of taking notes with free association.

Figure 5-1 represents just one possible free association from "To Lucasta, Going to the Wars." Your free association to "honor" may be completely different from mine and still be valid. You can extract even more from the poem by free-associating to other words. My choices for the next most interesting and important words are "fly" (line 4) and "faith" (line 7). "Fly" may open up the whole idea of freedom, and "faith" may deepen the religious parallels in the poem. Free-associate and see what you come up with. The "big ideas" in the poem, by the way, are *themes.* The speaker in Lovelace's poem is saying goodbye to his lover, but the poem deals with the themes of honor, freedom, and faithfulness.

Visualizing

When you're reading a poem, you may *visualize,* or play a film clip in your head so that you can "see" the poem. Don't visualize only the "real" scenes described in the poem. Also visualize the scenes evoked by comparisons, especially *similes* (comparisons with the words "like" or "as") and *metaphors* (comparisons without "like" or "as"). Add the sounds, smells, and tactile sensations to your visualization. When you visualize the poem, its meaning may become clearer to you.

Take a look at this William Wordsworth poem, "She Dwelt Among the Untrodden Ways," while you visualize what you read:

(01)　　　She dwelt among the untrodden ways

　　　　　Beside the springs of Dove.

　　　　　A Maid whom there were none to praise

　　　　　And very few to love;

(05)　　　A violet by a mossy stone

　　　　　Half hidden from the eye!

　　　　　Fair as a star, when only one

　　　　　Is shining in the sky.

　　　　　She lived unknown, and few could know

(10)　　　When Lucy ceased to be;

　　　　　But she is in her grave, and, oh,

　　　　　The difference to me!

This poem isn't the most complicated one ever written, but even so Wordsworth packed extra ideas into these 12 lines. After reading the poem, conjure up the scene in your imagination: Picture "untrodden ways" (line 1) — paths so remote that no one walks on them. See the "springs of Dove" (line 2), perhaps some water bubbling nicely. ("Dove" is the name of a couple of rivers in England, but you don't need to worry about that fact.) Now add the "violet by a mossy stone" (line 5). The stone's been sitting there a long time, so in your mental picture, make the stone look untouched and permanent. Visualize the hard rock and the delicate flowers next to each other. Then paint in a sky with just one star.

What does your whole mental picture now show you? You probably see a natural scene, something pretty and fragile (like the violets), and something that will never change (like the stone). You probably also see something that's unique — the fact that there's only one star in the night sky.

At this point, you now know what this "Maid" (line 3) means to the speaker: Lucy is natural, pretty, and unique. She's also dead, because she's "in her grave" (line 11), a permanent state echoed by the "mossy stone" (line 5). Her life was fragile, as violets are. The nature images reinforce the theme that life and death are natural elements of life. The single star (line 7) elevates this simple girl; because she's unique, Lucy can't be replaced.

Listening

On the AP exam, you can't read the poem aloud, but you can "hear" it in your head. Listen for words that stand out. Determine why those words are important. Also, identify sound patterns, if any are present. How does the pattern affect the reader/listener? Pay special attention to repeated sounds. Words that share sounds (rhymes or repeated letters) are linked. Determine whether those links reinforce or change the meaning.

Coming to terms with poetic language

English teachers are English teachers because they love language. Is it any wonder that they've coined a few words of their own? Literary terms abound when you're studying poetry, and if used properly, these terms warm the hearts of AP essay graders. However, even the most obsessed English teachers realize that students usually don't want to acquire a specialized vocabulary that's hardly ever useful at parties. After all, if you say, "Let me tell you about that asyndeton I read yesterday," the room will clear more quickly than if you say, "A rabid dog just walked in."

Literary terminology is fading fast on the AP exam. Therefore, I stick to the most common literary terms. Still, feel free to throw in words such as *asyndeton*

wherever you wish. You don't know what asyndeton is? Congratulations. You have a life. I don't, so I can define it. *Asyndeton* is the omission of conjunctions, words such as "and" that traditionally tie ideas together. "I sweated, I persevered, I scored a five on the AP exam" is an example of asyndeton. Aren't you sorry you asked?

Much more important than throwing around literary vocabulary is understanding the poem and, in the essay, communicating what you've gleaned from the text. In the multiple-choice section, of course, the most important thing to do is to come up with the right answer, which I can pretty much guarantee will never be asyndeton. But, it may be something more basic, such as *personification,* which is the attribution of human traits to nonhuman elements.

Read the poem "She Dwelt Among the Untrodden Ways," which appears in the previous section, aloud, or listen to it with your inner voice. The first thing you hear is that the poem has a regular, not an erratic, sound. Each stanza has four lines, with rhymes in the first and third lines and the second and fourth lines. In the first stanza, for example, "ways" (line 1) rhymes with "praise" (line 3) and "Dove" (line 2) rhymes with "love" (line 4). The only variation is in the second stanza, because "stone" isn't a perfect match for "one," but it's close enough. You may also notice that the first and third lines of each stanza are a bit longer than the second and fourth. Taken all together, you hear a song-like quality. The poem sounds simple and natural, qualities that Lucy has. (Check out Chapter 4 for more details on how poets use sound to manipulate their poems.)

Considering Context and Point of View

A good way to split the shell of a poem and allow more hidden meaning to spill forth is to consider context and point of view. By *context* I mean when the poem was written and in what situation. The AP exam writers are fairly discreet when it comes to context. They rarely tell you the name of the author or say anything about the selection other than "read this poem carefully." But, because you have reading experience, you may be able to infer more or less when something was written, and some of the references in the poem may help you determine the situation surrounding the poem.

For example, earlier in this chapter, I consider the traditional male and female roles in interpreting "To Lucasta, Going to the Wars." That context deepens the meaning of the poem. Here's another example: I know a thing or two about the Elizabethan era, when a big deal was made of "courtly love" (an idealized relationship that was never meant to come down to who does the dishes every night). Hence when I read an Elizabethan poem, I don't assume that lovers are married. In fact, I assume that they aren't.

Context can help you understand what you're reading, but unless you're sure, don't bring too much to the poem. If you're off by a hundred years or assume the wrong author, you may be completely wrong in your reading of the poem.

Point of view in poetry is also important, and it usually shows up in the following ways:

✔ If the poem has a speaker, you get his or her point of view.

✔ If you encounter other characters whose points of view differ from that of the speaker, you get their points of view.

✔ The poet may reveal his or her own point of view.

In Robert Browning's "My Last Duchess," for instance, the speaker is a Duke who had his wife, the Duchess, murdered because she smiled at everyone equally and didn't appreciate his "nine-hundred-years-old name." The poet conveys the Duke's tone of jealousy and pride, and you easily pick up the poet's condemnation of the monstrous speaker. The other characters in the poem are the Duchess, who appears only in a portrait on the wall looking "as if she were alive." You also run across an implied listener, who's visiting the Duke to make arrangements for the Duke's next marriage to the daughter of his employer, the Count. You can infer much about the Duchess from the Duke's comments, especially his criticisms of his dead wife. However, you don't get direct information about her point of view or the point of view of the marriage emissary, which I hope for the sake of the Count's daughter was highly unfavorable.

Bringing Your Own Experience to the Poem

A poem, according to many poets, is only partly finished when it reaches the page. The reader's reaction, which includes everything in the reader's life that helps him or her relate to the poem, is also part of the meaning. Recalling similar experiences may help you understand what the poet is getting at.

Going out on a limb, I'm going to guess that you've never hired a hit man or been murdered by an ego-tripping Duke. Nevertheless, you've probably met a snob or encountered jealousy at some point in your life. When you read Browning's poem, "My Last Duchess" (see the discussion in the preceding section), you can bring that snobbery or jealousy into your reading of the poem. You may, perhaps, have made a sarcastic comment about the Big Man on Campus who wouldn't shake hands because he didn't want to ruin his manicure. Your personal experience with sarcasm can help you see that Browning isn't presenting a grieving husband and a pretty picture of his dead duchess. Instead, he's showing you the nut case who murdered her and the attitude of snobbery that nurtured the Duke's egomania.

Be careful when you apply your own life experiences to a poem. Your experiences may be an entryway into the poem, but in the end, the work itself must contain enough evidence to support your interpretation. Take care to differentiate what you're bringing to the poem and what the text actually says.

Chapter 6

Acing Multiple-Choice Poetry Questions

In This Chapter
▶ Surveying multiple-choice poetry questions
▶ Creating a strategy for each type of question

*I*n a perfect world, one where homework is illegal, the AP English Literature and Composition exam wouldn't contain even one multiple-choice poetry question. Instead, test-takers would read beautiful poetry and write about it. The problem with multiple-choice poetry questions is simple. It's possible to come up with a great — and valid — interpretation of a poem and not find a single answer in the five choices that matches your idea. Then what do you do?

Panic! No, just kidding. To avoid running into this problem on the test, you simply need to read this chapter. It helps you examine the most common types of AP English multiple-choice poetry questions, pick up on the College Board lingo, and acquire strategies that maximize your score. (The basics — how many questions, how much time, and so on — are explained in Chapter 1.)

One point to note before you dive in: If you've read ahead, you may notice that the terminology that I use to describe the types of poetry questions in this chapter is the same as that in Chapter 11, but I've placed some terms in different categories. The reason? The questions that the College Board asks about poetry differ greatly from those that they ask about prose and drama. For example, most poetry syntax questions query you about meaning, perhaps because the meaning of poetry is sometimes difficult to grasp. In prose and drama, syntax questions usually revolve around the reason an author chose a particular syntax. The definition of syntax doesn't vary, but the questions about syntax do.

The Devil's in the Details: Factual Questions

Many of the poetry multiple-choice questions test simple reading comprehension and attention to detail, not interpretation. If you read carefully, the factual questions will breeze by as you darken oval after oval, each with the correct answer. This section deals with how to grasp the facts, all the facts, and nothing but the facts.

Reading comprehension: Extracting details

Lucky for you, quite a few questions on the AP English Lit exam ask nothing more than the meaning of a particular line. Granted, sometimes that line is no picnic. After all, it may contain hidden meanings (Chapter 5 helps you in this area) or weird vocabulary (see the next section). But your normal, everyday reading ability will get you to the correct answer more often than you think, because the questions are most times pretty straightforward; you just need to know how to take them apart and examine all the pieces. Check out this excerpt from Byron's poem *Don Juan*:

(01)   Don José and his lady quarreled — *why,*

   Not any of the many could divine,

Though several thousand people chose to try,

   'Twas surely no concern of theirs nor mine;

(05)   I loath that low vice — curiosity;

   But if there's anything in which I shine,

'Tis in arranging all my friends' affairs,

Not having, of my own, domestic cares.

A sample question about a poem such as the preceding one may read like this:

Line 3 may be restated in which way?

 (A) No one cared about the quarrel.

 (B) The quarrel's origins were well-known.

 (C) The couple's quarrel was the subject of much speculation.

 (D) The couple confided in their friends.

 (E) Everyone sided with either Don José or his wife.

Byron's poem is proof that gossip didn't begin with the Internet. Byron, who was as popular with the media of his own time as Brad Pitt is with modern journalists, understood celebrity. And this stanza of his poem mocks people who say they aren't interested in gossip. Answering the sample question calls for basic decoding skills. Check out the details in line 3, which tells you that "several thousand people" were discussing the couple and "chose to try" to figure out why Don José had a fight with his wife. Therefore the quarrel was the subject of "much speculation." (For a thorough review of methods that help you grasp the literal meaning of a poem, turn to Chapter 5.)

Decoding poems also goes hand in hand with vocabulary and syntax, which I discuss in the next two sections.

Vocabulary: Examining individual words

Poets are like kids in a sandbox surrounded by toys, only the toys are words — big words, little words, unusual words, and even made-up words. Maybe that's the reason vocabulary is often queried on the AP exam. The College Board wants to know that you can work your way through a difficult text and grasp the meaning of a word in context.

Questions that quiz your knowledge of literary terminology are becoming quite rare on the AP exam. However, they aren't totally extinct yet, so keep your eyes peeled. You may see a question asking which figure of speech appears in the poem or, more commonly, which figure of speech does *not* appear. Either way, you have to know the vocabulary to answer the question. (See Chapter 4 for a quick review of poetry-related vocab.)

Deciphering definitions in the context of a poem

One or two questions per selection generally ask for the meaning of a word *in the context of* a particular line. I italicized the bit about context because, as Hamlet says, "There's the rub": You may know a large percentage of the English language, but poets rejoice in bending language into word pretzels. And, as you can guess, exam writers rejoice just as heartily in bending answers (A) through (E) into word puzzles.

You have one point in your favor: Unusual or extremely difficult words are defined in footnotes, so you don't have to know, for instance, what a *zither* is. (It's a musical instrument, in case you're curious.) The words that the AP exam asks about are easier, though the questions aren't. Don't assume that the first definition that pops into your mind is the correct answer. The exam writers like to throw in five true definitions of the word they're asking about. The problem is that only one of those definitions is accurate *in the context of* the poem. Substitution is a good strategy for these cases. Look at the indicated line and restate it in your own words, inserting your own definition. Then check the five possible choices and choose the one that comes closest to the word you selected when you paraphrased.

If nothing matches your first attempt at paraphrasing, turn to your fund of real-world knowledge and try again. Suppose a line reads "gribbling in pain, her elbow was now in her eye and then in her nose." I made up the word *gribbling,* so don't be shocked if it's unfamiliar. Even though you can't know what *gribbling* means, you do know how people act when they're in pain. They may, for instance, groan, contort their bodies, or cry. If the elbow is moving around, contorting (or twisting) is the probable definition. Look at the choices, and find one that matches those ideas.

Check out this excerpt from Edward Arlington Robinson's poem, "Credo":

(01)   I cannot find my way: there is no star

        In all the shrouded heavens anywhere;

        And there is not a whisper in the air

        Of any living voice but one so far

(05)   That I can hear it only as a bar

        Of lost, imperial music, played when fair

        And angel fingers wove, and unaware,

        Dead garlands where no roses are.

A sample question about a poem such as the preceding one may read like this:

The word "bar" in line 5 may best be defined as

(A) a place that serves drinks

(B) an impediment

(C) a musical measure

(D) a metal rod

(E) a stripe

All of the choices correctly define the word "bar," but only choice (C) fits the context. You may know nothing about music except how to download it, but the words surrounding "bar," such as "Of lost, imperial music," take you to the correct answer. The real-world method also helps in this case. For example, you've probably seen sheet music somewhere, even if only on television or in the movies. And so, you probably know that the notes are divided into sections, or bars, which you can measure.

A question may appear to address vocabulary but instead deal with another, completely different issue such as figurative language, tone, or attitude. For instance, suppose you see the following question based on the previous poem "Credo."

Which of the following best expresses the meaning of "shrouded" (line 2)?

(A) a cloth that covers the dead

(B) grief

(C) cloudy

(D) mysterious

(E) cotton

A "shroud" is a covering for the dead, but Arlington Robinson isn't talking about a literal shroud. If you chose (A) or (B), you fell into that trap. Choice (B) may entice you because the poem is sad, but line 2 deals more directly with the appearance of the sky. (D) is tempting, but the poem refers to an absence of stars, which makes the night dark but not necessarily mysterious. (E) isn't supported by any details in the poem. Go for (C), because Arlington Robinson's "shrouded heavens" is a figure of speech describing a cloudy, starless night. (Check out "Finding value in figures of speech" later in this chapter for the best approach to these types of questions.)

Considering the meanings of the answer options

Some questions that challenge your vocabulary aren't asking about words in the poem. Instead, the question is worded simply and the answers contain the difficult vocabulary.

The mood of lines 1–8 is best described as

(A) elegiac

(B) optimistic

(C) aggressive

(D) nostalgic

(E) rueful

Okay, vocabulary fans, time to go to work. The best answer is (A). "Elegiac" comes from *elegy,* a lament for the dead. When you read the complete poem, you grasp the speaker's grief easily, but you can't answer the question unless you know the meaning of *elegiac.*

In this sort of question where the answers are more difficult to understand than the question, context or real-world knowledge is no help. You either know the word or you don't. Your best strategy is to eliminate answers that are clearly wrong. If you can cross off two or three, take a guess. Otherwise, skip the question entirely.

Syntax: Singling out grammatical structure

Syntax questions contain an element of revenge. Didn't pay attention when your teacher was droning on and on about pronouns? Wham! Here's your punishment: Explain the meaning of "that" in line 84. And *that* will teach you to call grammar irrelevant!

Okay, maybe the exam writers' intentions aren't exactly as I describe. In fact, the revenge may be purely accidental. However, *syntax,* the grammatical structure of the writing, is most definitely relevant and important. If you don't understand syntax, you may not be able to understand a poem. However, if you can decode the poem, you can often answer a syntax question with no trouble at all, simply by relying on your understanding of what the poem actually says.

Here's the great secret about syntax: You don't have to remember all the definitions that your sixth-grade teacher threw at you. Syntax questions can be answered purely on the basis of logic and reading comprehension. (For more help with decoding skills, flip to Chapter 5.)

Syntax questions tend to focus on a couple of grammatical principles that you can remember without all the fancy terminology. Here's a list of bare-bones examples showing common types of questions and how to answer them:

- ✔ **What is the subject of the verb _____ (line X)?** Ask yourself who or what is doing the action described by the verb in the blank. Or, in the case of a "be" verb (is, are, was, were, has been, and so on), ask yourself who or what is in the state of being expressed by the verb in the blank. The answer is the subject.

- ✔ **The subject _____ (line X) may be paired with which verb?** Ask yourself "What is the word in the blank doing?" or "In what state of being is the word in the blank?" The answer is the verb.

- ✔ **What does the pronoun _____ (line X) refer to?** Other versions of this question ask about the pronouns "which," "that," or "who." To answer this type of question, untangle the units of thought in the sentence. Attention to punctuation, if the poet uses any, pays off. Semicolons and periods divide major units from one another, and so the pronoun probably refers to something in the same unit. If the author of the selection is playful with punctuation marks, try using logic. Figure out what statement is being made about the pronoun and then find something in the poem that matches.

- ✔ **The structure of the sentence in lines X–Y serves to . . .** This sort of question pops up when the structure is unusual. The subject may follow the verb, for instance. This pattern stresses the importance of the subject ("arrived the honored guest" emphasizes "guest," for example). The sentence may include a number of similar structural elements. You may see something like "I sang and I danced and I ran away with the drummer." The repetition of "I-verb" elements may equate these actions, making each equally important. Or, in another context, the repetition may create rising tension.

- ✔ **The statements beginning with _____ in lines X and Y describe . . .** When you come across these questions, you have another reading comprehension issue on your hands; your best bet is to attack this type of question with logic. If the syntax is really complicated, remember that punctuation helps. You may see a bunch of commas around descriptions, and descriptions are usually in the same unit of thought as the word they describe. Periods and semicolons separate major thoughts.

Read this excerpt, from an Emily Dickinson poem, and then try the sample syntax question:

(01)   I said, but just to be a bee

         Upon a raft of air,

         And row in nowhere all day long,

         And anchor off the bar, —

(05)   What liberty! So captives deem

         Who tight in dungeons are.

A sample question about a poem such as the preceding one may read like this:

The word "So" (line 5) refers to

(A) dungeons

(B) the act of rowing

(C) the act of anchoring

(D) the way captives think about liberty

(E) a bee

If you're grammar-savvy, you know that "so" is an adverb that describes the verb "deem," which means "think" or "consider." (Fortunately, the terms "adverb" and "verb" aren't essential for nailing this question!) The word "So" in this sentence means "in this way." Therefore, the last sentence may be restated more simply as "Captives who are tight in dungeons think in this way." Just before this last sentence is "What liberty!" (line 5). Put these two ideas together and you know that choice (D) is the correct answer.

What Lies Beneath: Interpretation Questions

If AP English Lit multiple-choice questions stayed with the facts, the "what" and "who" of the poem, your life would be a lot simpler. Sadly, you also have to answer "why" and "how." These high-end questions move beyond fact into interpretation, querying the purpose, effect, and implied meaning created by poetic techniques such as imagery, diction, tone, and structure. These questions sound tough, but with the explanations of these techniques in the following sections, you'll be a pro in no time.

Considering the significance of sensations: Imagery

Imagery questions sit in the gap between literature and reality. In reality, thousands upon thousands of sensory impressions fill every single second of our lives. No poet can — or wants to — include them all. Instead, poets select the details that reinforce their meanings or *themes* (the ideas that a poet is pondering).

When you come across an imagery question, ask yourself "why." Why, for instance, does the poet use this detail and not another? Also ask yourself "how." How would a poem be different if a lion replaced the spider that's currently discussed in the poem? After you understand why and how the imagery functions, you can grasp the meaning that the imagery conveys.

Imagery questions resemble the following:

- ✔ **The description in lines 14–18 serves to _____.** Take the description out and read what's left. How has the meaning changed? Or consider substituting a different description. What else changes in the poem when you substitute descriptions? For example, a description of the speaker's ramshackle hut may emphasize poverty. If the poet had omitted the hut and instead focused on a description of a modern school attended by the speaker, the focus might shift to ambition or possibility.

- ✔ **The shift in imagery between the second and third stanzas may be characterized by . . .** Ah, shifts. The College Board exam writers love shifts! Here's how to take care of these questions: Take a look at the stanzas that you're provided, and then underline the imagery in the second stanza (or whatever stanza that you're analyzing). What do you see, hear, smell, and taste? Now underline the imagery in the third stanza (or the next stanza that you're supposed to be analyzing). What's the difference between the two sets of imagery? Has the author shifted from "ocean-clouds" to "clear blue sky"? If so, then perhaps the poet is shifting from pessimism to optimism. Make two lists in your head (you won't have time to write much) and compare.

- ✔ **Throughout the poem, the imagery suggests that . . .** As you do for an imagery shift, first pick out and underline the images. Substitute something different for the images and see how the poem changes. Now you probably know what the original imagery adds to the poem. You can also visualize or use free association (see Chapter 5) to unpack the deeper meaning of the imagery.

✔ **The _____ is characterized primarily by . . .** Depending on the poem, the answer may be imagery, dialogue, the speaker's reaction to whatever's in the blank, or any number of things. Ask yourself what you know about the word in the blank and then ask *how* you know it. If, for example, the blank contains the word "elephant" and the elephant's "rough gray skin," "lumbering gait," and "moist, prehensile trunk" dominate the poem, the answer is imagery.

✔ **The purpose of lines 20–23 is to . . .** If the lines are filled with imagery, the purpose may be simply to create a scene or to describe a person or object. However, even if you're dealing with straight description, the description may have another, deeper reason for being there. In this case, look for answers such as "to show the value of the vase" or "to create a sense of foreboding."

Take a look at this excerpt from "Misgivings," a poem by Herman Melville, and then try your hand at the sample question following it:

(01)   When ocean-clouds over inland hills

        Sweep storming in late autumn brown,

      And horror the sodden valley fills,

        And the spire falls crashing in the town,

(05)   I muse upon my country's ills. . . .

A sample question about a poem such as the preceding one may read like this:

The imagery in lines 1–3

(A) creates a sense of foreboding

(B) emphasizes the conflict between human beings and nature

(C) contrasts with the state of the nation

(D) heightens the drama of the spire's crash

(E) creates a feeling of peace

The imagery in the first three lines is all about nature, but it isn't the nature of a cheerful child's story or a rosy greeting card. After all, why have "ocean-clouds" (line 1) moved over "inland hills" (line 1)? I'm not a meteorologist, but when clouds from the ocean hit land, I know a storm is approaching. These clouds are a warning of bad weather to come. The next image in the poem is "late autumn brown" (line 2). How would the poem be different if the line read "early spring green"? Spring is associated with birth and with the beginning of the growing cycle. Autumn, on the other hand, is associated with the end of the growing cycle and the approach of winter, a symbol of death. This leads us to another negative image. Finally, check out the last image regarding the "valley" (line 3). You don't need to ask why the valley is "sodden" (line 3) because the "storming" (line 2) is clearly the cause. But why is it filled with "horror" (line 3)? If the valley had been filled with "joy" or "peace," the poem would have a very different meaning. All these factors add up to "foreboding," which means that choice (A) is the best.

Finding value in figures of speech

Figurative language, the parts of which are often called *figures of speech,* arises from the poet's imagination, so you need to employ your own imagination in answering questions about these elements. The exam writers, for example, may ask the meaning, purpose, or effect of a figure of speech — a simile, a metaphor, a symbol, personification, and the like. However, don't expect to see the term "figurative language" or the name of a particular figure of speech in the question. Instead, the questions simply ask for an interpretation of a few words from the poem.

Here are a few common figurative language questions and some info on what to do when you run into one:

- ✔ **Which poetic technique does NOT appear in the poem?** This type of question throws lots of terms at you. To answer one of these beauties, put on your catcher's mitt and work through the list of five, crossing off everything that you can find in the poem.

- ✔ **The second stanza relies on which poetic technique to convey the solemnity of the occasion?** To figure out the answer to this tricky question, reread your stanza to determine what's there. Then match your answer to the list of possible answers, which may contain figures of speech (symbols, metaphors, and so on) or other poetic techniques. (For more on figures of speech, see Chapter 4.)

- ✔ **The poet's attitude toward _____ is revealed primarily by . . .** How does the poet feel about whatever is written in the blank, and how do you know what he or she feels? This is actually a question about tone (see the next section), but I've included it here because your answer may be a figure of speech. (Your answer may be something else, of course — imagery, perhaps.)

- ✔ **The expression _____ in line X refers to . . .** This sort of question is easy because all you have to do is untangle the simile.

- ✔ **The speaker characterizes love as . . .** You may be in figurative-language territory here if the speaker has used figures of speech to convey a definition of love. Of course, the speaker may have ranted on and on about love, in which case your best answer may be "dialogue" or "dramatic monologue." Regardless, dust off your reading comprehension skills and you're home free.

Check out the following lines from a Henry Wadsworth Longfellow poem, and then try your hand at the sample question:

(01)   Pride and humiliation hand in hand

    Walked with them through the world where'er they went;

Trampled and beaten were they as the sand,

    And yet unshaken as the continent.

A sample question about a poem such as the preceding one may read like this:

The references to "sand" (line 3) and "continent" (line 4)

(A) express the suffering endured by "them" (line 2)

(B) contrast transience and permanence

(C) reveal the strength with which hardship was faced by "them" (line 2)

(D) emphasize a natural reaction to pride and humiliation

(E) create a setting for the events in the poem

Rearrange the words in line 3 to make the simile clear: They were as trampled and beaten as the sand. It isn't very difficult to see that the poet is talking about suffering. But before you latch onto (A), keep reading. The sand simile also relates to the "hardship" mentioned in choice (C). Now add the implied words to line 4 to check the other simile: They were as "unshaken as the continent." Here you find the "strength" of choice (C), which makes (C) the winner over (A). Notice that nobody (except me) mentioned the word "simile," and yet the basic idea of comparison is used. Nevertheless, this is a question about figurative language.

It's not just what you say, but how you say it: Tone and diction

The College Board is so hooked on how poets express themselves that it recently published a booklet for educators explaining how to teach *tone* (the author's attitude toward his or her topic or theme) in various works of literature. The AP English Lit exam is also rife with questions about *diction*, or word choice, which conveniently helps you to determine the tone of a selection. (Flip to Chapter 4 for a more detailed explanation of tone and diction.)

Tone and diction show up on the AP exam in questions such as these:

✔ **What attitude does the poet display toward . . .** To best answer this question, you need to check diction and direct, literal statements. Also examine figures of speech. (See the previous section for more info on how figures of speech help determine tone.)

✔ **It can be inferred from the poem that the author . . .** Inference questions like these turn you into Sherlock Holmes. The answers to these questions shouldn't be something that's actually stated in the poem. Instead, they should be something that's hinted at — the logical conclusion that always makes the great detective exclaim, "Elementary, my dear Watson." Go for the clues in the usual way (visualize, employ free-association, check connotation, and so forth), digging under the surface. (Chapter 5 explains in detail how to excavate for clues.)

Don't confuse the poet with the speaker or the other characters (if any appear in the poem). Tone questions are about the poet's attitude, which may differ markedly from the speaker's or characters'.

✔ **In line 9, the poem shifts from** . . . Depending on what's going on in line 9 and what was going on in lines 1–8, this question may have all sorts of answers. Be sure to check diction if you see an answer choice such as "formal to informal" or "colloquial to pedantic" or any words that describe diction. (*Pedantic,* by the way, means "teacherly" in the worst possible sense. A pedantic speaker wants to lecture you and impress you with the number of books he or she has read.) Also check tone; you may detect a shift from "I hate you for these reasons" to "we had some good times, didn't we?" You can have any number of possibilities.

✔ **Lines 3–9 reveal . . .** Again, the content of these lines tells you whether this question deals with diction and tone. If you see words such as "ain't," "whassup," and "gimme" and one of your answer choices is "lack of education," you know that you're in diction territory. And don't forget that the reasons the author provides for why the character speaks in a certain way may clue you in to the tone.

✔ **In line 20, the author uses the word "anguish" to . . .** Welcome to diction-land! To breeze through these questions, simply substitute another word, and then examine the way the poem changes. By substituting you determine what the word "anguish" accomplishes.

✔ **The word "beloved" (line 3) is ironic because . . .** With this type of question, you first have to remind yourself that with irony, people don't say what they mean. Therefore, the word "beloved" establishes that whatever "beloved" refers to is really hated, reviled, loathed, and . . . well, you get the point. Now search the poem for reasons, and then compare those reasons to the choices provided to get your answer.

Scan these lines by George Moses Horton, and then try the sample question:

(01)   Ha! tott'ring Johnny strut and boast,

          But think of what your feathers cost;

          Your crowing days are short at most,

            You bloom but soon to fade.

(05)   Surely you could not stand so wide,

          If strictly to the bottom tried;

          The wind would blow your plume aside,

            If half your debts were paid.

                Then boast and bear the crack,

(10)   With the Sheriff at your back . . .

A sample question about a poem such as the preceding one may read like this:

The tone of this selection may be described as

(A) nostalgic

(B) admiring

(C) regretful

(D) reasonable

(E) critical

The author isn't a big fan of "tott'ring Johnny" (line 1). How do you know? Look at the diction. "Strut and boast," for example, aren't activities to participate in if you want to have any friends. Also, look at the metaphor in line 3: "Your crowing days." A rooster crows to announce himself to the world, a kind of bragging. Now look at the poet's direct statements: "You bloom but soon to fade" (line 4) and even if you pay half of what you owe, you'll still have "the Sheriff at your back" (line 10). Bingo, choice (E) sums up the tone nicely, and diction helps get you to the correct answer. By the way, the answer makes even more sense when you know the title of the poem: "The Creditor to His Proud Debtor."

Reflecting on the whole enchilada: Structure

Structure questions require you to take a step back and consider the poem or the section that you're being asked about as a unit. Imagine that you have X-ray vision and are examining the bones. What unifies the poem? Content? Does the poem tell a story in chronological order or through flashbacks?

Consider whether the poem is organized by an element of style. For instance, does it present an idea metaphorically and then restate the idea with additional metaphors? Perhaps you can discern a rhyme scheme or a repetitious sentence pattern that holds everything together.

Structure questions may appear in the following forms:

> ✔ **Lines 5–8 are unified by . . .** To get your answer, reread the lines that you're being asked about, and then figure out what they have in common. Your answer will be whatever it is that the lines share.

> ✔ **The imagery in the fifth stanza serves to . . .** This question is the reverse of the preceding one. The answer may be "organize" or "unify" or a similar word. If the fifth stanza were altered, what would change in the poem? How would you perceive the meaning differently? The answers to these questions help you understand what the imagery in the fifth stanza accomplishes.
>
> ✔ **The structure of the poem . . .** This question has lots of possible answers. You may, for example, see a choice that refers to the rhyme scheme, something such as "has three quatrains and a couplet." Or, you may also see an answer that relies on reading comprehension ("is based on the speaker's journey away from his family," perhaps). Look for a pattern, and match the effect of that pattern to one of the answer choices.

Read the following part of Edward Arlington Robinson's famous poem, "Richard Cory," and then tackle the sample question:

(01)   Whenever Richard Cory went down town,

     We people on the pavement looked at him:

     He was a gentleman from sole to crown,

     Clean favored, and imperially slim.

     . . . .

(05)   And he was rich — yes, richer than a king

     And admirably schooled in every grace:

     In fine, we thought that he was everything

     To make us wish that we were in his place.

     . . . .

     And Richard Cory, one calm summer night,

(10)   Went home and put a bullet through his head.

A sample question about a poem such as the preceding one may read like this:

Which best describes the way in which this poem is structured?

(A) It is a series of facts about Richard Cory.

(B) It is a narrative of Richard Cory's life.

(C) It is a contrast between the attitude of the townspeople and Cory's true situation.

(D) It is a series of metaphors about wealth.

(E) It is a straightforward assessment of Cory's condition.

Talk about irony! The townspeople are envious, but apparently they don't know how Richard Cory's life feels from the inside. The last two lines make (C) the only possible choice. Notice the close-but-no-cigar answer: choice (A). It's almost there, because a fact about Cory's life is the envy of the townspeople, and Cory's suicide is also a fact about him. However, the poem revolves around the contrast between the supposedly perfect life the townspeople imagine for Cory and his despair. ***Remember:*** To answer a structure question, always go for the most specific answer that addresses the big picture.

Getting into the groove (or lack thereof): Rhyme and rhythm

Rhyme and rhythm (meter) don't really show up by themselves in multiple-choice poetry questions. Like packs of wannabe's trying to get into the hottest new club, these sound techniques are too insecure to go out alone. Look for them, if they're around at all, in questions about structure. For example, the question may concern how a poem is organized, with rhyme or rhythm (meter) as one of the answers. (Check out the structure discussion in the preceding section.)

You may also find rhythm or rhyme as one of the possible answers for a question that says something like "All of the following poetic techniques may be found in this poem EXCEPT. . . ." Answering this question correctly depends on two things: listening to the poem and knowing the literary terms that relate to sound. Chapter 4 helps you with both of these issues.

The sound qualities of poetry are especially important in the essay portion of the AP exam. Most essay prompts based on poetry ask you to relate poetic techniques to content. Because a lot of test-takers forget about rhythm and rhyme, you'll stand out from the crowd when you mention these elements.

Take a "listen" to this excerpt from a poem by Percy Bysshe Shelley:

(01)   Sometimes the living by the dead were hid.

Near the great fountain in the public square,

Where corpses made a crumbling pyramid

Under the sun, was heard one stifled prayer

(05)   For life, in the hot silence of the air;

And strange 'twas, amid that hideous heap to see

Some shrouded in their long and golden hair,

As if not dead, but slumbering quietly

Like forms which sculptors carve, then love to agony.

A sample question regarding the sound elements may read like this:

The rhyme scheme of this poem creates a division between which two lines?

(A) 2 and 3

(B) 3 and 4

(C) 4 and 5

(D) 5 and 6

(E) 6 and 7

The answer, of course, depends on the poem's rhyme scheme (pattern), which may be expressed this way:

    a b a b b c b c c

The sixth line introduces a new sound — "see," which is repeated in lines 8 and 9 with "quietly" and "agony." The meaning of the poem also changes between lines 5 and 6. The first five lines describe a battle scene with truly awful images. The last three lines are poignant, as the corpses with "long and golden hair" (line 7) appear to be "slumbering quietly" (line 8). The change of meaning and the change of rhyme show you that the division occurs between lines 5 and 6, which is answer (D).

Chapter 7

Mastering Essay Questions on Poetic Passages

● ●

In This Chapter

▶ Dissecting poetry questions

▶ Getting ready to write your essay

▶ Understanding how to -use evidence in your essay

▶ Determining deeper meanings with analysis

▶ Concluding your essay with ease

▶ Reviewing a sample prompt and essay

● ●

*1*magine the morning of the worst day ever — the kind of day when the alarm doesn't go off, your cat coughs up a hairball on your geometry homework, and you discover that the last rinse-cycle turned your entire load of laundry the color of raw salmon.

In your imagination, your AP English Literature and Composition exam testing morning, specifically the moment when you rip off the plastic wrap and open the green essay booklet, may be just as bad. You don't care that someone's immortal poem containing deep and important thoughts is sitting right in front of you. All you care about is getting the job done. The job, in this case, is to read a poem and write an essay demonstrating that you understand the meaning of the poem and the poetic techniques in it. And all this in 40 minutes or less.

Mission impossible? Nope. The disaster you envision doesn't have to happen. In this chapter, I zero in on poetry essays, explaining how to figure out the intention of a poetry *prompt* (the two- or three-sentence questions that "prompt" you to write an essay). I discuss how to gather and prioritize ideas and how to write an introduction, body, and conclusion for your essay. I also explain how to insert quotations from the poem smoothly and how to punctuate them properly. So that you can visualize the goal, I provide a sample poem and a polished essay.

Knowing What to Expect from Poetry Prompts

If you were to read a stack of AP poetry prompts, you would notice that the following two standard elements appear in the prompt for just about every essay:

✔ **"Read the poem."** There's a shock. You were planning to guess the content of the poem, right? The variation of this element is "read the poem carefully" or "read the following poem carefully." Sometimes the exam writers are daring enough to say, "Read the text carefully." No matter how they word the prompt, read the entire poem at least twice — once for an overview, and then again with your mind focused on the question. As you gather material for the essay, you may read all or part of the poem several more times. (The later section, "Making Notes and Preparing to Write," goes into detail on poetry reading, AP-exam style.)

✔ **"In a well-organized essay . . ."** And here you thought you should just randomly pour out ideas! You may also see the variation "in a well-written essay . . ." This one makes me wonder whether some future attorney once protested a grade because "no one ever said it had to be well written."

It's easy to make fun of AP questions, but really, you can see why the exam writers include this point in poetry prompts. After all, talking about a poem in class or answering a teacher's specific question about a poem is different from writing an essay about one. The exam tests your ability to gather ideas and communicate them clearly *in writing*. Remember, the test is called the AP English Literature and *Composition* exam.

One other item nearly always appears in prompts, and it's a crucial one. (Look for it and file it in the brain cell labeled "no-matter-what-don't-forget-me.") The basic phrase that I'm talking about is "poetic techniques" or "poetic elements." The variations include "literary techniques" or "literary elements." Whatever the AP writers call them, poetic techniques include rhyme, rhythm (meter), figurative language, imagery, and the like. (Turn to Chapter 4 for a complete review of these techniques.) You may see this question in the following forms:

✔ **"Analyze [or consider or discuss] techniques the poet uses in relation to . . ."** These words in the prompt are an open door to how the poem is written. Usually the rest of the prompt will ask you to relate those techniques to what the poem means or to something in the poem, such as the speaker's attitude, the setting, and so on.

✔ **"Consider [or discuss or analyze] the poetic techniques."** In this sort of question, go for a connection between poetic techniques and meaning or between poetic techniques and the effect on the reader.

In an open question like this, you may forget to look for an important element. So before you start gathering ideas from the poem, jot down a list of poetic techniques in the margin. As you read the poem, glance at the list so you don't skip something useful. Remember, however, that not every poetic technique is significant or even present in one particular poem. Don't be afraid to pick and choose.

✔ **"Consider how [a particular poetic technique] affects . . ."** This sort of question specifies only one particular technique that you're supposed to discuss (imagery, metaphor, or syntax, for example). In such a situation, hit that technique and nothing else. However, don't ignore the second half of the sentence — what the technique affects. Be sure to focus on what the exam writers want you to analyze. In that slot, you may see the following phrases (or any of the other million variations):

  • "the reader's perception of the speaker"

  • "the meaning of the poem"

  • "the contrast between the past and present"

✔ **"Discuss rhyme, diction, syntax, and the other poetic [or literary] elements found in the poem."** Certainly you should check for the listed elements, but don't stop there if you want your essay to stand out. When faced with this prompt, the vast majority of test-takers talk about rhyme, diction, and syntax and nothing else. Reading a thousand essays about the same three poetic elements isn't the most exciting activity on the planet. Therefore, if the prompt leaves the door open, for your grader's sake, venture into other territory (imagery, line breaks, and so forth). Your grader will be happy. (Need I explain the advantages of a happy grader?) However, be sure the poetic elements you discuss are actually significant in the poem that you're analyzing.

Poetry prompts nearly always require you to write something about *how* a poem is written. Look for that idea somewhere in the prompt. As you read the prompt, underline key words and restate the question in its simplest terms.

Making Notes and Preparing to Write

After carefully reading the poetry prompt, turn to the poem itself. Zoom through the poem once without writing anything. The first reading should take no more than a couple of minutes, depending on the length of the poem. (Chapter 2 discusses how to budget essay-writing time.) After you have an overview, reread the poem a bit more slowly, pen in hand. Underline and annotate anything important. (Chapter 3 explains and gives examples of how to annotate daily reading assignments for an English course.)

The definition of "anything important" when you're in the heat of battle with the AP English Lit exam is different from "anything important" when you're doing homework. Under test conditions, you have to concentrate and work as quickly as possible. Follow these steps:

1. **Keep the key words of the prompt in your mind and use them to locate relevant parts of the poem.**

   Return to those words again and again as you read, focusing your mind on what you're searching for. If the prompt asks you to consider diction, underline any words that seem odd or, conversely, any words that are typical of the particular poem. If the prompt queries you about imagery, underline all the sensory details.

2. **Whenever you have a relevant idea, write a couple of words in the margin.**

   Allow yourself about 5–7 minutes for this step. Don't waste time writing the whole idea, however. Instead, write just enough to help you remember the point you want to make. Your marginal notes should address both the meaning of the poem and the poetic techniques in it. If the prompt is very general, write all your ideas. If the prompt is more specific, on the other hand, concentrate only on that aspect of the poem (how the speaker resolves a conflict, what statement is made about poverty, the relationship between the speaker and her environment, or any of the gazillion other things prompts ask about). The prompt may also narrow your focus to one, or perhaps two or three, particular poetic techniques.

3. **Create a thesis statement and subtopics and craft your essay's introduction.**

   This step should take no more than 5 minutes. When you're writing an AP-exam poetry essay, the thesis statement is generally a restatement of the prompt, with an original idea (perhaps your understanding of the major theme or meaning of the poem) thrown in. The subtopics are usually the poetic techniques that you're writing about or the content points that you address in your essay. The thesis and subtopics then serve as the introduction for your essay. Generally one or two sentences do the job, because you need to get right to the point. Be specific so the reader knows right away what the essay is about.

   In your essay introduction, you must include the title of the poem (enclosed in quotation marks) and the author's name, if that information appears on the exam. Here are two examples:

   - **Prompt:** Carefully read the following poem, "The Thought Fox," by Ted Hughes. In a well-written essay, discuss how the speaker's attitude toward art is revealed through the poetic techniques in the poem.

     Introduction: In Ted Hughes' poem, "The Thought Fox," the speaker's attitude toward art is revealed by diction, imagery, and figurative language. As the speaker imagines the animal, he creates both the fox and the poem.

   - **Prompt:** Read this poem and analyze how the poetic techniques unify the poem.

     Introduction: This sonnet has only one simple message that is reinforced by the poetic techniques that the author employs. The speaker "count[s] the ways" she loves. The rhyme scheme, meter, form, and figurative language unify the poem.

In the preceding examples, both introductions include a reworded version of the prompt and one extra, original idea (the creation of the fox and the poem and the single message of love). These introductions get the job done without wasting time.

4. **Put the ideas in order.**

   Decide what topics you want to touch on and in what order. To help yourself organize your thoughts, go back and put a number on each underlined section of the poem (1 for something pertaining to the first subtopic, 2 for anything to do with the second subtopic, and so on down the line). Do the same thing for your marginal notes. Several items will have the same number; include all those ideas in the same paragraph of the essay.

5. **Choose quotations that support your main ideas.**

   When you select a quotation for your essay, take care not to write too many or too few words. Find the key phrase and leave out the rest.

   Here's what I mean, with a couple of examples in Goldilocks format:

   • **Example #1:**

     A Moment — We uncertain step
     For newness of the night —

     Poor response, too much excerpted: *In this poem the images of "A Moment — We uncertain step / For newness of the night —" lead the reader to think of children.* In this sentence, "A Moment" and "of the night" don't relate to the point at hand, so you shouldn't include them.

     Poor response, too little excerpted: *In this poem "step" and "newness" lead the reader to think of children.* In this sentence, "step" proves nothing. The important part is *how* the subject steps. The link to children is embodied in "uncertain step" — the way a toddler walks.

     Good response: *In this poem the images of "uncertain step" and "newness" lead the reader to think of children.* This response is strong because the writer is simply tying imagery to the idea of youth.

   • **Example #2:**

     Death be not proud, though some have called thee
     Mighty and dreadful, for thou are not so;
     For those whom thou think'st thou dost overthrow
     Die not, poor Death, nor cans't thou kill me.

     Poor response, too much excerpted: *The speaker addresses Death directly, in a way that diminishes Death's power, saying, "Death be not proud, though some have called thee / Mighty and dreadful, for thou are not so; / For those whom thou think'st thou dost overthrow / Die not, poor Death, nor cans't thou kill me."* This response contains every word from four lines, which is way more than necessary.

     Poor response, too little excerpted: *The speaker diminishes the power of Death, saying that death shouldn't be "proud" and "cans't thou kill me."* This response leaves out so much that the last point ("cans't thou kill me") actually says the opposite of the point that the writer is trying to make.

     Good response: *The speaker diminishes the power of Death by addressing "poor Death" and commanding, "Death, be not proud." Death is not "Mighty and dreadful" as people think and does not actually "overthrow" anyone, nor, as the speaker says, "cans't thou kill me."* Although the quotations in the preceding responses serve the same purpose as this one — to show that the speaker thinks Death is vastly overrated — this response is strong because it adequately supports the point without dribbling on and on.

I want to let you in on a secret of the AP English Lit exam: Most graders spend only two or three minutes per essay. They read with a mental notepad, on which they place a check every time you make a point. Here's what might go through a grader's mind as she reads: "He talked about the house image — check. He included a sentence about the window's symbolic importance — check. He mentioned a point about the open window — check." A test-taker who makes seven points about a poem isn't necessarily going to score more points than someone who makes only two points. However, in a speed-grading situation (which the AP definitely is), the odds favor those who include more ideas.

After you finish preparing to write (up to ten minutes that's time very well spent, I might add), slide the question booklet to one corner of your desk. Take out the answer sheet and get ready to transfer all your brilliance from green (the question booklet) to pink (the answer sheet). Remember that the graders won't see the green booklet. None of your writing counts until it hits the pink paper.

The Mechanics of Proving Your Case

Imagine, as you write your masterpiece, that the AP-grader is the jury and you're the prosecuting attorney. The jury doesn't need evidence of a crime (although some essays I've read most definitely could be considered literary felonies). Instead, the exam-grader needs evidence supporting the thesis statement that you set out in the introduction.

The evidence consists of quotations from the poem. And I won't lie — quotations are easy to find but difficult to insert correctly. Why? Because poetry is governed by some truly annoying punctuation rules (and that's a complaint coming from an English teacher!). In this section, I take you through the steps of inserting, punctuating, and citing evidence in a poetry essay.

Inserting quotations

When you write your essay, you want to slip your quotations into it so smoothly that they barely make a ripple. If possible, make the quoted words part of your sentence rather than a clunky addition tacked onto the beginning or the end of your sentence.

Check out these clunky and smooth examples:

- **Clunky insertion:** *The poet gives many descriptions of times when things are unclear. One example of this kind of description is "those Evenings of the Brain." On these "Evenings," you can't see anything. "When not a Moon disclose a sign." This last quotation shows the night is dark.*

  How is this response clunky? Let me count the ways. For starters, the second and the fifth sentences label the evidence ("One example of this kind of description is . . ." and "This last quotation shows . . ."). If the reader can't tell that you've provided an example, the example is poorly chosen. Also, the quotation, "When not a Moon disclose a sign," is just sitting there all by itself. The quotation should be embedded in the preceding sentence instead.

- **Smooth insertion:** *Hers is a description of "those Evenings of the Brain," which the reader comes to understand as simply times when something is unclear, or "When not a Moon disclose a sign."*

  You can probably tell that this quotation insertion is nice and smooth just by reading it aloud. The quotations arise from the sentence. For example, the first is the object of the preposition "of." The second quotation restates "when something is unclear." The "or" links them without a fuss.

Because poetry is sometimes difficult to decode, you may be tempted to insert the quotation and then restate it in your own words because you're not sure the reader will understand it without a "translation." Bad idea! Assume that the reader knows what the words mean (because the readers usually do). Adding a paraphrase wastes time and slows the flow of argument.

Punctuating quotations

Poetry essays require some ordinary punctuation marks — quotation marks, for example — and some that you hardly ever need in real-life writing. The oddballs include slashes, ellipses, and brackets. In this section, I show you how to punctuate poetry quotations properly, and I also explain how to block a quotation.

Quotation marks

When you quote from a poem (or from anything else for that matter), place quotation marks around the words that you're quoting. If the quotation is followed by a period or a comma, place the period or comma inside the closing quotation mark, unless you're citing a line number. (I explain how to cite quotations later in the chapter.) Here are examples of a line from a Shakespearean sonnet, properly enclosed in quotation marks:

> As Shakespeare writes, "You live in this, and dwell in lovers' eyes."
>
> Shakespeare's line, "You live in this, and dwell in lovers' eyes," recognizes the power of art to confer immortality.
>
> "You live in this, and dwell in lovers' eyes," writes Shakespeare.

Notice that the speaker identification ("Shakespeare writes") is followed by a comma when it appears at the beginning of the sentence.

Slashes and blocks

Poets spend a lot of time deciding where a line ends, so when you quote more than one line of poetry, you should indicate line breaks with a slash or with a blocked quotation. The slash has a little space before and after it, as in this example:

> Shakespeare writes, "Shall I compare thee to a summer's day? / Thou art more lovely and more temperate."

Another way to show line breaks is to *block,* or center, the quotation on separate lines. Blocks are best if you're quoting a large chunk of the poem, though strictly speaking, you can use them for as few as two lines. The lines should be indented about ten spaces from the left margin. However, remember that when you block a quotation, you don't use quotation marks. For example:

> Nature appears often in this sonnet:
>
> > Shall I compare thee to a summer's day?
> >
> > Thou art more lovely and more temperate.

Ellipses

If you drop any words from a poem, insert an *ellipsis* (the punctuation mark showing three little dots) to show the reader that something's missing. (Be very careful, however, not to drop words that are essential to the meaning of a line. Be true to the author's intentions.) If the missing words follow a punctuation mark, leave the punctuation mark if it helps the reader figure out the sense of the line. For instance, you might keep an exclamation point or a question mark but usually not a comma or a period. You don't need to place ellipses at the beginning or the end of a quotation. The reader assumes that words may precede or follow the quotation and that the words you've chosen don't constitute the entire poem. Consider the following lines from John Milton's "How Soon Hath Time":

> How soon hath Time, the subtle thief of youth,
>
> Stoln on his wing my three and twentieth year!
>
> My hasting days fly on with full career,
>
> But my late spring no bud or blossom shew'th.

Here are some examples, based on the preceding lines, of ellipses in action:

Quoted with words missing from one line: *The speaker acknowledges that Time has "[s]toln . . . my three and twentieth year!"* (Note: I explain later in the chapter the instances when you should write "Stoln" with a lowercase "s" in brackets.)

Quoted with words missing from two lines: *The speaker laments, "How soon hath Time . . . Stoln on his wing my three and twentieth year!"*

Quoted with a complete line missing: *The speaker laments,*

> *How soon hath Time, the subtle thief of youth,*
>
> *Stoln on his wing my three and twentieth year!*
>
> . . . .
>
> *But my late spring no bud or blossom shew'th.*

A better way to handle a long quotation with an entire line missing is to take small sections of the quotation and insert them into your own sentence, paraphrasing where necessary. For example, the preceding sample may be presented this way: *The speaker calls time "the subtle thief of youth," and laments that his "late spring no bud or blossom shew'th."*

Brackets

Most of the time you chop words from a quotation, but occasionally you have to add or change something for the sake of clarity or to avoid breaking the usual capitalization rules. (However, if the poet is playing with the capitalization rules to make a point, don't change anything.) You can avoid these confusing situations by using *brackets* (the things that look like squared-off parentheses). Brackets tell the reader that the quotation no longer appears as the writer intended. Check out these examples of brackets in action, based on the Milton lines in the preceding section on ellipses:

> Referring to the loss of his youth, the speaker says, it that was "[s]toln on his wing."
>
> The speaker regrets that his twenty-third year was taken "on [Time's] wing."

In the first example, the capital "S" changes to a lowercase "s" because the word appears in the middle of a sentence. In the second example, "his" has been changed to "Time's" because "his" is too vague.

Citing quotations

Citing sources is usually the bane of a student's existence. So before you run screaming from the room, let me explain that on the AP English exam citations aren't as big of a deal as they are in a research paper. (After all, with research papers, you have to indicate the source in a bibliography or source list and follow about a thousand rules for footnotes or parenthetical citations. Talk about instant headache material.) The English prof who slaps a grade on your work knows the source because the poem is right there on the exam. The only things you need to cite in an AP poetry essay are the line numbers. And of course, if you know the title and author of the poem, that information belongs in the introduction.

You aren't actually required to cite line numbers on the AP English exam. The graders have read the poem, and they know where everything is. However, I was once sitting in a room full of AP English teachers for a practice grading session (which was just slightly less enjoyable than a visit to my dentist). One of the four essays we read, graded, and discussed included line-number citations, and the other three didn't. Not only did the essay with citations score better than the other three, but nearly every teacher mentioned the fact that citations were included. What can I say? English teachers are suckers for stuff like that.

To insert a line-number citation, use parentheses, and don't worry about writing anything but the line number (the word "line" is unnecessary). The citation isn't part of the quotation, so it should follow the closing quotation mark. It precedes the period or comma or whatever punctuation mark that the sentence requires, as you see here:

> As Shakespeare writes, "You live in this, and dwell in lovers' eyes" (14).

> Shakespeare's line, "You live in this, and dwell in lovers' eyes" (14), recognizes the power of art to confer immortality.

> Shakespeare writes, "Shall I compare thee to a summer's day? / Thou art more lovely and more temperate" (1–2).

In a blocked quotation, place the citation after the last word:

> Nature appears often in this sonnet:

> > Shall I compare thee to a summer's day?

> > Thou art more lovely and more temperate. (1–2)

Knowing how to cite is important whether for an AP English Lit class or for any other class requiring research and writing. I cover citations in detail in *Webster's New World Punctuation: Simplified and Applied* (Wiley, 2006).

Adding Your Commentary: Analysis without the Couch

Believe it or not, analysis in a poetry essay actually has a lot to do with the kind of analysis associated with Sigmund Freud, who's the boss when it comes to psychology. Freud listened to what his patients said, and then he interpreted the hidden meanings. You do the same thing when you write a poetry essay, except that you're "listening" to the poem and interpreting the words in the context of the prompt.

All the skills I review in Chapters 4 and 5 — decoding the literal level and unearthing deeper meanings — make up the "toolkit" for poetry analysis. I can't cover every situation, because prompts vary. However, these guidelines will help you analyze an AP poetry selection:

✔ If the prompt queries you about content, figure out what the poem means and determine your answer. For example, suppose the prompt asks you about the speaker's attitude toward rural life. Well, what is the speaker's attitude toward rural life? Does she love it, hate it, or sit on the fence? Extract details from the poem that prove your point. Don't just list the details, however. Look for connotation, associations, allusions, and so forth. State what you find.

✔ If the prompt focuses on specific poetic devices, start by listing all you find in the poem. For instance, if the prompt queries you about the effect of figurative language, begin by locating these metaphors, similes, personification, and similar devices. Then ask yourself how the poem would be different if, for example, autumn were *not* personified. Now you know what the personification does to and for the reader. Declare that fact in your essay. Bingo! You've got an analytical statement.

> ✔ If the prompt requires you to link technique and meaning, as most prompts do, determine the meaning and then look for poetic elements such as rhythm (meter), rhyme, figurative language, imagery, diction, tone, and so on. Make as many statements as possible tying a particular poetic device to the ideas in the poem.

The most important word in analysis is *why*. Ask yourself *why* a particular word appears where it does, or *why* the speaker describes herself in a certain way. The answer to the question *why* is your analysis.

The following examples illustrate good and bad analytical technique. In the good ones, the writers examine the words and put them under a microscope to make a point. Yup — Freud would have been proud!

Bad analysis: The poem has assonance in line 14. The words "live," "in," and "this" all have short "i" vowel sounds.

Why it's bad: The writer has simply listed examples of assonance without explaining why anyone should care that these words share a vowel sound.

Good analysis: The short vowel sound of the letter "i" in line 14 ("You live in this, and dwell in lovers' eyes") links three words: "live," "this," and "in." The pronoun "this" refers to the poem. The repeated vowel sounds emphasize that the lover lives in the poem.

Why it's good: Now the assonance means something: a link between three words that serve to declare the main idea of the poem.

Bad analysis: The speaker uses a metaphor of "my late spring." The metaphor shows that the speaker is getting old.

Why it's bad: Yes, the metaphor does express the concept of aging. But why use a metaphor? Why not simply say, "I'm getting old"? The essay writer hasn't delved into the metaphor.

Good analysis: The speaker's metaphor, "my late spring" (4), expresses his frustration. Spring is a time of new life; nature comes into bloom in that season. However, the speaker says that "no bud or blossom shew'th" (4). He's barren, lacking even a little sign of productivity. However, there is hope because his spring is "late" (4). Perhaps the flower of creativity will come eventually.

Why it's good: Now the metaphor makes sense. The analysis brings in the idea of nature, seasons, barrenness, and lack of productivity. The speaker has gone way beyond saying that the speaker is getting old.

Wrapping Up with a Quick Conclusion

You have no time for a long, drawn-out conclusion when you're writing an AP essay. All you can do is hit one idea hard, perhaps in just one sentence. Take care not to repeat yourself and summarize your thoughts. Essay graders don't consider summaries proper conclusions. Instead, simply extend what you've already said.

Here are two conclusion samples, including some information about the essay so you can put them into context:

Essay content: Discussion of how the imagery in Nicholas Christopher's poem "The Palm Reader" reveals the author's attitude toward the title character, who lives in a cluttered room with a family that is alienated from her. The Palm Reader is a pathetic character.

Conclusion: The future is called "inescapable" and it "jumps out / at her from every stranger's hand." The Palm Reader may or may not be able to tell the future, but she must live it.

Essay content: Analysis of the poetic techniques that are used to characterize the speaker in Dylan Thomas's "Fern Hill." The speaker is an older person looking back at a seemingly idyllic boyhood that was lost as he aged.

Conclusion: The speaker concludes by stating, "I sang in my chains like the sea." The "sea" is natural, as is the speaker's loss of innocence and youth.

Notice that each conclusion adds just one tiny idea. Both of these examples refer to the end of the poem, which is a good spot to find a conclusion. After all, that's where the poet concluded! (I explain more about conclusions in Chapter 3.)

Aiming Your Ballpoint at the Goal: A Sample Poetry Essay

Your aim is always better when you can see the target, so here I provide a glimpse of the bull's-eye. I include Wilfred Owen's poem "Arms and the Boy," a sample prompt, a reasonably good essay, and commentary on the essay's merits and faults. (You can write your own practice essays with the prompts in Chapter 8.)

Sample poem and prompt: Wilfred Owen's "Arms and the Boy"

Carefully read the following poem "Arms and the Boy" by Wilfred Owen. In a well-written essay, discuss how the poetic techniques convey the poet's view of warfare.

(01)   Let the boy try along this bayonet-blade

        How cold steel is, and keen with hunger of blood;

        Blue with all malice, like a madman's flash;

        And thinly drawn with famishing for flesh.

(05)   Lend him to stroke these blind, blunt bullet-heads

        Which long to muzzle in the hearts of lads.

        Or give him cartridges of fine zinc teeth,

        Sharp with the sharpness of grief and death.

        For his teeth seem for laughing round an apple.

(10)   There lurk no claws behind his fingers supple;

        And God will grow no talons at his heels,

        Nor antlers through the thickness of his curls.

Sample essay about Owen's poem

The following essay is an example of one you might write about Owen's poem "Arms and the Boy." Give it a read through, and then head to the next section to see how it stacks up.

In Wilfred Owen's "Arms and the Boy," the poet's view of war is at first hidden from the reader. The boy of the title is introduced to weapons, presumably to become a good soldier. However, as the poem goes on, the weapons are associated with grief and destruction. Owen ultimately concludes that war is not natural and that young men must be brought to it against their nature. Owen's viewpoint towards war is conveyed through imagery, figurative language, syntax, and diction.

The first and second stanzas include several images of armaments: "bayonet-blade" (1), "cold steel" (2), "blunt bullet-heads" (5), and "cartridges of fine zinc teeth" (7). The reader sees the tools of war, the "arms" of the title. Owen begins these two stanzas with commands: "Let the boy try" (1) and "Lend him" (5). Because of these commands, the reader is led to believe that the poet wants the boy to become accustomed to war and armaments. However, the diction implies the opposite. The steel is "cold" (2), without human feelings. The blade is "keen" (2), which means "sharp," literally. However, "keen" may also mean "eager," and the blade is "keen with hunger of blood" (2). In other words, the blade is bloodthirsty. The bayonet is described with a simile, "like a madman's flash" (3) and is personified by "famishing for flesh" (4). The bullets are "blind" and "blunt" (5), so they do not see the damage they do. The dark side of war comes through.

At the end of stanza two, the poet's condemnation of war emerges clearly. The "fine zinc teeth" (7) have "the sharpness of grief and death" (8). Now the reader sees the consequences of these arms; they do harm. The third stanza begins with an innocent nature image of teeth "laughing round an apple" (9). The boy's natural innocence is emphasized by the fact that his fingers are "supple" (10) and have "no claws" (10). The verb "lurk" (10) is associated with claws and implies the secret behavior of a hunter or a criminal. The boy is the opposite. He is meant to laugh: "For his teeth seem for laughing round an apple" (9). Owen brings God into the poem in favor of innocence. God "will grow no talons" (11) or "antlers" (12). These are an animal's weapons, and the implication is clear. Animals hunt and kill and maim by instinct. Human beings, specifically the boy in this poem, must be taught to "try . . . this bayonet blade" (1) and learn "to stroke these blind, blunt bullet-heads" (5).

The poet's tone is ironic. Young men will go to war, but they will not mature there. Instead, they will betray both God's plan and their own nature. They will be changed by the "arms" they are given.

Evaluation of the sample essay

This essay isn't perfect, but for a 40-minute effort, it's very good indeed. Here's an analysis of its virtues and flaws. Overall, this writer did a fine job. If I were grading this essay, I'd award it an 8 out of a possible 9 points.

Here are the good points of the essay:

- ✔ The main ideas are all there. The prompt asks about Owen's attitude toward war, and the essay states what that attitude is (that war is an unnatural act that's harmful to young men). The prompt also requires a discussion of literary techniques, and the writer mentions diction, tone, syntax, imagery, and figurative language.

- ✔ The essay has a fairly sturdy structure. The writer includes an introduction with all the necessary elements, body paragraphs with evidence and line numbers, and a strong conclusion.

- ✔ Some of the analysis is fairly sophisticated. The word "keen," for instance, is discussed on the literal and figurative level.

- ✔ The essay is filled with good quotations from the poem, so every point is well supported by evidence.

✔ The writing is fluid. In other words, when you read it aloud, it flows. The quotations are tucked smoothly into the text.

✔ The essay has good mechanics. The spelling, grammar, and punctuation are all on target.

Here are the points of the essay that could use improvement:

✔ The body paragraphs are a little disorganized. The writer could have placed all the points about diction in one paragraph, everything about imagery in another, and so forth. Alternatively, the writer could have used the poem itself as an organizer, saying everything about the first stanza in the first body paragraph, everything about the second stanza in the second body paragraph, and everything about the third stanza in the last body paragraph.

✔ Here and there the writer repeats himself or herself or elaborates unnecessarily. For instance, the last sentence of the second paragraph isn't necessary. I'd also drop "In other words, the blade is bloodthirsty" from the second paragraph.

Chapter 8

Flexing Your Poetry Muscles: Practice Questions

In This Chapter

▶ Sampling multiple-choice poetry questions

▶ Writing practice poetry essays

▶ Checking your responses

Not quite ready for opening night on Broadway — er, I mean, the AP English Literature and Composition exam? Consider this chapter a dress rehearsal for the poetry act. First up is everyone's favorite: multiple-choice questions. Next are the essay prompts. (Go ahead, throw tomatoes.) Both are accompanied by answers and explanations, so you'll be ready to face the AP exam graders. Sharpen your pencil and take out some lined paper. It's almost show time.

Selecting an Answer from Multiple Options

If a mere glance at a multiple-choice poetry question makes you break out in hives, you're in the right spot. Also, you have a lot of company. Multiple-choice poetry questions are sometimes difficult, but with practice, you can face them with confidence. And that's what this section provides: four practice poems of varying styles and accompanying questions. (I tell you the title, author, and date of each poem to follow the publisher's citation style, but the real AP exam may not provide that information.) Take advantage of the wide margins in this chapter to annotate the questions and the poems. After you have an answer, write it on a sheet of lined paper.

I provide the answer and explanation for each question immediately after the multiple-choice options so you can have immediate feedback. When you've done the practice questions, study your mistakes and review as needed in Chapter 4 (poetry basics) or Chapter 5 (strategy for the test itself). If you're an early bird and the test is a couple of months away, you can address any areas of weakness with help from Chapter 3. For example, if you trip over vocabulary questions, Chapter 3 explains how to beef up your stock of words.

Practice set 1

Read the following poem, "Renters," by John Allman, and then answer the questions that follow. The poem is reprinted from *Lowcountry* (New Directions, 2007).

(01)   The egret's[1] platform of sticks no more permanent
        than my furnished room on West 58th Street —
        that shared toilet a marsh creek or slough[2]
        rich in mice. Think how all the wading birds
(05)   like to breed near each other, regurgitating night
        and day into the maws[3] of their young. Think of
        the apartments we inhabited on busy avenues,
        the honking of cars trapped by double parkers,
        the attic rooms with low dormers we hit our heads on,
(10)   the ghastly abstract mural a tenant painted on the green wall,
        its pretension of vitality and swirl and soft mire
        where the bittern[4] coughs. Think how the ring-billed
        gull[5] returns north, replenishing itself on farmers' pests,
        how we abandoned the Bronx to arrive on a snow-filled
(15)   midnight in Syracuse, our goods on the sidewalk like twigs
        for the picking.

1. Long-necked bird.

2. A marsh or swamp.

3. Animal's mouth.

4. Marsh bird.

5. Type of seagull.

1. The phrase "no more permanent" (line 1) compares

    (A) sticks and houses

    (B) birds and people

    (C) the speaker and a bird

    (D) a bird's nest and the speaker

    (E) a bird's nest and the speaker's rented room

The first two lines begin a lengthy comparison between the many rooms or apartments the speaker has inhabited and the "platform of sticks" that serves as a temporary home for the egret. Therefore, choice (E) is the correct answer.

2. Lines 3 and 4 imply that the "shared toilet" was

    (A) infested with mice

    (B) located near a marsh

    (C) used by both the speaker and the birds

    (D) wet

    (E) dirty

Lines 3 and 4 continue to compare the marsh birds' nests to the speaker's living conditions, a "furnished room on West 58th Street" (line 2) — which, by the way, probably rents for several thousand dollars a minute in today's overheated Manhattan real estate market. But I digress. As the "shared toilet" (line 3) is in Manhattan, not in a marshy area, (B) and (C) aren't the answers you want. The birds' toilet is probably wet and dirty — (D) and (E) — but you can't tell from the poem whether the speaker's toilet was in a similar state. All you know for sure is that it was "rich in mice," making (A) the answer you seek.

3. According to the poem, all of the following characteristics apply to both marsh birds and the speaker EXCEPT

   (A) living in close quarters

   (B) transience

   (C) a need to create a home

   (D) resistance to change

   (E) the ability to live in difficult conditions

The birds "like to breed near each other" (line 5) and the people live on "busy avenues" (line 7), so (A) is out. The egret's nest is "no more permanent" than the speaker's "furnished room" (line 2), so (B) bites the dust. Choice (C) doesn't make the grade because the birds are creating homes ("platform of sticks" in line 1) and so are people. Choice (E) appears in the poem in the "mire" (line 11) the birds live in and the many details of apartment life, including "low dormers we hit our heads on" (line 9) and the shared toilet (line 3). You're left with (D), a good choice because the birds move north (line 13) and so does the speaker (lines 14–15).

4. The predominant literary technique in lines 7–10 is

   (A) figurative language

   (B) imagery

   (C) narrative

   (D) monologue

   (E) alliteration

Imagery is lit-speak for description that appeals to the five senses (taste, touch, sight, hearing, and smell). Lines 7–10 cover most of those: "honking" (line 8) assaults the ear, the "ghastly abstract mural" (line 10) assaults the eye, and whacking one's head on the dormer (line 9) certainly relates to touch. The correct answer is (B). The other answers don't appear in lines 7–10. *Figurative language* includes metaphors, similes, personification, and the like. A *narrative* is a story. A *monologue* is one person speaking, but this term refers to a dramatic, "I-hear-your-voice" speech, not the plain comments of the speaker in this poem. *Alliteration* refers to sound, specifically the repetition of consonants, which occurs but doesn't dominate these lines.

5. The repetition of "Think" (lines 4, 6, and 12)

   (A) emphasizes the importance of an analytical approach to nature

   (B) reminds the speaker of the past

   (C) shows the reader how nature and human behavior are related

   (D) commands the speaker to pay attention to the similarities between human and avian behavior

   (E) reveals the speaker's desperation

The devilish part of this question is that many of the answers are true of the poem in general: the speaker *is* analyzing nature (A) and thinking of the past (B). Choice (E) is the only answer residing on Planet Wrong. Now you're left with (C) and (D). Both deal with the relationship between nature and human behavior. The key here, then, is to consider which answer relates to the word "Think." Each time the word appears, it's a command the speaker gives. The first time you see the word (line 4) it begins a statement about birds. The second time (line 6) it introduces a description of the speaker's living conditions. The last time the word is mentioned (line 12), it begins a sentence that includes both birds and people. (D) is best because it indicates the command, rather than the more general "show" of choice (C).

6. The primary purpose of line 11 is to

   (A) link the birds' habitat to the speaker's

   (B) emphasize the speaker's dislike of the mural

   (C) disconnect the speaker from nature

   (D) reveal the artist's lack of talent

   (E) show how nature and art are related

Line 11 contains three descriptions, "pretension of vitality," "swirl," and "mire." Line 10 describes the speaker's living conditions, and line 12 states, "where the bittern coughs." Therefore, line 11 is a link between the two, making (A) the best choice.

7. The "farmers' pests" (line 13) are analogous to

   (A) "platform of sticks" (line 1)

   (B) "that shared toilet" (line 3)

   (C) "regurgitating night" (line 5)

   (D) the mural (line 10)

   (E) "our goods on the sidewalk" (line 15)

Pests aren't valued and the "goods on the sidewalk" (line 15) are there "for the picking" (line 16), like garbage. Both are unwanted in some sense, but are valuable in another sense. The pest that the farmer wants to get rid of feeds the birds. And the goods that appear to be throwaways are the speaker's possessions. Therefore choice (E) is the answer that you're looking for.

8. The phrase "rich in mice" (line 4)

   (A) creates a distinction between the birds and the speaker

   (B) is an oxymoron

   (C) reveals the poet's cynicism

   (D) emphasizes the bounty of nature

   (E) is sarcastic

Beauty is in the eye of the beholder, as the saying goes, and so is the desirability of mice. You don't want them in your home, I imagine, unless you have a great love for little furry creatures. (If so, good for you. But I like mice in the field, not in the kitchen.) For the birds in the poem, however, a mouse might be dinner. Choice (A) expresses this distinction between human and avian life. An *oxymoron,* by the way, is not that meathead who failed math 12 times. It's an expression that seems to contradict itself, such as "jumbo shrimp."

9. The tone of this poem may be described as

   (A) argumentative

   (B) reflective

   (C) ironic

   (D) nostalgic

   (E) forceful

You can rule out (A) and (E) because the speaker isn't arguing about which is better, birds or people; nor is the speaker stating the opposite of what he or she means, placing the statement in ironic territory. You can therefore drop (C). That leaves you with reflective or nostalgic. Nostalgia has a bit of sweetness in it, and this poem doesn't. Go for the more neutral choice, (B).

10. The title of this poem is significant because it

    I.   expresses the transience of the birds' and the speaker's homes

    II. reveals the poverty renters face

    III. conveys a sense of powerlessness

    (A) I only

    (B) I and II

    (C) II and III

    (D) none of the above

    (E) all of the above

A renter may move at any time, and in this poem both the birds and the speaker move north. The speaker also moves at other times, as the poem refers to "apartments" (line 7). The second statement is only partly true; the speaker doesn't live in luxury, but some renters do. A renter is subject to a landlord, but "powerlessness" is too extreme. Go for (A), because only the first statement is justified.

Practice set 2

Carefully read the following poem, "Inland" by Edna St. Vincent Millay, and answer the questions that follow.

(01)   People that build their houses inland,
         People that buy a plot of ground
       Shaped like a house, and build a house there,
         Far from the sea-board, far from the sound

(05)   Of water sucking the hollow ledges,
         Tons of water striking the shore, —
       What do they long for, as I long for
         One salt smell of the sea once more?

       People the waves have not awakened,
(10)   Spanking the boats at the harbor's head,
       What do they long for, as I long for, —
         Starting up in my inland bed,

       Beating the narrow walls, and finding
         Neither a window nor a door,
(15)   Screaming to God for death by drowning, —
         One salt taste of the sea once more?

11. In the context of this poem, "plot" (line 2)

    (A) indicates that the speaker is scheming to return to the sea.

    (B) compares an area of land to a cemetery plot.

    (C) shows the narrowness of inland lives.

    (D) conveys stability.

    (E) reveals the uniformity of people's lives.

Literally the "plot" (line 2) is a parcel of land on which houses are built. However, the same word is used for a cemetery plot, the sliver of land that's your last address. Both meanings apply in this poem because the first stanza talks about "houses" and the last stanza refers to "[n]either a window nor a door" (line 14) and "death by drowning" (line 15). Choice (B) is therefore the best answer.

12. The poem compares

    I.   life on the sea and life on land

    II. a sailor's life before and after the sailor's return to land

    III. death by drowning to death on land

    (A) all of the above

    (B) none of the above

    (C) I and II

    (D) II and III

    (E) I and III

The speaker wonders about "People that build their houses inland" (line 1) and speaks of his or her own feelings about the sea: "as I long for / One salt smell of the sea once more?" (lines 7–8). Therefore, the first statement is valid. The speaker also talks about "[s]tarting up in my inland bed" (line 12), longing for the sea. Bingo: Statement II makes the cut. The third is tempting, because the poem mentions "death by drowning" (line 15). However, nothing in the poem speaks of death on land. The third statement drops out, and you're left with choice (C).

13. The lack of punctuation at the end of line 4

    (A) creates an incomplete sentence.

    (B) makes the first stanza more important.

    (C) weakens the beginning of the second stanza.

    (D) cuts the first stanza off from the second stanza.

    (E) allows "sound" to refer to an auditory sensation and to a body of water.

A line ending with no punctuation (which is called *enjambment* in literary terminology), both cuts and joins. The line break says stop, but the sentence continues. Poets get two meanings from this sort of trick. On the one hand, if you stop at the end of line 4, it reads "Far from the sea-board, far from the sound," with "sound" being a body of water. If you keep going, however, you have "far from the sound / Of water" (lines 4–5). Now "sound" means noise. As you see, choice (E) works nicely.

14. All of the following are found in the first stanza (lines 1–4) EXCEPT

    (A) parallel structure

    (B) enjambment

    (C) rhyme

    (D) metaphor

    (E) simile

Parallels in poetry are patterns that repeat. You can cross off choice (A) because the first stanza has two parallels ("People that . . ." and "Far from . . ."). You can also dump (B) because you see enjambment in lines 2 and 4. Rhyme occurs in lines 2 and 4, and a simile shows up in line 3 ("Shaped like a house"). Okay, you're left with (D), an implied comparison, which isn't in this poem.

15. Line 9 may be interpreted to mean that

    (A) some people are heavy sleepers.

    (B) anyone who lives inland hasn't truly lived.

    (C) inland life is less peaceful than life on the sea.

    (D) it is better not to experience life on the sea.

    (E) inland life is preferable to life on the sea.

Throughout the poem the speaker wonders what inland life is like. However, the speaker isn't neutral. By the fourth stanza the speaker is "[s]creaming to God" (line 15) for a "salt taste of the sea once more" (line 16). Keep that stanza in mind as you look back at "awakened" (line 9). The word has a double meaning — roused from sleep and opened to the fullness of life. Choice (B) fits both of these definitions.

16. Line 11 marks a shift between

   (A) formal and informal diction

   (B) a regular and an irregular rhyme scheme

   (C) analysis and opinion

   (D) relative detachment and increased emotion

   (E) vehemence and detachment

In the first ten lines of the poem, the speaker wonders about life inland but gives only one emotional clue: "as I long for / One salt smell of the sea once more" (lines 7–8). From line 11 onward, however, the emotion builds. The speaker would rather drown than die inland. The speaker is "beating" (line 13) and "screaming" (line 15). The other choices fall apart for various reasons. Choice (A) is out because the *diction,* or word choice, doesn't change. Nor does the rhyme scheme. The first ten lines speculate about those who live "inland"; no analysis appears, so (C) isn't a good answer. Choice (E) would be fine if it were reversed, with the detachment moving to vehemence — the pattern described by the correct answer, (D).

17. The "inland bed" (line 12) may be

   (A) a narrow cot

   (B) a grave

   (C) a sleeping bag

   (D) a jail cell

   (E) a shared accommodation

This poem is full of double meanings. If the speaker is "inland" (the title of the poem), he or she may actually be "in the land" as in "in the earth" or in a grave. That meaning fits the "narrow walls" (line 13) without windows and doors (line 14) and the reference to death in line 15. Now you've arrived at (B) as the best answer.

18. The speaker is probably

   (A) a former sailor

   (B) someone who has always longed to go to sea

   (C) someone who has always lived inland

   (D) a homeowner

   (E) on a ship

The speaker is longing to go to sea "once more" (lines 8 and 16), so choices (C) and (E) are easy to eliminate. You know the speaker wants to go to the sea now, but you don't know if that same wish was always present; drop (B). The speaker muses about people "that buy a plot of ground" (line 2), but you can't tell whether the speaker is in that category, and some lines suggest otherwise. All you can be sure of is (A), someone who once sailed and would like to do so again.

19. The dominant technique in the second stanza (lines 5–8) is

   (A) internal monologue

   (B) dialogue

   (C) narration

   (D) figurative language

   (E) imagery

The second stanza is all sensory description — the "water sucking the hollow ledges" (line 5), the "tons of water striking the shore" (line 6), and the "salt smell" (line 8). As you may know, imagery is defined as sensory description, so choice (E) is the one you're looking for.

20. In the context of line 12, "starting" may be defined as

   (A) beginning

   (B) opening

   (C) sudden awakening

   (D) originating

   (E) establishing

The speaker is "starting up" in an "inland bed" (line 12). What do you do in a bed? You wake up! The other choices all address the "moving to something new" definition of "starting." Because the speaker is in a bed, the only definition that fits is (C).

Practice set 3

Read the following poem, "The World Is Too Much with Us" by William Wordsworth, and answer the questions that follow.

(01)   The world is too much with us; late and soon,
            Getting and spending, we lay waste our powers:
            Little we see in nature that is ours;
            We have given our hearts away, a sordid boon!
(05)   This Sea that bares her bosom to the moon;
            The Winds that will be howling at all hours
            And are up-gathered now like sleeping flowers;
            For this, for every thing, we are out of tune;
            It moves us not — Great God! I'd rather be
(10)   A Pagan suckled in a creed outworn;
            So might I, standing on this pleasant lea[1],
            Have glimpses that would make me less forlorn;
            Have sight of Proteus[2] coming from the sea;
            Or hear old Triton[3] blow his wreathèd horn.

1. Meadow.

2. In Greek mythology, the "Old Man of the Sea."

3. In Greek mythology, a sea god.

21. The tone of this poem may be described as

    (A) passionate

    (B) humorous

    (C) detached

    (D) sarcastic

    (E) ironic

Tone describes the attitude of the author, and (A) is a perfect fit. Wordsworth doesn't hold back here. He's got a cause (people have lost touch with nature because they're too busy using it to make money), and he's screaming at the reader. Just look at the punctuation — two exclamation points in 14 lines. He's angry, not funny or calm, so you can drop (B) and (C). He's also straightforward, telling it like it is. Clearly, choices (D) and (E) don't do the job either.

22. Which statement best expresses the meaning of lines 1 and 2?

    (A) It is too late to change the way we relate to commerce.

    (B) We have ruined the natural world by our industry.

    (C) We waste time and energy making and spending money.

    (D) It is never too late to think about the world's welfare.

    (E) We do not take advantage of the power we have to change the world.

This question is straight reading comprehension. These lines are easier to decode if you change the sentence pattern into one resembling normal speech. The key words, for instance, are at the end of line 2: "We lay waste our powers." If you move "getting and spending," you have "We lay waste our powers getting and spending." The expression "lay waste" (line 2) means spoil or ruin, but you can still arrive at the correct answer is you go for the simpler meaning, "waste." From there it's a short hop to choice (C). Line 1 reinforces the meaning: "The world is too much with us" may be interpreted as "We think too much about worldly things, as opposed to spiritual or natural things." The punctuation of line 2 also helps you arrive at the correct answer. Line 2 ends with a colon, so the next statement must be either a list or an explanation of the preceding statement. Here, in line 3, you have an explanation, and that explanation is a statement that supports choice (C).

23. The shift in line 9 may be characterized as

    (A) idealistic to realistic

    (B) literal to figurative

    (C) descriptive to interpretive

    (D) scientific to artistic

    (E) universal to personal

The first eight lines employ first person plural (the *we/our/us* form), but halfway through line 9 the first person singular (the *I/my/me* form) appears. Clearly (E) is the best choice. The other answers don't come close. Choice (A) is out because the whole poem is idealistic, and (B) bombs because figurative language appears throughout the poem. (*Figurative language* is the literary term for similes, metaphors, personification, and other imaginative expressions.) The poem is neither descriptive nor scientific, so you're left with (E).

24. In the context of the poem, "creed outworn" (line 10) may be defined as

    (A) beliefs shown openly

    (B) prayers in archaic language

    (C) beliefs that have outlived their usefulness

    (D) religion no longer practiced

    (E) religion that is practiced publicly

The speaker in the poem wishes to return to an earlier time, when the connection with nature, expressed in mythology, was closer and more personal. The tricky part of this answer set is that some of the answers fit the meaning of "creed" (a statement or prayer of belief), and some attempt to trap you into thinking that "outworn" means "public," or "worn on the outside." In fact, "outworn" means "worn out." Choice (B) is tempting because an archaic language is one that is no longer spoken, but "prayers" and "creed" aren't exactly the same. Choice (C) doesn't work because the speaker thinks that such a creed would be useful. You're left with (D), the correct answer.

25. The allusions to Greek mythology in lines 13 and 14

    (A) emphasize the close connection of the speaker with the natural world

    (B) idealize the past

    (C) show how much progress has been made in the modern world

    (D) express the speaker's religious views

    (E) dismiss the speaker's views as fantasy

The speaker sees the past, represented by a "creed outworn" (line 10) as well as by the allusions to ancient Greek mythology as a better, purer time when the world wasn't "too much with us" (line 1). Just a quick glimpse of the old gods would make the speaker "less forlorn" (line 12). Choice (B) is the answer that you're looking for.

26. The dominant literary technique in lines 5–8 is

    (A) repetition of syntactic patterns

    (B) internal rhyme

    (C) figurative language

    (D) irregular meter

    (E) unusual word choice

Figurative language is all over lines 5–8, so (C) is the correct answer. The sea and the winds are personified (the sea bares her bosom, and the winds howl). The winds are also "up-gathered now like sleeping flowers" (line 7), a simile. In line 8, we're "out of tune," an implicit comparison between human beings and musical instruments. Figurative language rules! The only other answer that comes close is (E), because "up-gathered" seldom appears in everyday conversation. Neither does "bosom," unless you're reading a lingerie catalogue. No matter how you calculate, however, figurative language dominates.

27. The speaker would "rather be / A Pagan" (lines 9–10) because he or she would then

    (A) value "getting and spending" (line 2) more.

    (B) relate better to modern business.

    (C) consider religion more important.

    (D) be connected spiritually to nature.

    (E) have more control over nature.

The first part of the poem, which by the way is a sonnet, describes the disconnect between nature and human beings. The last bit (from "Great God!" to the end) shows what was lost according to the speaker — an intimate, spiritual connection to nature. Without a doubt, choice (D) is the best answer.

28. Which two lines are the closest in meaning?

    (A) 3 and 4

    (B) 3 and 8

    (C) 11 and 12

    (D) 11 and 13

    (E) 13 and 14

According to line 3, we see little in nature "that is ours," which is the equivalent of the statement in line 8 that "we are out of tune" with the sea and the winds. Line 4 concerns the waste of human energy and passion, because "[w]e have given our hearts away." These two meanings don't match, so you can rule out (A). Lines 11 and 12 tell a story. In line 11 the speaker is standing in a meadow, and in line 12 he or she is less sad. Because lines 11 and 12 aren't the same, (C) drops out. Line 13 also describes something the speaker sees (at least in his or her imagination), so line 13 pairs with 12 (not an answer choice), not with line 11. You can also rule out 13 and 14, because each tells of a different thing the speaker might see. The correct answer is (B).

29. The attitude of the speaker toward nature is

    (A) utilitarian

    (B) practical

    (C) idealistic

    (D) realistic

    (E) uninformed

Nature in this poem has no mosquitoes sending you running for the bug spray. Instead, you see a sea baring her breasts to the moon (line 5), howling winds compared to "sleeping flowers" (line 7), and a "pleasant lea" (line 11). The only other answer remotely in the running is (E), because you may conclude that the speaker is uninformed if he or she doesn't take wet feet, biting bugs, and other such annoyances into account. However, choice (C) fits best.

30. The rhyme scheme of the poem

    (A) divides the poem in half

    (B) unifies the first four lines and the last two

    (C) creates a divide between the first eight lines and the last six

    (D) is not related to meaning

    (E) works contrary to the syntax

The rhyme scheme is abbaabbacdcdcd. (For more information on rhyme scheme, turn to Chapter 4.) The break occurs after line 8, so (C) is the correct answer.

Crafting Solid Poetry Essays

Most people find writing an essay about a poem much easier than cracking the multiple-choice code. (If you aren't one of those people, turn to Chapter 7 for help.) No one ever said that writing essays was easy, so in this section I provide some great poems and some suggested essays. Before you start, take out a supply of lined paper. Just as you will on test day, use the margins in this book for scrap and the lined paper for the answer you would submit for grading.

The College Board suggests that you spend 40 minutes on each essay. To determine how close you come to that goal, keep a clock in front of you as you work.

Essay prompt 1

Read "You Get What You Pay For" by Dave Johnson (from *Dead Heat,* an audio CD released by Champion Records, 2007). Write a well-organized essay discussing the poetic techniques Johnson employs to create a particular mood.

YOU GET WHAT YOU PAY FOR

(01) I am in the middle of robbing a deli when a kid I taught last summer walks in.
    Hey. Hey, don't I know you? Hey, I do. It's the poetry guy.
Go away.
    What are you doing?
(05) *What does it look like?*
    Like you're robbing the store.
I am.
    That's cool.
Now get out.
(10)   *You're funny.*
There's nothing funny about it. Now get out.
    You. You're robbing this place.
Out. Now.
    Okay. Okay. Geez.
(15) I wave my gun at the owner. He gives me a bag of cash. The kid grabs a candy
    bar and a pack of gum.
He turns to walk out. I say,
    What are you doing?
        You're taking the money. Right?
Yes.
(20)   *So. I figure it's no big deal.*
Pay the man.
        What?
Pay, the man.
    I don't have the money.
(25) *Why are you coming into a store if you don't have the money?*
    I don't know.
*You should never go into any store, unless you're prepared to pay for what
they sell.*
I pull out my wallet. I take out two singles. I give them to the kid.
    Pay the man.
(30) The kid gives the owner the money. The kid leaves. And so do I.

Essay prompt 2

Read "After Apple-Picking" by Robert Frost. In a well-written essay, consider how the poet uses diction, figurative language, and other poetic techniques to convey meaning(s) beyond physical labor.

(01) My long two-pointed ladder's sticking through a tree
Toward heaven still,
And there's a barrel that I didn't fill
Beside it, and there may be two or three
(05) Apples I didn't pick upon some bough.
But I am done with apple-picking now.
Essence of winter sleep is on the night,
The scent of apples: I am drowsing off.
I cannot rub the strangeness from my sight
(10) I got from looking through a pane of glass
I skimmed this morning from the drinking trough
And held against the world of hoary grass.
It melted, and I let it fall and break.
But I was well
(15) Upon my way to sleep before it fell,
And I could tell
What form my dreaming was about to take.
Magnified apples appear and disappear,
Stem end and blossom end,
(20) And every fleck of russet showing clear.
My instep arch not only keeps the ache,
It keeps the pressure of a ladder-round.
I feel the ladder sway as the boughs bend.
And I keep hearing from the cellar bin
(25) The rumbling sound
Of load on load of apples coming in.
For I have had too much
Of apple-picking: I am overtired
Of the great harvest I myself desired.
(30) There were ten thousand thousand fruit to touch,
Cherish in hand, lift down, and not let fall.
For all
That struck the earth,
No matter if not bruised or spiked with stubble,
(35) Went surely to the cider-apple heap
As of no worth.
One can see what will trouble
This sleep of mine, whatever sleep it is.
Were he not gone,
(40) The woodchuck could say whether it's like his
Long sleep, as I describe its coming on,
Or just some human sleep.

Essay prompt 3

Read Sonnet 56 by William Shakespeare. In a well-organized critical essay, analyze how the poet conveys his attitude toward love.

(01)   Sweet love, renew thy force; be it not said
    Thy edge should blunter be than appetite,
    Which but today by feeling is allay'd,
    Tomorrow sharpened in his former might:
(05)   So, love, be thou, although today thou fill
    Thy hungry eyes, even till they wink with fullness,
    Tomorrow see again, and do not kill
    The spirit of love, with a perpetual dullness.
    Let this sad interim like the ocean be
(10)   Which parts the shore, where two contracted new
    Come daily to the banks, that when they see
    Return of love, more blest may be the view;
    As call it winter, which being full of care,
    Makes summer's welcome, thrice more wished, more rare.

Answer Guide for Poetry Essays

If 100,000 people buy this book and write these essays (oh, may that be true!), about 99,999 different answers will appear. (I'm allowing for one "I practiced, Mom, honest! The video game? Oh, that's just background noise.") Needless to say, I can't print — or even imagine — all possible answers. So here's the deal: For each poetry prompt, I provide a list of points that you *might* make about each poem, assuming you were working in an ideal world with no time limit. On the real AP exam, you can score a five without including everything on my list. My suggestions are simply there to help you see the possibilities. You may also come up with an idea that I haven't thought of. In that case, check to see whether you can justify your idea with evidence from the poem. If so, count your idea as correct and give yourself a gold star.

General essay requirements

Before I go into specifics on each individual poem, I want to give you a checklist for the elements that should be in every good AP essay. Reread your work and decide whether you've covered the basics. If not, try again. Here's what you need to strive for:

- ✔ The essay needs an introduction containing the title of the poem enclosed in quotation marks, the author's name, and a thesis statement.

- ✔ The essay should be organized logically. You may proceed through the poem in line order, making a point about each significant item. Or, you may group similar ideas into different paragraphs. For example, you may place everything about figurative language in one paragraph and everything about imagery in another.

- ✔ Ideally the essay should have a conclusion, not a summary or an abrupt stop.

- ✔ The essay must include evidence from the poem. Usually this evidence is given in the form of quotations, which need to be punctuated properly. You may cite line numbers in parentheses after the quotations.

- ✔ The essay should be written in present tense.

- ✔ You should have few grammar and spelling errors. Be sure to use complete sentences, each ending with a period or a question mark. (Exclamation points are okay grammatically but rarely justified in a formal essay.)

✔ You should check, check, and then recheck that you're answering the question from the prompt. Off-topic remarks should be crossed out.

Potential points for essay 1

I chose Dave Johnson's wonderful poem for two reasons: It's deceptively simple, and it gives you practice in looking below the surface. And the humor in it doesn't hurt either. Because English teachers tend to fill their reading lists with tragedy, you've probably had more experience with sad pieces than with humor. And believe it or not, many AP exams include humorous selections. This first essay gives you a chance to smile!

Main points

The crucial task, as explained in the prompt, is to decide how to characterize the mood of the poem. At first the scene is comical, almost as if you were watching a reality-show prank. By the end of the poem, however, you realize that the poet is working with more than humor. The speaker follows the student out of the store, knowing that the student received a bad lesson in dishonesty. Insisting that the student pay for the candy bar and the gum may have counteracted the initial lesson, but the poem ends without an answer. The dominant mood is uncertainty.

As long as you support your answer with evidence, you may be able to characterize the mood differently and still do well on your essay. I can imagine a fairly good case for a "serious," a "moral," or a didactic mood. (*Didactic* means that someone's teaching a lesson.) The points that I list later can be tweaked to support any of these answers. However, if you stay on the surface and say that the mood is "funny" or "comical," you'll likely write a fair essay but not a good one.

Evidence

An essay about the poem "You Get What You Pay For" may include these points about poetic technique and the mood of uncertainty:

✔ A few first-person narrative lines describe the situation, but the poem is mostly dialogue between the speaker and the student. By relying on dialogue, the poet stays on the surface, thereby increasing the uncertainty.

✔ The margins seesaw between the speaker and the student, reflecting the two paths — honesty and dishonesty. The seesaw emphasizes that the situation could go either way. Again, this pattern reinforces the mood of uncertainty.

✔ The diction is *colloquial* (the way people really talk). Examples of this colloquial diction include "That's cool" (line 8) and "Geez" (line 14). The diction makes the situation seem more real, as if the characters were actual people. With real people, the stakes seem higher.

✔ The dialogue consists of short, staccato lines, which add a sense of urgency. One example is "Out. Now." (line 13). Reinforcing the uncertain mood, much of the dialogue is in the form of questions ("Hey, don't I know you?" and "What are you doing? / What does it look like?" for example) Other dialogue expresses doubt: "I don't know" (line 26).

✔ Syntax is also important in this poem. The narrative in line 28 employs a repetitive pattern: *I-verb*. This pattern gives a sense of firmness and control. For example, consider this statement: "I pull out my wallet. I take out two singles. I give them to the kid." The individual sentences are short, and nearly every word is a single syllable, implying that the speaker is resolved; the student must be honest.

✔ The last line is very simple: "The kid gives the owner the money. The kid leaves. And so do I." The last bit — "And so do I" — isn't a complete sentence. This fragment implies that the speaker is now following the kid, who has been forced into honesty, but nothing is certain. The story is incomplete, just as one's decisions about life are often incomplete.

Organization

An essay about "You Get What You Pay For" may be organized in several different ways, including these:

- ✔ An introduction may identify the mood of the poem. Then you can devote one body paragraph for each poetic element (dialogue, diction, margins). The conclusion addresses *why* this mood is effective for the topic of honesty. This structure is probably the best, though you have to sort your information quickly in order to place it in the right paragraph.

- ✔ After an introduction identifying the mood of the poem, devote a body paragraph to the teacher and another to the student. The conclusion explains how the interplay between the two characters creates the mood. This structure is effective, but you have to be careful not to repeat information, a real pitfall because the two characters constantly interact.

- ✔ The quickest and simplest structure works through the poem, line by line, in order, commenting on the poetic devices employed in each line.

Overall assessment

If I were an exam grader, I would expect to see the first three points because they're the most obvious and also the most important. If you include only those points, your essay should score in the middle range. If you add two or three of the other ideas, your essay moves into the highest-scoring slot. Of course, the exam graders also take into account how well you've organized and presented the information. (For more details on scoring an essay, take a look at Chapter 17 or Chapter 19, where I present scoring grids for essay questions.)

Potential points for essay 2

The prompt for the second sample essay asks you to figure out what apple-picking symbolizes, taking into consideration diction and figurative language. However, the prompt also adds the phrase "and other poetic techniques." This phrase means that you must make sure that your answer includes more than diction and figurative language. If you stick with only those two poetic techniques, your essay will probably rise no higher than the mid-range of scores.

Main points

First you have to decide what apple-picking represents. Yes, the poem *is* about a tiring physical activity, but the story doesn't end there. The task of apple-picking also symbolizes the way a person views life — the choices made and things left undone — as death approaches. To use one of Frost's most famous lines, the poem also considers "the road not taken" and refers to the entire cycle of life.

You don't have to cover every point I mention in order to do well. An excellent AP essay on "After Apple-Picking" may focus on any single symbolic meaning cited in the preceding paragraph, assuming that you make a strong case with ample evidence for your assertions.

Evidence

Now for some specifics, which are divided according to the poetic technique that they represent.

Following are points about imagery:

- ✔ The ladder is "two-pointed" (line 1), and the two points may be life and death or heaven and hell. The ladder is reaching "[t]oward heaven" (line 2). This reference to heaven implies that the speaker has left the world. In other words, the speaker has died and is hoping to reach heaven.

- The speaker says "I am done with apple-picking" (line 6), a statement which is clearly another reference to death. The barrel "I didn't fill" (line 3) and the apples "I didn't pick" (line 5) symbolize tasks left undone. Life will continue without his presence.

- The reference to "hoary grass" (line 12) literally refers to ice upon the grass, probably frozen dew. However, "hoary" is also used to refer to gray hair and the age at which one gets gray hair — my age, which is old. Here you have yet another reference to the end of life.

- The extended description of the apples (lines 18–20) represents the clarity one has as death approaches. The moments of one's life and the relative importance of each become clear.

- The "rumbling sound" (line 25) has a link to thunder. Thunder alerts you to the fact that trouble — lightning — is coming. Here it may be a sign of death's approach.

Following are some points about diction:

- The vocabulary in the poem is quite simple, emphasizing the common, everyday aspect of the experience of apple-picking. Everyone works, and everyone eventually dies.

- "[S]till" (line 2) means "even now," but the word also means "motionless," which (you guessed it!) is an image of death. (Could this poem be any more of a downer?)

- The rhyme scheme is irregular, so the poet had no need to find a rhyme for "overtired" (line 28). Therefore, "desired" (line 29) catches the reader's attention, hinting at life's temptations and the way in which getting what one wants isn't always satisfying. The irregular rhyme scheme may also emphasize the unpredictability of life.

- The word "keep" is repeated twice (lines 22 and 24), emphasizing the dilemma — what in life is worth keeping, and what should be given up?

Following are some points about figurative language:

- "[W]inter sleep" (line 7) is a metaphor for death or for the last period of one's life.

- Many other references to sleep support the idea of death, including "I am drowsing off" (line 8) and "I was well / Upon my way to sleep" (lines 14–15).

- The final reference to sleep asks whether "this sleep of mine" (line 38) is "like his / Long sleep . . . [o]r just some human sleep" (lines 40–42). The speaker refers to the woodchuck but actually wonders what death will be like.

- The morning and night — which symbolize the life cycle — are both mentioned. In the morning, the ice sheet on the drinking water gives the speaker a "strangeness" (line 9) in his or her sight, which the speaker "cannot rub" (line 9) away. Only when the speaker is "[u]pon my way to sleep" (line 15) does the strangeness melt away. The implication is that death clarifies one's ideas.

- The "pane" of ice (line 10) represents a separation, perhaps the barrier between life and death.

- The "ten thousand thousand" (line 30) apples, clearly an exaggeration (which is a *hyperbole* in literary terminology), represent the events in the speaker's life or the tasks he or she had to accomplish. Each of the apples (tasks or moments) is something to "[c]herish in hand . . . and not let fall" (line 31).

- Any apple that "struck the earth" (line 33), even if undamaged, is dumped into the "cider-apple heap" (line 35), and is therefore worth less than the others. This tracks the idea that in death, one's value is diminished.

Following are some points about sound:

- The poem has no regular rhyme scheme, but some lines are grouped by similar words at their ends. For example, line 2 ends with "still" and line 3 with "didn't fill." When you link these words, you see that the poem is about what's left unfinished.

> ✔ Many of the words in the poem have just one syllable, giving the poem a simple beat. In the same way, the poet is declaring a simple truth: At the end of life, you evaluate what you've accomplished.

Organization

With so much material, this essay presents you with several potential structures. Here are three:

> ✔ An introduction may explain several possible meanings for "apple-picking." Then one body paragraph may be devoted to each meaning, supported by an analysis of poetic devices. The conclusion could address *which* meaning is most important. This structure calls on your organizational skills, because you have to pick apart the poem and sort the points you want to make to support each meaning.

> ✔ An introduction may identify one possible meaning for "apple-picking." Then you can discuss each poetic device (one for figurative language, one for sound, and so forth) in a separate body paragraph. The conclusion might step back and look at the poem as a whole, explaining which technique is most important in creating meaning for "apple-picking." Like the preceding structure, you have to decide what goes where before writing. (Pre-writing is always a good idea, as I explain in Chapter 7. However, some structures are more forgiving than others when it comes to last minute decisions.)

> ✔ An essay may work through the poem, line by line, in order, commenting on the poetic devices employed in each line and exploring possible meanings for "apple-picking." This structure allows you to make decisions as you write, so it's fast and easy. It's a little less sophisticated than the other two I explain, but it's still acceptable.

Overall assessment

After reviewing the previous lists, you may think that I've gone overboard in listing way too many ideas about "After Apple-Picking" — and you're right! I listed everything I could think of in order to increase the chances of covering what you may have noticed. If you made one or two points in each category or four or five points in just one category, you've done well.

If you came up with something I missed, it may be valid. Just be sure to support your ideas with evidence from the poem — not from your own experience picking apples or doing some other form of hard labor.

Potential points for essay 3

I couldn't resist throwing in a Shakespearean sonnet, because (a) I love Shakespeare and (b) so do the AP exam writers. Be grateful that the AP likes Shakespeare. Because just about every English class covers Shakespearean sonnets, you have a fund of knowledge to draw upon.

Main points

This beautiful Shakespearean sonnet begins with a plea to "Sweet love" (line 1). The speaker may be addressing a real person (the beloved) or the love that the speaker has inside himself for his beloved. Or, the speaker may be talking to love itself. These three meanings float around the poem. The best essays take all three meanings into account, because each reveals something different about the speaker's attitude toward love.

The basic idea of the poem is that the lovers aren't together — physically or emotionally. The break will be temporary, however. The lovers will reunite, and their love will be renewed and better. The speaker compares love to appetite; one may be hungry and eat, but the appetite always returns. The speaker also envisions the lovers parted by the ocean, with each of them on a different shore. Finally, the speaker sees the lover's return as summer, which is greeted with even more happiness after the iciness of the winter.

The ideas I provide in the preceding paragraphs, or at least most of them, should appear in your essay. And as always in an AP English poetry essay, you have to relate *how* the poem is written to *what* the poem means. The prompt asks you to convey the speaker's attitude toward love, so there's your focus.

Evidence

Specific points you may make include:

- As mentioned earlier, "Sweet love" (line 1) may be the beloved or it may be love itself. The technique used is called *apostrophe*. Apostrophe in a literary sense (not punctuation) is a direct address to an idea or to a person who isn't present. (You don't need to know the term apostrophe to receive a high score on the essay, but your grader will be *very* impressed if you do.)

- Syntax is important in line 1 also. (*Syntax* is the grammatical identity of words in a sentence.) First you have a command ("renew thy force") and then a decree ("be it not said"). You may expect the line to read, "renew . . . don't allow our love to decay." Instead, the strong command is followed by something more passive. The speaker has removed himself a little; he has placed a little space between himself and his desire.

- In line 2, love is compared to an edge, which may be blunt or sharp. This metaphor has a whiff of danger in it. You can get hurt (perhaps cut or stabbed) if you fall in love. This metaphor gives another hint that the relationship between the speaker and his beloved isn't going well.

- In line 6, the speaker mentions "hungry eyes" and a "wink." Your eyes may appear to wink when you're falling asleep. In other words, the literal meaning of this line refers to sleep. However, a wink may also be flirtatious, and the "hungry eyes" may be looking for nonfood sustenance (think sex). And if the hunger is satisfied, it still returns. The speaker assumes that love's (or his lover's) hunger, once fulfilled, will still return.

- Line 9 introduces the idea of "interim," which is a temporary period. However, the comparison with the ocean makes that interim awfully large! The speaker returns to the shore over and over again, waiting for love to return. While the poem expresses hope, it also contains an element of despair. After all, ocean travel, particularly in Shakespeare's time, was dangerous. The ocean metaphor suggests the possibility that the lover or the feeling of love will never return.

- Line 10 refers to "two contracted new." In other words, the speaker is referring to new lovers in the first flush of romance. They may be parted and do nothing more than return to the shore, waiting to see each other again. The word "contracted" implies a commitment, and "interim" (line 9) implies a temporary break. Both words add hope to the poem.

- The syntax is a bit odd in line 13, but the phrase "As call it winter" actually belongs to a sentence that was begun in line 9. The full sentence, paraphrased, is "This interim is like the ocean or like winter." Because summer always follows winter, the speaker is expressing hope (or at least more hope than the ocean metaphor).

- "More rare" (line 14) means "more valuable," as in the sense of a rare painting. Therefore, "summer's welcome" (line 14) will be more valuable because of the harsh winter or ocean that has parted the lovers.

- The poem is a sonnet, with three groups of four lines (a *quatrain,* in lit-speak) and a concluding *couplet,* or pair of lines. The rhyme scheme supports this division of the poem. Because the couplet contains the reference to summer and winter, the poem ends with hope, because seasons follow each other naturally. In other words, summer *must* happen; the lover or the love must return.

Organization

Sonnets are short, but as the list of points shows, you can say a lot about only 14 lines. Therefore, structure is still important in a sonnet essay. Any of these organizational patterns work well:

✔ The introduction states the poet's attitude toward love and identifies the nature of love in the poem — the beloved, the lover (speaker), and the emotion of love itself. Three body paragraphs discuss each of those aspects of love. The conclusion compares the human beloved to the abstract emotion, love. This structure follows the prompt closely and is easy to organize.

✔ The introduction identifies the poet's attitude toward love and then names the poetic devices that the poet employs. One body paragraph explains each poetic device. The conclusion identifies the most effective poetic device, the one that affects the reader most intensely. As always when you're sorting by poetic elements, you must take care to decide before writing exactly what you want to say. This structure allows little room for thinking as you write, unless you're very good at tucking in extra ideas. (If you do so, be neat and use a caret (^) for each insertion.)

✔ Follow the sonnet's organizational pattern. After identifying the poet's attitude, devote one paragraph to each of the three quatrains and one to the couplet. The couplet paragraph may serve as a conclusion, because that's its role in the sonnet. (Convenient, right?)

Overall assessment

As you rate your essay for the third sample prompt, consider yourself in great shape if you've identified all three aspects of love and made four or five points, including an analysis of the ocean/summer metaphors. If you found only two aspects of love, your grade may be a point lower — but only if you have provided ample evidence. An essay considering only a lover and his/her beloved would receive only a mid-range score, as would an essay relying only on one poetic element.

Part III
Getting the Story from Prose and Drama

The 5th Wave — By Rich Tennant

"You know, in Jane Austen's time a little well placed irony would have sufficed."

In this part . . .

Imagine a campfire in the days when campfires were the latest discovery. What do you see? I see a bunch of people sitting around telling stories — or, perhaps, acting out stories, particularly the one about the wooly mammoth that got away. "Honest, I was so close! If Akakak over there hadn't sneezed . . . " Then everyone chimes in: "We should hunt earlier in the day . . . when I was a kid the mammoths were bigger and woolier . . . " In other words, what I imagine is fiction (the stories), drama (acting out stories), and nonfiction (essays and memoirs). These types of writings are as old as humanity and as new as the AP English exam you're preparing to take.

In this part, I review the basics of prose and drama, telling you what to look for in each. I also explain what the College Board likes to test and how to approach each multiple-choice and essay question. Finally, I provide a wooly-mammoth-sized portion of practice.

Chapter 9

Reading Fiction and Drama Passages

· ·

In This Chapter

▶ Examining the building blocks of fiction and drama

▶ Appreciating how drama selections differ from story or novel excerpts

· ·

Meet Mr. Fiction and Ms. Drama, the fraternal twins of literature. On the outside, fiction and drama appear completely different, but inwardly, they're a lot alike. This chapter is a reconnaissance mission through their home territory, explaining the basic elements of each genre. The spotlight is on the twins as they usually appear on the AP English Literature and Composition exam. *Note:* Nearly every point about prose fiction in this chapter also applies to drama, with occasional, common-sense modifications.

Tell Me a Story: Fiction and Drama in the AP Exam

Prose fiction has a starring role on the AP English Literature and Composition exam, and drama makes cameo appearances fairly often. Here's what to expect:

✔ From a half to two thirds of the AP exam tests your ability to read fiction and drama. That's good news for those of you who break out in hives when you see a poem. (If you get poetry hives, you may want to spend some quality time in Part II.)

✔ Literary selections usually include slices of novels and plays or whole (but very short) stories.

✔ Most passages are about 800 words long, give or take a few paragraphs.

✔ Fiction and drama selections appear in both the multiple-choice and essay sections. (You may also encounter a nonfiction selection. Chapter 10 tackles that topic.)

✔ Fiction and drama are always the basis for the third essay on the exam, which is the open-ended one. What this means is that you get a prompt (a question), but no passage. Instead, the testers ask you to write about a novel or play of your own choice, from memory. (You can find more information on this particular form of torture in Chapter 14.)

Now that you know what's coming your way, you can follow the Boy Scout motto and be prepared.

Prose, not cons

You may hear the term *prose* in English class or when you're discussing the AP exam. Prose is easy to recognize, but difficult to define. Except for the bits of poetry tucked here and there, most of this book is written in prose. But the definition of prose is more than "anything that's not poetry." Prose is ordinary writing — the kind that has sentences and paragraphs. However, even that definition needs more explanation. After all, some poems are called *prose poems.* They look like run-of-the-mill paragraphs, but when you read them, you enter a dense, figurative world of meaning. (Chapter 18 contains a prose poem.) Prose may also shed its paragraphs and show up in drama; though some plays — Shakespeare's, for example — are written in verse. To make a long story short (if it's not too late for that already!), prose is a complicated term for simple writing.

What's Going On? Plot and Conflict

Short stories and novels are fueled by *plot,* or the set of events that propels the work forward. Not many people care to read a story without a plot, and it's also difficult to imagine a bestseller wholly lacking in *conflict,* which is the fight or dilemma that characters face. I explain both of these elements in detail in the following sections.

Plot: It's not just a piece of land

When you're writing an open-ended essay where you choose the literary work, plot is a big deal. Without a text in front of you, incidents in the story become Exhibit A, basic evidence for the case that you're trying to prove. On the other hand, when a passage is provided (in one of the other essays or in the multiple-choice section, for instance), plot sinks in importance. After all, unless the passage is a complete story, you see only a bit of the plot because you're reading less than a chapter's worth of material. However, you still have to answer a couple of questions or make some points based on plot. So you should have a solid understanding of how an author constructs a plot as well as how to locate those landmarks when all you have is a snippet of the story to go by — I cover both in this section.

Recalling plot structure

Years ago a television show about New York City began with these lines: "There are 8 million stories in the Naked City. This is one of them." In the world of literature, 8 million is a conservative estimate of the number of stories, or plots. Nevertheless, most fall into one classic pattern, illustrated here:

1. **The story begins with what English teachers call an *initiating incident,* the spark that ignites the flame.**

   In Toni Morrison's *Beloved,* for example, the attempted recapture of an escaped slave and her children provokes a murder. The murder and its consequences propel the action of the novel.

2. **After the initiating incident, authors may throw in some background information, or *exposition.***

   For example, in *The Adventures of Huckleberry Finn,* Mark Twain begins with a quick summary of the events in *The Adventures of Tom Sawyer,* the earlier novel that introduced Huck and his surroundings.

3. **At this point, the events of the story move along, gathering importance. In lit-speak, this progression is called *rising action*.**

   At some point the plot reaches its highest point of tension, where situations established in the story have to come to some sort of resolution, which is referred to as the *climax*. Herman Melville's novel *Moby-Dick* reaches its climax when the crew of the whaling ship Pequod battles the title character, a white whale.

4. **The climax is followed by *falling action,* also known as the *denouement,* a long word for the "how-it-all-worked-out" portion of the story.**

   Jane Austen's *Mansfield Park* has a very short denouement. For 300 pages the heroine, Fanny, has been pining away for this guy who thinks he's in love with someone else. The denouement simply tells the reader that in exactly the right amount of time, the guy realizes that he never loved Miss Wrong and turns his attention to Fanny, who agrees to marry him. This denouement takes about three paragraphs, tops. Other novelists — and even other Austen novels — devote a chapter or two to the denouement.

Not every plot proceeds in chronological order. The story may begin in the middle and then flash back to earlier events. You may also encounter *foreshadowing,* hints of future events, or a *frame story* that "bookends" another plot. Margaret Atwood's *The Handmaid's Tale,* for example, has a frame story in which a university professor lectures on a manuscript (the diary of the "handmaid" that forms the primary narrative). The lecturer's comments begin and end the novel.

If you're faced with a non-chronological plot, think about why the author has messed with the timeline. The reason may be relevant to your essay or may help you figure out a multiple-choice question.

Plots are often accompanied by *subplots* as well. Subplots are minor stories that weave around and through the main story line. In Charles Dickens' *Great Expectations,* for example, Miss Havisham's life story — and the reason she wears the same dress and only one shoe for decades — is only one of many intriguing subplots.

Pinpointing plot landmarks in an excerpted passage

Recognizing plot points in AP exam passages may be easy, especially if the information is presented in a straightforward manner. But don't expect to see too many paragraphs in a *here's-what-happened* format, because those would be way too easy for an AP test. The evil exam writers are more likely to choose their 800 words from a part of a novel or play that doesn't include background information. Without background, the task of answering questions becomes all the more difficult.

Don't worry. I'm here to arm you with some tips that will make detecting the plot points a bit easier. For instance, when reading fiction passages, be sure to ask yourself these questions about plot:

- ✔ **What happened?** Check the passage and make a mental list of events.

- ✔ **What events does the author leave out?** The AP exam tests your ability to "read between the lines" and make inferences. Reach beyond stated information into the realm of probability, always grounding your guesswork firmly in the passage.

- ✔ **What's the timeline?** In life, events happen one after another, but in fiction anything goes. Information may be revealed out of chronological order. Mentally reconstruct the order of events, and determine why the author may have chosen to structure the plot this way.

More likely than not, you'll see selections like the following one (albeit much longer) from Louisa May Alcott's novel *Jo's Boys:*

> Rob laughed, and, cheered by that unexpected sound, Nan bound up the wound with hands that never trembled, though great drops stood on her forehead; and she shared the water with patient number one before she turned to patient number two. Ted was much ashamed, and quite broken in spirit, when he found how he had failed at the critical moment, and begged them not to tell, as he really could not help it; then by way of finishing his utter humiliation, a burst of hysterical tears disgraced his manly soul, and did him a world of good.

The passage isn't impossible to read, but you have to fire up some brain cells to figure out what's going on. First, the basics: Rob laughs, and the sound makes Nan feel better. Nan seems to have acted as a doctor, but nervously. Ted faints, cries, and begs the others not to tell. Now you have to put on your Sherlock Holmes hat and stretch the basic plot points with an educated guess: Rob was hurt, and Nan came to help. The injury has to be serious, because Nan has "great drops" on her forehead. (She's so scared she's sweating.) Ted, instead of making himself useful, must have fallen apart, and so he became "patient number two," which appears to be a sarcastic title. And if you stretch a little further, you see that Ted is "ashamed" and the tears are "finishing his utter humiliation." In the end, something happened beyond the fainting and the tears. You don't know what, but you can guess that it was something serious.

Conflict: The element that brings in all the dra-ma!

Russian novelist Leo Tolstoy once commented that all happy families resemble each other, but each unhappy family is unhappy in its own unique way. Tolstoy's observation may be the reason why no one writes stories about perfect harmony. Conflict is simply easier to scrounge up, and it's almost always more interesting.

Conflict is essential to fiction, and so even a short AP passage generally depicts at least one instance of unrest. The characters' approach to the conflict, as well as its origin and resolution, may be the subject of AP questions.

Highlighting the conflict(s)

In a complicated work, some or even all of these conflicts may appear and interrelate:

- ✔ **One character against another:** This type of conflict is straightforward: One character in a story has a grievance against another, and a battle ensues. A variation of this conflict sets one character against a few others. For example, Ralph, the leader of the "good guys" in William Golding's *The Lord of the Flies,* gradually comes into conflict with Jack and later with Jack's "tribe" of hunters.

- ✔ **A character or group against society:** This kind of plot pits a character against society or a dominant group with a different agenda or values. In Harper Lee's *To Kill a Mockingbird,* lawyer Atticus Finch opposes the racist society in which he lives. Atticus has several sympathizers, but many in the town condemn his defense of a falsely-accused black man, Tom Robinson.

- ✔ **A character against nature:** Mother Nature, when she's having a temper tantrum, plays a central or supporting role in many novels and plays. Zora Neale Hurston's novel *Their Eyes Were Watching God,* for example, depicts horrors that the main character, Janie, endures as she struggles to survive a fierce hurricane and subsequent flood.

✔ **A character against himself or herself:** Centuries before Freud invited the first patient to lie down on the couch, psychology was already a part of literature. Writers have always been aware of the contradictory inner emotions and impulses everyone experiences. In Virginia Woolf's *To the Lighthouse,* Mrs. Ramsay struggles to preserve an authentic self in the context of marriage and motherhood.

Conflict is most often expressed through action (see the preceding section on plot) or dialogue and description (discussed later in this chapter). The best writers can inject lots of conflict into just a few words. Check out the technique in this tiny slice from *At the Cross,* a novel by Dana Crum (© Dana Crum, reprinted with permission), which communicates conflict in several different ways:

> "Affirmative action was never justified," snapped the thin pale girl with red hair.

> Sidney turned to the teaching assistant for help, but she was leaning forward, listening with apparent interest, nodding with apparent commiseration.

> The pale girl was looking right at Sidney now. "It's just not fair that some people have it easy while others are made to suffer. I'm from Scarsdale, New York, and some of my friends from Exeter couldn't even get into Princeton because the school lowered its standards to let minorities in. It's not my friends' fault they're White. Why should they lose out just because minorities can't score high enough?

> Beneath Sidney's shirt a trickle of sweat streaked from his armpit to his stomach. His lips fell apart. But no words came out. He wanted to say that standards weren't as high when it came to White athletes like the husky football player, who'd so far misspoken twice . . .

Several events set up the conflict in the preceding excerpt: The pale girl's comment and Sidney's silent glance at the teaching assistant, his physical reaction, and his thoughts. The conflict? Sidney's discomfort and disagreement with the pale girl and her views.

Looking at the conflict in its context

It isn't enough to know who's fighting whom or what. You also need to understand the context of the conflict — what caused or solved the fight and how the conflict affects the plot. Answering these questions helps you understand why the conflict is important in the novel, play, or story.

Ask yourself these questions to identify and determine the significance of conflict:

✔ **Has the question directed me toward one type of conflict?** If so, zero in on the conflict that the question asks about. If the prompt queries you about nature, you obviously don't want to write about a character pitted against society. Not addressing the question earns you a zero on an essay (no matter how well written your essay is).

✔ **Which characters are uneasy, angry, or fearful?** Find the unhappy camper, and chances are the conflict isn't far behind.

✔ **What caused the problem?** In a short selection, information regarding the problem may not appear, but you should always search for background information. Or, if you're desperate, you'll have to read between the lines and make an educated guess. (I discuss this tactic earlier in the chapter.)

✔ **What has to change in order to restore harmony or peace?** Answering this question helps you define the conflict.

✔ **Is the conflict resolved?** Not all stories have happy endings; many hinge on a character's unwillingness to change. In an AP passage, however, you may not find out the resolution.

✔ **What effect does the conflict have?** The easiest way to answer this question is to imagine the story without the conflict. What changes? Now you know the effect of the conflict.

Where It's At: Setting

Stories don't take place in a vacuum. They're embedded in a particular time and place, or _setting._ (Okay, maybe a couple of science fiction tales do take place in the vacuum of Outer Space, but in that situation the vacuum is part of the setting.) A surprising number of AP exam questions address setting, so you need to be aware of all the ways in which this literary element manifests itself. Keep the following points in mind:

✔ **Some settings are so specific that you know the date and place.** For instance, Arthur Miller's play _The Crucible_ is set in Salem, Massachusetts, during the witch trials of 1692.

The setting of the literary work may symbolize another era or situation entirely. For example, _The Crucible_ deals with Salem, but Arthur Miller wrote the play to protest the actions of the House Un-American Activities Committee, which investigated Communism in American society during the 1950s.

✔ **Some settings may be quite general.** Perhaps the author indicates that the action occurs in modern times — a period that includes anything from the early 20th century through the present day. Or, the action may occur in an unnamed small town or large city. William Golding's _The Lord of the Flies,_ for example, takes place on a deserted island sometime in the modern era. No other details are supplied. The vagueness of the setting, by the way, emphasizes the author's point, which is that every society is vulnerable to cruelty and inhuman behavior.

✔ **Much of the setting is created by description.** The author may not tell you where and when the scene takes place, but descriptive details often take the place of facts. In James Fennimore Cooper's novel _The Deerslayer,_ Natty Bumppo journeys through the wooded, sparsely inhabited Northeastern United States. Eloquent descriptions of the forest and Glimmerglass Lake place you right there with Natty.

✔ **Events and dialogue may contain clues regarding the setting, but these clues may be tough to interpret if you aren't knowledgeable about the time and place.** For example, characters who talk about "the bee's knees" (meaning "the height of fashion") probably inhabit the 1920s. However, you may not know that fact if you haven't read much about that time period. If you don't know the significance of a particular detail, don't guess. Rely on the information you understand to make your point.

It's nice to know when and where the story takes place, but it's much more important to consider how the setting affects the story's meaning. Ask yourself these questions:

✔ **Why here?** If the story were moved to another country or to a rural area rather than an urban area (or vice versa), what would change?

✔ **Why then?** If the story were moved to an earlier or a later time, how would the story be different?

✔ **How do the characters fit into the setting?** Are they in opposition to the setting — fish out of water — or are they well situated?

✔ **How does the action relate to the time and place?** Could these events happen at any time or just at one point in history? Similarly, could they happen in any place? Or is the story universal?

✔ **How do details of setting contribute to character development and/or theme?** The way a character's room or house looks may tell you quite a bit about his or her personality. Similarly, at times the setting may emphasize a theme. Again, the best way to see the effect of a setting is to imagine the story moved to a different time or place.

Be wary of bringing history to bear on an AP exam question. I once read an essay about Charlotte Bronte's *Jane Eyre* in which the writer discussed "Ms. Eyre's job opportunities." The writer knew very little about the early 19th century, including the fact that the term "Ms." didn't exist in that period. The essay, which advocated a career for Jane, made little sense because becoming an attorney wasn't an option for a woman of that era. Stay in the world of the literary work as much as possible, and venture into history only if you're absolutely sure of the facts.

Who's There? Characterization

I once attended an AP conference at which the presenter asked each of us to name a literary character that we identified with. What people said was interesting, but the way they spoke was amazing. Passion radiated from each speaker. Yes, everyone in the room was an English teacher, and yes, as a group we're nuts about literature. But ask the same question at other gatherings, and I believe you'll spark a similar amount of passion.

Why all this emotion? Because characters are people on paper, and people are interested in people. That's why *characterization* (the development of characters in a work) adds so much to fiction; it's the way writers manufacture fictional people. Recognizing the importance of characterization, the AP exam hits this topic hard, questioning you about all the approaches authors have at their disposal, including dialogue, description, actions, relationships with other characters, and the like.

Overarching questions to consider

When you're studying characterization and trying to figure out its effect on the story, ask yourself these questions:

- **Who's the most important character?** How do you know? After you examine your answer, you'll likely see the underpinnings of the characterization — the tools that the author used to create the character.

- **Which traits dominate?** Some characters are flat; you see one or two personality traits and nothing more. Other characters are more complicated, meaning that they're generally more important. Look for dominant characteristics and for contradictory or minor traits. For example, take note of a generous moment from a character that usually acts like a miser. The brief change may be important.

- **Does the character change?** Static characters stay the same, and they generally act as a background or foil for other characters. Dynamic characters are on the move, at least in terms of personality. If you note changes in a character, chances are those changes (and the character) are important.

- **How would the story be different if a character were altered?** The easiest way to determine a character's significance is to change the character's personality or attitude. Think of the effect that the change may have on the story. By working backward, you can figure out the character's role in the story as written.

What the characters look like

Looks can be deceiving. (Just ask smart, beautiful blondes how often they have to dispel the impression that their brains focus only on surfing.) However, authors aren't presenting reality in their descriptions; instead, they're stacking the deck by carefully selecting precisely the right details. The type of clothing, the hairstyle, and even footwear can signal economic level, insecurities, values, or personality.

Mrs. Joe in Charles Dickens' *Great Expectations,* for instance, wears a stiff apron with pins stuck into the bib. She's resentful of her position as a blacksmith's wife, and she's stricter than the teacher in your worst nightmare. The pin-filled apron perfectly mirrors her sharp tongue, prickly personality, and resentful attitude. Her husband, on the other hand, has blue eyes so light that they almost blend into the white surrounding them. Joe, as you may have guessed, likes to be as inconspicuous as possible.

What the characters say . . .

As you read a piece of prose or drama, be sure to listen closely to the character(s). The level of education, the age of the character, and the geographical home base of the character may be revealed by his or her manner of speaking. And of course, the content may tell you about the character's preoccupations and relationships. However, be aware that as you determine characterization the author may create a character who says one thing and means another or who is self-deluded. Pretend that you're listening to a real person, and then judge his or her character as you do in real life.

In poetry, the "I" voice you hear is called the *speaker.* In prose, the "I" is the *narrator,* and the main character is the *protagonist.* English teachers are picky about stuff like this, so don't confuse these terms.

. . . About themselves and to each other

Authors use dialogue to create a personality and background for their characters. Characterization lays the backdrop for a story, just as every storyteller uses personality to make a plot convincing and enticing. Here are some key points to remember:

✔ **The main character may narrate the story.** The first-person point of view is fun to write, because you enter the mind of one character and create the world seen through that character's eyes. For example, check out this excerpt from a Sherlock Holmes' story by Arthur Conan Doyle. The narrator is Dr. Watson:

> My marriage had drifted us away from each other. My own complete happiness, and the home-centered interests which rise up around the man who first finds himself master of his own establishment, were sufficient to absorb all my attention . . .

Watson's comments reveal that he's an educated man — a doctor, in fact. He also values proper behavior, as you see in his formal speech and his assumption that "home-centered interests" rise up around married men.

✔ **The characters may participate in dialogue.** If you've ever eavesdropped in a restaurant or elsewhere, you know how much you can learn from other people's conversations. Dialogue creates a literary "eavesdropping" opportunity. For instance, consider what Sherlock Holmes says to Watson in the same story as the previous excerpt:

> [M]y eyes tell me that on the inside of your left shoe, just where the firelight strikes it, the leather is scored by six almost parallel cuts. Obviously they have been caused by someone who has very carelessly scraped round the edges of the sole in order to remove crusted mud from it.

Sherlock Holmes' comments to Watson reveal his intelligence, logic, and sharp perception. The word "obviously" shows you that he thinks observation is easy, and he may look down on those who aren't able to match his own ability.

Notice the formal, correct diction in the preceding Sherlock Holmes examples. It's easy to perceive Watson's attachment to his home life and Holmes' analytical mind. Contrast these characters with Huck Finn, who's the narrator in the following passage:

> You don't know about me without you have read a book by the name of *The Adventures of Tom Sawyer;* but that ain't no matter. That book was made by Mr. Mark Twain, and he told the truth, mainly. There was things which he stretched, but mainly he told the truth. That is nothing. I never seen anybody but lied one time or another, without it was Aunt Polly, or the widow, or maybe Mary.

Huck's lack of education and straightforward, pull-no-punches manner come through clearly, as does his cynicism about human nature.

... About each other

The information one character gives about another is a gold mine when you're defining a character. A character may provide background information, description, or an assessment of another character's life or personality. However, be sure to filter out the character's bias. For example, a poverty-stricken character may refer to another character as snobbish, listing designer labels as proof. The assessment may be colored by the jealousy of the impoverished character.

Here's Dr. Watson, discussing his friend Sherlock, in which he tells about Sherlock's love life (actually, lack of love life), his unease with emotion, and his intelligence:

> To Sherlock Holmes she is always THE woman. I have seldom heard him mention her under any other name. In his eyes she eclipses and predominates the whole of her sex. It was not that he felt any emotion akin to love for Irene Adler. All emotions, and that one particularly, were abhorrent to his cold, precise but admirably balanced mind.

The narrator or character giving you information may not be reliable. Unreliable narrators are a lot of fun, and very popular on AP English exams. You know a narrator isn't trustworthy the same way that you know an acquaintance isn't; something the narrator says doesn't mesh with the reality you observe. For example, in Dorothy Parker's story, "You Were Perfectly Fine," a young woman reassures a very hung-over young man that he was "perfectly fine" the night before, even as she describes the many ways in which he made a fool of himself, such as pouring clam juice down a friend's back and greeting the waiter as a long lost relation. (And, of course, he can't remember any of these classy things that he did.)

How the characters behave and interact

Take note of the small, seemingly unimportant details when you're trying to figure out a character. Anything a character does — or fails to do — contributes to his or her characterization. Here's what I mean: When a character picks up a check in a restaurant or heads for the restroom just as the bill arrives, you learn something about that character's attitude toward money. When a character contemplates an action — to attend a party, perhaps — whether or not the character follows through reveals the character's strength, determination, and priorities.

Noticing important actions

AP exam writers include passages that cover life's major events — birth, death, freedom or captivity, and so forth. Just as you pay attention to the big stuff in real life, you should note it in literature as well. The way a character acts or reacts when the stakes are high reveals the essential nature of the character.

For example, in Mark Twain's *Huckleberry Finn,* Tom Sawyer's thoughtlessness and immaturity are revealed when Tom allows the escaped slave Jim to believe that he's been recaptured. (Jim is unaware that he was set free months before.)

Here's a passage (from Jane Austen's *Sense and Sensibility*) that allows you a glimpse at another important moment, a marriage proposal:

> "Mrs. Robert Ferrars!" was repeated by Marianne and her mother in an accent of the utmost amazement; and though Elinor could not speak, even HER eyes were fixed on him with the same impatient wonder. [Edward] rose from his seat, and walked to the window, apparently from not knowing what to do; took up a pair of scissors that lay there, and while spoiling both them and their sheath by cutting the latter to pieces as he spoke, said, in a hurried voice, "Perhaps you do not know — you may not have heard that my brother is lately married to — to the youngest — to Miss Lucy Steele."

You don't have to know much about Edward to grasp the fact that he's nervous. (He's about to propose to Elinor, having narrowly escaped marriage to Lucy Steele.) After all, anyone who cuts a scissor case into little pieces — when the case doesn't even belong to him! — is not exactly calm.

Being perceptive about body language

The response of one or more characters to another isn't always verbal. These responses can manifest themselves as body language as well. Therefore, you need to pay attention to the interplay between characters for clues to their personalities. Although crossing one's arms or planting one's feet firmly on the ground don't qualify as earth-shaking events, these actions tell you about emotions and personality.

Scan this excerpt from Jane Austen's *Sense and Sensibility* to see how interactions can help you glean clues about a character's personality:

> Marianne moved to the window. "It is Colonel Brandon!" said she, with vexation. "We are never safe from HIM."
>
> "He will not come in, as Mrs. Jennings is from home."
>
> "I will not trust to THAT," retreating to her own room. "A man who has nothing to do with his own time has no conscience in his intrusion on that of others."
>
> The event proved her conjecture right, though it was founded on injustice and error; for Colonel Brandon DID come in; and Elinor, who was convinced that solicitude for Marianne brought him thither, and who saw THAT solicitude in his disturbed and melancholy look, and in his anxious though brief inquiry after her, could not forgive her sister for esteeming him so lightly.

Marianne feels vexation (annoyance) at Colonel Brandon's visit and views him as someone "who has nothing to do." These two reactions may lead you to dismiss Colonel Brandon as a pest. However, Elinor's reaction counters Marianne's: Elinor sees the Colonel as "anxious" about Marianne, and she "could not forgive her sister for esteeming him so lightly." Who's right about Colonel Brandon? Actually, Elinor is, but the AP exam will never ask you something that requires knowledge beyond the passage. Questions on the preceding example would address the sisters' differing views, not the correctness of their opinions.

 A subset of "body language" is facial expression. When you're answering questions about characterization (what mood the character is in, for example), take note of smiles, frowns, eyebrow lifting, forehead wrinkling, and all sorts of physical reactions. In the preceding example, for instance, Colonel Brandon has a "disturbed and melancholy" look.

Significant objects associated with the character

Hester Prynne wears a red "A" as punishment for her sin of adultery in Nathaniel Hawthorne's classic *The Scarlet Letter*. The future King Arthur proves his royalty by extracting the sword Excalibur in T.H. White's *The Sword in the Stone*. And of course, Harry Potter is marked by his lightning bolt scar. These objects are forever associated with their characters and affect the reader's perceptions of them.

An author doesn't need to be super-dramatic when employing objects as a means of characterization. Something as small as a wallet or as commonplace as a hat may reveal a character's taste, income level, or aspirations. As an example, enter the dining room of Captain Nemo's submarine, as described in *Twenty Thousand Leagues Under the Sea* by Jules Verne:

> The dishes, of bell metal, were placed on the table, and we took our places. Undoubtedly we had to do with civilised people, and, had it not been for the electric light which flooded us, I could have fancied I was in the dining-room of the Adelphi Hotel at Liverpool, or at the Grand Hotel in Paris. . . . As to the dinner-service, it was elegant, and in perfect taste. Each utensil — spoon, fork, knife, plate — had a letter engraved on it, with a motto above it, of which this is an exact facsimile:

> MOBILIS IN MOBILI N

> The letter N was no doubt the initial of the name of the enigmatical person who commanded at the bottom of the seas.

What can you tell about Captain Nemo from the plates and silverware? Well, for one, he's a stickler for the nicetics. Who has ever heard of a five-star dining room on a sub! He's also proud (his initial is on every utensil), and he values movement (the motto means "Mobile in the mobile element [water]"). That's quite a bit of information from a dinner table.

What's in Style? Tone, Diction, and Point of View

Every novel (and every story) has a style created by many elements of writing. Chief among them are the author's tone and diction and the point of view that he or she adopts. At a lecture on grammar (yes, I'm nerdy enough to go to things like that), the speaker explained that in the English language, double negatives make positive statements. He commented that "I didn't do no homework" actually means "I did some homework." (In my opinion, however, it means, "You have detention today.") The lecturer added that double positives add emphasis and are never negative. "Yeah, right!" commented someone in the audience.

I probably don't need to explain that the tone of "Yeah, right" is sarcastic. Someone learning English may need a little help decoding the expression, but most people catch the tone immediately, especially when they hear the words spoken. *Tone* in literature functions much the same as tone in an oral comment. The attitudes of both the characters and the author come through. However, because you can't actually hear the characters or talk with the author, you have to gather clues from the text in order to determine tone. One of the most important clues is *diction*, the particular words the author chooses.

The *point of view* of a story basically determines which demands the story places on the reader. For example, in the first-person point of view (when the narrator speaks directly to the reader), you must evaluate the narrator's biases. You see the other characters from the narrator's point of view.

Tone and diction

In a story or novel, both tone and diction are usually more complex than they are in a poem. (I discuss poetic devices in Chapter 4 — some of those ideas apply to fiction as well.) For one thing, generally prose and drama have more characters than a poem (which may have no characters at all). The diction and tone may differ for each character, and the author's impersonal descriptions may have still another tone or diction. All these factors complicate your life, but when you untangle the various voices in a literary passage, you learn more about the characters' personality and the author's views of his or her subject.

Knowing what's worth noting

Some questions worth asking when assessing tone and diction include the following:

- ✔ **How many narrators and characters does the text have?** In a short AP selection, chances are you'll hear the voice of only one narrator. Full-length novels, which you may discuss for the open-ended essay, may employ more than one narrator, and you need to keep tabs on who's saying what in the story. Tracking characters, of course, is also essential, because you need to know the people who propel the story forward. Tone and diction often differentiate one character from another. A dockworker sounds different from an attorney, for example.

- ✔ **Does a character's tone shift?** Particularly in a novel, but even in a short story, a character's tone may shift from, say, nostalgic to analytical to depressed. The shift often signals a plot development or adds depth to the characterization, as the character evolves personally or reacts to events.

- ✔ **Does the author's tone or diction differ from that of the characters?** The author's tone and diction may create a gap between what the characters say and do and the point the author is making. For example, the author's description may reveal the sadness beneath a character's sarcasm.

- ✔ **If any words were changed, how would the story be affected?** This question relates directly to diction. Try rewording a sentence or two and watch what changes.

Figures of speech — similes, metaphors, personification, and a bunch of other imaginative devices — are the building blocks of creative writing. And, creative writing, especially of the AP variety, requires close reading, which is the English teacher term for "pay careful attention to language." As you investigate diction, keep your eyes open for symbolism and nonliteral expressions. (For a complete discussion of figurative language, turn to Chapter 4.)

Practice take #1 on noting tone and diction

The easiest way to understand tone and diction is to note them as they appear in a literary work. Take a look at this excerpt from Oscar Wilde's short story, "The Canterville Ghost." As you read, ask yourself how the narrative voice of the author and the language of each character affect your perception of the work:

> Standing on the steps to receive them was an old woman, neatly dressed in black silk, with a white cap and apron. This was Mrs. Umney, the housekeeper, whom Mrs. Otis, at Lady Canterville's earnest request, had consented to keep in her former position. She made them each a low curtsey as they alighted, and said in a quaint, old-fashioned manner, "I bid you welcome to Canterville Chase." Following her, they passed through the fine Tudor hall into the library, a long, low room, paneled in black oak, at the end of which was a large stained glass window. Here they found tea laid out for them, and, after taking off their wraps, they sat down and began to look round, while Mrs. Umney waited on them.

> Suddenly Mrs. Otis caught sight of a dull red stain on the floor just by the fireplace, and, quite unconscious of what it really signified, said to Mrs. Umney, "I am afraid something has been spilt there."

"Yes, madam," replied the old housekeeper in a low voice, "blood has been spilt on that spot."

"How horrid!" cried Mrs. Otis; "I don't at all care for blood-stains in a sitting-room. It must be removed at once."

The old woman smiled, and answered in the same low, mysterious voice, "It is the blood of Lady Eleanore de Canterville, who was murdered on that very spot by her own husband, Sir Simon de Canterville, in 1575. Sir Simon survived her nine years, and disappeared suddenly under very mysterious circumstances. His body has never been discovered, but his guilty spirit still haunts the Chase. The blood-stain has been much admired by tourists and others, and cannot be removed."

"That is all nonsense," cried Washington Otis; "Pinkerton's Champion Stain Remover and Paragon Detergent will clean it up in no time," and before the terrified housekeeper could interfere, he had fallen upon his knees, and was rapidly scouring the floor with a small stick of what looked like a black cosmetic. In a few moments no trace of the blood-stain could be seen.

"I knew Pinkerton would do it," he exclaimed, triumphantly, as he looked round at his admiring family; but no sooner had he said these words than a terrible flash of lightning lit up the sombre room, a fearful peal of thunder made them all start to their feet, and Mrs. Umney fainted.

How many tones can you identify throughout this passage? Make your way through the following list to see whether you found the ones that I did:

1. **First, check out the housekeeper, Mrs. Umney.**

   She speaks in a "low voice" and a "low, mysterious voice" about blood from a centuries-old murder. Her tone is serious, slightly spooky, and self-important, as is her diction. Only she can give the vital information about the "guilty spirit" that "still haunts" the house — and she "smiled" while giving this information. (Talk about spooky!)

2. **Next up is Mrs. Otis.**

   This lady doesn't "care for blood-stains in a sitting-room." She's used to getting her way: "It must be removed at once." Her tone is commanding. She speaks, as does her husband, with formal diction, and she knows her power. Notice that she says, "I don't at all care for blood-stains in a sitting-room." What Mrs. Otis cares about is obviously vitally important (in Mrs. Otis's view).

3. **Now look at Washington Otis.**

   His tone is completely different from Mrs. Umney's. "That is all nonsense," he declares and praises "Pinkerton's Champion Stain Remover and Paragon Detergent." His remark, "I knew Pinkerton would do it," is said "triumphantly." Otis is a man of action, a believer in his own ability to get things done, a believer in progress. His tone is confident, and his diction is plain and straightforward. No fancy words for him! And no hints of underlying meanings.

4. **Finally, what about the author? Step back and look at the passage as a whole.**

   Can you see the humor in the interplay between Mrs. Umney and the Otis family? Notice how the passage begins like a classic gothic novel, with an aged housekeeper "neatly dressed in black silk" leading the family into a library paneled in dark oak, where tea is laid out. How many horror stories have begun this way? Lots! And how many of these stories have Pinkerton's Champion Stain Remover and Paragon Detergent"? Only this one. These two facts clue you in to Wilde's mocking tone. He inserts practical Americans into an English manor and, more importantly, into a gothic story, which includes supernatural elements, mysteries, old houses, scary housekeepers, and the like. He especially has fun in the long last sentence, which forms one paragraph: Just as Otis erases the stain, "a terrible flash of lightning lit up the sombre room . . . and Mrs. Umney fainted."

Practice take #2 on noting tone and diction

Now take a crack at determining the tone and diction of another literary passage. Here's an excerpt from "A Scandal in Bohemia," a Sherlock Holmes story narrated by Dr. Watson:

> One night — it was on the twentieth of March, 1888 — I was returning from a journey to a patient (for I had now returned to civil practice), when my way led me through Baker Street. As I passed the well-remembered door, which must always be associated in my mind with my wooing, and with the dark incidents of the Study in Scarlet, I was seized with a keen desire to see Holmes again, and to know how he was employing his extraordinary powers. His rooms were brilliantly lit, and, even as I looked up, I saw his tall, spare figure pass twice in a dark silhouette against the blind. He was pacing the room swiftly, eagerly, with his head sunk upon his chest and his hands clasped behind him.

What tone do you "hear" in Watson's narration? I hear precision; Watson takes care to specify the date. I also hear fussiness; he backtracks to insert information (his return to civil practice, the associations of the "well-remembered door," and so on). Finally, I hear admiration. Watson describes Holmes' rooms as "brilliantly lit." His choice of words echoes the doctor's admiration for Sherlock Holmes' "extraordinary powers." Watson's diction is formal, educated, but a bit fussy. He speaks of "wooing" and "dark incidents."

Point of view

Literature provides a lens through which readers look at the world. Skillful authors can fix their readers' attention on exactly the detail, opinion, or emotion the author wants to emphasize by manipulating the point of view of the story. Point of view is the way the author allows you to "see" and "hear" what's going on.

Point of view comes in three varieties, which the English scholars have handily numbered for your convenience:

✔ **First-person point of view** is in use when a character narrates the story with "I-me-my-mine" in his or her speech. The advantage of this point of view is that you get to hear the thoughts of the narrator and see the world depicted in the story through his or her eyes. However, remember that no narrator, like no human being, has complete self-knowledge or, for that matter, complete knowledge of anything. Therefore, the reader's role is to go beyond what the narrator says.

For example, Harper Lee's *To Kill a Mockingbird* is told from the point of view of Scout, a young child. She doesn't grasp the complex racial and socioeconomic relations of her town — but the reader does, because Scout gives information that the reader can interpret. Also, Scout's innocence reminds the reader of a simple, "it's-not-fair" attitude that contrasts with the rationalizations of other characters.

✔ **Second-person point of view,** in which the author uses "you" or "your," is rare; authors seldom speak directly to the reader. When you encounter this point of view, pay attention. Why? The author has made a daring choice, probably with a specific purpose in mind. Most times, second-person point of view draws the reader into the story, almost making the reader a participant in the action.

Here's an example: *Desperate Characters* is a book-length poem by Nicholas Christopher in which all sorts of magical events occur — libraries appear and disappear, characters sort out karma from another life, and Thomas Jefferson makes a cameo appearance in the 20th century. Christopher said that he chose the second-person point of view because that's how most people explain their dreams.

✓ **Third-person point of view** is that of an outsider looking at the action. The writer may choose *third-person omniscient,* in which the thoughts of every character are open to the reader, or *third-person limited,* in which the reader enters only one character's mind, either throughout the entire work or in a specific section. Third-person limited differs from first-person because the author's voice, not the character's voice, is what you hear in the descriptive passages.

In Virginia Woolf's wonderful novel, *Mrs. Dalloway,* you're in one character's mind at a time. You know the title character's thoughts about Peter, the great love of her youth, for example, and then a few pages later, you hear Peter's thoughts about Mrs. Dalloway. Fascinating! When you're reading a third-person selection, either limited or omniscient, you're watching the story unfold as an outsider. Remember that most writers choose this point of view.

Consider these issues when you discuss point of view in an AP essay:

✓ **What does the point of view add to the story?** Do you get to know one character extremely well? Has the author created a unique voice? Is the author's attention fairly divided among several characters?

✓ **What are the limitations of the point of view?** Are you getting only part of the story? What must you add, as the reader? Be alert to the details you can't get from the point of view that the author chose. Spend a moment considering what you aren't being told.

What's the Big Idea? Themes

When you read great literature, you come away from it with deep thoughts about The Meaning of Life. In other words, literature explores *themes,* the big ideas that philosophers contemplate for a living. Regular books, such as this one, don't. A theme is different from a subject, however. The *subject* is what the book is actually about — the people or events in the story. The theme is the idea expressed by means of the subject.

Consider Miguel de Cervantes' novel *Don Quixote,* for example. The subject of the novel is a crazy old man's quest for the ideal of knighthood. On the other hand, the themes of *Don Quixote* include the nature of reality, the extent to which human beings need illusions to get through life, and other important issues. I first read *Don Quixote* four decades ago, and I still revisit it from time to time. With each reading, I wonder again: Is it better to work toward an impossible goal or to give up and take life as it is? In other words, I ponder the book's theme.

AP literary selections, not surprisingly, are dense with themes. The exam usually includes at least one or two multiple-choice questions addressing theme, and it may be an element to include in one of your essays.

To identify the theme(s) of a work, ask these questions:

✓ **Why should I read this literary work?** You aren't allowed to answer, "Because it's on the test." Instead, think about why a literary work has value. What can you learn from it? Jane Austen's *Pride and Prejudice,* for instance, has lasted for more than 200 years — and not just because it's funny. The lovers' struggle to grow up and to give up their preconceived ideas strikes a chord in readers, as does the characters' belief that they're smart enough to know what they're doing — even when they aren't! Modern readers can identify with the themes of pride and prejudice.

The title of a work is often a clue to its theme. (*Pride and Prejudice* is a case in point.)

✔ **What does the story reveal about life?** Erich Maria Remarque's *All Quiet on the Western Front* follows troops in the trenches of World War I. This specific situation is interesting and historically important, but the book also reveals how people behave when they're in mortal danger; it surveys their courage and concerns. It also shows the callousness of people on the home front who don't really want to know what the soldiers are going through. The novel addresses the themes of honor, cowardice, violence, and willful ignorance.

✔ **What will you be thinking about after you read the book?** Ten years later, what will matter? That Elizabeth marries Darcy or that prejudice gets in the way of a good relationship? Chances are that when the details of the plot fade, the ideas — the themes — remain.

The Play's the Thing: Drama Particularities

Your AP English exam (three hours of nonstop fun!) may include a drama passage that's written in either prose or verse (poetry). Even though some exams have no drama passages, every exam gives you the option of writing about drama when you answer the third, open-ended essay question.

Theater is a collaborative art, and playwrights must resign themselves to the fact that human actors will inhabit the characters, giving a physical body and a unique interpretation to the dialogue. Set designers, directors, costume designers, and many others have roles in the creation of a play.

On the AP English Lit exam, however, you don't see a play. You read one. You have to work from the script provided (or remember the play, in the case of the open-ended essay). With drama passages, you have three elements to help you: set description, stage directions, and lines of dialogue. Not a lot! Plus, at times you may find that one of the three elements is missing. From such minimal material you have to deal with questions about plot, conflict, characterization, theme, and so forth.

Treat a dramatic selection as you would any piece of fiction, but pay special attention to what the characters say (dialogue), how they say it (tone), and what they do (plot). Also, take note of any directions from the playwright about setting, movement, and so forth.

Plot, conflict, and theme

Plot, conflict, and theme are present in plays as well as in novels and stories. The difference between these elements in prose and in drama is that you have to flesh out the skeleton of a dramatic script by imagining the play on a stage. As with prose AP questions, expect to find slices of a play that leave you with some plot points to figure out.

Plays often begin with heavy doses of *exposition,* the background information that helps you understand the scene in front of you. If you're writing about a play, you don't need to provide that exposition in your essay, however. You can assume that the readers know the background of the classic, taught-everywhere works. (If you're writing about a lesser known work, a bit of exposition is a good idea. Check out Chapter 14 for instructions about how to include background material on open-ended essays concerning non-classic literature.)

The same conflicts outlined earlier in this chapter show up in plays. However, the limitations of performance decrease the instances of the "character versus nature" conflict (though I did once get soaked at a too-realistic performance of the storm scene from Shakespeare's *The Tempest*.)

One element of theater lends itself nicely to the depiction of internal conflict: the *dramatic monologue*. In a dramatic monologue, a character speaks at length to an implied listener. The character may be alone on stage or in the presence of other, silent observers. When the character is strictly alone and is simply voicing his or her thoughts, the speech picks up another title: *soliloquy*. Shakespearean tragedies are filled with wonderful monologues and soliloquies; Prince Hamlet alone recites four soliloquies. Because the plays are written in verse, you may see a Shakespearean soliloquy and assume that you're reading a poem. And you're sort of correct: You're in drama-land, but all the techniques for decoding poetry apply. (See Chapter 4 for the lowdown on poetic devices.)

Themes, the ideas that the playwright considers, are every bit as important in dramatic works as they are in novels and stories. As in prose fiction, plot and dialogue help you figure out the themes of a work. And because you have little more than dialogue to work from on the AP English exam, you need to turn a microscope on the words in a drama passage. Consider not only a character's particular situation but also the broader level beneath his or her words.

In Arthur Miller's *Death of a Salesman,* for example, Willy Loman's long-suffering wife makes a passionate case that "attention must be paid" to Willy. The specifics of Willy's predicament — that he has lost his job, he's heavily in debt, and he's losing his grip on reality — are important. The theme, however, is universal: the common or "low man" (notice how the name relates?) is just as valuable as someone with a prominent position in society.

As another example, here's a bit of Oscar Wilde's comedy *The Importance of Being Ernest*:

> ALGERNON — You have invented a very useful younger brother called Ernest, in order that you may be able to come up to town as often as you like. I have invented an invaluable permanent invalid called Bunbury, in order that I may be able to go down into the country whenever I choose. Bunbury is perfectly invaluable. If it wasn't for Bunbury's extraordinary bad health, for instance, I wouldn't be able to dine with you at Willis's tonight, for I have been really engaged to Aunt Augusta for more than a week.

> JACK — I haven't asked you to dine with me anywhere tonight.

> ALGERNON — I know. You are absurdly careless about sending out invitations. It is very foolish of you. Nothing annoys people so much as not receiving invitations.

The plot of Wilde's play revolves around these two bachelors, Algernon and Jack, and their social obligations and relationships. However, even if you aren't familiar with the work, you can still get a lot from this short excerpt. Algernon and Jack excuse themselves from undesirable social invitations by pleading other obligations. Jack uses a fictitious younger brother, "Ernest," and Algernon tends to an imaginary sick friend, "Bunbury." Algernon has accepted an invitation to dine with his Aunt Augusta, but he will cancel because "Bunbury" needs him.

Setting: The fine print

If you see a play performed, the stage set literally shows where the characters are. If you're reading a dramatic selection, you have to rely on stage directions or author's notes to clue you in, so don't — I repeat, *do not* — breeze past them! If you do, you'll likely miss some very important information.

Even without a description of the stage set, you may still be able to determine when and where the action happens. How? From the dialogue and plot. (The section "Where It's At: Setting" earlier in this chapter explains how.)

Here are Eugene O'Neill's notes about the setting of *Anna Christie:*

> SCENE — "Johnny-The-Priest's" saloon near South Street, New York City. The stage is divided into two sections, showing a small back room on the right. On the left, forward, of the barroom, a large window looking out on the street. Beyond it, the main entrance — a double swinging door. Farther back, another window. The bar runs from left to right nearly the whole length of the rear wall. In back of the bar, a small showcase displaying a few bottles of case goods, for which there is evidently little call. The remainder of the rear space in front of the large mirrors is occupied by half-barrels of cheap whiskey of the "nickel-a-shot" variety, from which the liquor is drawn by means of spigots. On the right is an open doorway leading to the back room. In the back room are four round wooden tables with five chairs grouped about each. In the rear, a family entrance opening on a side street.

It doesn't matter where the bar is or how long it is, but if you see information like this on the exam, you can pick up some details to help you interpret the scene. Notice, for example, that there is "little call" for the more expensive "case goods" and that the "half-barrels of cheap whiskey of the 'nickel-a-shot' variety" occupy a lot of space. These are all indications that the patrons of the bar have little money.

Characterization: Monologue, dialogue, and brackets tell all

The playwright may tuck in a few stage directions, which are usually placed in square brackets, about the character's mood, actions, or tone of voice. However, you're mostly working from dialogue in determining characterization. Therefore *diction* (word choice) and *syntax* (the way the words are put together grammatically) deserve special attention because they're the most important clues to the character's ideas, values, background, and emotions. (See the earlier section "What's in Style? Tone, Diction, and Point of View" for a discussion of tone and diction in prose. The information there also applies to dramatic passages.)

Check out this excerpt from Eugene O'Neill's play *Anna Christie,* in which two longshoremen (dockworkers) enter a bar:

> FIRST LONGSHOREMAN — [As they range themselves at the bar.] Gimme a shock. Number Two. [He tosses a coin on the bar.]
>
> SECOND LONGSHOREMAN — Same here. [Johnny sets two glasses of barrel whiskey before them.]
>
> FIRST LONGSHOREMAN — Here's luck! [The other nods. They gulp down their whiskey.]
>
> SECOND LONGSHOREMAN — [Putting money on the bar.] Give us another.
>
> FIRST LONGSHOREMAN — Gimme a scoop this time — lager and porter. I'm dry.

The dialogue here is minimal; these guys want to drink, and they aren't interested in socializing or etiquette. The stage directions indicate actions (tossing a coin, gulping the whiskey), but you get just as much information from the slang "gimme" as you do from the author's comments. And look at the difference between the two men: The first is interested only in himself ("gimme"), but the second says, "Give us another."

Chapter 10

...And Nothing but the Truth: Reading Nonfiction Passages

In This Chapter

▶ Exploring nonfiction AP passages

▶ Identifying nonfiction literary techniques

▶ Analyzing selections from essays, memoirs, and biographies

Although nonfiction (my favorite genre!) is defined mostly by what it is *not* — made-up stories such as those found in novels and plays — it has its own set of defining characteristics: Nonfiction *is* argument, discussion, life stories, instruction, and more. It's creative, because although you can't mess with the subject matter, you do have to come up with an effective and interesting way to get your message across to the reader. You won't see many nonfiction passages on the AP English Literature and Composition exam, but you still need to be prepared just in case. You don't want to be caught unaware. This chapter whisks you through the types of nonfiction that the AP exam writers favor. Read on for the truth, the whole truth, and nothing but the truth about AP English nonfiction.

A Preview of Nonfiction on the Exam

Once in a blue moon — that's how often to expect a nonfiction passage on the AP English exam. Not often, but more importantly, not never either. When nonfiction shows up, you should be prepared to tackle it. Remember that the AP exam includes only seven or eight literary selections. Do you really want to risk one seventh or one eighth of your points? I didn't think so.

If you see nonfiction on the exam at all, you'll have just one passage, usually of 800 words or less. Here are the types of excerpted nonfiction passages you may see on the exam:

✔ **Essays:** An essay may discuss an idea without taking a stand or may advocate a particular viewpoint, which you have to identify.

✔ **Autobiographies, memoirs, or biographies:** Real events told by real people about their own or others' lives. What could be more interesting? Expect to see one "episode" in someone's life or perhaps an overview.

With these types of passages, the exams usually pose questions about content and technique. Literal questions test your ability to decode the text, which may be on a difficult reading level. Interpretive questions address your ability to infer information that isn't stated directly. The AP writers also want to know *why* a particular writing technique appears and *how* the style affects the readers' perception of the text.

In what are called *paired-passage questions,* you may see a nonfiction passage coupled with another nonfiction passage or with a fiction selection. In this situation you have to compare and contrast information, purpose, tone, and so forth. (See Chapter 15 for more information on this two-for-the-price-of-one deal.)

Because you've been reading and writing nonfiction all your life, you probably know a lot about this genre already. But to improve your score on AP nonfiction questions, you need to bone up on a few terms — what various techniques are called — and pay attention to how a piece of writing is constructed. Then you're on the way to a high score. I explain everything you need to know in this chapter.

Arguing and Exploring Ideas: The Essay

It seems strange to explain how to read and analyze an essay to someone who's preparing to write three of them on the AP exam. After all, at this point in your academic career you've probably written enough homework and test essays to wallpaper your room. The essays you write and the ones you have to read on the AP exam are related, but not closely. Think of them as second cousins once removed. AP exam essays are dense with ideas, and they generally feature difficult vocabulary and complicated sentences. Nevertheless, with the right approach, you can crack the code.

When you're reading an AP exam essay selection, you need to pay attention to structure. Also take note of diction, syntax, and tone. As a bonus, besides preparing you for AP questions, a close reading of sample essay selections teaches you a couple of writer's tricks to improve your own creations.

College admissions essays, those delightful tasks facing high school seniors every autumn, are generally quite different from the essays you read and write on the AP English exam. College essays have one goal: to reveal more about you to the admissions office. (I know, you have one goal too: to get in.) College admissions essays include statements about your ideas and beliefs, but they mostly resemble short narratives. They usually fall closer to the category of memoir or autobiography. By the way, if you're having trouble writing your college essays, feel free to boost my ego by consulting my book on the subject, *College Admissions Essays For Dummies* (Wiley, 2003).

Finding meaning in essay structures

An essay is an exploration of ideas. The author is often arguing — and sometimes screaming — a point of view. A few basic structures dominate essays. After you identify the structure, you can usually follow the logical thread of the author's discussion fairly easily. Here are the most common structures, with some examples:

- ✔ **Problem and solution:** This type of essay is heavy with evidence — supporting facts for both the problem and the solution. For example: *The high cost of radishes has ruined the world (or the nation, the kitchen, the dog, or whatever). Strict price controls will solve the problem.*

- ✔ **Cause and effect:** The conclusion of this kind of essay generally evaluates the effect. It comes to the conclusion that a particular result is the best outcome ever or that it will lead to the end of the world, the galaxy, and quite possibly the universe. For example: *You slapped me, so I'm aiming my supercharged blaster ray at you.*

   A variation of "cause and effect" is "effect and cause": *I blasted you with my supercharged blaster ray because you slapped me.* The order of the essay is different, but the content is the same.

✔ **Compare and contrast:** Similarities and differences are the meat of this kind of essay. For example: *Potato chips were better in the old days. They're still salty, but they're not as crispy because now they're fried in spring water.*

✔ **Assertion and defense:** You write this sort of essay in school all the time; you state a thesis and then support it with evidence. For example: *The best things in life aren't free! Cable TV is expensive.*

✔ **Anecdote and interpretation:** This type of essay tells a story and explains its significance. For example: *One day Boris tripped on a crack in the sidewalk. That trip changed his life because . . . . Everyone else should trip on the sidewalk too.*

✔ **Question and answer:** This essay poses a question and then answers, or attempts to answer, it. For example: *Why do fools fall in love? They need a date for the prom, a reason to fail math, and so on.* Another example: *What's the basis of existence? Library books, watermelons, the Yankees, and similar stuff.*

Care to test-drive your structural skills? Here's a paragraph by one of the most famous essayists in the English literary tradition, Francis Bacon. Read the excerpt and determine how it's structured.

> TRAVEL, in the younger sort, is a part of education, in the elder, a part of experience. He that travelleth into a country, before he hath some entrance into the language, goeth to school, and not to travel. That young men travel under some tutor, or grave servant, I allow well; so that he be such a one that hath the language, and hath been in the country before; whereby he may be able to tell them what things are worthy to be seen, in the country where they go; what acquaintances they are to seek; what exercises, or discipline, the place yieldeth. For else, young men shall go hooded, and look abroad little.

Even in this short passage, you can detect the author's structure: assertion and defense. Bacon is famous for packing a whole lot of ideas into a small space, as you see in the preceding sample, so he isn't always easy to decode. He doesn't bother with stories (for example: *Mike went to Antarctica alone and did nothing but chase penguins.*). Nor does Bacon spend a lot of time elaborating. After he has the idea on paper, he moves on. In this slice of his essay entitled "Of Travel," the point he's asserting is simple: Because travel is educational for young people, "the younger sort" should travel with a "tutor" or "grave servant" who "hath the language" of the country being visited. He backs up this assertion with reasons: The tutor/servant "may be able to tell [the youngster] what things are worthy to be seen . . . what acquaintances . . . to seek" and what may be learned there ("what exercises, or discipline, the place yieldeth"). His punch line may be restated this way: If young travelers don't travel as he suggests, they may as well "go hooded" because they're flying blind.

Here's another example. This time the excerpt comes from American essayist Ralph Waldo Emerson. Again, read the passage and then check out the structure:

> It has been said that "common souls pay with what they do, nobler souls with that which they are." And why? Because a profound nature awakens in us by its actions and words, by its very looks and manners, the same power and beauty that a gallery of sculpture or of pictures addresses. Civil and natural history, the history of art and of literature, must be explained from individual history, or must remain words. There is nothing but is related to us, nothing that does not interest us, — kingdom, college, tree, horse, or iron shoe, — the roots of all things are in man. Santa Croce and the Dome of St. Peter's are lame copies after a divine model. Strasburg Cathedral is a material counterpart of the soul of Erwin of Steinbach. The true poem is the poet's mind; the true ship is the ship-builder. In the man, could we lay him open, we should see the reason for the last flourish and tendril of his work. . . .

As you may have guessed, this excerpt rests on a question-and-answer structure. Emerson takes his time, so his style differs from the text-message effect Bacon achieves in the previous example. The question is why do "common souls" matter because of "what they do" and "nobler souls" because of "that which they are"? The answer is that once you're "nobler" or "profound," you radiate "power and beauty" just as art does. The rest of the excerpt equates art with the artist, who presumably is as profound as possible, whether designing a cathedral or writing a poem.

If you're writing an essay about an essay (for some reason I love saying that) or answering multiple-choice questions about an essay, X-ray the passage until you detect the structure. Understanding how the piece is organized helps you decode its meaning more efficiently and accurately. Working from an understanding of the structure, you can break down the many parts and analyze each.

Paying attention to rhetorical techniques

In the old days — the very old days, as in ancient Greece and Rome — students practiced *rhetoric,* the art of persuasive speaking. The students' goals were to become orators who were capable of convincing and thrilling their audiences. More recent writers have employed many of the same techniques to get their messages across. (Then they take jobs in advertising.) Many rhetorical techniques, especially those tested on the AP exam, relate to *diction* (word choice) and *syntax* (the grammatical design of a sentence). Diction and syntax help you identify the *tone* of the essay — the attitude the author takes toward the subject.

A few hundred terms describe rhetorical techniques, and a few thousand more relate to grammar. Fortunately for you, almost none of this specialized vocabulary shows up on the exam. You just have to dissect the essay and characterize what you find there.

Close reading of an essay pays off. Going through the following points when you're answering questions about an essay will force you to take the time to read a passage closely:

- **What overall impression does the language make?** Is it formal or informal? Conversational? Observational? Detached? Judgmental? Are the words simple or unusual? Relate the diction to the content, if possible.

- **Why did the essayist choose this particular word or phrase?** To find out, substitute another word and see what changes.

- **What is the sentence pattern?** In other words, are the sentences long or short? Do you see repetition? Does the sentence follow the usual subject-verb order, or do you detect a different pattern? After you've answered these questions, try to link the answers to the content of the essay.

- **What does the author think about the subject?** Identifying the author's attitude helps you understand the points that he or she makes in the essay.

The easiest way to understand diction, syntax, and tone is to observe them in action. Read this passage, excerpted from an essay by Leslie Stephen, and consider the rhetorical techniques he uses:

> Goethe says somewhere, that as soon as a man has done any thing remarkable, there seems to be a general conspiracy to prevent him from doing it again. He is feasted, fêted, caressed; his time is stolen from him by breakfasts, dinners, societies, idle businesses of a thousand kinds. Mr. Buckle had his share of all this; but there are also more dangerous enemies that wait upon success like his. He had scarcely won for himself the place which he deserved, than his health was found shattered by his labors. He had but time to show us how large a man he was, time just to sketch the outlines of his philosophy,

and he passed away as suddenly as he appeared. He went abroad to recover strength for his work, but his work was done with and over. He died of a fever at Damascus, vexed only that he was compelled to leave it uncompleted. Almost his last conscious words were: "My book, my book! I shall never finish my book!" He went away as he had lived, nobly careless of himself, and thinking only of the thing which he had undertaken to do.

To crack this passage, you need to examine diction, syntax, and tone. Use the guidelines I provide earlier in the section to come up with your own analysis, and then compare your observations to what I discovered when I dissected Stephen's prose:

- **Note observations about diction.** The first thing that hits you in the preceding essay is the formality; Stephen discusses "Mr. Buckle," not simply "Buckle." And a first name is never mentioned. You probably noticed that some words are unusual, such as "fêted" and "vexed." However, many of the words also are quite simple. For example, Buckle "had his share of all this" and had "time just to sketch the outlines of his philosophy." The mixture of commonplace and unusual words implies complexity; therefore, the ideas here may not be as straightforward as they seem.

  In this particular passage, you need to dig a bit deeper into the diction to grasp Stephen's subtle message. Time "is stolen," not "taken up by" or "spent on." The implication is that the time belonged to the man who did something remarkable, and "idle businesses" committed a crime. The word "idle" tells you that "breakfasts, dinners, societies" are a waste of time. The word "businesses" as Stephen uses it here suggests "keeping busy," not "making money."

  Take a look at the description of Buckle's illness and death. As you can see, even when mortally ill, he's still in work mode. Buckle was "compelled" to leave his work "uncompleted," and he died "thinking only of the thing which he had undertaken to do." The word "compelled" here is a strong one. Imagine that sentence without it: Buckle was "vexed only that he left it [the work] uncompleted." In this alternate version, Buckle is less attached to his work. With "compelled" in the sentence, the reader senses that Buckle was wrenched forcibly from his book.

- **Examine the syntax of the passage.** The second sentence of the passage contains two lists. This structure emphasizes the disadvantages that come with fame. The passage also includes many *he/verb* combinations: "He is feasted . . . He had scarcely won . . . He had but time . . . he passed . . . he appeared . . . He went abroad . . . He died . . . He went away . . . he had undertaken." This repetitive sentence structure places the focus on Buckle's actions; it helps you focus on what he *did* and not on what he *was*. The syntax of the last sentence reiterates this idea by ending with the word "do."

  Other, subtle syntactical touches reinforce Stephen's idea about "man" and "his work." Most of the sentences in this essay are quite long. The long sentences give a sense of urgency; the reader has few places to stop and catch a breath. In the same way, Buckle was driven by an urgent desire to complete his work.

- **Consider the author's tone.** When you put diction and syntax together, what do you get? The author's tone, of course! In this passage, the tone is complicated, as are the sentences (syntax) and the vocabulary (a mix of ordinary and unusual words). The overall tone is approving, but before you settle on that verdict, check out the last sentence. Buckle "went away as he had lived, nobly careless of himself." The word "nobly" implies approval, but a hint of disapproval remains. True, Buckle had "more dangerous enemies," such as too great a devotion to his work. Stephen trivializes the illness at Damascus; after all, overwork, not an illness, was the true cause of Buckle's death. However, society's tendency to celebrate great work (those "idle businesses of a thousand kinds") and Buckle's participation in that tendency played a role in his early death and his failure to complete "that which he had undertaken to do." In other words, here's the disapproval: Buckle didn't fulfill his commitment.

✔ **Pay attention to figurative language.** No, I'm not talking about language that describes figures — *slender, athletic, bikini-challenged*. I'm talking about the imaginative figures of speech that spice up writing: personification, metaphor, hyperbole, and so forth. I go into this topic in greater detail in Chapter 4, because figurative language is plastered all over poetry. However, plenty of figurative language shows up in nonfiction too. In fact, it's a favorite AP exam topic, so be on the lookout when you're reading nonfiction.

Here are a couple of examples, drawn from a variety of authors:

- **Metaphor:** "[Woman] was created to be the toy of man, his rattle, and it must jingle in his ears, whenever, dismissing reason, he chooses to be amused." (Mary Wollstonecraft)

- **Simile:** "[The slave's] going out into the world [being sold], is like a living man going into the tomb, who, with open eyes, sees himself buried out of sight and hearing of wife, children and friends of kindred tie." (Frederick Douglass)

- **Personification:** "Nature is full of a sublime family likeness throughout her works, and delights in startling us with resemblances in the most unexpected quarters." (Ralph Waldo Emerson)

Once in a Lifetime: Memoir and Biography

Everybody has a life, and therefore we all have lots to write about. (Okay, I admit that some folks' lives are more interesting than others.) And because we all have stuff to write about, that's how we get biographies, memoirs, and autobiographies. A *biography* is about someone else, and a *memoir* or *autobiography* is about the author. All of these occasionally provide AP material.

As with all nonfiction, you're searching for structure and style, and you want to relate those elements to meaning. You should also pay extra attention to the details that the author includes and those that he or she omits. The following sections guide you in these tasks.

Clocks and calendars: Chronological structure

Biography and memoir usually punch a time clock, and you should always keep your eye on the clock or calendar when you're reading one of these selections. Every deviation from strict chronological order has meaning. Chronological structure comes in the following varieties:

✔ **Strict chronological order:** The most obvious and therefore most common way to structure a life story is to start at the beginning, move through the middle, and then hit the end. For example: *I was born, I lived and did some things along the way, and then I died.*

Because AP-exam excerpts are just that — excerpts — you obviously won't see the whole thing. But you should be able to tell more or less where you are in someone's life. Furthermore, within the excerpt you normally see straight chronological order.

✔ **Flashback:** AP passages are generally too short for fully developed flashbacks, but you may find one. More likely to appear are brief references to earlier events — just a sentence or two about the past plopped into the story. For example: *An equally horrible thing happened to my neighbor's dog once. He got attacked by a cat and then he fell in the neighborhood hot tub. But anyway, now back to my original story.* However, remember that the essayist won't be so blunt as to say "Now back to my original story." The exam passages shift time frames more subtly.

> ✔ **Flash-forward:** Lots of memoirs are written from the point of view of an older person reflecting on his or her life. As older writers look back, they tend to evaluate earlier events. Sometimes this "now I get it" point of view leads the writer to explain, out of order, what happened after the life-changing event. In other words, the writer moves forward in time for a bit and then returns to the main narrative. For example: *So I was elected Dog-Catcher-in-Chief, a position which led, fifty years later, to my being named "Cat-Napper-in-Chief."*

When you encounter a passage from a memoir or a biography, follow these steps:

1. **Construct a timeline of the events described in the passage.**

   Insert information that's stated and add what you infer. However, don't waste time actually writing or drawing the timeline; just keep it in your head or jot down a couple of words to remind you what happened when.

2. **Consider the order of events.**

   Authors move things out of sequence on purpose. If you find a flashback or a flash-forward, analyze the effect on the story. A flashback may deepen your knowledge of the motivations or experiences of the subject. A flash-forward may create a tone of irony or a sense of inevitability.

Here's a bit from Frederick Douglass's autobiography that begins when the slave owner dies. Douglass, along with other slaves, is waiting to hear his fate. Read the passage, make a timeline, and then decide why some of the events are out of chronological order:

> In contemplating the likelihoods and possibilities of our circumstances, I probably suffered more than most of my fellow servants. I had known what it was to experience kind, and even tender treatment; they had known nothing of the sort. Life, to them, had been rough and thorny, as well as dark. They had — most of them — lived on my old master's farm in Tuckahoe, and had felt the reign of Mr. Plummer's rule. The overseer had written his character on the living parchment of most of their backs, and left them callous; my back (thanks to my early removal from the plantation to Baltimore) was yet tender. I had left a kind mistress at Baltimore, who was almost a mother to me. She was in tears when we parted, and the probabilities of ever seeing her again, trembling in the balance as they did, could not be viewed without alarm and agony. The thought of leaving that kind mistress forever, and, worse still, of being the slave of Andrew Anthony — a man who, but a few days before the division of the property, had, in my presence, seized my brother Perry by the throat, dashed him on the ground, and with the heel of his boot stamped him on the head, until the blood gushed from his nose and ears — was terrible! This fiendish proceeding had no better apology than the fact, that Perry had gone to play, when Master Andrew wanted him for some trifling service. This cruelty, too, was of a piece with his general character. After inflicting his heavy blows on my brother, on observing me looking at him with intense astonishment, he said, "That is the way I will serve you, one of these days;" meaning, no doubt, when I should come into his possession. This threat, the reader may well suppose, was not very tranquilizing to my feelings. I could see that he really thirsted to get hold of me. But I was there only for a few days. I had not received any orders, and had violated none, and there was, therefore, no excuse for flogging me.

> At last, the anxiety and suspense were ended; and they ended, thanks to a kind Providence, in accordance with my wishes. I fell to the portion of Mrs. Lucretia — the dear lady who bound up my head, when the savage Aunt Katy was adding to my sufferings her bitterest maledictions.

> Capt. Thomas Auld and Mrs. Lucretia at once decided on my return to Baltimore. They knew how sincerely and warmly Mrs. Hugh Auld was attached to me, and how delighted Mr. Hugh's son would be to have me back; and, withal, having no immediate use for one so young, they willingly let me off to Baltimore.

> I need not stop here to narrate my joy on returning to Baltimore.

The passage begins with a moment in the "present" during which Douglass is thinking about the future that awaits him and his fellow slaves. Douglass describes several events that happened before that moment and a few that happened after. The following events occurred prior to the "present moment" in the passage:

- Douglass experienced "kind . . . treatment." He wasn't whipped. He left "a kind mistress at Baltimore."

- Douglass visited the home of Andrew Anthony. During this visit, Anthony wanted some small service from Perry (who had been out playing), and Anthony "stamped" on Perry's head because the boy wasn't immediately available.

- Anthony told Douglass that the same thing would happen to Douglass "one of these days."

- Douglass left Anthony's home and returned to the "kind mistress."

- At some time (not specified), "savage Aunt Katy" hurt Douglass's head and "Mrs. Lucretia" dressed the wound.

- Other slaves lived in Tuckahoe with a cruel overseer who whipped them.

Now that you've defined the past, turn to the future. The following events occurred after the "present moment" in the passage:

- The decision on Douglass is made: He goes to Mrs. Lucretia.

- Mrs. Lucretia and Thomas Auld decide that Douglass should return to Baltimore.

- Douglass returns to Baltimore.

Getting the timeline is fairly easy, but figuring out its significance is a bit tougher. However, it's certainly possible to determine the significance of a time change if you think about *why* Douglass inserted these specific events from the past, just at the moment when he's contemplating the future. For instance, you may have noticed that nearly everything Douglass mentions is terrible: He's thinking about the hard lives of other slaves, whose backs are "parchment" and are written on with scars from a slavemaster's whip. He's thinking about Perry, who was "stamped" in the head simply for playing. He remembers Anthony's threat during Douglass's brief time with Anthony. All these references deepen the reader's sense of Douglass's peril. His relative happiness with a "kind mistress" could be transformed into a nightmare. The events that Douglass reports stress the horrible possibilities that Douglass faces. The events that follow the flashback feel like a reprieve, but the reader and Douglass know that nothing is certain or permanent for a slave — exactly the point that Douglass emphasizes with this structure.

Rhetorical techniques

The points about diction, syntax, and tone in essays (which I discuss earlier in this chapter) hold true for memoir and biography as well. However, when you're reading an excerpt from someone's life story, you have to check for another element of style: *how* the information is conveyed. Here are some things to look for, each with an example:

- **Direct statements by the subject about the subject:** Most people describe themselves when they're writing a memoir, and biographers often quote the subject they're writing about. For example: *I'm very musical, though my musical education was cut short the day I threw my violin out of the window after my teacher instructed me to play the same piece yet again.* (The person quoted may believe that he or she is speaking only of music, but the reader easily gleans the fact that the speaker has a problem with authority.) Look for these statements, and take care to evaluate them. You may see qualities that the writer didn't mean to reveal. This extra information helps you understand the person who's the subject of the memoir or biography.

- **Quoted statements from others about the subject:** As you can imagine, it's also important to evaluate what other people say about the subject of a memoir or biography. For example: *He was always concerned about my welfare. That push in front of the bus was a complete accident. Honestly!*

- **Summary and narrative:** Every author has a ton of material to choose from when writing a life story. Thus the choices are important. What's glossed over quickly? What gets full detail (dialogue, action, description)? Even in a short AP passage, you still see some of each. For example: *Mort never shopped at the same place twice, except for the hot day in June when . . .* This sort of sentence signals that "the hot day in June" is particularly important, either because it breaks Mort's pattern or because of some event that occurred then. Either way, you know that "the hot day in June" has significance. The proportion of summary to narrative and the events the author emphasizes slant the work in a particular direction. After you know the slant, you can easily grasp the author's purpose.

When you're reading memoir or biography, keep these questions in mind:

- **Who's telling you the story?** If you know who's talking, you know how to evaluate the information. For example, if a fired employee is talking, you can assume that at least some of the information may be influenced by whatever bitterness accompanied the employee's exit.

- **How's the story told?** Summary, narrative, dialogue, and thoughts all have different effects on the reader. For example, summary glosses over long periods of time, but narrative nails your attention to one specific scene. You can assume that the scene is crucial to the life story you're reading.

- **Where's the emphasis?** Some ideas or events get more attention than others. Why? The answer to that little question tells you a lot about the author, the subject, and the author's attitude.

- **Which details stand out?** If you know very little about the subject of the memoir other than the fact that his parakeet flew away, chances are that the parakeet is pretty gosh darn important. So examine the parakeet to determine its significance.

Read the following passage from Frederick Douglass and consider what's summarized and what's described in detail. Then think about the author's reasons for these style choices:

> Now all the property of my old master, slaves included, was in the hands of strangers — strangers who had nothing to do in accumulating it. Not a slave was left free. All remained slaves, from youngest to oldest. If any one thing in my experience, more than another, served to deepen my conviction of the infernal character of slavery, and to fill me with unutterable loathing of slaveholders, it was their base ingratitude to my poor old grandmother. She had served my old master faithfully from youth to old age. She had been the source of all his wealth; she had peopled his plantation with slaves; she had become a great-grandmother in his service. She had rocked him in infancy, attended him in childhood, served him through life, and at his death wiped from his icy brow the cold death-sweat, and closed his eyes forever. She was nevertheless left a slave — a slave for life — a slave in the hands of strangers; and in their hands she saw her children, her grandchildren, and her great-grandchildren, divided, like so many sheep, without being gratified with the small privilege of a single word, as to their or her own destiny. And, to cap the climax of their base ingratitude and fiendish barbarity, my grandmother, who was now very old, having outlived my old master and all his children, having seen the beginning and end of all of them, and her present owners finding she was of but little value, her frame already racked with the pains of old age, and complete helplessness fast stealing over her once active limbs, they took her to the woods, built her a little hut, put up a little mud-chimney, and then made her welcome to the privilege of supporting herself there in perfect loneliness; thus virtually turning her out to die!

The advantages the slave owner and his family received from the author's grandmother are summarized. For instance, he notes her cradle-to-grave service to the slave owner and the children she gave birth to and their descendents (all "property" of the slave owner and thus an increase in his wealth). The family's treatment of the grandmother, on the other hand, is given much more detail. You hear of "her frame racked with the pains of old age," "her once active limbs" that can't function well now, and her "little hut" in the woods. Douglass even includes the fact that the chimney was made of mud. The effect of this division of summary and narrative is to focus on the ill-treatment the grandmother received and her virtual abandonment by the family she had served.

Chapter 11

Conquering Multiple-Choice Prose and Drama Questions

In This Chapter

▶ Surveying multiple-choice prose and drama questions

▶ Creating a strategy for each type of question

Sometime in elementary school, you probably opened a book and encountered an intriguing story, interesting characters, and a stirring climax. But just as your imagination went into high gear — wham! — down came a worksheet. There went the fun.

If I've described your experience, I'd like to apologize on behalf of every single teacher in the entire world, including myself. And if the educational establishment hasn't yet succeeded in ruining good books for you, I'm hopeful that the AP English Literature and Composition exam, which in part resembles a giant worksheet, won't do so either. Regardless, keep in mind that on the exam, you should be thinking about strategy, not the beauty or wisdom of the works that you read. (However, those last two qualities are, I believe, what you get from literature in its natural, untested state.) This chapter focuses on effective approaches to the most common types of AP multiple-choice prose and drama questions, which fall into two broad categories: what the passage means and how the passage is constructed.

You may notice that the terminology that's in this chapter matches the terminology in Chapter 6. However, questions about literary technique in poetry differ from questions about prose or drama technique. Poetry questions tend to query how literary devices uncover meaning, whereas prose and drama questions tend to focus on the *effects* that the writer achieves by using various techniques. Don't skip a section here just because you read about the same technique in Chapter 6!

Attacking a Prose or Drama Passage: A Quick How-To

The AP exam is a war, and every multiple-choice passage is a different battle. Your army of brain cells needs orders. Here's your plan of attack:

1. Read the entire passage quickly.

Don't underline or take notes the first time, because frankly, you probably won't know on the first read-through what's important and what isn't.

If you read the passage once and find that you're totally at sea, don't give up the ship. The wisest course may be to skip the whole passage. Later, if you have time, you can paddle back and have another go at it. But if you skip the section, be sure to slot your remaining answers into the right line of ovals.

2. **After the first read-through, skim the questions.**

   Don't read all the choices; just get a general idea of what they want to know.

3. **Read the passage again, but this time more slowly.**

   Annotate the passage as you read. Underline a couple of phrases that stand out or impress you. Jot down words in the margin, identifying what's going on in that paragraph ("conflict with Katy," for example) or ideas that occur to you ("theme = loneliness" perhaps). You won't have time to write much, but those few words will help you with the whole question set.

   The most common mistake is to underline and write too much, not too little. Keep it short! (For more help with annotation, see Chapter 3.)

4. **Begin to answer the questions.**

   Every question — both easy and difficult — is worth one point. If a question stumps you, circle it in the question booklet and move on. Return later to anything that puzzled you.

Testing Your Observation: Basic Reading Comprehension Questions

Quite a few multiple-choice questions based on prose and drama passages measure basic reading comprehension skills and vocabulary. You've probably been answering this sort of question for years. Before you breathe a sigh of relief, however, remember that AP selections tend to be tough compared to the ones you may have seen on other standardized tests. To discover the best strategy for each type of question, read on.

Pointing out the "obvious": Literal questions

Gleaning information from an AP prose or drama selection has one huge advantage: You don't have to search for or remember the facts. Being the merciful people that they are, the exam writers even supply line numbers with most questions. When you're facing a question about Roger's flight from home, for example, you don't have to comb the passage looking for the spot describing his departure. Instead, the question says something like "Roger leaves (line 44) because . . ."

Sadly, the exam writers' compassion has limits; for instance, they don't tell you which line contains the reason Roger went out for the newspaper one morning and didn't return until 20 years had elapsed. Roger's motive may appear in line 12 or in line 51 — or nowhere, in which case you have to infer the answer. (Later in this chapter, I explain more about beefing up your inference skills.)

Paying attention to straightforward facts

Some (though admittedly not many) AP questions stay on the surface. The key to answering straightforward factual questions is to examine the entire sentence or paragraph referred to in the question. You may even need to review more of the text if the answer isn't obvious. The question may address the setting or the personality of a particular character or a similar issue. You may be asked to clarify the meaning of something in the paragraph.

It's time to test-drive a simple fact question. Read this passage and answer the question that follows it:

(01)   There was until last winter a doorway in Chatham Square, that of the old Barnum clothing store, which I could never pass without recalling those nights of hopeless misery
with the policeman's periodic "Get up there! Move on!" reinforced by a prod of his club
or the toe of his boot. I slept there, or tried to when crowded out of the tenements in the
(05)   Bend by their utter nastiness. Cold and wet weather had set in, and a linen duster was
all that covered my back. There was a woolen blanket in my trunk which I had from
home — the one, my mother had told me, in which I was wrapped when I was born; but
the trunk was in the "hotel" as security for money I owed for board, and I asked for it in
vain. I was now too shabby to get work, even if there had been any to get. I had letters
(10)   still to friends of my family in New York who might have helped me, but hunger and
want had not conquered my pride. I would come to them, if at all, as their equal, and,
lest I fall into temptation, I destroyed the letters. So, having burned my bridges behind
me, I was finally and utterly alone in the city, with the winter approaching and every
shivering night in the streets reminding me that a time was rapidly coming when such a
(15)   life as I led could no longer be endured.

According to the narrator, the "tenements in the Bend" (lines 4-5) are

(A) where he keeps a special woolen blanket

(B) in terrible condition

(C) overpopulated

(D) likely to turn him away

(E) located near Chatham Square

As you know, the question helpfully points you to lines 4-5. Reread lines 4 and 5. The
narrator sleeps in the doorway when he's "crowded out of the tenements in the Bend by
their utter nastiness." The nastiness isn't described, but you do know that the doorway is
cold, wet, and public. Plus, the police aren't exactly sleeper-friendly. Hence, the tenements
must be even worse. They must be "in terrible condition," so choice (B) is the one you're
looking for.

A favorite trick of the AP exam writers is to supply a wrong answer that snags test takers
who read only part of a passage. In the preceding question, for example, the narrator says
that he sleeps in the doorway when "crowded out of the tenements in the Bend" (lines 4–5).
If you stop reading at that point, you think "too many people," so you end up opening door
(C). And by choosing that answer, you lose a quarter point because the narrator is "crowded
out . . . by their utter nastiness" (lines 4-5). In other words, the conditions "crowded" him
out, not the number of people.

Practicing the process of elimination: What's missing?

Another type of question zeroes in on what's absent from the passage rather than what's
present. To help you, AP exam writers capitalize the crucial word. For example, look for key
phrases such as "all of the following EXCEPT . . ." or "reasons for Roger's flight do NOT
include . . .". The best approach to this question is the process of elimination. Cross off
everything that *is* included and bingo, you've got the answer.

Here's a sample question based on an excerpt from Susan Glaspell's play *Trifles*. In this
scene, two women are in the kitchen of the Wright home. Mr. Wright was murdered, and his
wife is a suspect. Read this passage, and then answer the question that follows:

(01)   MRS. HALE — [examining the skirt] Wright was close. I think maybe that's why she kept so much to herself. She didn't even belong to the Ladies Aid. I suppose she felt she couldn't do her part, and then you don't enjoy things when you feel shabby. She used to wear pretty clothes and be lively, when she was Minnie Foster, one of the town girls

(05)   singing in the choir. But that — oh, that was thirty years ago. This all you was to take in?

         MRS. PETERS — She said she wanted an apron. Funny thing to want, for there isn't much to get you dirty in jail, goodness knows. But I suppose just to make her feel more natural. She said they was in the top drawer in this cupboard. Yes, here. And then her little shawl that always hung behind the door. [opens stair door and looks] Yes, here it is.

(10)   [quickly shuts door leading upstairs.]

         MRS. HALE — [abruptly moving toward her] Mrs. Peters?

         MRS. PETERS — Yes, Mrs. Hale?

         MRS. HALE — Do you think she did it?

         MRS. PETERS — [in a frightened voice] Oh, I don't know.

(15)   MRS. HALE — Well, I don't think she did. Asking for an apron and her little shawl. Worrying about her fruit.

         MRS. PETERS — [starts to speak, glances up, where footsteps are heard in the room above. In a low voice] Mr. Peters says it looks bad for her. Mr. Henderson is awful sarcastic in a speech and he'll make fun of her sayin' she didn't wake up.

(20)   MRS. HALE — Well, I guess John Wright didn't wake when they was slipping that rope under his neck.

Mrs. Hale and Mrs. Peters know all of the following EXCEPT

(A) Mr. Wright's attitude toward money

(B) Mrs. Wright's social life

(C) the identity of Mrs. Wright's lawyer

(D) the murder method

(E) Mrs. Wright's habits prior to marriage

Let the cross-out process begin! Line 3 tells you that Mrs. Wright "couldn't do her part" in the local "Ladies Aid" (line 2) and probably felt "shabby" (line 3). Line 1 explains that Mr. Wright was "close"; he didn't like to spend money. Therefore, you can cross out (A). The same speech tells you that Mrs. Wright "kept so much to herself" (lines 1–2) and that "when she was Minnie Foster" (line 4), she wore "pretty clothes" (line 4) and was "lively" (line 4). Now you can rule out (B) and (E). The last comment by Mrs. Hale (lines 20–21) indicates that Mr. Wright was strangled. Now you can eliminate choice (D). The only choice left is (C). You can infer the identity of the prosecutor from lines 18–19, but no information about her lawyer appears in the passage. Thus choice (C) is your answer.

Understanding vocabulary in context

If you're taking an AP English Lit course (and even if you aren't), you probably have a good stock of words in your vocabulary. However, vocabulary-in-context questions may still stump you if you ignore the "in-context" part of the question. The exam writers like to choose a simple word used in an unusual way, and then they list all the ordinary meanings as options. Pretty evil, huh? Don't worry. Your strategy is simple:

1. **Read the sentence in which the word appears.**

   As best as you can, figure out what the sentence says. If it's a tough sentence, restate it in your own words.

2. **Look for clues that signal the meaning of the word.**

   Suppose I tell you that at the grocery store I bought "oranges, melons, and other globular fruit." You may not be familiar with the word "globular," but you know that oranges and melons are shaped like balls. (You may also detect a resemblance to the word "globe.") Now you have a clue (or two).

3. **Insert a possible synonym into the sentence.**

   For instance, in your head say, "I bought oranges, melons, and other ball-shaped fruit."

4. **Find a matching choice within the list of answers.**

   "Ball-shaped" may not appear, but you may find "round" or something similar.

Some "vocabulary" questions actually test your ability to interpret figurative language (metaphors, symbols, and so forth). When you answer a question about the meaning of a particular word or phrase, consider this level of meaning as well as the literal level of meaning. (For help with figurative language, check out Chapter 4, which reviews figurative language in poetry. Figurative language appears most often in poetry, but it can show up in prose and drama too.)

Now you can try your hand at a vocabulary-in-context question. Refer to the preceding passage from *Trifles* (see the earlier section "Practicing the process of elimination: What's missing?") to answer this question. Reread the passage and then answer the following question.

In the context of line 1, "close" may be defined as

(A) near

(B) intimate

(C) aware

(D) shut

(E) miserly

"Close" may be defined in general by (A), (B), (D), and (E). Stretching the point a bit, even choice (C) can define "close" if the context is "close to understanding." However, the sentences following the word "close" talk about Mrs. Wright's inability to spend money. You can substitute "tightwad," "penny-pincher," or something similar. Check out the five choices, and you see that (E) is the answer that fits the context.

Matching twin to twin: Equivalent statements

Another "more-fun-than-a-barrel-of-piranhas" question asks you to find something in the passage that says exactly the same thing as another part of the passage. When seeking out these types of questions, look for expressions such as "the same meaning is expressed by" or "states a similar sentiment." Your approach with these questions is simple:

1. **Go back to the passage and read the line referred to in the question.**

2. **Restate it in your own words.**

3. **Check each of the choices offered.**

4. **As soon as you find one that's a good match, darken the oval and move on.**

Read this passage and answer the question following it:

(01) Square and triangular houses are not allowed, and for this reason. The angles of a Square (and still more those of an equilateral Triangle,) being much more pointed than those of a Pentagon, and the lines of inanimate objects (such as houses) being dimmer than the lines of Men and Women, it follows that there is no little danger lest the points (05) of a square or of a triangular house might do serious injury to an inconsiderate or perhaps absentminded traveler suddenly running against them; and therefore, as early as the eleventh century of our era, triangular houses were universally forbidden by Law, the only exceptions being fortifications, powder-magazines, barracks, and other state buildings, which is not desirable that the general public should approach without (10) circumspection.

At this period, square houses were still everywhere permitted, though discouraged by a special tax. But, about three centuries afterwards, the Law decided that in all towns containing a population above ten thousand, the angle of a Pentagon was the smallest house-angle that could be allowed consistently with the public safety.

Which statement most closely expresses the same idea as "there is no little danger lest the points of a square or of a triangular house might do serious injury" (lines 4–5)?

(A) Square and triangular houses are not allowed (line 1)

(B) [T]riangular houses were universally forbidden (line 7)

(C) [T]he only exceptions being fortifications (line 8)

(D) [T]he general public should approach without circumspection (line 9–10)

(E) [T]he angle of a Pentagon was the smallest house-angle that could be allowed consistently with public safety (lines 13–14)

This passage speaks of the danger of running into sharp angles, such as those of triangles and squares. A triangle has three corners, a square four. The next shape has to be a pentagon, which has five corners. The statement in the question says that the triangle and the square are dangerous. The pentagon is therefore "the smallest house-angle that could be allowed" safely, which means the statement in (E) is correct.

Say again? Interpretation questions

Oh, if interpretation questions were only as simple as moving from one language to another. ¡Sí, sí! (Sorry. I got carried away. That's just Spanish for "Yes, yes!") To interpret an AP English Lit passage is a bit complicated, but it isn't impossible.

Identifying the main idea

Main-idea questions may cover the entire passage or a portion of the passage (one paragraph, perhaps). The question may be worded in several ways:

✔ **The passage as a whole indicates . . .** The key words in this question are "as a whole." If you choose an answer that applies to only one paragraph, you're going to come up with the wrong answer.

✔ **Taken as a whole, the passage is . . .** The answers here may fall into several categories. You may see five terms that refer to how the passage is written (more on technique appears later in this chapter) or five words that refer to content (an apology, a request, a rebuttal, and so forth).

✔ **The main idea asserted in lines 12–23 is . . .** Be careful with the line numbers. Choose an answer that fits *only that portion* of the passage.

When you're answering a main-idea question, imagine an umbrella. The umbrella must be large enough to ensure that your shoulders don't get soaked, but not so large that you put someone's eye out with a spoke. Similarly, the main-idea statement must cover all the crucial points in the designated passage, but it can't be so broad that it covers everything in the printed universe. The best strategy for a main-idea question is a simple one: Imagine a title for the designated lines. Check your imagined title for fit. Is it too tight (doesn't cover important ideas), too loose (goes way beyond the passage), or just right? Then look at the answers for one that matches your title.

A variation of the usual main-idea question asks for a word that sums up a situation or a character. To answer this sort of question, follow the umbrella method, but concentrate only on the designated situation or character.

Practice makes perfect, so have a go at this main-idea question, which is based on the following excerpt. The narrator of this passage is named Aronnax.

(01)   My two companions stretched themselves on the cabin carpet, and were soon sound asleep. For my own part, too many thoughts crowded my brain, too many insoluble questions pressed upon me, too many fancies kept my eyes half open. Where were we? What strange power carried us on? I felt — or rather fancied I felt — the machine sinking

(05)   down to the lowest beds of the sea. Dreadful nightmares beset me; I saw in these mysterious asylums a world of unknown animals, amongst which this submarine boat seemed to be of the same kind, living, moving, and formidable as they. Then my brain grew calmer, my imagination wandered into vague unconsciousness, and I soon fell into a deep sleep.

Which of the following most closely expresses the main idea of lines 1–9?

(A) sinking under the sea

(B) worries about safety under the sea

(C) dreams of unknown animals

(D) ocean travel

(E) Arronax's worries

This passage comes from Jules Verne's sci-fi masterpiece, *Twenty Thousand Leagues Under the Sea*. The title of the novel, however, is too general for this passage; anyway, it's not one of the choices. Choice (E) expresses the "fancies" (lines 3–5) that worry Arronax when he's awake. It also covers the "nightmares" (lines 5–7) that hit him when he's asleep. Line 1 also relates to (E); the companions can sleep and Arronax can't. The only lines left out of (E) are the last two — when Arronax finally calms down and gets some rest — but they aren't crucial. Choices (A) and (C) are too narrow; (B) and (D) are too broad. Therefore, (E) is the correct answer.

Reading between the lines: Inference

Inference is what your brain does when it builds a bridge between what actually appears in the passage and what's probably true. Acting like Sherlock Holmes, you put on your detective hat and work from clues when you solve — er, answer — an inference question. For example, if the passage features an irate parent, shards of glass, and a muddy baseball, chances are someone was playing baseball in a wet yard — and that someone who hit the unfortunately aimed ball is probably now grounded for two weeks.

Inference questions show up in several different formats, including these:

- ✔ **Lines 12–18 imply that . . .** "Imply" is a fancy way to say "hint," and hints are the foundation on which inference rests.

- ✔ **The description of sewing class suggests that . . .** "Suggest" is another synonym for "hint."

✔ **The sewing class probably meets frequently because . . .** When you're in "probably" territory you're rubbing shoulders with inference.

✔ **The most likely reason Hilda drops a stitch is . . .** "Most likely" means that you have to stretch further than what the passage actually says.

✔ **Hilda may have taken the class because . . .** The verb "may" opens the door to interpretation *based on the passage*. Not just any interpretation will do!

One type of inference question that shows up quite often asks you what probably precedes or follows the excerpt on the exam. In this case, just imagine the excerpt in a larger context and work from the clues, as you do with any other inference question.

The best approach to an inference question is to follow these steps:

1. **Look for what's actually stated in the selection.**

2. **Underline information that appears relevant, and then call on your knowledge of human nature.**

3. **Rearrange the evidence from the passage until it fits a plausible theory.**

When answering inference questions, take care not to extend yourself too far. Make a logical step forward, not a long jump into imagination territory.

Check out this passage and take a stab at the inference question following it:

(01)   The superintendent of Lowood (for such was this lady) having taken her seat before a pair of globes placed on one of the tables, summoned the first class round her, and commenced giving a lesson on geography; the lower classes were called by the teachers: repetitions in history, grammar, etc., went on for an hour; writing and arithmetic suc-
(05)   ceeded, and music lessons were given by Miss Temple to some of the elder girls. The duration of each lesson was measured by the clock, which at last struck twelve. The superintendent rose. "I have a word to address to the pupils," said she. The tumult of cessation from lessons was already breaking forth, but it sank at her voice. She went on. "You had this morning a breakfast which you could not eat; you must be hungry: I have
(10)   ordered that a lunch of bread and cheese shall be served to all."

The teachers looked at her with a sort of surprise.

"It is to be done on my responsibility," she added, in an explanatory tone to them, and immediately afterwards left the room.

The reaction of the students and teachers to the superintendent indicates which of the following?

I. The students respect the superintendent.

II. Bread and cheese is a luxury at the school.

III. The teachers do not agree with the superintendent's plan.

(A) All of the above

(B) None of the above

(C) I only

(D) I and II only

(E) III only

This passage comes from *Jane Eyre* by Charlotte Bronte. The format of this question appears from time to time on the AP exam. It's no more difficult than any other format; just check the validity of each statement and then choose the letter that corresponds to your opinion. Statement I is easily inferred; the moment the superintendent begins to speak (line 7), the "tumult of cessation from lessons was already breaking forth, but it sank at her voice." Such instant obedience indicates respect. Statement II is probably true because the teachers "looked at her with a sort of surprise" (line 11) when the superintendent announced the lunch menu. She explains that the menu "is to be done on my responsibility" (line 12). From the surprise and the "I'll-take the-blame" comment, you have to assume that the students don't usually get bread and cheese. It's likely that such a meal is a luxury. Statement III goes a little too far. After all, the teachers show "a sort of surprise" (line 11), but they don't show disapproval. Because I and II are correct, the best choice is (D).

Sizing up attitude and tone

A reputable site on the Internet lists 76 different tones that may be discerned in literature. That's a lot, but really I'm surprised that the number isn't even higher. *Tone,* a term that may be applied to the *attitude* of the author or characters, is a popular AP-exam topic. (Chapter 9 goes into more detail on tone in prose and drama.)

Approach a question on tone or attitude with these steps:

1. **Read the question carefully, and be sure you know what it asks.**

   The attitude of the author or of a specific character may be quite different, and you can be sure that the exam writers will include words that apply to both. In other words, don't answer the wrong question!

2. **"Hear" the relevant portion of the passage in your head as you read.**

   Can you identify the emotions you hear? Does the passage sound playful or sad, sarcastic or admiring, regretful or analytical?

3. **Look closely at the words.**

   Does the diction (word choice) slant toward a particular attitude?

4. **Check the content.**

   Can you imagine a fit between what's being said and the tone you've selected? Jane Austen's *Pride and Prejudice,* for example, begins with a famous sentence: "It is a truth universally acknowledged, that a single man in possession of a large fortune, must be in want of a wife." Can anyone say that sentence with a straight face? I don't think so! Clearly Austen's tone here isn't serious. If this sentence appeared in a tone question, you'd look for "mocking" or a similar answer.

Test your attitude-detector by reading this passage and answering the tone question that follows:

(01) There only remain an hundred and twenty thousand children of poor parents annually born. The question therefore is, How this number shall be reared, and provided for? which, as I have already said, under the present situation of affairs, is utterly impossible by all the methods hitherto proposed. For we can neither employ them in handicraft or
(05) agriculture; we neither build houses, (I mean in the country) nor cultivate land: they can very seldom pick up a livelihood by stealing till they arrive at six years old; except where they are of towardly parts, although I confess they learn the rudiments much earlier; during which time they can however be properly looked upon only as probationers. . . . I shall now therefore humbly propose my own thoughts, which I hope will not be liable to
(10) the least objection.

I have been assured by a very knowing American of my acquaintance in London, that a young healthy child well nursed, is, at a year old, a most delicious nourishing and whole-some food, whether stewed, roasted, baked, or boiled; and I make no doubt that it will equally serve in a fricassee, or a ragout.

The author's tone may be described as

(A) ironic

(B) argumentative

(C) detached

(D) sincere

(E) sympathetic

This passage comes from Jonathan Swift's famous work, "A Modest Proposal," and is one of the best examples of irony in English literature. You find *irony* when a gap yawns between what the author or character says and what he or she means. In this excerpt, Swift pretends to offer a solution to the problem of poverty in Ireland. His answer? The Irish should eat their children. What?! You can't get much more ironic that that! Look at the evidence. The first paragraph explains that children can't "pick up a livelihood by stealing" (line 6) until they're 6 years old. For a moment, perhaps, you may think that Swift is serious. But only for a moment, because as soon as you think a bit more, you know that theft will not be offered as a serious career option. The next clue is the author's declaration that he will now "humbly propose [his] thoughts" (line 9), which he hopes "will not be liable to the least objection" (lines 9–10). If the author actually intended to encourage cannibalism, he would have expected some objections (okay, quite a lot of objections!). Obviously, the answer is (A).

Assessing the Role of Style and Technique

Writing a piece of literature is easy. As the great sportswriter Red Smith once said, "All you have to do is sit down at a typewriter and open a vein." (These days, of course, a computer has replaced the typewriter.) Smith's remark captures the emotional investment writers make in their work, but it omits an important factor: technique.

Each page of prose represents hundreds of decisions. What should I put in? What should I leave out? In what order should the information be presented? Should I use dialogue or description? This word or that one? All these decisions add up to writing style or technique, which are major categories tested by AP multiple-choice questions.

Identifying the author's purpose in choosing elements of style

A slew of multiple-choice questions ask the purpose or effect of some lines or paragraphs. And sometimes questions address the type of writing involved (dialogue, description, thoughts, and so on). Look for questions resembling these:

✔ **The description of the** _____ **(lines 2–7) serves primarily to . . .** In other words, the exam writer wants you to think about why the author wants you to know what the element identified in the blank looks like.

✔ _____ **is quoted in line 4 in order to . . .** Why not give the information another way? What happens when the reader knows the exact words of the character named in the blank?

✔ **What is the function of paragraph** _____ **?** A variation of this question asks about the "purpose" of the paragraph specified in the question.

To answer these types of questions, follow these steps:

1. **Reread the portion of the passage referred to in the question.**

   Be sure you know what it says, and then determine what it is: description, dialogue, argument, objection, and so forth.

2. **Imagine a change in the passage.**

   Take out the designated lines or alter them in some other way. However, don't take the time to write down the alternate-universe passages you create. Just think about the changes.

3. **Determine how the passage is affected by the alteration.**

   After you know how the passage comes across in the alternate-universe version, you know why the writer made the original choice. You know the purpose, the function, the effect, and anything else the AP writers throw at you!

Rev up your brain, read this selection, and answer the question that follows:

(01) FIRST LONGSHOREMAN — [Abruptly.] Let's drink up and get back to it. [They finish their drinks and go out left. The POSTMAN enters as they leave. He exchanges nods with JOHNNY and throws a letter on the bar.]

THE POSTMAN — Addressed care of you, Johnny. Know him?

(05) JOHNNY — [Picks up the letter, adjusting his spectacles. LARRY comes and peers over his shoulders. JOHNNY reads very slowly.] Christopher Christopherson.

THE POSTMAN — [Helpfully.] Square-head name.

LARRY — Old Chris — that's who.

JOHNNY — Oh, sure. I was forgetting Chris carried a hell of a name like that. Letters
(10) come here for him sometimes before, I remember now. Long time ago, though.

THE POSTMAN — It'll get him all right then?

JOHNNY — Sure thing. He comes here whenever he's in port.

THE POSTMAN — [Turning to go.] Sailor, eh?

The postman's conversation with Johnny serves to

(A) introduce the character "Christopher Christopherson"

(B) show that Johnny is unfamiliar with his customers

(C) create an atmosphere of uncertainty

(D) prepare the way for a confrontation between Larry and Johnny

(E) indicate the informality of the bar

This passage from Eugene O'Neill's play *Anna Christie* gives quite a bit of data about Chris: he's a sailor, he received letters a "long time ago" (line 10), and he visits the bar when he's in port. The implication is that Chris has no fixed address on land and that he has few ties to others, as the bar is his only point of contact. What a great, economical introduction to this character. Choice (A), then, is the correct answer.

Pondering the order of events: Structure questions

Structure questions ask you to consider *location* — where everything is in the passage — and why the author chose that order of events. Structure questions also require you to note when something changes and, of course, what effect the change has on a reader's perception of the passage. Some common structure questions include the following:

✔ **The passage as a whole moves from . . .** The answers to this type of question will be something like these: From description to narration? From present to past — and back? From argument to resolution?

✔ **The shift to first-person point of view (lines 8–10) . . .** The exam writers love *shifts* — changes in point of view, tone, and so forth. Sometimes they ask you to describe the change (from happy to sad or from past to present, perhaps). Other times they want to know the purpose or effect of a shift.

A variation of the "shift" question asks about *juxtaposition,* placing two things next to each other. Why these two, and why together?

✔ **The last paragraph (lines 50–66) primarily serves to . . .** To answer this question correctly you need to think about why that paragraph is at the end of the passage. What does it do in this position?

Solving structural puzzles is easy. Just follow these steps:

1. **Take a close look at the designated lines.**

   What do they add to the passage? What do they accomplish?

2. **Check out the lines or paragraphs before and after the designated lines.**

   Context is everything! Step back from the passage and consider the big picture.

3. **Decide how the designated lines relate to neighboring paragraphs or lines.**

   Does the third paragraph, for example, serve as a bridge between the discussion of the past (the second paragraph) and the future (the fourth paragraph)? Does it set the scene for the dialogue that follows? Does it explain what happened after the events of the second paragraph?

4. **Look for a matching answer.**

   If you don't find one that fits your theory, test out the answers provided. You may not find an identical twin, but a second cousin may pop in for a visit.

Read this passage and answer the question following it:

(01)   There was even an ease and cheerfulness about her air and manner that I made no pretension to; but there was a depth of malice in her too expressive eye that plainly told me I was not forgiven; for, though she no longer hoped to win me to herself, she still hated her rival, and evidently delighted to wreak her spite on me. On the other hand, Miss

(05)   Wilson was as affable and courteous as heart could wish, and though I was in no very conversable humor myself, the two ladies between them managed to keep up a pretty continuous fire of small talk. But Eliza took advantage of the first convenient pause to ask if I had lately seen Mrs. Graham, in a tone of merely casual inquiry, but with a sidelong glance — intended to be playfully mischievous — really, brimful and running over

(10)   with malice.

"Not lately," I replied, in a careless tone, but sternly repelling her odious glances with my eyes; for I was vexed to feel the color mounting to my forehead, despite my strenuous efforts to appear unmoved.

"What! Are you beginning to tire already? I thought so noble a creature would have

(15)   power to attach you for a year at least!"

"I would rather not speak of her now."

Overall, the passage shifts from

(A) first to third person

(B) description to narration

(C) narration to dialogue

(D) action to narration

(E) conflict to resolution

This excerpt from Anne Bronte's *The Tenant of Wildfell Hall* portrays a vicious fight that's conducted in the super-polite setting of a drawing room. The first paragraph summarizes what's going on — the attitude of the ladies, their motives, their methods of attack. Then the fight begins. As this is a verbal, not a physical fight, the characters talk. There you have your answer: The first paragraph is *narration,* ("here's-what-happened" statements). Then the *dialogue* (characters' speech) begins. Clearly, (C) is the best choice.

Questioning word choice and arrangement: Syntax questions

Syntax refers to the grammatical structure of a sentence. The AP English exam tests your understanding of syntax in questions such as these:

- **The introductory clauses (lines 2–6) act as . . .** This kind of question names a grammatical element and asks you to figure out why the author chose that particular grammatical element.

- **The repetition of**   **in lines 12 and 55 suggests that . . .** With this question, the exam writers want to know why the author repeated this word. What's being tied together?

- **The structure of the last sentence serves to . . .** This question asks you to determine why the sentence is put together in this particular way.

    Questions about the sentence structure sometimes revolve around emphasis — what's stressed or what's downplayed. Look for parts of the sentence that can stand alone, and then look for parts that are dependent (incomplete ideas that rely on the rest of the sentence in order to make sense). The stand-alone portions generally draw the reader's attention.

- **In line 12, "that" refers to . . .** This question addresses pronoun reference; it asks you to determine what word a pronoun replaces. A variation of this question may look like this: The antecedent of "that" (line 12) is . . .

If you're grammar-challenged, don't panic. Usually, syntax questions can be answered without much knowledge of grammar terminology. The following steps should get you through most syntax questions:

1. **Reread the designated lines.**

   Be careful to focus on the portion that the exam writers are questioning you about.

2. **With your best reading comprehension skills, determine what the lines mean.**

   Don't worry about whether "that" is a pronoun, an adverb, an astronaut, or a watermelon. Just figure out which other word in the paragraph "that" represents.

3. **Restate the exam question in your own words.**

   The question "The introductory clauses (lines 2–6) act as . . ." would be reworded to sound something like this: "What purpose do the introductory words serve?" The question "The repetition of _____ in lines 12 and 55 suggests that . . ." would become "Why did he say _____ two times?"

4. **Answer the question in your own words, and look for a choice that comes close to your own.**

   If nothing matches, test likely candidates from the five choices offered.

A syntax question — just what you need to complete your day! Answer the following question after reading this bit of nonfiction, which may ring a (Liberty) bell:

(01)   We hold these truths to be self-evident, that all men are created equal, that they are endowed by their Creator with certain unalienable Rights, that among these are Life, Liberty, and the pursuit of Happiness. That to secure these rights, Governments are instituted among Men, deriving their just powers from the consent of the governed, That

(05)   whenever any Form of Government becomes destructive of these ends, it is the Right of the People to alter or to abolish it, and to institute new Government, laying its foundation on such principles and organizing its powers in such form, as to them shall seem most likely to effect their Safety and Happiness.

The successive clauses beginning with "that" serve to

(A) de-emphasize each individual clause

(B) create a sense of uncertainty

(C) stress logical reasoning

(D) prepare the way for more important ideas

(E) focus on the "Right of the People to . . . institute a new Government" (line 6)

This excerpt comes from the Declaration of Independence. You won't find the Declaration on the AP exam, but you may find similar syntax, and similar questions about syntax, in nonfiction passages. The term, *clause,* is nice to know, but not crucial. (A clause, by the way, is a subject-verb statement.) To answer this question, read the paragraph "aloud" in your inner voice. Can you hear how each "that" goes back to the "truths" that are "self-evident" (line 1)? No clause beginning with "that" stands alone; it's dependent on another statement. Each "that" clause adds a link to the chain of logic. That means (C) is the answer that you're looking for.

Chapter 12

Writing Stellar Essays on Prose and Drama Passages

. . . .

In This Chapter

▶ Extracting crucial information from the prompt

▶ Reading the passage and determining what you'll write

▶ Selecting evidence from the passage

▶ Creating a workable structure for your essay

▶ Reviewing a sample essay

. . . .

Writing an AP English Literature and Composition exam essay on a prose or drama selection is both easier *and* harder than writing one in response to a poem. Most people feel more comfortable with prose and drama selections than they do with poetry. Plus, prose or drama passages are generally longer, and on first reading they appear to offer more points to include in an essay. However, the length of the material may create a time problem. You have to read the passage, gather ideas, and slide a polished essay into the booklet in less than three quarters of an hour. The great thing about poems, on the other hand, is that they're short. (For more on poetry essays, see Chapter 7.)

In this chapter, I explain how to approach prose and drama passages and write about them with ease and intelligence while under a time crunch.

Cracking Open the Essay Prompt

Like poetry prompts, prose and drama questions usually contain some standard elements. Thus, you should read every word of an essay prompt and underline key words, because you don't want to risk missing something that you need to include. However, don't waste precious seconds pondering the following phrases:

✔ **"Read the passage below."** Yawn. How else can you write the essay? Often, the prompt orders you to "read the passage carefully." Good thing they reminded you not to skim.

✔ **"In a well-written essay . . . "** I'm sure without this reminder you'd write a terrible essay on purpose or skip around just to keep the grader guessing about what comes next.

Also like poetry prompts, prose and drama prompts usually — but not always — specifically ask you to relate meaning (what's going on in the passage) to writing style (how the meaning is conveyed). Aspects of meaning queried in prose and drama prompts include plot, conflict, setting, characterization, attitude, purpose, and theme. The elements of style (which are also known as "literary elements," "literary devices," or "stylistic devices,") include dialogue, description, diction, syntax, tone, point of view, selection of detail, and figurative language. (Turn to Chapter 9 for a review of these prose and drama terms.) In short, these prompts ask how technique conveys meaning/theme.

Even though you have a chance to see just about any of the preceding elements in an essay prompt, a survey of the last two decades of prose and drama essay prompts shows that the most commonly asked questions concern attitude and characterization. The exam writers like to query you about a character's attitude (especially if that character is the narrator) or about a change in attitude. For instance, the attitude of the author toward his or her characters, the author's viewpoint on a social or political issue, or the way an author views an event have all made appearances on the AP English exam.

Characterization — how a character is portrayed — pops up so often that I imagine the College Board has a special computer command for it (control+A or F5 or something like that). For example, the AP has asked about techniques that define so-and-so's character, how narrative techniques create characterization, and which literary techniques characterize such-and-such a character. (For more on characterization, turn to Chapter 9.)

Even if a prose or drama essay prompt on your AP exam doesn't mention literary technique, you should incorporate references to style in your essay anyway. The graders expect you to pick apart the passage and to read below the surface. If you're asked about the characterization of Emily, write about Emily's characterization and then write about how you determined Emily's characterization.

This style portion of the question may be worded in many ways, including these:

- ✔ **Analyze how point of view and diction affect . . .** I used "point of view and diction" here, but you may encounter any literary technique. And in some prompts, the word "affect" may be replaced with "produce" or "reveal." How does this question end? The possibilities for prose and drama prompts are more varied than those for poetry, and they depend on what's in the passage. You may find a general category ("the comic effect" or "the reader's perception," for example) or something more specific (perhaps "the impact of the experience on Jamie" or "the dramatization of the conflict between the father and the son").

- ✔ **Discuss how literary devices convey . . .** The verb in this sort of prompt may also be "analyze," "consider," or "discuss." Also, "reveal" or "express" show up fairly often as synonyms for "convey." The prompt may ask how the stylistic devices convey an event, a conflict, a relationship, an attitude, a comparison, the author's purpose, or something else. The key here is to comb through the passage with style in mind.

- ✔ **Consider selection of detail, point of view, and other such elements . . .** I've chosen three elements of style for this sample prompt, but you may see two, four, or even more than that. The important part of this prompt, however, isn't the stylistic devices mentioned (though you should pay extra attention to anything listed). Instead, the crucial phrase is "other such elements," which asks you to go beyond what the prompt specifies.

  The trend in recent AP English exams is toward more general questions that mention a couple of literary elements plus "other techniques" or "similar literary devices." When the door is open in this way, don't slam it shut and discuss only the one or two things asked about in the prompt. The graders look kindly upon essays that discuss items not mentioned in the question because variety is the spice of life — especially in lives that are spent grading tons of papers that pretty much say the same thing.

It's important to know upfront that AP prose and drama essay prompts sometimes break from tradition. (Poetry prompts seldom bust loose. They're more predictable than prose and drama prompts.) One AP exam, for example, presented two versions of the same prose passage and asked for an essay commenting on the author's reasons for revision. (That one must have been fun to write.) Another prompt asked the test taker to explain how comic, grotesque, and pathetic aspects of a selection were blended. (Also fun to write, I'm sure.) Prompts have queried satirical effects and how they're created, a heroine's adventures and how they're dramatized, and the relationship between narrative voice and social commentary.

If you get an unusual question, don't panic. Chances are the graders will read your response with an open mind. If you make a point and back it up with evidence from the selection, you should be fine. Graders also look kindly upon those who know what they're talking about when they use literary terminology, and they're checking to see whether you've really thought about what you're writing and have support for your assessment. (For more information, see the later section "Choosing Your Evidence.")

No matter what kind of prompt you face, follow the dissecting procedure I outline in Chapter 3. In this procedure, you briefly underline key words in the prompt, restate the question in your own words, and concentrate on what the exam writers want you to do.

Digesting the Passage and Deciding on a Focus

You read novels, stories, and plays all the time, but during the AP English exam, you have to do more than just read. You have to chew up the passage and digest its contents, and you have to work fast. (Then you have to spit it back, in new and improved form, onto the pink answer booklet.)

Don't even think about reading an essay passage until you've spent a couple of minutes reviewing the prompt. Understanding the prompt allows you to read with purpose, to focus on what you need to unearth from the passage.

You're not required to write the essays in order. The best tactic, therefore, is to start with the essay that's easiest for you. If you're a poetry fan, write about the poetry selection first. If you spend half your life in the theater (and if your exam includes a drama passage), start with the drama essay. Leave the most difficult essay for last.

Here's a plan for reading prose and drama passages when the time clock is ticking:

1. **Read and annotate right away.**

    When you first read a poem, you probably shouldn't take notes because you'll likely need to use every available brain cell simply to decode the meaning. The surface meaning of a prose or drama passage, on the other hand, is generally easier to grasp the first time through. Just pick up a pen and underline as you read through the first time. Jot down your notes in the margin. For instance, if you're queried about a relationship between two characters, note their interactions. If the question asks about the techniques that create a comic effect, pay attention to every sentence that makes you smile.

    If you find yourself underlining too much or taking too many notes, you need to narrow your focus. Suppose the prompt asks you to define the narrator's attitude toward Reverend Hilton and to discuss the literary devices that convey that attitude to the reader. You begin to read, and every time the narrator says something about Reverend Hilton, you underline the comment. The only problem with this tactic is that the entire passage is narrated, and the whole thing is about Reverend Hilton. What do you do? No, you don't throw the booklet at the ceiling fan. You think about the available literary devices. In fact, you may even make a list in the margin to help you remember what you're looking for: diction, syntax, figurative language, description, dialogue, and so forth. Then you read the passage looking for those literary devices, noting each device you find.

2. **Read what you've underlined or noted.**

    By reading your initial notes, you can get an idea of what's in the passage and which parts relate to the essay that you have to write.

Putting your funny bone to the test

The common wisdom — Jane Austen's "truth universally acknowledged" — is that the worst AP essays are written about comedy. The theory is that English teachers tend to overload their classes with tragedy, so test takers are less prepared to read something lighter. If you encounter a comic selection, loosen up as you read. Allow the author's sense of humor to reach you through the fog of anxiety that permeates an AP test room. Then look for all the things that make comedy. Here's a list of the most common comedy elements:

✔ **Hyperbole:** *Hyperbole* is a fancy term for overstatement, such as American humorist Heywood Broun's comment that a censor "is a man who . . . believes that he can hold back the mighty traffic of life with a tin whistle and a raised right hand."

✔ **Understatement:** *Understatement* is the opposite of hyperbole, when you play down the importance, size, or intensity of an event. Here's an example from Beowulf — an Old English hero versus monster story with surprising touches of comedy: "The [sword] was not useless to the warrior now." In case you haven't read this story, the warrior is facing a gruesome monster and definitely needs his sword.

✔ **Incongruity:** *Incongruity* occurs when something is wildly out of place or weird things show up together. For example, in James Thurber's story, "The Macbeth Murders," an American tourist reads Macbeth, the famous Shakespearean play, as if it were a detective novel. She applies the usual detective-story methods to the play, and of course they don't fit at all. In this case, the incongruity creates the humor. (She decides that Macbeth and his wife were innocent because they appear to be guilty!)

✔ **Irony:** *Irony* arises from a gap between what is said and what is meant. Consider Alexander Woollcott's comment on his childhood visits to the theater: "[S]ome of our classmates not only avoided these orgies, but sincerely believed that we, who indulged in them, were simply courting Hell's fire." Woolcott, a playwright, employs irony when he calls the shows "orgies."

Also look for witty dialogue, silly situations, and the like. And smile! Not only will you feel better, you'll write a better essay too.

3. **Reread the passage.**

Go through the whole thing again, but this time read more slowly. Add to your notes or underline anything useful, always keeping the prompt in mind. If you realize that something you wrote the first time isn't helpful, put a single vertical line through it. However, don't obliterate the text. You still want to be able to read what you wrote or underlined, in case you later change your mind and decide it's relevant after all.

Two readings ought to be enough. If at that point you still feel like you don't have enough to write about, consider going through the passage a third time. Timing, of course, is the deciding factor here. The third read may be the charm. However, if you're a fairly slow reader and the clock is running faster than an Olympic sprinter, cut your losses. Fashion the best essay possible from what you've gleaned so far. Or, hit another essay and return to this one later. The short break may make all the difference.

4. **Construct a thesis statement and subtopics and craft your introduction.**

Your introduction should be a separate paragraph and must contain the title and author of the passage (if you know these facts) and a thesis statement. *Remember:* The title of a full-length work (a play or a novel) should be underlined. The title of a short story is placed in quotation marks and not underlined. The *thesis statement* — the main point you set out prove in the essay — is easy to create on the AP English exam. In fact, usually all you have to do is restate the prompt, inserting specifics where the prompt remains in general territory. (For a complete explanation of how to write a thesis statement, turn to Chapter 3.)

Consider two examples of effective introductions:

> In this passage from Virginia Woolf's <u>To the Lighthouse</u>, Lily is painting an abstract portrait of Mrs. Ramsay and her son James. Through dialogue, Lily's thoughts, and the description of her painting, Lily's attitude toward art becomes clear.

> Willy Loman, of Arthur Miller's <u>Death of a Salesman</u>, is a quintessential tragic hero. Much like a doomed character in a Greek tragedy, Willy slowly destroys his career, his family, and eventually himself due to hubris over which he has no control: the infinite power of his crippling self-delusion.

The thesis statement in each of these examples is the last sentence of the paragraph. In the first example, the thesis statement sets the stage for a discussion of Lily's view of art. In the second, the reader knows that the essay will analyze how Willy deludes himself. These introductions are short, but they accomplish their goals.

When my brain is fried and my inspiration has taken a vacation, physical activity often helps me. You obviously can't go for a bike ride during the AP exam, but you can drop your head and roll it in a circle or wriggle your toes. (However, if you're moving your head around, be sure to keep your eyes closed. You don't want to risk a cheating charge.) Even a minute's break may open a pathway through your head that originally had been blocked. Then you can return to the problem essay and charge ahead.

Choosing Your Evidence

Much trickier than creating a thesis statement is selecting the best evidence. See yourself as a literary crime scene investigator, with the passage as the murder site. When you're working on a poetry passage, nearly all your evidence takes the form of quotations from the poem, because every word in a poem is dripping with meaning. However, prose and drama are different. The evidence for essays about these passages comes in two forms: non-quoted references to the passage and quotations.

In most prose and drama selections, stuff happens. A story (or, more likely, a slice of a story) is told. People converse or do things — wipe sweaty brows, throw shoes at each other, overthrow the government, and so forth. Or, in a nonfiction passage, the writer strings together a logical train of thought, taking the reader from problem to solution, from cause to effect, from similarities to differences. The point is that prose and drama passages contain readily identifiable content. Just to be clear: I'm not saying that poetry is content-free. Poetic content, however, is different. Poetry usually works on a more imaginative, thematic level. Prose and drama passages, on the other hand, tend to give you more literal content to work with as you write an essay.

Deciding whether to quote or summarize

When you're writing about fiction or drama, the key to success is to avoid summarizing the plot or quoting content unless you have a good reason to do so. The College Board frowns so deeply on irrelevant plot summary that sometimes the prompt explicitly tells you to avoid it. Similarly, when you're writing about an essay or another nonfiction piece, don't waste time summarizing or quoting content unless doing so helps answer the question posed by the prompt. The goal: Choose whatever supports your assertions and ignore the rest of the passage.

If you're describing a literary device (an element of style) and if you're going to explore how that device contributes to the piece, you should quote directly from the passage. However, at times quotations aren't important, and inserting them only slows you down. I explain specifically when and when not to quote in the following sections.

Knowing when you can get away without quoting

Keep these guidelines in mind when identifying what you don't need to quote:

- ✔ **It's seldom worth the trouble to quote plot points.** If a character shows up, you don't need a quotation giving that information — unless, of course, the diction (word choice) affects the way you perceive the arrival. For instance, if the passage says, "Godfrey slid into town" or "Godfrey stomped up Main Street," a quotation is justified. The first sentence sounds sneaky, and the second sounds aggressive. But don't bother quoting, "Godfrey came to town." Just refer, if need be, to Godfrey's arrival.

- ✔ **You can often summarize dialogue, unless you want to make a point about diction and syntax or characterization.** Imagine this conversation, which is all too common in the school lunchrooms of America: Mary declares, "I hate this food." Her friend Sally answers, "Me too." You can state in your essay that Mary and her friend hate cafeteria food without going into more detail. The exception, of course, is when even commonplace dialogue reveals character. If you're writing about Mary's domination of Sally, for example, Sally's response ("Me too") may bolster your case.

- ✔ **If you need background information for your essay, you can often summarize it.** Perhaps the passage tells you that Mary and Sally attend elementary school and that they're best friends. Unless the diction slants that information in a certain direction (for example, "Mary and Sally had been stuck with each other since kindergarten" or "Sally glued herself to Mary on the first day of kindergarten"), simply state the facts and move on.

- ✔ **If you're writing about a nonfiction passage, you can sometimes paraphrase the author's arguments without quoting.** As always, restate material only if it's needed for your essay, and quote whenever the exact words affect the reader's perception.

Don't quote simply to show that a particular literary element exists in the passage. The AP-graders hate laundry lists and will likely downgrade you if they see one. Quote only words or phrases that you're going to interpret or analyze.

Take a look at this passage from "Over Tilly," a story by F. Scott Fitzgerald (in it, Jim is also known as "Jelly-bean"):

(01)   Clark took out his handkerchief and wiped his damp brow. "Reckon you're not the only one it shook up," he admitted gloomily. "All this thing of girls going round like they do is going to stop right quick. Too bad, too, but everybody'll have to see it thataway."

"Do you mean," demanded Jim in surprise, "that all that's leaked out?"

(05)   "Leaked out? How on earth could they keep it secret. It'll be announced in the papers tonight. Doctor Lamar's got to save his name somehow."

Jim put his hands on the sides of the car and tightened his long fingers on the metal. "Do you mean Taylor investigated those checks?"

It was Clark's turn to be surprised. "Haven't you heard what happened?" Jim's startled
(10)   eyes were answer enough. "Why," announced Clark dramatically, "those four got another bottle of corn, got tight and decided to shock the town — so Nancy and that fella Merritt were married in Rockville at seven o'clock this morning."

A tiny indentation appeared in the metal under the Jelly-bean's fingers. "Married?"

"Sure enough. Nancy sobered up and rushed back into town, crying and frightened to
(15)   death — claimed it'd all been a mistake. First Doctor Lamar went wild and was going to kill Merritt, but finally they got it patched up some way, and Nancy and Merritt went to Savannah on the two-thirty train."

Imagine that you're writing in response to a prompt about the characterization of Jim. These points can probably be mentioned in your essay without direct quotations:

- ✔ Any statement about Clark
- ✔ Jim's surprise that information has leaked out
- ✔ His worry about the town's finding out about the checks
- ✔ The tightening of Jim's fingers on the metal of the car when he asks about the checks
- ✔ His learning of Nancy's marriage in conversation with Clark

The fact that you aren't quoting doesn't give you license to make vague references to the passage. Specifics nearly always top generalities in literary essays. For example, write that "Jim is surprised to hear of Nancy's marriage" — not that "Jim is surprised at Clark's news."

Recognizing when quotations are essential

"Use a quotation!" That's the neon sign that should blink on and off in your brain whenever you face prompts about the following factors:

- ✔ **Attitude:** Attitude is a common AP topic. Because the author's voice is heard most directly there, quoting from the narrative portions of a prose piece (when no character is speaking) is often the easiest way to establish the author's attitude. You can also quote from the playwright's stage directions and character descriptions. When writing about a character's attitude, look closely at the dialogue and actions of the character and quote relevant words.

- ✔ **Characterization:** Some characters are educated, and some aren't. Some are angry, and others are elated. The way a character is described, the way he or she speaks, and the comments others make about him or her may all be important enough to quote. In the F. Scott Fitzgerald passage earlier in this chapter, for instance, this quotation from Clark reveals his lack of education and his views of women's roles: "Reckon you're not the only one it shook up . . . this thing of girls going round like they do is going to stop right quick. Too bad, too, but everybody'll have to see it thataway."

- ✔ **Diction:** Anytime that you're analyzing diction (word choice), you have to quote the words that the author has selected. This point holds true when you're discussing either the author's or a character's diction. Take a look at this excerpt from Emily Bronte's *Wuthering Heights:*

  > The nearer I got to the house the more agitated I grew; and on catching sight of it I trembled in every limb. The apparition had outstripped me: it stood looking through the gate.

  You may state that the author's word choice reinforces the extreme emotions of the person in this passage, but without quoting "agitated," "trembled," and "outstripped," you haven't made your case.

- ✔ **Literary techniques:** If, for example, you're writing about the impact of figurative language, you need to quote the similes or metaphors that you're analyzing. However, be sure you're analyzing these devices and not simply stating that a particular literary technique is present in the passage.

- ✔ **Mood:** Emily Bronte's masterpiece, *Wuthering Heights,* is set in the moors of England. Her descriptions in this story are heavy with words establishing the somber mood of the moors: "On that bleak hill-top the earth was hard with a black frost, and the air made me shiver through every limb." Had I not inserted the quotation showing Bronte's exact descriptions ("bleak," "hard with a black frost," "air [that] made me shiver"), you would have had to take my word for it when I declared that the moors are gloomy. The quotation proves my point.

- **Motivation, emotion, or state of mind:** You may mention (without quoting) what a character does, but once you get into *why* the character acts in a certain way or *how* a character feels or thinks, you're almost always in quotable territory. For example, the title character of Shakespeare's tragedy *Macbeth* defends himself after his wife attacks his manhood: "I dare do all that may become a man. / Who dares do more is none." This quotation shows Macbeth's ideas about masculinity and bravery in a way that an unquoted reference to his actions can't.

- **Selection of detail:** A fair number of AP prompts mention the author's "selection of detail." You should quote details the author includes as you discuss them. Otherwise, your comments will be too general.

    For example, in your essay, don't write that the den is described meticulously. Instead, state that the author mentions "the dusty television that hasn't worked for years," the "slightly puckered wallpaper," and the "bowl of stale potato chips next to crusted, moldy onion dip."

- **Shifts:** The AP loves shifts — shifts in point of view, shifts in tone, shifts in attitude, shifts in technique, and so on. If you claim that something in the passage has shifted, you sometimes have to quote to prove your point. When? If the shift is simple, say, from one narrator to another, just mention the change. If the shift is more complex — from sarcastic to sincere, perhaps — you may need to quote.

- **Symbols:** If you're interpreting a symbol, chances are the text reveals the meaning of the symbol. Therefore, quotations are particularly important. For instance, in Virginia Woolf's *To the Lighthouse,* the lighthouse represents (depending on the literary critic you consult) God, Mrs. Ramsay, death, adulthood, and maybe a dozen other things. To make a case of any of these meanings, you have to dig into the text and quote from it.

- **Syntax:** If you're making a point about how a sentence is put together, you probably need to quote the sentence. Exceptions, of course, exist. For instance, you may say something like "Every sentence in the second paragraph is a command" without writing every word in the paragraph in the answer booklet.

- **Tone:** Is the author sarcastic, depressed, optimistic, or aggressive? The only way you can support a statement about tone is by quoting, because diction and syntax are so closely related to tone.

Selecting and inserting appropriate quotations

Reading on the AP level requires that you dig into the text, analyzing not only what the passage says but how the passage says it. Thus the words in the passage remain the best source of evidence, and you won't end up with a good essay unless you insert quotations into your essay (if they're appropriate; see the earlier section "Knowing when you can get away without quoting" for more on when quotations aren't necessary). The key is selecting the best quotations and using them properly.

You probably already know the basics of quotation punctuation and citation (and if you don't, Chapter 7 explains them). But a couple of points about quoting prose and drama can be tricky. Because prose and drama passages offer so much potential evidence, you may be tempted to quote too often or at too great a length. So how many quotations do you need? Here's my answer: As many as it takes to make your point clear, and as many as you have time to insert. Don't leave any point unsupported by evidence of some kind. However, don't throw five quotations into a paragraph as support for just one assertion, unless that assertion is really important.

When you do choose to quote, grab the best words and leave out the rest. Insert *ellipses* (three spaced dots) wherever you've cut something from within one sentence. Four spaced dots do the job when more than one sentence is missing. The first dot is the period, and the other three dots show the omission. If you're chopping off the end of a sentence that has a question mark or an exclamation point, think twice before sharpening your ax. Why? The reader should be able to tell that the words belong to a question or to an emphatic statement. In other words, don't take out anything that changes the meaning of the quotation.

If you're quoting more than three lines (measured by your own handwriting in the answer booklet), you should *block* the quotation by centering it on the page and indenting both the right and left margins. In a blocked quotation, omit quotation marks unless you're quoting dialogue embedded in the narrative, as in this example from F. Scott Fitzgerald's "Over Tilly":

> The Jelly-bean hesitated. "I don't know," he began slowly, "somethin' about — about that girl last night talkin' about a lady named Diana Manners — an English lady, sorta got me thinkin'!" He drew himself up and looked oddly at Clark, "I had a family once," he said defiantly.

If you're quoting an exchange between characters in a play, you also can block the dialogue. Here's an example from Eugene O'Neill's *Anna Christie:*

> ANNA — [half-frightenedly — trying to laugh it off] You have? When? I thought you was saying —
>
> BURKE — [boldly and forcefully] This night. [hanging his head — humbly] If she'll be having me. [Then raising his eyes to hers — simply] 'Tis you I mean.

If you leave a line or more of dialogue out of a blocked quotation, insert a line of dots to show the omission:

> ANNA — [half-frightenedly — trying to laugh it off] You have? When? I thought you was saying—
>
> . . . .
>
> CHRIS — Anna! [he comes toward them, raging, his fists clenched.] Anna, you gat in cabin, you hear!

If you're blocking a quotation, however, you may be writing too much. After all, remember that the clock is always ticking your exam minutes away. Instead of blocking, try selecting relevant words from the text and tucking them into your own sentence, like so:

Anna's confusion is evident when she asks Burke, "You have? When?" He replies, "If she'll be having me."

Building on the Intro: Organizing and Discussing Your Ideas

AP English exam graders don't expect you to wow them with an original, never-before-seen organizational pattern. They do love to see creativity, but they also know that you're under pressure. And face the facts: In 40 minutes, you don't have time to reinvent the wheel. Save your experiments in structure for take-home papers! Go with the traditional introduction, body paragraphs, and conclusion for your prose or drama essay.

The grand presentation: Body paragraphs

The body paragraphs of an essay on prose and drama may be organized in several different ways, such as the following:

- ✔ **One paragraph for each literary device (element of style) that you're discussing.** For example, your essay may be divided into three body paragraphs: one for dialogue, one for a character's thoughts, and one for a description of an important topic from the story.

- ✔ **One paragraph for each subtopic.** If you're writing about a character's conflict with her mother, for example, you may have subtopics about the origin of the fight, the way the mother and daughter communicate, and the effects of their struggle on other characters. The literary devices may be placed in each body paragraph as needed. For instance, if the origin of the fight is explained metaphorically, discuss that technique in the paragraph devoted to the initial stage of their conflict.

- ✔ **In a compare and contrast essay (a format often useful for nonfiction selections), one paragraph may address similarities and another one may discuss differences.** Or, one paragraph may be devoted to the first element that you're comparing and another to the second element. This structure is particularly helpful for an essay about two different attitudes or characters or for some sort of shift.

- ✔ **Body paragraphs may follow the organizational pattern of the passage.** With this structure, you work your way through the passage, making every point possible along the way. Whenever you find a natural break (say, a shift in emphasis or tone), start a new paragraph.

If you have 15 minutes left and one whole essay is incomplete, try this structure. It's made for speed. You think as you write, recording what you see. Of course, budgeting your time to allow the full 40 minutes is a better strategy, but if you get caught short, at least you'll rescue some credit.

Regardless of how you structure the essay, be sure to analyze the text in relation to the prompt. Don't simply retell the story or list literary techniques. Take a peek at this example illustrating both good and bad analysis in a prose or drama essay:

Bad analysis: The scene between Jane and Mrs. Reed is composed almost entirely of dialogue, so dialogue is the dominant technique here.

Why it's bad: The writer has simply mentioned the technique, not discussed its effect on the reader. Also, the writer has said the same thing twice! Repetition wastes time — yours and the graders'.

Good analysis: Because the scene between Jane and Mrs. Reed is composed almost entirely of dialogue, the reader has little information about their appearance or location. The struggle between the two is highlighted; nothing distracts the reader from their conflict, just as nothing distracts the characters from their fight.

Why it's good: Now the essay explains *why* dialogue is important in this scene.

Making a statement based on your evidence: The conclusion

In Chapter 3, I explain in detail how to come to a conclusion in an AP essay, and I tell you what to avoid ("In this essay I have proved," summaries, repetitive remarks, and so forth). In this section, I simply illustrate a couple of good conclusions for prose and drama essays:

Essay content: A discussion of Thomas Friedman's essay on American values.

Conclusion: Friedman's description of the graduation at Eastern Middle School, where children from every ethnicity, religion, and race are in harmony, creates a striking contrast to the single-minded intolerance of the September 11th terrorists.

Essay content: Analysis of Willy Loman as a tragic hero whose downfall arises from his inability to face reality.

Conclusion: Willy's suicide at the end of the play is tempered with a sense of inevitability. Like an animal that cannot adapt to a new environment, his shortcomings were bound to his downfall. The hope, then, is that the others who were affected will be able to overcome the challenges that ruined Willy — that they will not be tragic figures as he was. "We are free," sobs Linda at Willy's funeral — the ultimate acceptance of reality.

Notice that both conclusions are quite short, but each packs a punch. The second conclusion is particularly effective because the final quotation sums up the play, Willy's relationship with his family, and the possible future of the remaining characters — quite an accomplishment for four sentences!

On Your Mark, Get Set, Go! A Sample Prose Essay

I couldn't possibly publish this essay chapter without showing you a complete essay based on a prose passage, complete with an evaluation of its strengths and weaknesses. Check out the following sections, which give you just that.

Sample excerpt and prompt

Read this excerpt from Joseph Conrad's novella, *The Secret Sharer*. In a well-organized essay, discuss the stylistic devices Conrad uses to reveal the relationship between the captain and Leggatt.

(01) "What's the matter?" I asked in my ordinary tone, speaking down to the face upturned exactly under mine.

"Cramp," it answered, no louder. Then slightly anxious, "I say, no need to call anyone."

"I was not going to," I said.

(05) "Are you alone on deck?"

"Yes."

I had somehow the impression that he was on the point of letting go the ladder to swim away beyond my ken — mysterious as he came. But, for the moment, this being appearing as if he had risen from the bottom of the sea (it was certainly the nearest land to the
(10) ship) wanted only to know the time. I told him. And he, down there, tentatively:

"I suppose your captain's turned in?"

"I am sure he isn't," I said.

He seemed to struggle with himself, for I heard something like the low, bitter murmur of doubt. "What's the good?" His next words came out with a hesitating effort.

(15) "Look here, my man. Could you call him out quietly?"

I thought the time had come to declare myself. "I am the captain."

I heard a "By Jove!" whispered at the level of the water. The phosphorescence flashed in the swirl of the water all about his limbs, his other hand seized the ladder.

"My name's Leggatt."

(20) The voice was calm and resolute. A good voice. The self-possession of that man had somehow induced a corresponding state in myself. It was very quietly that I remarked: "You must be a good swimmer."

"Yes. I've been in the water practically since nine o'clock. The question for me now is whether I am to let go this ladder and go on swimming till I sink from exhaustion, or —
(25) to come on board here."

I felt this was no mere formula of desperate speech, but a real alternative in the view of a strong soul. I should have gathered from this that he was young; indeed, it is only the young who are ever confronted by such clear issues. But at the time it was pure intuition on my part. A mysterious communication was established already between us two — in
(30) the face of that silent, darkened tropical sea. I was young, too; young enough to make no comment. The man in the water began suddenly to climb up the ladder, and I hastened away from the rail to fetch some clothes.

Before entering the cabin I stood still, listening in the lobby at the foot of the stairs. A faint snore came through the closed door of the chief mate's room. The second mate's
(35) door was on the hook, but the darkness in there was absolutely soundless. He, too, was young and could sleep like a stone. There remained the steward, but he was not likely to wake up before he was called. I got a sleeping suit out of my room and, coming back on deck, saw the naked man from the sea sitting on the main hatch, glimmering white in the darkness, his elbows on his knees and his head in his hands. In a moment he had con-
(40) cealed his damp body in a sleeping suit of the same gray-stripe pattern as the one I was wearing and followed me like my double on the poop[1]. Together we moved right aft[2], barefooted, silent.

"What is it?" I asked in a deadened voice, taking the lighted lamp out of the binnacle, and raising it to his face.

(45) "An ugly business."

He had rather regular features; a good mouth; light eyes under somewhat heavy, dark eyebrows; a smooth, square forehead; no growth on his cheeks; a small, brown mustache, and a well-shaped, round chin. His expression was concentrated, meditative, under the inspecting light of the lamp I held up to his face; such as a man thinking hard
(50) in solitude might wear. My sleeping suit was just right for his size. A well-knit young fellow of twenty-five at most. He caught his lower lip with the edge of white, even teeth.

1. A deck.

2. Toward the rear of the ship.

Sample essay

Here's a sample essay written in response to the prompt shown in the previous section:

This excerpt from Joseph Conrad's <u>The Secret Sharer</u> describes an encounter between two men, one the captain of a ship and the other a desperate, naked man in the water. Through dialogue, description, and the narrator's evaluation of the swimmer, the men become mirror images of each other.

The identification between the two is made immediately when the narrator says that the swimmer's face was "upturned exactly under mine." Water reflects light, and it is as if the captain were looking in a mirror. The identification continues when the narrator hears the swimmer's voice, which is "calm and resolute." The tone of the swimmer's voice brings about "a corresponding state in myself." The swimmer is naked, and when he boards the ship, the captain gives him a "sleeping suit of the same gray-stripe pattern as the one I was wearing" and which is "just right for his size." Once again, the two characters are equated. Also, it's important that the characters are identified with each other by means of a sleeping suit because in dreams, peoples' true selves come out and daytime facades drop away.

The swimmer, whose name is Leggatt, "followed me [the captain] like a double." The captain says that he is young, and later refers to Leggatt as young also. When Leggatt follows the captain, the captain says that they moved toward the back of the boat together.

When the two men converse, they are both terse. The captain's "I am the captain" is answered by "By Jove" and "My name's Leggatt." Later the captain asks, "What is it?" and Leggatt replies, "An ugly business." Neither goes into detail, and both are surprisingly calm, despite Leggatt's situation, even though the captain speaks of Leggatt's "desperate speech."

The fact that the two men are alone is also significant. The rest of the sailors are asleep, and the solitude of the men binds them. They are, as the title implies, "secret sharers" in each other's life. When the captain holds a lamp up to Leggatt's face, the captain sees "a man thinking hard in solitude," which is what the captain was doing on deck.

Finally, the captain explains that "a mysterious communication was established already between us two." These characters are connected, as Conrad makes clear.

Evaluation of the sample essay

The sample essay has its flaws, but it accomplishes its basic task — to define the relationship between the men and to explain how that relationship is conveyed. If I were grading this essay, I would award it an 8, which is close to the highest mark and generally in "5" territory when it comes to the overall exam grade. (For more information on how the exam is scored, see Chapter 1.)

Here are the good points of the sample essay:

- ✔ The essay addresses the prompt, stating correctly that the captain and Leggatt mirror each other.
- ✔ The essay quotes frequently from the text, supporting the mirror-image assertion with quite a bit of evidence.
- ✔ The quotations are well chosen and snipped down to just what's needed. The writer has included no unnecessary words.
- ✔ The quotations are inserted smoothly into the text and punctuated properly.
- ✔ The essay addresses literary technique fairly well, pointing out dialogue and the narrator's description.
- ✔ The essay is reasonably well organized. It has a good introduction and, for the most part, has logical body-paragraph divisions.

The following are points for improvement:

- ✔ The introduction is a bit fuzzy when it comes to correctly identifying the literary techniques that Conrad employs. Dialogue and description are, in fact, literary techniques. What the writer calls "the narrator's evaluation of the swimmer" would be better described as "narrative" or "the narrator's point of view."

- ✔ The organization isn't bad, but the second and third paragraphs are divided without good reason. They would be better combined into one paragraph.

- ✔ The conclusion is weak, probably because the writer ran out of time. The last sentence is repetitive and general.

- ✔ The quotations aren't cited by line number. (Strictly speaking, you don't absolutely have to cite line numbers, but if you have time, go for it.)

Chapter 13

Practice Makes Perfect: Prose and Drama Questions

In This Chapter
▶ Sharpening skills with multiple-choice sample questions
▶ Writing practice essays on prose and drama selections
▶ Analyzing your strengths and weaknesses

You can't learn to ride a bike by reading an instruction manual. You have to hit the road and start peddling. Similarly, you can't perfect your prose- and drama-question skills until you go around the block a couple of times, answering multiple-choice questions and writing practice essays. Conveniently, this chapter contains samples of both types of questions. Try some, check your answers, and read the explanations. If you come across any wrong answers or any essays that miss the target, review the basic concepts in Chapter 9 (fiction and drama) or Chapter 10 (nonfiction). If the problem you're having concerns the format of the questions, head for Chapter 11 (multiple-choice strategy) or Chapter 12 (essay instructions). Then go out for a real bike ride; you deserve a break!

Choosing an Answer from Multiple Options

The dreaded letters A–E stub the toes of many a fine English student. But don't worry. Your toes are safe because in this section, I'm going to make sure that you can sprint through prose and drama multiple-choice questions. On the actual exam, you'll see excerpts of novels or stories, and you'll probably encounter a nonfiction selection. Drama has a cameo role every once in a while. I've labeled the practice sets in this chapter as nonfiction, fiction, or drama so that later you can figure out where your strengths and weaknesses lie. The AP exam writers generally aren't as nice. The only information they might give you is the title and author of a passage (and that's usually only when there are copyright requirements).

Practice set 1 (nonfiction)

Carefully read the following essay by Henry David Thoreau and answer the questions that follow.

(01)   I, who cannot stay in my chamber for a single day without acquiring some rust, and when sometimes I have stolen forth for a walk at the eleventh hour, or four o'clock in the afternoon, too late to redeem the day, when the shades of night were already beginning to be mingled with the daylight, have felt as if I had committed some sin to be

(05)   atoned for — I confess that I am astonished at the power of endurance, to say nothing of

the moral insensibility, of my neighbors who confine themselves to shops and offices the whole day for weeks and months, aye, and years almost together. I know not what manner of stuff they are of — sitting there now at three o'clock in the afternoon, as if it were three o'clock in the morning. Bonaparte[1] may talk of the three-o'clock-in-the-morn-

(10) ing courage, but it is nothing to the courage which can sit down cheerfully at this hour in the afternoon over against one's self whom you have known all the morning, to starve out a garrison to whom you are bound by such strong ties of sympathy. I wonder that about this time, or say between four and five o'clock in the afternoon, too late for the morning papers and too early for the evening ones, there is not a general explosion

(15) heard up and down the street, scattering a legion of antiquated and house-bred notions and whims to the four winds for an airing — and so the evil cure itself.

How womankind, who are confined to the house still more than men, stand it I do not know; but I have ground to suspect that most of them do not STAND it at all. When, early in a summer afternoon, we have been shaking the dust of the village from the skirts of

(20) our garments, making haste past those houses with purely Doric or Gothic[2] fronts, which have such an air of repose about them, my companion whispers that probably about these times their occupants are all gone to bed. Then it is that I appreciate the beauty and the glory of architecture, which itself never turns in, but forever stands out and erect, keeping watch over the slumberers.

(25) No doubt temperament, and, above all, age, have a good deal to do with it. As a man grows older, his ability to sit still and follow indoor occupations increases. He grows vespertinal[3] in his habits as the evening of life approaches, till at last he comes forth only just before sundown, and gets all the walk that he requires in half an hour.

But the walking of which I speak has nothing in it akin to taking exercise, as it is called,
(30) as the sick take medicine at stated hours — as the Swinging of dumb-bells or chairs; but is itself the enterprise and adventure of the day. If you would get exercise, go in search of the springs of life. Think of a man's swinging dumbbells for his health, when those springs are bubbling up in far-off pastures unsought by him!

Moreover, you must walk like a camel, which is said to be the only beast which rumi-
(35) nates when walking. When a traveler asked Wordsworth's servant to show him her master's study, she answered, "Here is his library, but his study is out of doors."

Living much out of doors, in the sun and wind, will no doubt produce a certain roughness of character — will cause a thicker cuticle to grow over some of the finer qualities of our nature, as on the face and hands, or as severe manual labor robs the hands of

(40) some of their delicacy of touch. So staying in the house, on the other hand, may produce a softness and smoothness, not to say thinness of skin, accompanied by an increased sensibility to certain impressions. Perhaps we should be more susceptible to some influences important to our intellectual and moral growth, if the sun had shone and the wind blown on us a little less; and no doubt it is a nice matter to proportion

(45) rightly the thick and thin skin.

1. Napoleon Bonaparte, famous general and Emperor of France.

2. Architectural styles.

3. Referring to the late afternoon.

1. In the context of line 1, the "rust" that the narrator acquires may be defined as

(A) mental illness

(B) metallic corrosion

(C) ill-effects of inactivity

(D) physical weakness

(E) emotional disturbance

The narrator can't stay inside "without acquiring some rust" (line 1). The remedy is to go out for a walk. Therefore, you can assume that he feels the ill-effects of sitting inside all day, a concept best expressed by choice (C). Did (D) tempt you? Old, creaky joints (I have some!) may certainly indicate "physical weakness," but you don't get them in one day, the length of time specified in the passage. Because of this fact, (C) is a better answer.

2. The purpose of lines 1–7 ("I, who cannot . . . years almost together") is to

    (A) describe the late afternoon hours

    (B) equate indoor inactivity with moral failing

    (C) explain the narrator's habits

    (D) compare the narrator to shop and office workers

    (E) establish the context of the narrator's remarks

The passage opens by informing you that the narrator gets ants in his pants if he doesn't go outside for a walk at least once. Then the narrator thinks about the "endurance" (line 5) and "moral insensibility" (line 6) of those who are stuck inside all day, every day — the shop and office workers. These lines establish a comparison, as (D) specifies.

3. In the context of line 8, "stuff" may best be defined as

    (A) character

    (B) physical properties

    (C) material goods

    (D) personal possessions

    (E) habits

The narrator harshly judges those who work in shops and offices. He even speculates that they're less moral because they're alienated from nature, and he wonders how they can stand their lives. He wonders what *stuff,* or character, allows them to stay inside for years on end. Choice (A) wins the prize.

4. The purpose of the allusion to Bonaparte in line 9 is to

    (A) imply that people all over the world feel the same as the narrator does

    (B) make the reader consider the nature of courage

    (C) establish that the narrator is an insomniac

    (D) emphasize the courage needed to forgo outdoor activity

    (E) belittle the courage of indoor workers

An *allusion* refers to an element outside the literary work that brings into the work all the associations, information, and emotions attached to that element. In lines 9–10, Thoreau alludes to a statement by Napoleon Bonaparte, and the notes tell you that Napoleon was both a general and an emperor. The courage Napoleon needed to go into battle was considerable. By alluding to Napoleon's comment, Thoreau emphasizes that "three-o'clock-in-the-morning" courage pales in comparison to the courage of those who stay in at three in the afternoon. You may have been tempted by choice (E). The paragraph does contain a comparison, but some key words are omitted. In fact, Thoreau is employing irony by saying the opposite of (E), that Napoleon's courage "is nothing [when compared] to the courage" (line 10) of those who "can sit down cheerfully" (line 10) at 3 p.m.

5. The "garrison to whom you are bound by such strong ties of sympathy" (line 12) most likely refers to

   (A) ideas

   (B) the townspeople

   (C) shop and office workers

   (D) Napoleon's soldiers

   (E) walkers

The "garrison" of line 12 (another military image), refers to brain cells or the ideas they generate. Because only the second of those two items appears in the multiple-choice list, go with (A). The key to figuring out this question is the reference in line 11 to "one's self whom you have known all the morning" and the reference in line 15 to "antiquated and house-bred notions." "Notions" are ideas, and philosophically, your "self." As the French philosopher Descartes put it, "I think; therefore I am."

6. What is the narrator's attitude toward the "general explosion" (line 14)?

   (A) He is surprised that it takes place.

   (B) He fears it.

   (C) He cannot understand why it occurs.

   (D) He thinks it would be a positive event.

   (E) He sees it as evil.

The narrator says "I wonder" (line 12), not in the sense of speculation but more along the lines of Alice in Wonderland; he's surprised and awed that "there is not" (line 14) an explosion, which would have a positive effect, "scattering a legion of antiquated and house-bred notions and whims" (lines 15–16) and bringing about a "cure" (line 16). Thus, (D) is the correct answer.

7. Overall, the second paragraph (lines 17–24) marks a shift from

   (A) a male to a female narrator

   (B) a light to a serious tone

   (C) indoors to outdoors

   (D) military to religious metaphors

   (E) personal to universal

The first paragraph talks about how terrible it is to be inside all day. True, it ends with a reference to "the street" (line 15), but the question says "overall," and the bulk of the first paragraph concerns indoor life. The second paragraph begins with a reference to women, whom the narrator views as even more housebound than men. However, the narrator doesn't change, so you have to rule out choice (A). The second paragraph goes outside, when you're "making haste past those houses" (line 20) and have been "shaking the dust of the village" off (line 19). Clearly, (C) is the answer you want. Were you fooled by (D)? True, the first paragraph is army-oriented; Thoreau alludes to Napoleon (a general) and talks about a "garrison" (line 12), an "explosion" (line 14), and a "legion" (line 15). The second paragraph, however, doesn't venture into religious territory.

8. The pronoun "it" (line 17) refers to

   (A) temperament

   (B) confinement

   (C) the ability to walk

   (D) age

   (E) the advantages of walking

Womankind, the narrator says, "are confined to the house" (line 17) but, he suspects, do not "stand it" (line 18). Hence "it" refers to confinement, choice (B).

9. The purpose of the fourth paragraph (lines 29–33) is to

   (A) emphasize the importance of mental exercise

   (B) explain the physical benefits of exercise

   (C) discuss the value of exercise

   (D) persuade the reader to exercise in varied ways

   (E) emphasize the superiority of walking to other forms of exercise

Thoreau, I think it's safe to say, would not join a gym and settle in on a treadmill. For him, outdoors is the place to be, walking and thinking at the same time. The fourth paragraph belittles the fitness crowd, referring to "the Swinging of dumb-bells or chairs" (line 30) as inferior to walking, which is the "adventure of the day" (line 31). Therefore, choice (E) is the answer you're looking for.

10. The comment from Wordsworth's servant (line 36)

    (A) implies that Wordsworth thinks less in his library than outdoors

    (B) implies that Wordsworth studies nature

    (C) disparages Wordsworth's connection with books

    (D) emphasizes Wordsworth's appreciation of nature

    (E) criticizes Wordsworth's study habits

Wordsworth's "study" is the place where he thinks. The comment stands by itself, but it's reinforced by the reference to a camel, "which is said to be the only beast which ruminates [thinks] when walking" (lines 34–35). True, Wordsworth did appreciate nature. His poetry is filled with flowers, oceans, rocks, and everything else under the sun. (The sun's in his poetry too.) However, the servant's comment isn't about Wordsworth's views on nature but rather about what he does when he's in contact with nature. And like a camel, he thinks when he's walking. Choice (A) is the correct answer.

11. The "cuticle" (line 38) is most likely meant to be interpreted as a

    (A) physical barrier

    (B) natural process

    (C) deadening of physical sensation

    (D) sign of honest labor

    (E) lessening of moral and intellectual sensibility

The cuticle is a metaphor, not a physical reality. Thoreau cautions that too much time outdoors can have an effect on "the finer qualities of our nature" (lines 38–39). Later in that paragraph, the finer qualities are described as "intellectual and moral growth" (line 43). Go for (E) as your answer.

12. Which of the following is the best interpretation of "it is a nice matter to proportion rightly the thick and thin skin" (lines 44–45)?

    (A) Care is needed to find the correct balance between indoor and outdoor activity.

    (B) Kind, friendly people balance indoor and outdoor activity.

    (C) Sensitivity and roughness must be in balance.

    (D) You control the amount of sensitivity in your life.

    (E) Physical activity has unpredictable results.

The word "nice" has come to mean "friendly" or "good-natured," but it also means "neatly" or "with precision," which is the definition that's operating in this passage. The "thick and thin skin" are metaphors for too much time outdoors (thick) and indoors (thin). Thoreau advocates a balance, so (A) is the best choice.

Practice set 2 (fiction)

Carefully read the following passage, which is an excerpt from a comic novel written in the late 18th century, and answer the questions that follow.

(01)   No one who had ever seen Catherine Morland in her infancy would have supposed her born to be an heroine. Her situation in life, the character of her father and mother, her own person and disposition, were all equally against her. Her father was a clergy-man, without being neglected, or poor, and a very respectable man, though his name

(05) was Richard — and he had never been handsome. He had a considerable independence besides two good livings — and he was not in the least addicted to locking up his daughters. Her mother was a woman of useful plain sense, with a good temper, and, what is more remarkable, with a good constitution. She had three sons before Catherine was born; and instead of dying in bringing the latter into the world, as anybody might

(10) expect, she still lived on — lived to have six children more — to see them growing up around her, and to enjoy excellent health herself. A family of ten children will be always called a fine family, where there are heads and arms and legs enough for the number; but the Morlands had little other right to the word, for they were in general very plain, and Catherine, for many years of her life, as plain as any. She had a thin awkward figure,

(15) a sallow skin without colour, dark lank hair, and strong features — so much for her person; and not less unpropitious for heroism seemed her mind. She was fond of all boy's plays, and greatly preferred cricket not merely to dolls, but to the more heroic enjoyments of infancy, nursing a dormouse, feeding a canary-bird, or watering a rose-bush. Indeed she had no taste for a garden; and if she gathered flowers at all, it was

(20) chiefly for the pleasure of mischief — at least so it was conjectured from her always pre-ferring those which she was forbidden to take. Such were her propensities — her abili-ties were quite as extraordinary. She never could learn or understand anything before she was taught; and sometimes not even then, for she was often inattentive, and occa-sionally stupid. Her mother was three months in teaching her only to repeat the "Beggar's

(25) Petition"; and after all, her next sister, Sally, could say it better than she did. Not that Catherine was always stupid — by no means; she learnt the fable of "The Hare and Many Friends" as quickly as any girl in England. Her mother wished her to learn music; and Catherine was sure she should like it, for she was very fond of tinkling the keys of the old forlorn spinner; so, at eight years old she began. She learnt a year, and could not

(30) bear it; and Mrs. Morland, who did not insist on her daughters being accomplished in spite of incapacity or distaste, allowed her to leave off. The day which dismissed the music-master was one of the happiest of Catherine's life. Her taste for drawing was not superior; though whenever she could obtain the outside of a letter from her mother or seize upon any other odd piece of paper, she did what she could in that way, by drawing

(35) houses and trees, hens and chickens, all very much like one another. Writing and accounts she was taught by her father; French by her mother: her proficiency in either was not remarkable, and she shirked her lessons in both whenever she could. What a strange, unaccountable character! — for with all these symptoms of profligacy at ten years old, she had neither a bad heart nor a bad temper, was seldom stubborn, scarcely

(40) ever quarrelsome, and very kind to the little ones, with few interruptions of tyranny; she was moreover noisy and wild, hated confinement and cleanliness, and loved nothing so well in the world as rolling down the green slope at the back of the house.

    Such was Catherine Morland at ten. At fifteen, appearances were mending; she began to curl her hair and long for balls; her complexion improved, her features were

(45) softened by plumpness and colour, her eyes gained more animation, and her figure

(50) more consequence. Her love of dirt gave way to an inclination for finery, and she grew clean as she grew smart; she had now the pleasure of sometimes hearing her father and mother remark on her personal improvement. "Catherine grows quite a good-looking girl — she is almost pretty today," were words which caught her ears now and then; and how welcome were the sounds! To look almost pretty is an acquisition of higher delight to a girl who has been looking plain the first fifteen years of her life than a beauty from her cradle can ever receive.

13. One can infer from the passage that the traditional characteristics of a heroine include all of the following EXCEPT

(A) being born into an impoverished family

(B) ill-treatment from family members

(C) being orphaned or left motherless

(D) great beauty

(E) average intelligence

This wonderful excerpt from *Northanger Abbey,* a novel by Jane Austen, begins with an explanation of why it was unlikely that Catherine Morland would be considered a heroine. All the things that Catherine lacks are listed, and by implication, those qualities are assigned to heroines. The only thing she does have is average — or even at times below-average — intelligence. Hence (E) is the answer you seek.

14. The passage as a whole may be characterized as

(A) vicious sarcasm

(B) straightforward exposition

(C) gentle mockery

(D) sentimental reflection

(E) incisive analysis

This question addresses *tone,* and Austen's tone is mocking, but not vicious, as indicated in choice (A). Therefore, (C) is the best answer. Can't you hear the little laughter at such tongue-in-cheek comments as "instead of dying in bringing the latter [Catherine] into the world, as anybody might expect, she still lived on" (lines 9–10)? By the way, the *exposition* referred to in (B) is background information, the explanation that sets up the story. This passage tells a lot about Catherine, but it doesn't begin a story. Nor do (D) and (E) make the cut. This author is anything but sentimental, as Catherine is evaluated critically in the passage. Nor does the passage delve into the reasons for Catherine's behavior, so "incisive analysis" doesn't fit.

15. The characterization of Catherine Morland is achieved primarily by

(A) a recital of what she is not

(B) a description of her family

(C) a list of her pastimes

(D) an account of her accomplishments

(E) an explanation of her mother's point of view

The whole first paragraph is negative and describes what Catherine is not: She was not poor, her parents weren't cruel, her mother didn't die when Catherine was born, and Catherine wasn't pretty. True, some of her accomplishments are listed (she learned a fable and, eventually, a poem), but they also illustrate her lack of brain power and talent. Thus, go with choice (A).

16. The statement that Catherine's father was named Richard (line 5) implies that

    (A) Richard is not a suitable name for the father of a heroine.

    (B) The fathers of other heroines have that name.

    (C) Men named Richard are generally not respectable.

    (D) Men named Richard are generally respectable.

    (E) The father's name should be unusual.

The fact that Catherine's father is named Richard (line 5) is introduced by the word "though." Just before that statement, Catherine's father is described as "respectable" (line 4). The implication is that men named Richard aren't usually respectable. (Don't blame me. I like the name Richard.) Clearly (C) is the best answer.

17. Which of the following statements is closest in meaning to "a family of ten children will always be called a fine family, where there are heads and arms and legs enough for the number" (lines 11–12)?

    (A) The label "fine family" is frequently applied without much thought.

    (B) Any family with ten children is fine.

    (C) The criteria for the label "a fine family" are very strict.

    (D) The label "fine family" is usually applied inappropriately.

    (E) People who say that a family is "fine" are generally lying.

The key to this answer is tone and context. For instance, if you're counting fingers, you may miss one and not suffer a huge deficit. However, if you're counting heads, the proper number is a lot more important. The author's tone is mocking, and she implies that the label "fine family" is slapped on without much consideration of the family's quality. You should choose (A) as your answer.

18. The author mentions "the Beggar's Petition" (lines 24–25) and "The Hare and Many Friends"
(lines 26–27) probably to show

    (A) that children in England were required to memorize literary works

    (B) Catherine's inconsistent efforts in learning

    (C) Mrs. Morland's inadequate teaching ability

    (D) that poems are easier to learn than fables

    (E) Catherine's dislike of literature

Catherine can learn, but sometimes she learns slowly and sometimes "as quickly as any girl in England" (line 27). Thus she's inconsistent, and choice (B) is the winner.

19. "The day which dismissed the music-master was one of the happiest of Catherine's life" (lines 31–32) is an example of

    (A) hyperbole

    (B) exposition

    (C) irony

    (D) characterization

    (E) dramatization

Okay, maybe Catherine was happy, but "one of the happiest" days of her life? You're in exaggeration territory here, which, in lit-speak, is *hyperbole,* or choice (A). Just for the record, however, *exposition* occurs when the author gives background information that's necessary to understand the plot. *Irony* shows up when you say the opposite of what you mean, and *characterization* is everything the author does to illustrate character. Choice (E), dramatization, isn't really a literary term. You dramatize a novel by turning it into a play, a meaning that doesn't apply here.

20. According to the passage, why is Catherine's character deemed "strange" (line 38) and "unaccountable" (line 38)?

    (A) She has "interruptions of tyranny" (line 40).

    (B) Catherine refuses to conform to gender roles.

    (C) Catherine does not live up to her potential.

    (D) Her character is unnaturally consistent.

    (E) Her failings are not accompanied by antisocial tendencies.

The crucial word here is "for" (line 38), which in this sentence means "because." After you crack that definition in context, you're home free, because the second half of the sentence explains exactly *why* Catherine's character was "strange" and "unaccountable": She "had neither a bad heart nor a bad temper, was seldom stubborn, scarcely ever quarrelsome, and very kind to the little ones" (lines 39–40). In other words, she was a normal girl with some failings and inconsistencies. Therefore, choice (E) is the winner here.

21. The change in Catherine at fifteen (lines 43–52)

    (A) marks a shift in point of view

    (B) places Catherine in the context of her society

    (C) is consistent with the tone of the rest of the passage

    (D) marks a shift in tone

    (E) implies that Catherine will never be as beautiful as a girl who has been "a beauty from her cradle" (lines 51–52)

The gentle mockery of the rest of the passage continues when Catherine matures. She's less happy to be dirty and loves to hear that she's "almost pretty today" (line 49). Without a doubt, (C) is the best answer.

22. The word "mending" in the context of line 43 may best be defined as

    (A) sewing

    (B) improving

    (C) reconciling

    (D) altering

    (E) healing

Catherine's appearance has improved; her hair, figure, features, and habits are all "mending." True, choice (D) is a possibility, because Catherine is in fact changing, and "alter" does mean "change." However, (B) is more specific and thus a better choice.

Practice set 3 (fiction)

Read the following excerpt from *At the Cross,* a novel by Dana Crum (© Dana Crum, reprinted with permission) and answer the questions that follow.

(01)   "Where you want this stuff!" Joe asked.

"Anywhere," Sidney said.

The boxes clunked as Joe knelt and dropped them beside Sidney's portable stereo. Mr. Lewis and his potential fiancée slogged up the stairs, the things they carried clatter-
(05)   ing against the banister.

"There you are," she said, looking at Sidney as she stepped inside the room. "It's a good thing you got the door open. 'Cause we wouldn't have known what room to come to."

"Sorry about that," Sidney said.

Against a wall she and Mr. Lewis placed luggage and boxes.
(10)   She exhaled deeply. "I must be getting old." She smiled and caressed her flaccid biceps. "That one little suitcase had my arms hurting."

"Mom, this is Brian, one of my roommates."

"Nice to meet you."

Brian shook her hand. "It's nice to meet you, too."
(15)   "And this is Mr. Lewis," Sidney said with all the courtesy he could muster but with-out looking at the man.

"Call me 'William,' Mr. Lewis said, shaking Brian's hand. "I've been trying to get Sidney to do the same, but he insists on calling me by my last name. Like I'm his boss or something."
(20)   Sidney knew he should banter with Mr. Lewis to show there were no hard feelings. But he said nothing.

"So, Brian," Sidney's mom began and Sidney wondered if she was intentionally relieving the mounting tension, "I see you're an early riser. I thought we were early. But you beat us here."
(25)   "Yeah, I don't think my parents could have waited another moment to get me out of the house."

"We heard that, Brian," a baritone voice said, its Boston accent even sharper and swifter than Brian's. At the bottom of the stairs appeared a man with a bald, perfectly round head and a short, stocky body. He took two steps at a time, a glass coffee table in
(30)   his hands and a stuffed backpack over one shoulder. Behind him trailed a woman with bright eyes and red wavy hair, which she wore in a bob. She carried a lamp. . . in both hands.

"Dad, did you get lost?" Brian asked, in the doorway now.

"Only in conversation," his father said, pausing on the landing and facing Brian, who
(35)   was much taller. Brian's father hadn't made room for his wife, so she stood behind him and beneath him, on the top stair. "We met some fellow parents outside. It seems they — unlike your mother and I, of course — were at first glad to be rid of their daughter. All summer she worried them to no end, anxious, able to think and talk about nothing but how fun and challenging Princeton would be. She and her parents couldn't wait for the
(40)   fall. But now that the moment of parting has come, neither the parents nor the child wants to say goodbye. Typical, isn't it, dear?" he asked, turning to his wife.

"It is," she said and beamed.

"I know what you mean," Sidney's mom began, and Brian stepped out of the door-way, apparently so that his parents could see who was talking. "A lot of times this week,
(45)   I caught Sidney here just sitting on the couch, lost in thought."

Sidney's skin flushed hot.

He and his mom exchanged a look that communicated their acknowledgement of what he'd really been thinking about last week, that communicated their ready agree-ment to make no mention of the subject here.
(50)   "At first, I was worried," she continued, still watching him. "Then I realized. . . he's just got school on his mind. It's a big step. The biggest they've taken so far."

Sidney exhaled and realized he hadn't been breathing at all. And now to inhale and exhale was so soothing to his body it seemed he'd discovered life's greatest luxury.

As he watched his mom talk, watched her lips move and her hands gesticulate, it
(55)   seemed he was meeting her for the very first time. He'd never known she was capable of such subtlety: just now, while making small talk with Brian's parents, she'd managed to simultaneously carry on an inaudible conversation with him. This was the second time today she'd surprised him. First, his realization of why she'd dyed her hair and always wore trendy clothes. Now, this. And why did she tacitly broach the events and near-
(60)   events of that hot August night? Probably to reprimand him yet again.

23. The "potential fiancée" (line 4) refers to

   (A) Mrs. Lewis

   (B) Brian's mother

   (C) Mr. Lewis

   (D) the woman Joe intends to marry

   (E) Sidney's mother

Sidney's mother accompanies Mr. Lewis into the room, and shortly thereafter Sidney calls her "Mom." Bingo: (E) is the answer.

24. In this passage, Sidney's relationship with Mr. Lewis is portrayed as

   (A) close

   (B) antagonistic

   (C) professional

   (D) discourteous

   (E) filial

"Antagonistic" means "hostile." Sidney answers Mr. Lewis "with all the courtesy he could muster but without looking at the man" (lines 15–16), a statement implying trouble between the two, or at least trouble from Sidney's point of view. Did I stump you with choice (E)? "Filial" is the term for "son-to-father" sentiments and carries a connotation of respect and obligation. Sidney's behavior — not looking at Mr. Lewis, not bantering with him — may certainly characterize some filial relationships, but in this case, "antagonistic," choice (B), is a better fit.

25. In this scene, Sidney reevaluates his mother in terms of which of the following?

   I.   Her understanding of what he's thinking.

   II. Her social skills.

   III. Her choice of clothing.

   (A) I only.

   (B) I and II.

   (C) II and III.

   (D) I and III.

   (E) All of the above.

Sidney isn't surprised that his mother knows what he's thinking. The look that they exchange in line 47 implies that she has been aware of his concerns before. However, the passage states that Sidney had "never known she was capable of such subtlety" (lines 55–56) and he marvels at her ability to make small talk, a social skill. The passage also refers to Sidney's understanding of "why she'd dyed her hair and always wore trendy clothes" (lines 58–59). Therefore, II and III are correct, but I isn't. Go for (C).

26. The characterization of Brian's mother implies that she

   (A) takes a subservient role

   (B) dominates her son

   (C) feels superior to Sidney's mother

   (D) is too attached to her son

   (E) is happy to be parted from her son

Brian's mother stands "behind and beneath" (lines 35–36) her husband and says very little. In fact, her only lines are a short statement agreeing with her husband's comment. Sounds subservient to me! You may have been tempted by choice (E), because Brian says that his parents were glad to get rid of him. However, Brian's statement is contradicted by his father, who says "unlike your mother and I" (line 37), the other parents they met were glad to part from their child. The reader has no way of knowing whether Brian or his father is more accurate, so (E) is at best a guess, making choice (A) the winner.

27. Sidney's character is revealed by all of the following EXCEPT

    (A) reactions of other characters to him

    (B) his surroundings

    (C) physical description

    (D) thoughts

    (E) actions

Sidney doesn't do anything in this passage; he doesn't even talk much. Therefore, choice (E) is the winner. You can also arrive at the correct answer by eliminating the losers. The other characters react to Sidney, so (A) is out. Sidney has just arrived at his dorm room, which doesn't yet reflect his personality, so you can drop (B). On the other hand, you see quite a bit of physical description, including the fact that his skin "flushed hot" (line 46), eliminating (C). The entire passage is written from Sidney's point of view, so choice (D) — thoughts — isn't the one you want. That leaves you with (E), which is the correct answer.

28. "[W]hat he'd really been thinking about" (line 48) and "their ready agreement to make no mention of the subject here" (lines 48–49) suggest that

    (A) Sidney is ashamed of his upbringing.

    (B) Sidney chooses not to reveal something from his past.

    (C) Sidney's mother does not understand her son.

    (D) Sidney's mother does not understand his new environment.

    (E) Sidney is uncomfortable with his mother.

Whatever past event Sidney was worrying about, as well as the tacit agreement between Sidney and his mother not to speak of it, implies that Sidney doesn't trust that his new roommate will accept some aspect of Sidney's past. Sidney feels the need to hide something, which his mother apparently knows about. But the relationship between Sidney and his mother is close. He admires her social skills and isn't ashamed of his upbringing. Thus choice (B) is a better answer than (A). The other choices aren't even close.

29. The tone of the passage is

    (A) judgmental

    (B) critical

    (C) nostalgic

    (D) sarcastic

    (E) ironic

The passage is written from Sidney's point of view, and Sidney makes quite a few judgments about those around him; he doesn't approve of Mr. Lewis, for example, and he raises his opinion of his mother as he sees her handle a totally new situation. Sidney isn't nostalgic or critical. *Sarcasm* and *irony* arise from a gap between what's said and what's meant, and these elements aren't present here. Thus, the correct answer is (A).

30. The phrase "Sidney exhaled and realized he hadn't been breathing at all" (line 52) implies that he

   (A) is nervous in his new surroundings

   (B) trusts his mother

   (C) is embarrassed by his mother

   (D) assumes his mother may reveal a secret

   (E) believes that Brian will not like him

Sidney's rediscovery of breathing shows the tension and worry that he experiences as his mother speaks about his "sitting on the couch, lost in thought" (line 45). He thinks she may spill the beans about something, though the reader doesn't know what. Bingo, choice (D) is the one you want.

Writing Engaging Prose and Drama Essays

This section requires more ink than the multiple-choice questions, but the same amount of brain power. You need some lined paper, either loose-leaf or notebook pages, and a pen. Don't forget to annotate the passage as you would during the real AP exam. Also, keep to the recommended 40 minutes for each essay. If you go over a bit, turn back to Chapter 2 for speed suggestions. After you write an essay, check out the later section "Answer Guide for Prose and Drama Essays" to evaluate your work.

Essay prompt 1 (drama)

The following passage is from Henrik Ibsen's play *An Enemy of the People*. In it, Dr. Stockmann has just discovered that the water in the town spa is tainted. His brother, Peter Stockmann, is the mayor. Petra is Dr. Stockmann's daughter. Katherine Stockmann is the doctor's wife. After reading the passage carefully, write a well-organized essay exploring how Ibsen conveys the ethical stance of the characters in this excerpt.

(01)   PETRA — Uncle, that is a shameful way to treat a man like father!
         MRS. STOCKMANN — Do hold your tongue, Petra!
         PETER STOCKMANN [looking at PETRA] — Oh, so we volunteer our opinions already, do we? Of course. [to MRS STOCKMANN] Katherine, I imagine you are the most
(05)   sensible person in this house. Use any influence you may have over your husband, and make him see what this will entail for his family as well as —
         DR. STOCKMANN — My family is my own concern and nobody else's!
         PETER STOCKMANN — for his own family, as I was saying, as well as for the town he lives in.
(10)   DR. STOCKMANN — It is I who have the real good of the town at heart! I want to lay bare the defects that sooner or later must come to the light of day. I will show whether I love my native town.
         PETER STOCKMANN — You, who in your blind obstinacy want to cut off the most important source of the town's welfare?
(15)   DR. STOCKMANN — The source is poisoned, man! Are you mad? We are making our living by retailing filth and corruption! The whole of our flourishing municipal life derives its sustenance from a lie!
         PETER STOCKMANN — All imagination — or something even worse. The man who can throw out such offensive insinuations about his native town must be an enemy to
(20)   our community.
         DR. STOCKMANN [going up to him] — Do you dare to — !
         MRS. STOCKMANN [throwing herself between them] — Thomas!
         PETRA [catching her father by the arm] — Don't lose your temper, father!

(25) PETER STOCKMANN — I will not expose myself to violence. Now you have had a warning; so reflect on what you owe to yourself and your family. Goodbye. [goes out]

DR. STOCKMANN [walking up and down] — Am I to put up with such treatment as this? In my own house, Katherine! What do you think of that!

MRS. STOCKMANN — Indeed it is both shameful and absurd, Thomas —

PETRA — If only I could give uncle a piece of my mind —

(30) DR. STOCKMANN — It is my own fault. I ought to have flown out at him long ago! — shown my teeth! — bitten! To hear him call me an enemy to our community! Me! I shall not take that lying down, upon my soul!

MRS. STOCKMANN — But, dear Thomas, your brother has power on his side.

DR. STOCKMANN — Yes, but I have right on mine, I tell you.

(35) MRS. STOCKMANN — Oh yes, right — right. What is the use of having right on your side if you have not got might?

PETRA — Oh, mother! — how can you say such a thing!

DR. STOCKMANN — Do you imagine that in a free country it is no use having right on your side? You are absurd, Katherine. Besides, haven't I got the liberal-minded, inde-

(40) pendent press to lead the way, and the compact majority behind me? That is might enough, I should think!

MRS. STOCKMANN — But, good heavens, Thomas, you don't mean to?

DR. STOCKMANN — Don't mean to what?

MRS. STOCKMANN — To set yourself up in opposition to your brother.

(45) DR. STOCKMANN — In God's name, what else do you suppose I should do but take my stand on right and truth?

PETRA — Yes, I was just going to say that.

MRS. STOCKMANN — But it won't do you any earthly good. If they won't do it, they won't.

(50) DR. STOCKMANN — Oh no, Katherine! Just give me time, and you will see how I will carry the war into their camp.

MRS. STOCKMANN — Yes, you carry the war into their camp, and you get your dismissal — that is what you will do.

DR. STOCKMANN — In any case I shall have done my duty towards the public —

(55) towards the community, I, who am called its enemy!

MRS. STOCKMANN — But towards your family, Thomas? Towards your own home! Do you think that is doing your duty towards those you have to provide for?

PETRA — Ah, don't think always first of us, mother.

MRS. STOCKMANN — Oh, it is easy for you to talk; you are able to shift for yourself, if

(60) need be. But remember the boys, Thomas; and think a little of yourself too, and of me —

Essay prompt 2 (nonfiction)

Read this passage carefully and, in a well-organized essay, analyze the literary devices the author employs to make the setting both reflect and emphasize the changes in the family.

(01) The next morning we made the last stage of our journey, our hearts filled with the joy of nearing our new home. We all had an idea that we were going to a farm, and we expected some resemblance at least to the prosperous farms we had seen in New England. My mother's mental picture was, naturally, of an English farm. Possibly she had

(05) visions of red barns and deep meadows, sunny skies and daisies. What we found await-ing us were the four walls and the roof of a good-sized log-house, standing in a small cleared strip of the wilderness, its doors and windows represented by square holes, its floor also a thing of the future, its whole effect achingly forlorn and desolate. It was late in the afternoon when we drove up to the opening that was its front entrance, and I shall

(10) never forget the look my mother turned upon the place. Without a word she crossed its threshold, and, standing very still, looked slowly around her. Then something within her seemed to give way, and she sank upon the ground. She could not realize even then, I think, that this was really the place father had prepared for us, that here he expected us to live. When she finally took it in she buried her face in her hands, and in that way she

(15) sat for hours without moving or speaking. For the first time in her life she had forgotten us; and we, for our part, dared not speak to her. We stood around her in a frightened group, talking to one another in whispers. Our little world had crumbled under our feet. Never before had we seen our mother give way to despair.

(20) Night began to fall. The woods became alive with night creatures, and the most harmless made the most noise. The owls began to hoot, and soon we heard the wildcat, whose cry — a screech like that of a lost and panic-stricken child — is one of the most appalling sounds of the forest. Later the wolves added their howls to the uproar, but though darkness came and we children whimpered around her, our mother still sat in her strange lethargy.

(25) At last my brother brought the horses close to the cabin and built fires to protect them and us. He was only twenty, but he showed himself a man during those early pioneer days. While he was picketing the horses and building his protecting fires my mother came to herself, but her face when she raised it was worse than her silence had been. She seemed to have died and to have returned to us from the grave, and I am sure (30) she felt that she had done so. From that moment she took up again the burden of her life, a burden she did not lay down until she passed away; but her face never lost the deep lines those first hours of her pioneer life had cut upon it.

That night we slept on boughs spread on the earth inside the cabin walls, and we put blankets before the holes which represented our doors and windows, and kept our (35) watch-fires burning. Soon the other children fell asleep, but there was no sleep for me. I was only twelve years old, but my mind was full of fancies. Behind our blankets, swaying in the night wind, I thought I saw the heads and pushing shoulders of animals and heard their padded footfalls. Later years brought familiarity with wild things, and with worse things than they. But tonight that which I most feared was within, not outside of, the (40) cabin. In some way which I did not understand the one sure refuge in our new world had been taken from us. I hardly knew the silent woman who lay near me, tossing from side to side and staring into the darkness; I felt that we had lost our mother.

Essay prompt 3 (fiction)

Read this excerpt from Sinclair Lewis's novel *Main Street*. In a well-written essay, discuss how this scene reveals societal norms. Do not limit yourself to plot summary.

(01) Even while they were removing their overshoes they were peeping at the new decorations. Carol saw Dave Dyer secretively turn over the gold pillows to find a price-tag, and heard Mr. Julius Flickerbaugh, the attorney, gasp, "Well, I'll be switched," as he viewed the vermilion print hanging against the Japanese obi. She was amused. But her (05) high spirits slackened as she beheld them form in dress parade, in a long, silent, uneasy circle clear round the living-room. She felt that she had been magically whisked back to her first party, at Sam Clark's.

"Have I got to lift them, like so many pigs of iron? I don't know that I can make them happy, but I'll make them hectic."

(10) A silver flame in the darkling circle, she whirled around, drew them with her smile, and sang, "I want my party to be noisy and undignified! This is the christening of my house, and I want you to help me have a bad influence on it, so that it will be a giddy house. For me, won't you all join in an old-fashioned square dance? And Mr. Dyer will call."

She had a record on the phonograph; Dave Dyer was capering in the center of the (15) floor, loose-jointed, lean, small, rusty headed, pointed of nose, clapping his hands and shouting, "Swing y' pardners — alamun lef!"

Even the millionaire Dawsons and Ezra Stowbody and "Professor" George Edwin Mott danced, looking only slightly foolish; and by rushing about the room and being coy and coaxing to all persons over forty-five, Carol got them into a waltz and a Virginia (20) Reel. But when she left them to disenjoy themselves in their own way Harry Haydock put a one-step record on the phonograph, the younger people took the floor, and all the elders sneaked back to their chairs, with crystallized smiles which meant, "Don't believe I'll try this one myself, but I do enjoy watching the youngsters dance."

(24)   Half of them were silent; half resumed the discussions of that afternoon in the store. Ezra Stowbody hunted for something to say, hid a yawn, and offered to Lyman Cass, the owner of the flour-mill, "How'd you folks like the new furnace, Lym? Huh? So."

    "Oh, let them alone. Don't pester them. They must like it, or they wouldn't do it." Carol warned herself. But they gazed at her so expectantly when she flickered past that she was reconvinced that in their debauches of respectability they had lost the power of play as well as the power of impersonal thought. Even the dancers were gradually

(30) crushed by the invisible force of fifty perfectly pure and well-behaved and negative minds; and they sat down, two by two. In twenty minutes the party was again elevated to the decorum of a prayer-meeting.

    "We're going to do something exciting," Carol exclaimed to her new confidante,

(35) Vida Sherwin. She saw that in the growing quiet her voice had carried across the room. Nat Hicks, Ella Stowbody, and Dave Dyer were abstracted, fingers and lips slightly moving. She knew with a cold certainty that Dave was rehearsing his "stunt" about the Norwegian catching the hen, Ella running over the first lines of "An Old Sweetheart of Mine," and Nat thinking of his popular parody on Mark Antony's oration.

(40)   "But I will not have anybody use the word 'stunt' in my house," she whispered to Miss Sherwin.

    "That's good. I tell you: why not have Raymond Wutherspoon sing?"

    "Raymie? Why, my dear, he's the most sentimental yearner in town!"

    "See here, child! Your opinions on house-decorating are sound, but your opinions of

(45) people are rotten! Raymie does wag his tail. But the poor dear' — 'Longing for what he calls 'self-expression' and no training in anything except selling shoes. But he can sing. And some day when he gets away from Harry Haydock's patronage and ridicule, he'll do something fine."

    Carol apologized for her superciliousness. She urged Raymie, and warned the plan-

(50) ners of "stunts," "We all want you to sing, Mr. Wutherspoon. You're the only famous actor I'm going to let appear on the stage tonight."

    While Raymie blushed and admitted, "Oh, they don't want to hear me," he was clearing his throat, pulling his clean handkerchief farther out of his breast pocket, and

(54) thrusting his fingers between the buttons of his vest.

Answer Guide for Prose and Drama Essays

Hello, all you creative people out there! How do I know you're creative? Because you're reading a *For Dummies* book and not some other boring AP practice volume. I can't come to your house to read your essay (though if you offer me an ice cream sundae with caramel sauce, I'll make an effort). So in this answer guide, I explain the basic elements that every grader looks for. Then I provide a list of points you *might* make about each selection, which is pretty much everything I can think of about each passage. When you take the AP English exam, you can score a five without including all the ideas on my list. Also, you may come up with something I neglected to include. Good for you! Just be sure you can justify your idea with evidence from the passage.

General essay requirements

Here are the basic elements that every AP essay grader looks for:

    ✔ The essay needs an introduction containing the name of the author and the title of the literary work (assuming you have that information). The title of a novel or a play should be underlined. Story titles are enclosed in quotation marks.

    The essay prompt helps you deal with the punctuation needed for a title. If the AP writers used quotation marks, so should you. If the title is italicized, you should underline it.

- ✔ The introductory paragraph should contain a thesis statement. (Chapter 3 explains how to create a thesis statement.)

- ✔ The essay needs to be organized logically. You can proceed through the passage in line order, making a point about each significant item. Or, you can group similar ideas, with everything about a particular character in one paragraph, for example.

- ✔ Ideally the essay should have a conclusion, not a summary or an abrupt stop.

- ✔ The essay must include evidence, in the form of quotations, from the selection. The quotations should be punctuated properly. You can cite line numbers in parentheses after the quotations, but you don't have to do so.

- ✔ The essay should be written in present tense, unless you need to indicate an order of events. Here's an example: "As the play begins, Macbeth is praised for his courage. The captain describes how Macbeth defeated the rebels." "Defeated" is in past tense to show that the praise takes place after the battle.

- ✔ You should have a minimum number of grammar and spelling errors. Be sure to use complete sentences, each ending with a period or a question mark. Stay away from exclamation points, which are out of place in a literary essay.

- ✔ You should check, check, and then recheck that you're answering the question the prompt asks. Off-topic remarks should be crossed out. Stay focused!

Potential points for essay 1

I chose Ibsen's play because it's often cited on the AP exam as one of the works to analyze in the third, open-ended essay question. The AP writers like this play for very good reason: The characters' interactions are more subtle than they first appear, and the overall conflict is compelling and relevant to current issues. It's a great play; I suggest that you read all of it when you have some extra time.

Main points

The prompt asks you to analyze "how Ibsen conveys the ethical stance of the characters." Therefore, your first task is to define each character's views of right and wrong. Here are some of the general ideas:

- ✔ Peter Stockmann is pragmatic, and if he has any ethics, he's willing to ignore them because he wants the town's economy to survive. He doesn't care that the water may be dangerous in the long run. He's thinking about the *here and now*. Lying isn't a problem for Peter.

- ✔ Dr. Stockmann sees the world in absolute terms. The water is tainted, and therefore he has to disclose that fact, regardless of personal cost.

- ✔ Petra backs her father. Right is right and wrong is wrong. End of story.

- ✔ Katherine Stockmann's primary concern is her family's welfare. She's practical rather than idealistic. She thinks that Dr. Stockmann will lose if he battles the mayor. She also thinks that her husband should be loyal to the mayor because the mayor is family. For her, "family values" isn't a cliché but an ethical imperative.

Evidence

After you understand who believes what, zero in on how those beliefs are portrayed, the most important part of the prompt. Simply reporting the basic ethical stance of each character won't earn you much credit. Identifying the way in which Ibsen conveys each character's ethical stances is more impressive, but it's also tougher. You can't just note that he uses dialogue. After all, it's a play! But analyzing the stage directions and the punctuation in this selection turns an okay-but-not-great essay into a wow-listen-to-this-answer essay.

Here's the evidence dealing with dialogue:

- ✔ Peter Stockmann acknowledges the doctor's duty to his family ("see what this will entail for his family," line 6), but his attention is focused on the town ("for the town he lives in," lines 8–9). He adds that his brother's "blind obstinacy" (line 13) will "cut off the most important source of the town's welfare" (lines 13–14). He condemns his brother as "an enemy to our community" (lines 19–20).

- ✔ Dr. Stockmann is repelled by the fact that "our flourishing municipal life derives its sustenance from a lie!" (lines 16–17). However, his comments also show that his ethical stance is mixed with something else — competition with his brother. Dr. Stockmann says, "Am I to put up with such treatment as this?" (lines 26–27) and challenges his brother: "Do you dare to — " (line 21). Dr. Stockmann tells his wife that he should have "shown [his] teeth" (line 31) long ago. Mostly, however, he rests on moral certainty: "I have right on [my side]" (line 34). He believes that the press and the majority will back him as he says, "That is might enough" (lines 40–41). He declares, "[I] take my stand on right and truth" (lines 45–46).

- ✔ Katherine Stockmann challenges her daughter, trying to keep peace in the family: "Do hold your tongue, Petra" (line 2). She also supports her husband when he complains that he has been attacked in his own home: "Indeed it is both shameful and absurd" (line 28). However, she fears the consequences of her husband's stance ("What is the use of having right on your side if you have not got might?" lines 35–36, and "you get your dismissal," lines 52–53). She emphasizes family: "To set yourself up in opposition to your brother" (line 44) and "towards your family . . . your own home!" (line 56). She reminds her husband that he must think of "the boys . . . and of me" (line 60).

- ✔ Petra berates her uncle, saying her uncle's treatment of her father is "shameful" (line 1). She dismisses her mother: "[H]ow can you say such a thing?" (line 37) and "[D]on't always think of us first, Mother" (line 58). She praises her father: "I was just going to say that" (line 47).

Here are some lines of evidence you might use regarding the stage directions:

- ✔ The mayor appeals to the women, looking at Petra and Mrs. Stockmann (lines 3–4).

- ✔ The doctor confronts his brother physically, "going up to him" (line 21).

- ✔ Mrs. Stockmann is so anxious to make peace that she is described as "throwing herself between" the men (line 22).

Here are some ideas you can bring up regarding punctuation:

- ✔ All the dashes, indicating unfinished thoughts, are important. An unfinished thought may show hesitation or conflict. Or, if another character jumps in, the dash may display the unity between two characters or their impatience.

- ✔ The mayor, interrupted in line 6, goes back to his original thought in line 8 as if the interruption had not happened. The dashes indicate here that he's obstinate; the interruption won't slow him down.

- ✔ The dashes show changes of thought or increased emotion. In lines 30–31, for example, the doctor says "I ought to have flown out at him long ago! — shown my teeth! — bitten!"

- ✔ The dash in line 35 between "right" and "right" reveals Mrs. Stockmann's ambivalence. She wants to support her husband's views, but she questions his definition of right because it may hurt her family.

- ✔ The many exclamation points throughout the passage intensify the emotions of the characters. Petra, for example, says, "Oh, mother! — how can you say such a thing!" (line 37).

Organization

The essay may be organized in a couple of ways. You can devote one paragraph to each character, perhaps combining Petra and her father, as their views are similar. Or, you can devote one paragraph to dialogue, one to stage directions, and one to punctuation.

Overall assessment

Overall, rate your essay as "poor' if all you did was identify the main ethical stance of each character. Move yourself to "fair" if you captured the complexity of Mrs. Stockmann's and Dr. Stockmann's views. These ideas, of course, have to be supported by quotations from the dialogue. Step into the "good" category if you mentioned stage directions and punctuation, perhaps making two or three points about these elements. The exam graders will also take into account how well you've organized and presented the information, so be sure your essay is logical and well written. (For more details on scoring an essay, take a look at Chapter 17 or Chapter 19, where I present scoring grids for essay questions.

Potential points for essay 2

This selection describes the brutal homecoming of a pioneer family to a homestead prepared by the father. The details of the family's living conditions and reactions take you right into this scene. As soon as you're immersed in the scene, you realize that the setting is only a way to tell you what's going on in the family.

Main points

The prompt asks you to explain how the setting works to "reflect and emphasize the changes in the family." You can make several points about the setting and the family:

- The setting is a wilderness in which the father of the family has built a cabin. No specific time period is identified, though the family is clearly in the "pioneer" category.

- The mother experiences a mini–nervous breakdown in this scene. Her strength and confidence seem to desert her as she views her new living conditions. Eventually, she accepts her fate.

- The brother rises to a new level of maturity and responsibility as the mother becomes incapacitated.

- The narrator loses her innocence, realizing that her mother doesn't have all the answers. This new idea makes the narrator fearful.

Evidence

This prompt is a complicated one because it requires you to deal with three elements: the changes in the family, the setting, and the literary devices that convey the setting. To write a really good essay, you also have to link these three elements and use evidence to prove how the setting mirrors the changes in the family.

Here's evidence you can use regarding changes in the family:

- The mother breaks down by "standing very still" (line 11) as she first enters her new home and having "something within her . . . give way" (lines 11–12) as she collapses. She sits "for hours" (line 15) and "buried her face in her hands" (line 14). The narrator says that "[f]or the first time in her life she had forgotten us" (line 15). When the mother begins to function again, she "seemed to have died and to have returned to us from the grave" (line 29). She now carries "a burden she did not lay down until she passed away" (line 31), and her face "never lost the deep lines those first hours of pioneer life had cut upon it" (lines 31–32).

✔ The children change also. At first, they "stood around her in a frightened group, talking to one another in whispers" (lines 16–17). The children's "little world had crumbled" (line 17) from the sight of their mother's despair, and they "whimpered around her" at nightfall (line 23). However, the brother finally takes charge, bringing the horses closer to the house; he "showed himself a man during those early pioneer days" (lines 26–27). The narrator is sleepless, explaining that "we had lost our mother" (line 42).

You can use the following ideas as evidence for showing how the author conveys the setting:

✔ The events take place during "pioneer days" in a wilderness setting. The location is not disclosed, but the house is contrasted with "prosperous farms . . . in New England" (lines 3–4) and "an English farm" (line 4). It's late afternoon when the family arrives (lines 8–9).

✔ The "good-sized log-house" (line 6) has only walls and a roof. The windows are open "square holes" and the floor is "a thing of the future" (line 8). The family sleeps on "boughs spread on the earth" (line 33) with blankets over the windows and door.

✔ The natural world is threatening. The "woods became alive with night creatures" (line 19), with owls and wildcats and wolves crying in the night.

The following are lines of evidence regarding literary devices:

✔ In describing the imagined setting, the author selects details that create an idyllic scene — "red barns and deep meadows, sunny skies and daisies" (line 5). These details emphasize the idyllic view the children have of their mother. She's strong and unbreakable, they think. That strength means that her breakdown is all the more shocking to them.

✔ The hyperbole in line 17 ("our little world had crumbled under our feet") matches the earthen floor of the house.

✔ The diction is plain; all the words are simple and the syntax is natural. The diction and syntax emphasize the plainness of the house and the naturalness of the change in the family. All children, at some point, realize that their parents aren't all-powerful.

✔ The simile in line 21 ("a screech like that of a lost and panic-stricken child") expresses what the children are going through. Also, the wolves howl, just as the children whimper.

✔ The boughs (line 33) symbolize the family's entry into nature. They're in the wilderness, and again, the children realize that their mother isn't the rock they thought she was — a natural part of their maturation process.

Organization

Putting all the necessary information together into one essay isn't easy. You can structure the essay by devoting one paragraph to family changes, one to setting, and one to literary devices. Or, you can split the essay into two sections, devoting one part to the mother and her changes and another to the children and their maturation. In each of these sections you would include the literary devices and refer to elements of the setting that you encounter, taking care to relate those elements and devices to each other and to the characters' changes.

Overall assessment

A good essay in response to this prompt should include comments about the mother, the children, and the setting, plus at least two or three points about literary devices (all with supporting evidence from the passage). A fair or poor essay lacks some of these elements and fails to support the main ideas. I've included a ton of quotations, but if you have half as many as I do, you've written a good response. And of course, don't forget that you need to express yourself clearly and fluently to impress an AP grader.

Potential points for essay 3

This prompt is your invitation to Carol's party, and what a drag that party appears to be! The prompt sends you inside the society, where your mission is to figure out what the norms are. As usual in an AP exam prompt, a super-important word here is "how." When you're in "how" territory, you're looking for writing techniques, the infamous literary devices.

This prompt, like many AP prompts, specifically tells you to avoid plot summary. Why? The exam graders don't want to read that Carol gave a party at which the guests danced, sneaked looks at price tags, had boring conversations, and then listened to somebody perform karaoke without the music. The graders know all that. Instead, they want you to use the information from the passage to answer the question.

Main points

An essay in response to this prompt should deal with individual characterization (action, dialogue, thoughts, description, diction, figurative language, point of view, and so forth), especially of Carol, who's the most important character. She's set up in opposition to the group; she's the punk rocker of her society. (Okay, maybe not a punk, but she _is_ a rebel.) The party guests, in turn, serve as a foil for Carol; they have different values and traditions. Analyze the way in which the characters interact, and take a long look at the few, but important, physical details of the setting. (And they say the AP exam is no fun . . .)

Evidence

Now for some specifics. I've divided these points into two camps — one for Carol and one for everyone else. Interspersed are some specific literary devices you may mention.

Here are the points of evidence for Carol's characterization:

- Carol sees herself as superior to her guests, but she feels responsible for changing their behavior — a heavy burden. "Have I got to lift them, like so many pigs of iron?" she asks (line 8). She whirls around and demands that her party be "undignified" (line 11), implying that serious behavior is the norm.

- Carol "sang" (line 11) and "exclaimed" (line 34) rather than "said" or "spoke." This word choice contrasts her liveliness with the dullness of the other people. Her variation from the norm helps indentify rules that the others obey.

- Carol is described as a "silver flame in a darkling circle" (line 10). The circle is dark and joyless; again, this metaphor indicates that having fun is the exception, not the rule in this society. "Darkling" implies nightfall, the end of something. The society is on its way out; it's already dead in some ways, and Carol is trying to liven it up.

- She asks her guests to be "a bad influence" on her house (line 12). The house is symbolically tied to Carol, who wants to be "bad" but with group support.

- Carol "flickered past" the guests (line 28). The word choice (diction) here depicts her as a flame (fire flickers), dangerous but also bringing light and heat to the town.

The following is evidence for the characterization of other characters:

- Discretion seems to be important in this society. The guests are "peeping at the new decorations" (lines 1–2), and Dave Dyer "secretively" looks for price tags (line 2).

- Money is a big deal; people want to know how much you're worth. For example, Dave Dyer tries to find out how much Carol spent on her pillows, and the Dawsons are described as "millionaires" (line 17).

✔ Conformity rules. The decorations feature a "vermilion print" (line 4) and a "Japanese obi" (line 4). The obi, a sash, shocks the guests; Mr. Julius Flickerbaugh gasps when he sees it and says, "Well, I'll be switched" (line 3). Obviously anything new is a surprise in this social group. "Switched" is an interesting word choice. He's almost saying that the surprise makes him become someone else.

The guests enter in "dress parade" (line 5) and form a "long, silent, uneasy circle" (lines 5—6). The military metaphor and the description of the seating arrangement reinforce the conformity of this society.

✔ When Carol leaves, the guests "disenjoy themselves" (line 20). Later the guests are said to have "lost the power of play as well as the power of impersonal thought" (lines 29–30). In this group, fun is off limits, as are new ideas.

✔ Carol sees her guests as having "debauches of respectability" (line 29). A "debauch" is usually an out-of-control event such as a keg party or an orgy. Here the debauch is respectable. In other words, frat-party guests get drunk on beer; these guests get drunk on "respectability," which appears to be a synonym for their nearly joyless lives.

✔ The dancers are gradually crushed by "the invisible force of fifty perfectly pure and well-behaved and negative minds" (lines 31–32), and the party becomes a "prayer-meeting" (line 33). "Pure," "well-behaved," and "prayer-meeting" are normally good labels, but here they're linked with "negative" (line 31). These people are pure because they won't allow anything to happen.

✔ Appearances are important among this conservative crowd. The dancers are said to be "looking only slightly foolish" (line 18), but the guests have "crystallized smiles" (line 22). That metaphor emphasizes the unchanging, stolid character of the group. In the same vein, the guests talk with "lips slightly moving" (lines 36–37).

✔ The guests value conformity to the unvarying rituals and conversations they're used to. Ezra Stowbody "hunted for something to say" (line 25), and many guests resume conversations they had started earlier in the day.

✔ Self-expression and individuality are no-nos. Vida Sherwin tells Carol that Raymie is "longing for what he calls 'self-expression'" (lines 45–46). The quotation marks around "self-expression" distance Raymie from that sentiment. She's more likely to see "self-expression" as "self-indulgence." However, Vida has some affection for Raymie, expecting him to "do something fine" (lines 47–48) when he's removed from the bad influence of another member of the group.

Organization

This prompt asks for a lot of information, and so organizing all of it — or even some of it! — is tough. To make the task easier, you can divide the essay in these ways:

✔ One body paragraph for Carol and one for everyone else. This structure is easy, but you have a lot to cram into two paragraphs. Still, it could work.

✔ One body paragraph for each norm you identify: conformity, respectability, money, appearances, and so forth. (There are a lot of possibilities; you may find only three or four depending on how you define the categories.) This structure is more sophisticated and therefore more impressive, but you have to get organized fast to place everything in the right spot.

✔ The fastest way to tackle this prompt is to devote one body paragraph to each section of the story. The first body paragraph covers the guests' arrival, the second discusses the dancing, and the third handles the conversation (or lack thereof) and singing. The problem with this organizational structure is that you have to keep moving back and forth between Carol and the others. Plus, you have to find a way to include evidence for the same societal norm without repeating yourself.

Avoid repetition not only because you lack time but also because reading the same thing twice is B-O-R-I-N-G. If you discuss money in the first body paragraph, when Dave turns the pillows over, don't say the same thing about money later, when the Dawsons are described as millionaires.

Overall assessment

If you recognized all the points that I listed for this essay, you should drop out of school and take my job. I spent a long time gathering these points — far longer than those measly 40 minutes you have on the AP exam. If you correctly characterized three or four of the societal norms (conformity, deadening respectability, money, appearances, and all other possibilities) and if you made six or seven supporting points, you're in good shape. You don't need fancy labels (metaphor, diction, and the like), but literary terminology does enhance your essay. However, it's only a positive addition if you analyze the impact of each element that you identify.

Part IV

Paired Passages and the Open-Ended Essay

The 5th Wave   By Rich Tennant

THE RELATIONSHIP ANALYSIS PROMPT

Listen to your boyfriend's decision to skip the AP English Literature and Composition practice session and go to a hockey game instead. Then write an essay on what a moron you are for supporting his decision to forgo college and become a Zamboni operator instead.

In this part . . .

Figure skating routines are designed by the contestants, who skate to music of their choice. This aspect of skating is similar to the *open-ended question,* the third and last AP English Literature and Composition exam essay. The open-ended question comes without a literary passage. You choose a work to write about in response to a question that the College Board supplies.

Another aspect of figure skating is the pairs competition, in which twirling couples compete with gravity-defying leaps and tight spins. Sometimes the AP English exam has a pairs competition too. In this case, the trophy is a 9 (the highest essay score). The slippery surface you're working on consists of two literary selections, side by side, and a prompt that asks you to compare and contrast them in a well-written essay. Let me guess! You'd probably rather slide into the wall of the rink than work on such an essay?

Never fear. In this part, I show you how to train for these two questions. You'll find open-ended essays in Chapter 13 and paired-passages in Chapter 14. When the Olympic competition — er, I mean the AP exam — begins, you'll be ready.

Chapter 14

Free at Last: The Open-Ended Essay

- -

In This Chapter

▶ Preparing literary works in advance

▶ Getting used to the elements in open-ended prompts

▶ Handling evidence without a text to work from

▶ Understanding how to discuss a selected topic in context of an entire work

▶ Examining an example open-ended essay

- -

*I*magine how it feels to loosen your tie or slip out of your high heels. That's what the open-ended essay feels like: a bit of sweet freedom. Only a bit, though! You're still taking an exam. But after you arrive at the third, open-ended essay question, you're free from the literary passages that the College Board plopped in front of you for the first and second essay questions. Instead, the open-ended essay hits you with a prompt and a list of perhaps 30 titles. You respond to the prompt by discussing a work from the list or something "of comparable quality." Ah, the sweet freedom of choice.

However, not so fast. Freedom isn't all fun and games. As philosophers have often pointed out, with freedom comes responsibility. Choosing the right text can be a make-or-break decision. Also, analyzing a literary work that isn't in front of you presents unique challenges.

Not to worry, though. In this chapter, I explain everything you need to know about the open-ended essay, from prompt decoding and text selection to evidence collection. I also go into detail on how to arm yourself for AP English Literature and Composition exam with prepared material — enough information on four or five literary works to cover nearly all possible prompts. (Just for the record, I'm talking about mental preparation, not notes etched on your contact lenses.) I also show you a good open-ended essay, so you can visualize the goal.

Preparing Literary Works for AP Use

Put yourself in this scene: You're sitting in a classroom, sweat dripping slowly onto a desk, working your way through the two-hour endurance test known as the essay section of the AP English Literature and Composition exam. You turn to the open-ended prompt. You read it, figure out what the exam writers actually want to know, and search your memory bank and the list of suggested works for something suitable to write about. You come up with absolutely nothing. Nada. Zippo.

Nightmare time, right? Fortunately, it's a scenario that never has to happen. Why? Because before exam day arrives, you can prepare four or five literary works that ride to your rescue no matter what questions the AP writers dream up. Here's the secret: AP open-ended questions tend to focus on large, somewhat hazy (though still important) ideas. Handily, great works of literature also tend to deal with large, somewhat hazy (though still important) ideas. So the odds are one or more of your prepared works will make a match.

Adhering to standards of literary quality

No, you can't get credit for writing about your favorite Dr. Seuss book, as one daring but misguided student tried to do a few years ago. The College Board wants to evaluate how well you understand and write about *serious* literature. Therefore they expect you to analyze a full-length, unified work that contains these elements:

- ✔ **Layers of meaning:** Not every idea in the work comes across after a brief skim-read. Good literature rewards attention and offers something new every time you read it.

- ✔ **Important issues:** If the only topic covered in the work is whether the ideal prom date is available, you can be sure that you're not in serious literature territory. Important issues include art, war, love, mortality, truth, and other such topics.

  Sometimes a book that appears to deal only with trivial issues actually addresses universal human situations. Virginia Woolf's *To the Lighthouse,* for example, contains a scene in which the characters eat dinner and chat about nothing. In one corner of the table, however, a young woman moves a salt shaker and silverware. The character's thoughts roam from the role of art to the pressure on an artist to conform to society's expectations to gender roles and a lot more. Don't shy away from works that seem to tackle everyday life. Just be sure that the work addresses important issues on some level.

- ✔ **Fully-developed characters:** The minor characters may display only one personality trait, but the important characters need to embody complexity, as real people do.

- ✔ **Adult-level vocabulary and sentence structure:** The AP program offers college credit, so not surprisingly it expects you to read college-level material. Unless the writer has created a narrator who speaks simply, look for difficult words and complicated sentences.

The full-length-only rule has one advantage: it takes the mystery away from title punctuation. The titles of full-length works — novels, plays, book-sized poems — are underlined, not placed inside quotation marks. However, if you merit special accommodations and are typing your AP essay (see Chapter 1 for more information), you may italicize the title instead of underlining it.

Staying on the safe side

If you don't enjoy gambling, which is probably the best attitude for an AP exam, you can feel safe and confident when you choose one of the following types of works for your essay:

- ✔ **Anything you studied in English class:** If you spent six weeks on a particular work in a high-level English class (11th or 12th grade), it's a good bet that you can use that work on the AP exam. However, proceed at your own risk if it's something you read in tenth grade or earlier.

- ✔ **Classics:** These are the titles you've heard a million times (*Pride and Prejudice, Moby-Dick,* or *King Lear*). They come in special editions with plain but dignified covers. Not sure if the one you've chosen is a classic? Check Appendix A for a list of classics and worthy newer works.

- ✔ **Anything from the list provided on the exam:** If the exam writers tell you that *Important Novel* or *Classic Play* is a possible choice, you can be sure that it's super-safe. As my students put it, duh!

If you're writing about a book that has been made into a movie, be extremely careful to write only about the book. Ignore the movie completely! Hollywood often destroys (sorry, *adapts*) literature. One horrifying example is Bernard Malamud's novel *The Natural,* which concerns a baseball player. The book is serious; the player is a flawed hero who often makes poor choices and has to suffer the consequences. At the end of the book (spoiler alert here!), the baseball player strikes out at a crucial moment. In the movie, however, he hits a home run, which is filmed in slow motion with inspiring background music. Writing about that (inaccurate) cinematic moment — as a student of mine once did — can seriously annoy any teacher or AP exam grader who expects you to read and write about the text, not the film.

Taking a chance

Are you the creative type who would rather score a low grade than compromise your integrity? Okay, I'm not going to argue with you. Just remember that you may be able to do well with one of the following types of literature, but these choices are definitely risky:

- **Recent books or plays:** It takes a while for literature to work its way into what teacher-types call "the canon" of English literature. After all, when a new work appears, some people like it, some love it, some are indifferent, and some ignore it completely because they refuse to read anything published after the 19th century. (A couple of people I know are in that category.) Thus, even if the book was published to "critical acclaim," as the jacket blurb brags, the grader may not consider it a worthy choice.

  If you do go off the beaten path, you risk writing about a work that the grader hasn't read. The AP Graders-in-Chief have a strategy for such cases; they try to give that exam to someone who's familiar with the work. I have a strategy for you also; read the later section "Detecting and Selecting Evidence" for information on how to deal with plot points in an essay about lesser-known literature.

- **Young adult works:** An unfair fact of life is that books perceived as children's or "young adult" literature seldom get the respect they deserve (despite the fact that quite a few books devoured by not-old-enough-to-vote people are worthy of your attention and analysis). On the AP exam, however, such titles as *Alice in Wonderland* and *The Secret Garden* may not make the cut.

- **Graphic novels:** I'm not a particularly visual person, but I appreciate serious graphic novels, which convey meaning through drawings and text. For instance, I loved reading Art Spiegelman's *Maus,* an account of a Holocaust survivor and his son, as well as Marjane Satrapi's *Persepolis,* which deals with her childhood in Iran. However, some English teachers look down on graphic novels, mistakenly viewing them as souped-up comic books. Also, because you're proving that you can handle text, not pictures, you may not be able to discuss the work adequately in the context of an AP exam.

- **Novellas:** A novella is shorter than a novel but generally just as complex as the longer work. You're in a gray area if you opt for a novella because the essay prompt generally asks you to write about a novel or play. However, the AP often lists a few novellas, such as Franz Kafka's *The Metamorphosis,* so sometimes the graders do approve of these shorter works.

Don't go there

A few types of writing send your essay right off a cliff (without a parachute). Avoid these works at all cost:

- **Short stories:** Even a collection of short stories is a bad idea for the open-ended essay. The exam writers are looking for analysis of a full-length, unified work. In fact, the prompt often specifically rules out short stories.

- **Poems:** In general you aren't allowed to write about poems in response to the open-ended question. The prompt sometimes states that poems should be avoided. One exception: You may write about a book-length poem or a play written in verse, such as Homer's *Odyssey* or Dante's *Divine Comedy.* As long as you choose a classic, book-length poems or verse plays are great subjects for the open-ended essay.

- **Non-print works:** No films, no television shows, no song lyrics, no operas, and no blogs.

- **Non-published works:** If your Uncle Oscar wrote the best play ever, you can't write about it unless it's in print. How would the graders evaluate your work? You can't rely on the fact that Oscar's play was performed ten times and may have picked up an English teacher or two in the audience.

Choosing works to prepare

When choosing works to prepare for the AP exam, your goal is to have four or five arrows ready to fire. (Each arrow is one literary work, either a novel or a play or a book-length poem.) The basic principle is simple: Go for variety.

If your favorite books are *Pride and Prejudice, Mansfield Park,* and *Persuasion,* you can claim membership in the Jane Austen fan club. (I'm a life member.) And with these three works prepared, you're all set if the open-ended prompt concerns societal norms, male-female or parent-child conflicts, comedy, or coming-of-age stories. But if the prompt asks you to consider the effect of a tragic hero on the people surrounding him or her — a real AP question one year — you're in trouble if you have nothing prepared other than these novels. As much as I love Jane, even I have to admit that she was right when she called her writing "a little bit . . . of Ivory, on which I work with so fine a Brush." In other words, her scope was definitely narrow.

Variety, in literary terms, means works containing different issues, types of characters, situations, and themes. (Turn to Appendix A for a list of great literary works and some information on their content and themes.) When choosing four or five works to prepare, I suggest that you have at least one from each of the following categories:

- **Tragedy:** This work may be either a play or a novel or a book-length poem, but it should be a tragedy in the classical sense, featuring a flawed hero or heroine who suffers partly through his or her own actions.

- **Comedy:** Comedy doesn't always get the attention it deserves, but it may deal as seriously with the human condition as tragedy does. Sometimes it's the best choice for an open-ended essay question.

- **One novel and one play:** Frequently the same question may be answered by either a prose or a dramatic work, but if you have one of each ready to go, you won't be caught short.

- **Works not written by a dead white male (DWM):** Okay, before you start screaming at me, let me admit that Shakespeare's work includes just about any issue you can think of, and old Will is one of the deadest, whitest, male writers you can find. Plenty of other DWMs are amazing also. However, diversity in your reading and in your AP preparation is still a good idea. Why? Well, for one, you encounter some great literature if you move beyond DWMs, and you also may find some AP questions easier to answer with works not from the DWM category. For example, in recent years, many AP questions have dealt with a character who's outside of mainstream society, either for cultural or personal reasons. Other open-ended questions have addressed stereotypes, opposition to society, and social or political change.

- **A work that you love:** Every once in a while you fall under the spell of a book, and it becomes part of who you are. If a work makes you passionate, you can write about it with passion too. Keep in mind this well-known formula: passion equals a good essay.

Some of these categories overlap. A tragedy may also be a play, for example. Just be sure you end up with four or five varied, ready-to-rumble works. Then you're all set. Turn to Chapter 3 for an explanation of how to keep track of works that might be suitable for the open-ended essay.

Compiling notes on your chosen works

Unless you have a photographic memory, you've probably forgotten a lot of details from the books you read in previous school years or even from the current year. Luckily for the non-memorizers out there, notes help you keep track of Mr. Darcy, Celie, Fortinbras, Estella, and all the other wonderful characters in literature, along with their exploits. This section explains how to compile notes that will help you on the exam.

Free verse!

In general, you aren't allowed to write about poems in response to the open-ended question. However, writing about a book-length poem or a play written in verse is fine. If you do write about a poetic work for the third essay, keep these ideas in mind when you're recording the must-have info for your work:

- ✔ **Pick and choose plot points to support your thesis, just as you do when writing about prose literature.** Most book-length poems and all plays written in verse have some sort of plot, even if it's one of those avant-garde works where the actor eats his socks or the poet creates words that have no formal meaning. (Call me old-fashioned, but I'm much happier when I can make sense of what's going on.)

- ✔ **If you remember anything about the poet's technique, by all means feel free to mention it, as long as it relates to the prompt that you're answering.** I doubt that you've memorized many lines from a book-length poem or a verse play, so you can't dig into the text in the same way you do when you're dealing with a poem printed on the exam. You can, however, discuss a literary technique in general, with few or no quotations.

For example, much of the figurative language in Shakespeare's *Macbeth* deals with sight, eyes, and morality. In your essay, you might mention that Macbeth asks the stars in the sky to "hide [their] fires" so they won't see his desire to kill the king. Similarly, you might note that after the murder, Macbeth is afraid to return to the murder scene because he doesn't want to look at what he's done.

- ✔ **If you do insert a quotation into the essay, punctuate it correctly.** The line break should be signaled with a forward slash (/), or you can block the quotation. (Chapter 7 explains in detail how to punctuate poetry quotations.)

Recording the must-have info

When recording the important information from a work, your goal is to know the following specifics *cold*:

- ✔ Title, author, names of all major characters and some significant minor characters
- ✔ Setting
- ✔ Important events in the plot
- ✔ Themes and symbols
- ✔ Significant quotations

Don't try to memorize a ton of quotations. Aim for one or two quotations from each work or none at all if you have a lot of trouble memorizing. It's better to paraphrase than to quote badly. The graders don't want to read your thoughts on "Hamlet's soliloquy about 'being or not being.'"

Flip to Chapter 3 for guidance on preparing good notes, and see the yellow tear-out card at the front of the book for a blank note-taking form.

No shortcuts! Don't read an online or printed summary of a book rather than the book itself. It's fairly easy for an experienced English teacher — a category that includes all AP exam graders — to differentiate between canned analysis and the real thing, which arises from a reader's unique interaction with a text.

Adapting your notes to answer several question types

In his famous poem, "Thirteen Ways of Looking at a Blackbird," Wallace Stevens constantly shifts the reader's reality. One moment you're looking at the contrast between the blackbird's eye and a snowy landscape, the next you see the bird in relation to human watchers. Stevens gets a lot of mileage out of that feathered fellow because he understands that the blackbird's meaning changes, depending on how you look at it. So too with other literary works. If you prepare a novel or a play by reviewing character, plot, and theme, you're ready for any number of prompts.

William Shakespeare's *Hamlet* is a staple of high school English courses — and for good reason! Not only does it represent one of the greatest writers at the height of his powers, it also provides tons of discussion material. It's stuffed with themes! In this section, I show you how to record notes on that play (see Figure 14-1) and how to slice and dice the notes to fit many prompts.

Title: *Hamlet*

Author: Shakespeare

Date of Publication or Writing: Elizabethan England

Main Characters:
Hamlet — Prince of Denmark. About 30, returned from his studies at Wittenberg after his father's death. Resents his mother's remarriage to Claudius, Hamlet's uncle. Broods constantly. Tries to avenge his father but can't make himself act.
Gertrude — Hamlet's mother. Hamlet says she was in love with her first husband, King Hamlet. She probably doesn't know about the murder.
Claudius — murderer of King Hamlet. Feels some guilt but doesn't want to give up Gertrude and the kingdom.
Polonius — advisor to the king. Windbag. Loving father to Laertes and Ophelia. Accidentally killed by Hamlet.
Ophelia — was "dating" Hamlet and ordered to stop by her father. Allows herself to be used by her father and the king as "bait" to catch Hamlet. Goes mad and drowns.
Laertes — mad for revenge when his father dies and sister goes mad. Agrees to Claudius's plot to kill Hamlet.

Setting: The castle, Denmark

Important Plot Points:
Ghost's appearance, Hamlet pretends to be mad as he plots revenge.
Polonius tells Ophelia to stay away from Hamlet. Reports that Hamlet came to her, upset, and spoke nonsense.
Hamlet's soliloquys reveal his thoughts of suicide, his obsession with his mother's remarriage, his self-loathing stemming from his inaction.
Play-within-a-play. Claudius's guilty reaction.
Hamlet's visit to his mother, fight about Claudius, killing of Polonius. Reappearance of the ghost.
Hamlet sent to England, "rescued" by pirates.
Ophelia's mad scene. Her brother's return, her suicide. Plot to kill Hamlet.
Final duel. Death of Gertrude (poison), Laertes (exchange of swords), Claudius (Hamlet stabs him), and Hamlet (poisoned sword).

Themes and Symbols: Appearance and reality, death, the Oedipal complex, action versus intellect and emotion, role of women, role of supernatural. The skull, cosmetics, gardens, and weeds.

Important Quotations:
Seems, madam? I know not seems.
To be or not to be.
Hyperion to a satyr.
Something is rotten in the state of Denmark.

Figure 14-1:
A sample evaluation of Shakespeare's *Hamlet*.

If you've prepared _Hamlet_ with a form like the one in Figure 14-1 and have reviewed your notes, you should be ready to attack any number of prompts. In the following lists, I show you some points that you can extract to answer four different questions. (However, I don't answer the questions for you; I just get you started.)

If the prompt asks how the theme of appearance and reality relates to the work, you could mention any of the following points:

- ✔ Hamlet isn't really mad (or is he?).
- ✔ Ophelia only pretends to read a book so that Hamlet will reveal his true feelings to hidden observers.
- ✔ Claudius appears to repent when he kneels to pray but actually refuses to change his ways.
- ✔ The play contains much discussion of prostitutes who cover their faces with makeup. Similarly, the skull (death) that the gravediggers unearth is covered during life by smiles.

If the prompt asks how parallel characters or situations affect the readers' reactions, you could mention any of the following points:

- ✔ Laertes loves his father Polonius.
- ✔ Hamlet loves his father, the late king.
- ✔ Laertes rushes to vengeance, but Hamlet stalls.
- ✔ King Hamlet has a talk with his son (the two ghost appearances).
- ✔ Polonius gives Laertes advice.
- ✔ Fortinbras of Norway attacks Denmark to avenge his father's defeat and death in battle.

If the prompt asks how parent-child relationships are depicted, you could mention any of the following points:

- ✔ Hamlet idealizes his father ("Hyperion to a satyr") and displays anger toward his mother. He berates her for having sex with Claudius.
- ✔ Laertes accepts his father's advice respectfully.
- ✔ Fortinbras attempts to avenge his father's death in battle by invading Denmark.

If the prompt asks how minor characters affect your view of a major character, you could mention any of the following points:

- ✔ Ophelia reveals Hamlet's cruelty; he calls her a prostitute and frightens her. She allows herself to be used by her father and the king; when Hamlet suspects that she's deceiving him, he becomes enraged.
- ✔ Horatio, Hamlet's best friend, shows Hamlet's appreciation of sincerity and loyalty. Hamlet is natural and unforced in his conversations with Horatio. Horatio admires Hamlet and thinks Hamlet would have made a good king.

I haven't created thesis statements for these four potential essays, but you can do so easily from the information on the form and from data in your memory bank. Notice that the points for each prompt are slightly different, but each set could support a good essay.

Familiarizing Yourself with Open-Ended Essay Prompts

Creating essay prompts is one of those nerdy activities that English teachers love to do. We find interesting quotations and insert them into our questions. We ponder timeless ideas and ask students to relate them to the works that they're writing about. We even throw in things that puzzle us. The sky's the limit, because we don't have to answer the prompt. Sadly, you do. This section gives you an overview of open-ended essay prompts so the territory will be familiar on exam day. (For detailed instructions on decoding prompts, turn to Chapter 3.)

Standard elements of open-ended prompts

When you write an essay, half the battle is figuring out what the exam writer (or teacher) is asking. Unfortunately, open-ended prompts tend to be longer than passage-based prompts, making open-ended prompts not only a battle, but an uphill one. However, the basic format is simple:

> Famous person once said, "Important philosophical-sounding statement." Select a literary work illustrating "important philosophical-sounding statement." In a well-organized essay, apply "important philosophical-sounding statement" to [a specified aspect of the literary work]. Show how this aspect of the literary work contributes to the work as a whole. Select a title from the list below or choose a work of similar quality. Avoid mere plot summary.

Got the general idea? Good. Now I can dive into the specifics. Here are the standard ingredients of an open-ended essay prompt:

- ✔ **A statement about life or literature:** This statement may be a quotation from a literary critic or an author. I always picture the exam writers hunched over a computer when I see a quotation in an essay prompt. They're typing "literature," "life," "war," "peanut butter," or whatever into a search engine and then cutting and pasting the result. However, sometimes the life/lit statement is a simple sentence from the exam writers themselves. Maybe the search engine turned up nothing interesting?

    The quotation or statement is included only to start you off. The important information generally follows it. Take a look at this example, which is a product of my fevered imagination and *not* a quotation from a real person:

    > Critic Alden Birch once remarked, "Literature creates relentless and inevitable confusion." Choose a work from the list below or another work of recognized literary merit in which a character or an event creates "relentless and inevitable confusion." Discuss how this confusion contributes to the work as a whole.

    All the action is in the second sentence, which contains the assigned task. In this case, the second sentence instructs you to describe a character or an event that creates confusion.

- ✔ **A list of literary works:** On this list of works, expect to see novels and plays and an occasional book-length poem drawn from works taught in high school or college English courses. Unless your school is located on the planet Mars, you'll likely run into a couple of works that you have read in your own classes. ***Note:*** Once or twice a decade, the AP doesn't supply a list of works. If that sort of exam appears in front of you, don't panic. Just turn to your prepared works!

- ✔ **The words ". . . or a work of similar literary merit [or quality or value]" or "a work of recognized literary value":** These phrases mean that you get to pick any work that you want as long as it ranks high in the literary world. How do you know which works make the cut? Check out the earlier section "Adhering to standards of literary quality" for details.

- ✔ **The statement ". . . relates [or contributes] to the work as a whole":** This statement, which nearly always appears in some form or another in open-ended essay prompts, is about context. In fact, it's so important that I devote a whole section of this chapter to this part of the prompt. Flip to the later section "Relating the Part to the Whole" for more information.

- ✔ **The phrase "Avoid mere plot summary" or "Do not limit yourself to plot summary":** This part of the prompt represents the exam graders' defense against reading *Hamlet Lite* instead of a true literary essay on *Hamlet*. Because this statement is important enough to warrant its own sentence in an AP prompt, I comment on using, not summarizing, plot in "Detecting and Selecting Evidence" later in this chapter.

The variable elements of open-ended prompts

The ideas that exam writers want you to discuss vary enormously, but some large categories show up regularly. The open-ended essay prompt has to contain an idea that's broad enough to apply to many literary works. As the following list illustrates, the prompts address universal issues:

- ✔ **Characterization:** Good, evil, or some of both? Mad, irrational, or just eccentric? Sidekick or star?

- ✔ **Conflict:** Internal or external? What's the solution or response?

- ✔ **Genre:** Mystery, comedy, or tragedy? How do the mysterious, comic, or tragic elements affect the reader?

- ✔ **Parts of the work:** What does the setting, the opening scene or line, the climax, or the title accomplish?

- ✔ **Social norms:** Upheld or betrayed? How does an individual or a society respond to pressure?

- ✔ **Identity, culture, or memory:** What's the influence of the past on the present? On a particular character?

- ✔ **Appearance and reality:** Do appearance and reality differ? Why?

Detecting and Selecting Evidence

After you understand the prompt and have chosen a literary work to write about, you need to create a *thesis statement* — the point you're going to prove in your essay — and select evidence to support your case. Then, of course, you have to write the essay. I discuss thesis statements and general essay-writing in Chapter 3. This section concentrates on evidence.

When choosing evidence for an open-ended essay, you have to decide how to focus your energy. You have two choices:

- ✔ **You can make your coverage broad.** If you "go wide" (as they say in football), you cover a lot of ground. You may, for example, write about four characters from a novel. The downside of this approach is that you can't delve into each point you make because you have too many. As a result, this sort of essay often feels like an overview, and it can come across as shallow in the eyes of the essay grader.

✔ **You can narrow the scope of your essay.** The benefit of this approach is that you have time to analyze every subtopic in depth. For instance, you may discuss, say, two characters. Then you have time to dig into the pair, giving lots of information about each and providing many insightful comments and bits of evidence to support your assertions. This approach also has its problems, though. The grader may say, "Where's character X or protagonist Y?" And if your luck goes sour, you may end up leaving out the grader's all-time favorite character.

What's a harried — and hurried — AP essay-writer to do? Well, unfortunately, I can't give you an ironclad rule. My own preference is to keep essays narrow and deep, but I also know teachers who prefer to see a wider range. You just have to decide for yourself. However, whatever you do, take care to distribute your attention more or less evenly. Don't end up with a lopsided essay, with a long discussion of two subtopics and only two sentences about a third. In that situation, it's best to drop the third and use the extra time to polish what you've written about the other two.

As you select evidence, remember that you're writing an analytical essay, not a book report that rehashes the story. Because exam graders hate unnecessary plot summary, you face the tricky task of deciding how much to include about the plot and how much to leave out. Use these guidelines to decide:

✔ **If you choose a work from the list provided on the exam or another well-known work, assume that the exam graders know the story.** Trust me: they do. In fact, each of them has probably taught the book at one point or another.

✔ **If the work that you're writing about isn't on the list or isn't well known, you can add an introductory paragraph summarizing the plot.** One paragraph. That's it! And don't make it a ten-page paragraph, either. Simply write enough to keep the grader in the loop. Here's an example of an appropriate summary:

> Zora Neale Hurston's novel <u>Jonah's Gourd Vine</u> traces the life story of John, a character based on the author's father. Set during Reconstruction, the novel begins when John leaves his stepfather's house and takes a job at the plantation where his mother had been enslaved. John doesn't realize that his employer is his biological father. John's charisma earns him a career as a preacher and a loyal wife, Lucy. However, John's infidelity to Lucy and his lack of self knowledge lead to her death and his expulsion from his church.

See what I mean? Short but comprehensive — that's exactly what you want. Now the stage is set for whatever the prompt requires, and you can proceed as if you were writing about a more famous work.

✔ **Imagine that the exam grader doesn't agree with you.** Every time you assert a point, picture the grader's wagging finger signaling "No, you're wrong!" Your job is to argue, changing that wagging finger to a nodding head that says, "Yes, you've convinced me."

✔ **Choose bits and pieces of the story that make your point, but try to be global with your consideration of the text by showing textual knowledge of the entire work.** The most difficult aspect of writing an open-ended essay is that the text isn't available to you during the test. (No matter how good you are at stuffing books into your socks, stay on the right side of the academic law. Nobody likes a cheater!) And because you don't have the text in front of you, you can't quote much unless you have a terrific memory. Therefore, you have to bolster your case with references to events in the plot or to characters' interactions.

Suppose, for example, that you're writing about Lily, a character in Virginia Woolf's *To the Lighthouse*. Your point is that as a young woman she bows to societal pressure. Even though you can't quote the text, you can still support your point. For instance, simply refer to the dinner-party scene, in which Lily asks Mr. Tansley silly questions, just because this politeness is expected of her. You can also note that as he replies, Lily seethes with anger at her own weakness, thinking that she should have stayed silent. All she really wants to do is think about a picture that she's painting.

Not all of your supporting events must fall into the once-in-a-character's-lifetime, never-to-be-forgotten category. In fact, sometimes a small (yet important) detail sticks in your mind and is just what you need for your essay. For example, in F. Scott Fitzgerald's novel *The Great Gatsby,* Daisy looks at Jay Gatsby's shirts. Her resistance to his love begins to melt as she notes their many colors and soft cloth. This supporting point may be evidence for any number of ideas: Daisy's materialism or Gatsby's momentary success in erasing his humble origins, perhaps.

If you refer to the plot, be sure to focus on specifics and not generalizations. This bullet, for example, gives details about Lily's reaction to societal pressure in one particular situation. It isn't enough to say that she caves in. You have to show that she caves in by providing specific examples.

Relating the Part to the Whole

Nearly every open-ended essay prompt asks you to discuss the selected topic in the context of the entire work. To answer this part of the question, imagine that the topic is a piece from a jigsaw puzzle. How does it contribute to the big picture? To put it another way, how is the work changed if that puzzle piece is missing? You don't have to write a lot when responding to this part of the essay prompt. One or two ideas, each described in four or five sentences, should suffice.

When the prompt asks you to relate the topic to the work as a whole, consider how the aspect of the work you've discussed changes the way the reader perceives the novel or play or book-length poem.

Suppose, for example, a prompt asks you to discuss a clash of cultures (which was a real AP question one year). You dig into a literary work — say, Shakespeare's *Othello.* Here are a few paragraphs that you might include to discuss the culture clash:

> The title character is a Moor (a North African), a minority in white Venetian society. Even though Othello is accepted for his skills as a military leader, he isn't accepted socially. In fact, when he marries a white woman, Desdemona, her father accuses Othello of winning her love through witchcraft. Othello defends himself, explaining that he wooed Desdemona with accounts of his adventures in the army.

> Othello's identity as a military man also leads to a culture clash. He's straightforward, honest, and naive; he's also a man of action. Shortly after his marriage to Desdemona, he's sent to defend the island of Cyprus from an invasion by Turkish forces. He's ready for battle, but he's not ready for the romantic world (his relationship with Desdemona), or for the political world, as represented by Iago. Iago, one of the great villains in literature, was passed over as Othello's lieutenant. He gets his revenge through an elaborate plot to make Othello doubt Desdemona's fidelity. Iago twists and manipulates every situation.

The preceding paragraphs explain the culture clash. Now it's time to relate that clash to the work as a whole. You can say, for instance, something like this:

> Othello's straight-shooting style makes him more vulnerable to Iago's plots. The military is all about giving and receiving orders: attack, retreat, clean your rifle, and so on. Political or personal manipulation of that sort practiced by Iago is exactly the opposite. Iago never says what he means; he says what he thinks will ruin Othello's life.

Another possible part/whole relation comes from the fact that Othello's military mindset places him at a disadvantage in dealing with women and contributes to his tendency to deal with problems violently. Othello's all-male army experience didn't exactly prepare him for love and marriage. This aspect of the culture clash arouses the reader's sympathy, even after Othello murders his wife in a fit of jealous rage.

Aiming for a Bull's Eye

You can't hit an invisible target (unless you get super-lucky), so in this section I provide a sample essay written in response to an open-ended prompt. I also include an evaluation of that essay.

An open-ended essay example

The following essay was written by a student practicing for the AP exam in response to a prompt that asked how a tragic hero caused others to suffer and how that suffering affects the tragedy as a whole.

In <u>Beloved</u> by Toni Morrison, the tragic character of Sethe is the cause of much of the unhappiness in the book. She is the main catalyst for action and is portrayed as slightly scary. However, the book is also a historical novel and as such, the tragedy that surrounds her leads the reader to a greater understanding of the tragedy of slavery as a whole. The way that Sethe treats Paul D., Denver, and the community as represented by Stamp Paid shows both how she creates suffering in others and how the tragedy inherent in any story about slavery actually exists.

In her interactions with Paul D., Sethe brings him suffering, even though he loves her. Although at first Paul D. appears to be happy with Sethe, eventually he becomes unhappy because he is seduced by Beloved and feels unmanned. While Paul D. was a slave, he couldn't love anything too much, so metaphorically he put his heart in a tin can so that it wouldn't have to hurt. After Beloved and Sethe become close with him, his tin can is broken and all of the emotions that Paul D. has kept inside come out. The self-loathing that Paul D. feels because he was a slave and not fully a man are finally revealed. Through the pain that Paul D. feels from finding that Sethe, the woman he loves, killed her baby and from the way that Beloved emasculates him, we see not only the tragedy of Paul and Sethe's relationship but also the tragedy of the book as a whole in how it deals with the corruption of society and people caused by slavery.

Sethe's relationship to Denver has similar problems. The stories that Denver has been told about her childhood lead her to be scared of her mother. Since Sethe broke the rule of not loving things as a slave and she loved her children too much, she had to kill her daughter. The pain that Sethe has caused Denver shows us again just how much slavery has disturbed society. Even the scars on Sethe's back, where the schoolteacher's nephews beat her after they took her milk, have led to Sethe's corrupt love for her children. Sethe felt an incredibly strong need to give her children milk after that incident, another example of the way Sethe loved her children so much that she killed one of them. The tragedy of a child's being afraid that her mother will kill her shows just what the experience of slavery can do to family relationships.

Sethe also brings tragedy to the community at large and to Stamp Paid, the symbolic leader of the community. The way that she breaks down and murders her child ruins their vision of happiness. Stamp Paid and the community are horrified at the way Sethe has acted because she is an example of a woman following animal instincts, which is something the ex-slaves are very anxious to prove they do not follow. Sethe ruins their vision of themselves also, since they feel partly to blame for not warning her. This tragedy of misunderstanding and pride shows us just how much the African American community as a whole has lost to slavery.

All of the tragedy that happens to Sethe and that is caused by Sethe contributes to our understanding of the novel as a whole. Toni Morrison wrote a work dealing with the utter tragedy of slavery, and she succeeds in that task admirably. Each individual tragedy is a piece of the whole tragedy of the historical period the novel captures.

Evaluation of the open-ended essay example

The example essay makes many good points, though it isn't perfect. It accomplishes the task — to show how Sethe causes others to suffer and to relate that suffering to the novel as a whole. If I were grading this essay, I'd give it 7 or 8 points out of a possible 9.

Here are the good points of this essay example:

- The essay addresses the question, stating correctly that Sethe hurts Paul D., Denver, and the larger community represented by Stamp Paid.

- The essay places the individual events (Sethe's murder of her baby, Paul D.'s fears about his masculinity, Denver's traumatic childhood, and the community's flawed sense of itself) in the context of slavery and its aftermath.

- The references to the text are, for the most part, specific and clear.

- For the most part the essay is written in a mature style, with good command of language.

- The writing is grammatically correct, with proper spelling.

- The essay is reasonably well organized, with a good introduction, logical body paragraph divisions, and a fairly strong conclusion.

Here are the areas for improvement:

- The essay includes some repetitive statements.

- A few sentences are worded awkwardly.

- Though Stamp Paid is mentioned, the evidence and analysis relating to him is short. More could be said about his situation. One solution is to drop him from the essay and use the extra time to discuss Denver or Paul D. in greater depth.

- Sethe's suffering is alluded to, but her status as a tragic hero isn't supported by evidence. A couple of sentences about her beating and degradation while enslaved and her desperate murder of her baby just as the slave catchers appear should be included in the essay.

- The evaluative statement in the last paragraph could be cut. The graders don't want to know whether you like or dislike a work. They want you to analyze it!

Chapter 15

Double Trouble: Paired-Passage Essays

- -

In This Chapter

▶ Understanding paired-passage prompts

▶ Gleaning ideas from pairs of passages

▶ Examining effective structures for paired-passage essays

▶ Practicing and evaluating paired-passage essays

- -

*L*ife, especially AP life, is unfair. Consider this fact: Paired-passage questions force you to read two literary works and then compare and contrast specific elements in them. After you're finished writing, however, you get credit for only one essay. Fortunately, paired-passages are like Category 5 hurricanes: They don't appear often, but they seem to show up more and more frequently these days. Nearly all paired-passage essays on the AP English Literature and Composition exam are based on poetry. But a handful have addressed prose, and so you should be ready for those passages also. (Thus far, the exam writers haven't paired drama passages. Stay tuned, though. They could be coming around the bend.)

In this chapter, I show you the quickest, most effective way to deal with paired-passage questions on the AP exam. I also provide some sample questions and evaluation guidelines so that you're prepared if your very own AP exam contains double trouble. As a bonus, the strategies outlined in this chapter work well for the compare and contrast essays that you write for homework or tests during the school year.

Seeing Double: Paired-Passage Prompts

They look different from the other AP essay prompts, but at heart, paired-passage prompts require you to write an essay, and you already know how to tackle that task. However, paired-passage essays differ from single-work essays just enough to make your life interesting: Paired-passage prompts ask you to compare and contrast *two* works. Sometimes the prompt specifies a particular literary element, and sometimes the question is more general. (Feeling shaky about the single-work essays? Turn to Chapter 3 for essay basics. Chapter 7 zeroes in on poetry essays, and Chapter 12 focuses on prose and drama essays.)

Here are some of the most common types of paired-passage prompts:

> ✔ **Comparison of the speakers' attitudes and the poets' techniques:** For example, consider this prompt:
>
> > Read the following two poems carefully. Then, in a well-organized essay, compare the speakers' attitudes toward dreams and the techniques the poets use to convey the speakers' views.
>
> As you can see, this sample prompt focuses on the attitude of each speaker and allows you to choose the poetic devices that you want to analyze.

✔ **Significance of an image and a comparison of poetic technique:** Here's an example of this type of prompt:

> Read these poems, taking note of the significance of the color red. Then write a well-organized essay comparing and contrasting the color red in the poems, discussing such literary techniques as imagery, figurative language, and diction.

This prompt zeroes in on the color red, specifying three literary elements — imagery, figurative language, and diction — but allows you to expand beyond those literary elements.

Whenever the door is open, walk through it! Discuss imagery, figurative language, and diction, but add something else if you can. That way your essay will stand out from the crowd.

✔ **Comparison of two poems by one author and the literary elements in them:** Take a look at this example prompt:

> The following two poems by William Wordsworth were published in 1800 and 1810. In a well-organized essay, compare and contrast the two poems, taking into account the literary devices used in each.

This prompt leaves everything up to you. You get to choose the literary devices you want to mention and how much consideration to give the content.

When you're faced with a general prompt that allows you to choose what to write about, spend most of your energy and time commenting on how the poem or passage is written. The AP exam is a test of your ability to analyze literature, so content plays a secondary role while literary technique is the star.

Twice in the last 30 years, AP test takers have faced "wildcard" prompts — strange, paired-passage questions that break the mold. One wildcard, vintage 1977, displayed two poems by D.H. Lawrence and asked for an essay explaining why the second poem was better. Another wildcard prompt showed up in 1985. This time test takers were asked to compare two drafts of one prose passage, suggesting reasons for the changes and explaining the effect of the writer's revisions. Nothing like these two prompts has ever appeared again, I suspect because the graders vetoed a repeat performance.

Annotating and Gathering Ideas from Pairs

When two literary works appear on an exam, a reader's instinctive reaction is to compare and contrast one to the other. And that instinct guides you to the correct path! In fact, you should follow that instinct even if the words "compare and contrast" don't appear in the prompt. The basic technique is to zigzag between one passage or poem and the other. Here are some steps you can follow to gather your thoughts:

1. **Read both selections.**

   Don't write anything the first time through. Just read, keeping in mind what the prompt asks you to address.

2. **Read the first selection again, annotating as you read.**

   With the second selection in the back of your mind, reread the first. Underline everything in the first passage that stands out, particularly anything that seems different from the second passage. In the margin, note possible effects for each difference that you spot. (Check out Chapter 3 for more details on annotating text as you read.)

3. **Read the second selection again, annotating as you read.**

   Let the first passage be your background music as you read the second passage. Consider how key elements in this passage differ from those in the first passage; also consider how the passage would change if those key elements were removed.

4. **Create a thesis statement that responds to the prompt and takes both selections into account.**

   A thesis statement is generally confined to one sentence, but paired-passage essays sometimes call for a two-sentence thesis. In either case, start on the road to a thesis by making a statement about each passage or poem. Combine the statements if you can. If not, leave them as separate sentences.

5. **Gather supporting evidence.**

   Read the passages or poems once more, looking for significant details in each that support your thesis.

 The appearance of the words "juxtapose" or "juxtaposition" in an AP English essay sets off flutters in graders' hearts. "Juxtapose," the verb, means to place two things next to each other. "Juxtaposition" is the noun. For reasons unknown, these words make your essay sound more mature and thoughtful — but only if you use them correctly and only if you actually have something to say about the effect of the juxtaposition. In paired-passage essays, you might consider how the reader's reaction to each selection changes because of the juxtaposition of the two. The literary analysis should center on the way the pair works as a unit in the reader's mind.

Building for Two: Structuring Paired-Passage Essays

When you're writing about a pair of literary works, you resemble the parents-to-be of twins. The happy-but-terrified future mom and dad have to decide how to preserve the individual identity of each sibling and how to deal with the fact that twins naturally form a unique partnership. Similarly, you, the lucky AP test taker facing a paired-passage essay, have to divide the essay so that each literary selection gets the attention it's due without forgetting the fact that the pair is, in fact, a pair. Creating a sturdy structure to hold your ideas is the key to handling paired passages.

One size doesn't always fit all, especially on the AP exam. In the following sections, I present a couple of possible structures for paired-passage essays. Depending on the literature and prompt you must respond to, you may find one easier to use than another. You may even come up with something unique. No problem. As long as you have a logical path that the grader can walk on, you're fine.

The half-and-half approach: Dividing the essay in two

The easiest structure for a paired-passage is one that divides the essay into two large chunks. One chunk discusses the first literary selection, and the other analyzes the second. The strength of this design lies in its simplicity. You don't have to make many decisions about where each supporting point belongs, and you can practically fly through the body paragraphs.

Here's a bare bones outline of the different paragraphs in an essay written with the half-and-half approach:

Introduction: Titles and authors of both works, if known, and a thesis statement

First body paragraph: Analysis and evidence for the first passage

Second body paragraph: Analysis and evidence for the second passage

Conclusion: Statement about the pair, relating one to the other or building on what you said in the body of the essay

The conclusion to this sort of essay can make or break your score, because this paragraph is where you tie the two selections together. You have to end with a punch or your reader (who is — need I point out? — the exam grader) will feel that you honored the individuality of the selections but didn't really deal with them as a pair.

Here are a couple of good, bring-it-all-together conclusions:

> Smyth's ironic tone makes the naïveté of the speaker in Adamson's poem all the more poignant. The world-weary Smyth seems centuries older than Adamson's speaker, despite abundant imagery indicating that Smyth is relatively young. These poems illustrate that age is partly a matter of experience and one's unique reactions, not simply a matter of the calendar.

> William Tenger glorifies winter with a series of idealized metaphors and formal, almost elegiac diction, while Olivia May presents a more realistic view through choice of her detail and her natural, unforced word choices.

Notice that both of these sample conclusions make one statement about each separate selection, relating them to each other.

If you select the half-and-half structure for your essay, take care that your "twins" don't resemble Danny DeVito and Arnold Schwarzenegger in terms of height. In other words, your essay should give equal attention to each selection. If you write three pages on one selection and a quarter page on the other, your essay will be lopsided, and your score will suffer. You don't need an exact 50/50 divide, but stay as close as you can to this proportion.

The thematic approach: Sorting by ideas

With the thematic approach, you structure your essay by sorting your information according to the different ideas derived from each of the selections. The ideas, or *subtopics,* vary depending on the selections and the prompt. Each body paragraph discusses *both* selections. The advantage of this structure is that it forces you to consider the works as a pair. And by constantly moving from one work to another, you discover more about the relationship between the two as you plan the content of each body paragraph.

The thematic essay looks like this:

Introduction: Titles and authors of both works, if known, and a thesis statement

First body paragraph: Analysis of one literary element or aspect of meaning, along with evidence from each work

Second body paragraph: Analysis of a second literary element or aspect of meaning, along with evidence from each work

Additional body paragraphs: Analysis of any additional literary elements or aspects of meaning, along with evidence from each work, with as many additional paragraphs as needed

Conclusion: Final thoughts about the overall effect of each work, perhaps how they're similar and how they're different

The drawback of this approach is that you have to organize your thoughts very quickly. And if you aren't well prepared before you begin to write on the answer sheet, this structure can sink you. True, you can always tuck in one or two extra thoughts — neatly! — with a caret symbol (^). However, graders may tolerate only a few insertions and a bit of rearrangement. Simply remember that a standard element of an AP prompt is the phrase "in a well-organized essay."

The similarities-and-differences approach: Grouping like and unlike

On the second read-through of a paired-passage question, you may begin to see a pattern of similarities and differences emerging. If you'd like, you can go with the pattern and organize your essay around these two categories. The benefit of this structure is its simplicity. You probably make a same/different list automatically. Perhaps these classifications are hard-wired into the human brain!

The similarities-and-differences structure looks like this:

Introduction: Titles and authors of both works, if known, and a thesis statement

First body paragraph: Discussion of the way in which the two selections are similar, with supporting evidence from each work

Second body paragraph: Discussion of the way in which the two selections are different, with supporting evidence from each work

Conclusion: Final thoughts about the overall similarities and differences of each work, perhaps speculating about the intentions of the authors and about the effect that each work has on the reader

The pitfall of a similarities-and-differences essay is that this structure may ping-pong the grader. You may end up with sentences like "Poem A relies on imagery to create an ominous mood, as the speaker describes . . . and poem B creates the same mood through diction. . . . Poem A's speaker appreciates the spring, calling it . . . in the same way that poem B's speaker finds the season. . . ." The back and forth is inevitable with this structure, but it's a little less annoying if you make substantial statements — a couple of sentences, perhaps — about one selection before turning to the other. With a little more to chew on, the grader is less likely to experience whiplash.

Practicing Effective Compare/Contrast Essays

I'm guessing that every New Yorker is familiar with the old joke in which a tourist asks how to get to the famous concert venue, Carnegie Hall. The answer: "Practice!" That's the answer for you, too, if your destination is a good grade on the AP English exam. In this section, you have three chances to prove your brilliance. Write one, two, or all three essays, and then check your work using the evaluation guide at the end of the chapter.

Essay prompt 1

The following poems, "Civil War" by Hettie Jones and "Returning" by Abby Wender, both deal with family visits. In "Civil War," the speaker visits her sister. In "Returning," the speaker and her husband visit the husband's ancestral home in Sri Lanka. Read the poems carefully. In a well-written essay, compare and contrast each speaker's attitude and the poetic devices used to convey it.

"Civil War" by Hettie Jones (Reprinted from *Drive*, ©1998, by Hettie Jones, by permission of Hanging Loose Press)

(01) Into my sister's kitchen

light pours

       across the patio

of American dreams

(05)   outside

a bird calls

       sometimes

you can hear him

as I hear my indefatigable sister

(10)   bounding through

    her dream house

where the jungle waits

   twenty feet

   away

(15) lush impenetrable

       the bird is loud

       I have come

       into the sun

       to be with him

(20) and when I hear his long and varied

riff against the background

of air conditioners

how easy it is for me to imagine

that he is singing to me

(25)   or to my sister

       my indefatigable sister

against whose screen

lizards run

against whose heart

(30) I hold no weapon

against whose dream

I am forever

    committed

"Returning" by Abby Wender

(01) The armoire opens: I smell mildew.

It's the salt in the air," my husband says.

Hair plump as a watered bush, he paces

the house he was born in,

(05) reacquainting himself as if a part of him

had been left here,

unsuitable for the cold climate of an immigrant's life,

and so that part is stored

in the cabinet alongside his batik[1] shirts and sandals.

(10) What do I make of him?

He wraps an orange and black sarong[2] around his waist,

struts the garden. He is the son of kings.

A sari[3] halves my stride, I'm hobbled.

Baby Hamu, the servants call, as in Baby Master.

(15) I am *Suddu Hamu*, Ghost Mistress.

His feet absorb the dark polish of the old stone floors.

On the veranda, squatting like an old pelican, a palm reader trills,

"No master! Believe me, your time is good, very good. The bad time is over!"

From Galle and Kandy[4], aunties and uncles arrive

(20) with packages of tea and teardrop-shaped ashtrays

of pounded silver, each engraved *From Sri Lanka*.

"We don't smoke," I say. They nod *yes,* meaning *no.*

At 3 a.m., tripping over a servant asleep at our door,

I mumble, "Workers of the world unite!"

(25) and walk past shelves of *National Geographic,* circa 1950,

flakes of gold crumble to the floor.

My husband's reading old letters.

On the desk a typewriter sits open, no new fingerprints on its keys.

On the wall, his father stares from a black and white photo,

(30) arm raised: A son could do so much for his country.

Yes, I say, meaning *no.*

1. *Printed fabric.*
2. *A garment tied around the waist.*
3. *A traditional dress.*
4. *Locations in Sri Lanka.*

Essay prompt 2

Carefully read each of the following poems, "Sunset in the Tropics" by James Weldon
Johnson and "A London Thoroughfare. 2 A.M." by Amy Lowell. In a well-organized essay,
analyze how each poet depicts the night.

"Sunset in the Tropics" by James Weldon Johnson

(01) A silver flash from the sinking sun,

Then a shot of crimson across the sky

That, bursting, lets a thousand colors fly

And riot among the clouds; they run,

(05) Deepening in purple, flaming in gold,

Changing, and opening fold after fold,

Then fading through all of the tints of the rose into gray,

Till, taking quick fright at the coming night,

They rush out down the west,

(10) In hurried quest

Of the fleeing day.

Now above where the tardiest color flares a moment yet,

One point of light, now two, now three are set

To form the starry stairs, —

(15) And, in her fire-fly crown,

Queen Night, on velvet slippered feet, comes softly down.

"A London Thoroughfare. 2 A.M." by Amy Lowell

(01) They have watered the street,

It shines in the glare of lamps,

Cold, white lamps,

And lies

(05) Like a slow-moving river,

Barred with silver and black.

Cabs go down it,

One,

And then another.

(10) Between them I hear the shuffling of feet.

Tramps doze on the window-ledges,

Night-walkers pass along the sidewalks.

The city is squalid and sinister,

With the silver-barred street in the midst,

(15) Slow-moving,

A river leading nowhere.

Opposite my window,

The moon cuts,

Clear and round,

(20)   Through the plum-coloured night.

She cannot light the city;

It is too bright.

It has white lamps,

And glitters coldly.

(25)   I stand in the window and watch the moon.

She is thin and lustreless,

But I love her.

I know the moon,

And this is an alien city.

Essay prompt 3

In the following passages, Heywood Broun and Alexander Woollcott express their views on the origins of moral behavior. In a well-written essay, compare and contrast their views and discuss the literary devices each writer employs.

Selection 1 by Heywood Broun

(01)   The guardians of morals hold that if the spectator sees a picture of a man robbing a safe he will thereby be moved to want to rob a safe himself. In rebuttal we offer the testimony of a gentleman much wiser in the knowledge of human conduct than any censor. Writing in *The New Republic,* George Bernard Shaw advocated that hereafter public read-
(05)   ing-rooms supply their patrons only with books about evil characters. For, he argued, after reading about evil deeds our longings for wickedness are satisfied vicariously. On the other hand there is the danger that the public may read about saints and heroes and drain off its aspirations in such directions without actions.

We believe this is true. We once saw a picture about a highwayman (that was in the days
(10)   before censorship was as strict as it is now) and it convinced us that the profession would not suit us. We had not realized the amount of compulsory riding entailed. The particular highwayman whom we saw dined hurriedly, slept infrequently, and invariably had his boots on. Mostly he was being pursued and hurdling over hedges. It left us sore in every muscle to watch him. At the end of the eighth reel every bit of longing in our
(15)   soul to be a swashbuckler had abated. The man in the picture had done the adventuring for us and we could return in comfort to a peaceful existence.

Selection 2 by Alexander Woollcott

(01)   A cigarette addict who, in a spartan moment, swears off smoke, is familiar enough with the inner gnaw that robs him of his sleep and roils his dinner for days and days. His body, long habituated to the tobacco, had dutifully taken on the business of manufactur-ing its antidote. When the tobacco is abruptly removed, the body continues for a while
(05)   to turn out the antidote as usual and during that while, that antidote goes roaming angrily through the system seeking something to oppose and destroy.

(10)   A somewhat analogous condition has agitated the body politic ever since the late Fall of 1918. The passage of the Eighteenth Amendment[1] had robbed the prohibitionists of their chief excitement; then the signing of the Armistice[2] took away the glamor of public-spiritedness from all those good people who had had such a splendid time keeping an eye on their presumably treasonable neighbors. Behold, then, the Busy Body (which is in every one of us) all dressed up and nowhere to go. The itch became tremendous. The moving pictures caught it first. No wonder the American playwright is uneasy. He ought to be.

(15)   He dreads a censorship of the theatre because he suspects (not without reason) that it will be corrupt, that it will work foolishly, and that, having taken and relished an inch, it will take an ell.[3]

1. An amendment prohibiting alcoholic beverages.
2. The end of World War I.
3. A measure.

Answer Guide for Compare/Contrast Essays

All done? Great! Now it's time to see how your efforts rate on the AP grading scale. In this section, I provide a list of possible points to make about each set of literary works and a discussion of the suitable structures for each essay.

General essay requirements

Before I get to the specifics, I want to go over the basics that are important to your success. Be sure to read your essay with these general standards in mind:

- ✔ Your essay should deal with each of the two selections.
- ✔ Your essay should relate one selection to the other, comparing and contrasting content and literary technique as specified by the prompt.
- ✔ The essay should be organized in a logical way with an introduction, body, and conclusion.
- ✔ You should support your assertions with evidence (quotations or references to the texts).
- ✔ The essay should display good grammar and spelling and a mature writing style.

Potential points for essay 1

Both poems referred to by essay prompt 1 express affection and frustration, understanding and miscommunication — the staples of family life. In the following sections, I list the ways that the poems are alike and different, and then I show you the evidence that you can use to support your statements about similarities and differences. Finally, I discuss the best organizational structures for your essay.

Main points

The similarities and differences between "Civil War" and "Returning" include the following:

- ✔ Both poems express uneasiness; these aren't purely joyous visits. Neither poem expresses open anger or disagreement, however. The war is "civil" in the first poem, and the speaker in "Returning" says "yes," though she means "no."

✔ Both poems rely on description of the setting to represent the human relationship.

✔ "Civil War" is more visual; the margins echo the conflict (see Chapter 4 for more on how a poem's form can affect meaning). Wender's poem includes more details, such as the *National Geographic* magazines and the photo of the father. She uses dialogue and description to get her point across. Jones, on the other hand, is more indirect; the bird and screen represent the barrier between the sisters.

Evidence

Here's some evidence from "Civil War" that you can use as support in your essay:

✔ The speaker visits her sister, who's in her "dream house" (line 11). The allusion in line 4 to "American dreams" calls to mind picket fences, apple pie, two-car garages, and all the other staples of the traditional American image of happiness.

✔ The sister is "bounding through" (line 10) her house, but the speaker has "come / into the sun" (lines 17–18) to be with the bird. In lines 23–24, the bird symbolizes the speaker: "how easy it is for me to imagine / that he [the bird] is singing to me." "Bird" calls to mind "free as a bird," and the speaker is outside, associated with nature. But the sister is inside, where the air conditioner attempts to control nature. The house is walled off from nature; the lizard (a part of nature) runs against a screen of the house. The "jungle waits" (line 12) outside; this line links the speaker to wild and untamed nature.

✔ The title of the poem has several meanings: A "civil war" takes place within a family unit, and the sisters are part of that unit. The last lines "against whose dream / I am for- ever / committed" (lines 31–33) plainly state the speaker's opposition to her sister's aspirations. The speaker's dream is different from her sibling's "American dreams" (line 4). "Civil" also means "polite," and the speaker "hold[s] no weapon" (line 30) against her sister's heart. In other words, even though they don't agree, they don't fight either.

✔ Line 30 in the poem shows that the speaker is vulnerable to her sister, because she can't fight her sister's love; the speaker is defenseless when it comes to her sister. The fact that the sister is "indefatigable" (lines 9 and 26) reveals that she never stops trying to achieve her dream or to convince her sister of the rightness of "American dreams" (line 4).

✔ The speaker's attitude is revealed through figurative language — the symbols of the bird, lizard, jungle, and air conditioner — and allusion ("American dreams" in line 4). The margins also seesaw, visually representing the back-and-forth of a "civil war" between sisters.

If you need a refresher course on figurative language, symbolism, and allusion, flip to Chapter 4.

Here's supporting evidence for the second poem, "Returning":

✔ The poem contrasts the experiences of the husband and wife during their visit to the husband's childhood home. The husband expands; he's described as having "[h]air plump as a watered bush" (line 3). He regains "that part" (line 8) of himself that's "stored / in the cabinet alongside his batik shirts and sandals" (lines 8–9). He "struts . . . the son of kings" (line 12).

On the other hand, the speaker, his wife, contracts. She is "hobbled" (line 13) by the sari that "halves" (line 13) her stride. He becomes "Baby Master" (line 14), but she turns into a "Ghost Mistress" (line 15). In other words, he gains the power that a baby has over a family. The wife, instead, loses herself and becomes a ghost.

✔ The speaker is exasperated during the trip. She wakes "tripping over a servant asleep at our door" (line 23) and mutters a pro-workers'-rights slogan (line 24). She also states a fact to the relatives — "We don't smoke" (line 22) — but they don't really listen: "They nod *yes,* meaning *no*" (line 22). In line 10, she's also surprised at the change in her husband. She wonders, "What do I make of him?"

✔ The last few lines illustrate the speaker's urge to rebel. While her husband reads "old letters" (line 27), she interprets the photo of her father-in-law as a call to come back home — "A son could do so much for his country" (line 30) — but rejects that comment with an ironic reference to the relatives' statement: "*Yes,* I say, meaning *no*" (line 31).

✔ The imagery and choice of detail reveal the speaker's belief that her husband has gained importance during the visit. Figurative language is also important. Notice the simile in line 3 ("plump as a watered bush") and the metaphor in line 12 ("He is the son of kings").

✔ The title of the poem, "Returning," may signify that the husband is "returning" to former prominence. If he's "returning," he must be in a different state outside of the ancestral home, so the implication is that the husband-wife relationship is more balanced when they aren't in Sri Lanka.

Organization

You can structure essay 1 in several different ways. One possibility is to devote a body paragraph to each poem and then to compare and contrast the works in the conclusion.

You could also devote one body paragraph to imagery, another to figurative language, and another to allusion, margins, and dialogue. The downside of this structure is the awkwardness of that third group; the literary elements don't easily fit together. However, you can make this structure work by specifically stating that the two poems are alike in employing imagery and figurative language (body paragraphs one and two) and differ in other ways (body paragraph three). In body paragraph three, explain that Jones employs allusions and visual arrangement of lines to make her point and Wender relies more on dialogue and description.

Overall assessment

I've listed a lot of points you may make about these two wonderful poems. If you got every single one, consider applying for my job. In 40 minutes, however, it's likely that you had time to state each speaker's attitude and mention perhaps three supporting points, with evidence, from each poem. Consider yourself in great shape if you identified those six. If you analyzed only one literary technique for each poem but correctly identified the speakers' attitudes, you have probably written a fair but not great essay.

Potential points for essay 2

Setting is important in both poems. Johnson's poem is set in "the tropics," though the reader doesn't know exactly where. The time is dusk, as night arrives. Lowell's poem describes a London street at 2 a.m. In the following sections, I list the ways that the poems are alike and different, and then I show you the evidence you can use as support for your statements about those similarities and differences. Finally, I discuss the best organizational structures for your essay.

Main points

The similarities and differences between "Sunset in the Tropics" and "A London Thoroughfare. 2 A.M." include the following:

✔ Both poems depict night as separate from human experience. For instance, in Johnson's poem, night is personified and replaces the human element. In Lowell's poem, the city fights against the night.

✔ Johnson's poem sees night as powerful and victorious; Lowell's poem sees night as unable to dominate the city.

✔ Johnson relies on figurative language and color imagery; Lowell also employs figurative language, but line breaks and sound also play a role.

Evidence

Here's some evidence from "Sunset in the Tropics" that you can use as support in your essay:

✔ This poem's depiction of night is generally positive. The color imagery is beautiful and lively. However, notice the hint of danger: "silver flash" (line 1), "shot of crimson" (line 2), and colors that "riot" (line 4) and "flam[e]" (line 5). The colors also flee in "quick fright" (line 8).

✔ The colors are personified. For instance, they "run" (line 4) and "rush out" (line 9). Because they've become "human," the colors may have human emotions.

✔ The night is personified as "Queen Night" (line 16).

✔ The order in the poem suggests a royal court; the colors precede the arrival of the "Queen Night" (line 16) in "her fire-fly crown" (line 15).

✔ The poet also employs other types of figurative language that glorify night, such as metaphor. These metaphors include "starry stairs" (line 14) and "fire-fly crown" (line 15).

✔ One pattern emerges when you examine the rhyme scheme. You see *couplets* (pairs of lines), each separated by either one or two lines. The couplets suggest that the events are predictable; order exists in this poem.

Check Chapter 4 for details regarding imagery, personification, and rhyme scheme.

Here's supporting evidence for the second poem, "A London Thoroughfare. 2 A.M.":

✔ Unlike "Sunset in the Tropics," this poem is set in the city of London, where night arrived some hours earlier. Here night isn't a beautiful arrival; it's something to fight. The "cold, white lamps" (line 3) battle the darkness. "The moon cuts" (line 18) but "[s]he cannot light the city" (line 21). The city is alienated from night, which is depicted almost as an occupying power.

✔ Night in the city isn't pleasant. The street is like "a slow moving river" (line 5) that's later deemed to be "leading nowhere" (line 16). Feet are "shuffling" (line 10) and "[t]ramps doze on the window-ledges" (line 11) while prostitutes, or "Night-walkers" (line 12), pass. The speaker makes a judgment: "The city is squalid and sinister" (line 13).

✔ The speaker says, "I know the moon" (line 28), and sees the city as "alien" (line 29). Thus the speaker allies herself with nature and against the city. The implication is that the city, which represents the majority of human beings, is alienated from nature.

✔ Diction is particularly effective in this poem. The fact that the lamps are "cold" (line 3) and feet are "shuffling" (line 10) evokes old age, sickness, and death. Adding to this impression is the personification of the moon, which is "thin and lustreless" (line 26). The street is "silver-barred" (line 14), which is a description suggesting confinement.

✔ Sound patterns link ideas in this poem as well. Listen to the long "I" sounds at the beginning of the poem in "shines" (line 2), "white" (line 3), and "lies" (line 4). The moon looks beautiful, but that impression is false — a *lie*. Similarly, take note of the "S" sounds: "squalid and sinister" (line 13), "silver-barred" (line 14), "Slow" (line 15). All of these words have negative connotations.

✔ The sense of alienation is emphasized by line breaks. The cabs travel "One, / And then another" (lines 8 and 9). The break after "one" implies disconnection.

For information regarding how diction and sound can affect poetry, flip to Chapter 4.

Organization

The easiest way to organize the information in your essay is to write a paragraph about similarities and a paragraph about differences in the depiction of night, using the bullets in the "Main points" section. Another simple plan is to devote a paragraph to each poem and then sum up the differences and similarities in the conclusion.

Overall assessment

A very good AP essay correctly identifies the depiction of night in each poem. Supporting points should include at least three ideas about each poem, identifying at least two of the poetic techniques that each poet employs and relating these techniques to the way in which the night is depicted. If you had time to make only one or two points about each poem, or if you didn't address the literary techniques, your essay is only fair.

Potential points for essay 3

The selections for essay 3 are excerpted from *Noncensorship,* a volume of essays protesting censorship. In the following sections, I list the ways that the essays are alike and different, and then I show you the evidence you can use as support for your statements about those similarities and differences. Finally, I discuss the best organizational structures for your essay.

Main points

The similarities and differences between Broun's and Woollcott's passages include the following:

✔ Both writers employ irony. The writers, acclaimed American humorists, question moral crusades. In general, they mean the opposite of what they say.

✔ Broun's tone is less bitter than Woollcott's. Woollcott sees the end of World War I primarily as depriving moralists of their favorite pastime — spying on the neighbors to root out treasonable behavior. Broun's remarks about the highwayman mock his own love of ease and comfort. It's significant that Broun uses first person plural point of view (the "we" form) and that Woollcott uses third person (the "he" form). By using these points of view, Broun includes himself in the group to be mocked, but Woollcott places himself in a superior position.

Evidence

Here's supporting evidence from Broun's passage that you can use in your essay:

✔ Broun says, tongue-in-cheek, that movies should feature villains because doing so discourages immoral behavior and promotes morality. His long description of the highwayman is comical, as in this sentence: "We had not realized the amount of compulsory riding entailed" (line 11) in this profession.

✔ Broun relies on hyperbole to create humor: "At the end of the eighth reel every bit of longing in our soul to be a swashbuckler had abated" (lines 14–15).

✔ The super-formal (and at times antiquated) diction also creates humor. Broun writes of "evil deeds" (line 6), "wickedness" (line 6), and "swashbucklers" (line 15).

Here's evidence from Woollcott's passage:

✔ Woollcott sees the crusade against drinking and draft-evasion as fulfilling a need to find "something to oppose and destroy" (line 6) after being deprived. Morality, in Woollcott's view, is a hammer that disappointed or bored people use to club someone else.

✔ Woollcott's critique of moralists comes through clearly when he refers to "the Busy Body (which is in every one of us) all dressed up and nowhere to go" (lines 11–12). His irony is evident when he cites "all those good people who had had such a splendid time keeping an eye on their presumably treasonable neighbors" (lines 10–11).

✔ Woollcott alludes to several common sayings, changing the wording just a bit to make a satiric point. These sayings include "all dressed up and nowhere to go" (line 12) and "having taken and relished an inch, it will take an ell" (lines 16–17). These allusions emphasize that this "moral" stance is commonplace. And of course, Woollcott doesn't see this stance as moral at all.

Organization

This essay nicely fits a compare-and-contrast format. The introduction may cite each author and explain his view of morality, perhaps in one or two sentences. One body paragraph tackles similarities (irony, diction, and use of examples, for example) and one tackles differences (point of view and attitude). Or, you can devote one body paragraph to diction, one to tone, and one to attitude. The conclusion in either format could address point of view, as described in the earlier "Main points" section.

Overall assessment

The point that each of these passages makes is simple: Censorship is bad. (It isn't exactly a huge surprise that Broun and Woollcott feel this way. They're writers, and they don't like limitations on their freedom of expression.) Because the content is relatively simple, most AP essay writers will get it right. Therefore, the best way to stand out from the crowd is to do a good job analyzing the techniques each writer employs to make his point. Specifically, a good essay should discuss diction and tone. A fair essay hits only one of these two literary elements, and a great essay delves into irony and hyperbole.

Part V

Dress Rehearsal: Practice Exams

The 5th Wave   By Rich Tennant

"I'm always surprised at the amount of figurative language inspired by the AP English Lit. and Comp. exam."

In this part . . .

You can't hit the big time on the AP English Literature and Composition exam without a dress rehearsal. Consider this part your costume, sets, script, and director. It contains two full-length exams (and their answer chapters). Each exam takes three hours, not counting a short break between the sections. Put the dog in the yard, the cat in the kitchen, and your cell phone in the attic. Do everything you can to simulate real test conditions. Then set the timer, pick up a pencil, and go to it. After you're finished, check your answers and read the explanations. Good luck!

Answer Sheet

1. Ⓐ Ⓑ Ⓒ Ⓓ Ⓔ
2. Ⓐ Ⓑ Ⓒ Ⓓ Ⓔ
3. Ⓐ Ⓑ Ⓒ Ⓓ Ⓔ
4. Ⓐ Ⓑ Ⓒ Ⓓ Ⓔ
5. Ⓐ Ⓑ Ⓒ Ⓓ Ⓔ
6. Ⓐ Ⓑ Ⓒ Ⓓ Ⓔ
7. Ⓐ Ⓑ Ⓒ Ⓓ Ⓔ
8. Ⓐ Ⓑ Ⓒ Ⓓ Ⓔ
9. Ⓐ Ⓑ Ⓒ Ⓓ Ⓔ
10. Ⓐ Ⓑ Ⓒ Ⓓ Ⓔ
11. Ⓐ Ⓑ Ⓒ Ⓓ Ⓔ
12. Ⓐ Ⓑ Ⓒ Ⓓ Ⓔ
13. Ⓐ Ⓑ Ⓒ Ⓓ Ⓔ
14. Ⓐ Ⓑ Ⓒ Ⓓ Ⓔ
15. Ⓐ Ⓑ Ⓒ Ⓓ Ⓔ
16. Ⓐ Ⓑ Ⓒ Ⓓ Ⓔ
17. Ⓐ Ⓑ Ⓒ Ⓓ Ⓔ
18. Ⓐ Ⓑ Ⓒ Ⓓ Ⓔ
19. Ⓐ Ⓑ Ⓒ Ⓓ Ⓔ
20. Ⓐ Ⓑ Ⓒ Ⓓ Ⓔ
21. Ⓐ Ⓑ Ⓒ Ⓓ Ⓔ
22. Ⓐ Ⓑ Ⓒ Ⓓ Ⓔ
23. Ⓐ Ⓑ Ⓒ Ⓓ Ⓔ
24. Ⓐ Ⓑ Ⓒ Ⓓ Ⓔ
25. Ⓐ Ⓑ Ⓒ Ⓓ Ⓔ
26. Ⓐ Ⓑ Ⓒ Ⓓ Ⓔ
27. Ⓐ Ⓑ Ⓒ Ⓓ Ⓔ
28. Ⓐ Ⓑ Ⓒ Ⓓ Ⓔ
29. Ⓐ Ⓑ Ⓒ Ⓓ Ⓔ
30. Ⓐ Ⓑ Ⓒ Ⓓ Ⓔ

31. Ⓐ Ⓑ Ⓒ Ⓓ Ⓔ
32. Ⓐ Ⓑ Ⓒ Ⓓ Ⓔ
33. Ⓐ Ⓑ Ⓒ Ⓓ Ⓔ
34. Ⓐ Ⓑ Ⓒ Ⓓ Ⓔ
35. Ⓐ Ⓑ Ⓒ Ⓓ Ⓔ
36. Ⓐ Ⓑ Ⓒ Ⓓ Ⓔ
37. Ⓐ Ⓑ Ⓒ Ⓓ Ⓔ
38. Ⓐ Ⓑ Ⓒ Ⓓ Ⓔ
39. Ⓐ Ⓑ Ⓒ Ⓓ Ⓔ
40. Ⓐ Ⓑ Ⓒ Ⓓ Ⓔ
41. Ⓐ Ⓑ Ⓒ Ⓓ Ⓔ
42. Ⓐ Ⓑ Ⓒ Ⓓ Ⓔ
43. Ⓐ Ⓑ Ⓒ Ⓓ Ⓔ
44. Ⓐ Ⓑ Ⓒ Ⓓ Ⓔ
45. Ⓐ Ⓑ Ⓒ Ⓓ Ⓔ
46. Ⓐ Ⓑ Ⓒ Ⓓ Ⓔ
47. Ⓐ Ⓑ Ⓒ Ⓓ Ⓔ
48. Ⓐ Ⓑ Ⓒ Ⓓ Ⓔ
49. Ⓐ Ⓑ Ⓒ Ⓓ Ⓔ
50. Ⓐ Ⓑ Ⓒ Ⓓ Ⓔ
51. Ⓐ Ⓑ Ⓒ Ⓓ Ⓔ
52. Ⓐ Ⓑ Ⓒ Ⓓ Ⓔ
53. Ⓐ Ⓑ Ⓒ Ⓓ Ⓔ
54. Ⓐ Ⓑ Ⓒ Ⓓ Ⓔ
55. Ⓐ Ⓑ Ⓒ Ⓓ Ⓔ

Chapter 16

Killing Three Perfectly Innocent Hours: Practice Exam 1

$\mathcal{P}$ut the cat in the yard and turn off your phone. Lock the door and throw away the key. In this chapter, I've got you — or more accurately, the AP's got you — for three whole hours, plus one 15-minute break. Aren't you thrilled? Okay, if you're a normal person, you're not thrilled. But remember that these three hours, plus some time for checking your answers, may make the difference between a good score and a great score on the AP Literature and Composition exam. As someone in corporate America once said, "No boredom, no gain." Or something like that . . .

This test consists of two sections:

> **Section 1:** Multiple-choice — one hour. This section has a total of 55 questions and counts as 45% of the exam score.

> **Section 2:** Three essays — two hours. This section counts as 55% of the exam score.

Some last-minute instructions:

1. **Make sure that anyone who's likely to interrupt you (parental unit, friend, parole officer) has been warned that you are *not* available until the test is completed.**

2. **Place a timer or a watch on the desk or table where you're working. Set the timer for one hour, the time allotted for the multiple-choice section.**

   No timer? Write the start and end time on a piece of paper and tape the paper to the side of the clock. When wrestling a poem to the mat, you may forget exactly when you're supposed to stop.

3. **Carefully tear out the multiple-choice answer sheet that precedes this chapter. Grab a No. 2 pencil and indicate your answers by filling in the ovals that correspond to your choices.**

   You may write in the margins of the exam, annotating as you wish. However, nothing but the scoring grid and the essay forms will be graded. Answers or remarks written next to the question will receive no credit.

4. **After you've completed the multiple-choice section, get up and stretch for 15 minutes.**

5. **When your break is over, set the timer or check the clock for two hours, the time you have to write three essays. Write your essays on loose-leaf paper.**

On the real test day, you have to take the entire exam in one horrible morning or afternoon. Resist the urge to chop this sample exam into bite-sized pieces: multiple-choice on Friday night, one essay on Saturday morning, and the last two essays on Monday. You won't have the luxury of that kind of schedule when it counts! Face the AP grind as it truly is *now* so that you'll be better prepared *later*.

Section 1: Multiple-Choice

Time: 1 hour

55 questions

This section contains six selections, each of which is followed by a set of questions. Read each selection and answer the questions following it, choosing the best possible answer. Fill in the corresponding oval, being sure to darken the entire oval. Do not select more than one answer. If you erase an answer, take care to do so completely. Questions with more than one oval darkened are automatically scored as wrong. Blank answers receive no credit; one quarter of a point is deducted for each wrong answer.

Questions 1–12 are based on the following excerpt from "Lines Composed a Few Miles Above Tintern Abbey," by William Wordsworth.

(01) Five years have past; five summers, with the length
Of five long winters! And again I hear
These waters, rolling from their mountain-springs
With a soft inland murmur. — Once again
(05) Do I behold these steep and lofty cliffs,
That on a wild secluded scene impress
Thoughts of more deep seclusion; and connect
The landscape with the quiet of the sky.
The day is come when I again repose
(10) Here, under this dark sycamore, and view
These plots of cottage-ground, these orchard-tufts,
Which at this season, with their unripe fruits,
Are clad in one green hue, and lose themselves
'Mid groves and copses. Once again I see
(15) These hedge-rows, hardly hedge-rows, little lines
Of sportive wood run wild: these pastoral farms,
Green to the very door; and wreaths of smoke
Sent up, in silence, from among the trees!
With some uncertain notice, as might seem
(20) Of vagrant dwellers in the houseless woods,
Or of some Hermit's cave, where by his fire
The Hermit sits alone.
                         These beauteous forms,
Through a long absence, have not been to me
As is a landscape to a blind man's eye:
(25) But oft, in lonely rooms, and 'mid the din
Of towns and cities, I have owed to them
In hours of weariness, sensations sweet,
Felt in the blood, and felt along the heart;
And passing even into my purer mind,
(30) With tranquil restoration: — feelings too
Of unremembered pleasure, such, perhaps,
As have no slight or trivial influence
On that best portion of a good man's life,
His little, nameless, unremembered acts
(35) Of kindness and of love. . . .

1. The mood of the poem may be characterized as

   (A) playful

   (B) nostalgic

   (C) argumentative

   (D) analytical

   (E) regretful

2. All of these poetic devices appear in the poem EXCEPT

   (A) onomatopoeia

   (B) personification

   (C) metaphor

   (D) apostrophe

   (E) alliteration

3. The "unremembered pleasure" (line 31) is probably

   (A) something the speaker does not wish to recall

   (B) an action that can be described only vaguely

   (C) a scene the poet can't describe adequately

   (D) a memory that is primarily felt, not recalled literally

   (E) pleasure that the speaker does not want to explain

4. The pronoun "them" (line 26) refers to
   (A) "rooms" (line 25)
   (B) "towns and cities" (line 26)
   (C) nature
   (D) "sensations" (line 27)
   (E) "forms" (line 22)

5. The poet's attitude toward nature may best be described as
   (A) appreciative
   (B) critical
   (C) elegiac
   (D) contemptuous
   (E) dismissive

6. The poem shifts in line 22 from
   (A) melancholy to joy
   (B) first to second person viewpoint
   (C) description to interpretation
   (D) formal to informal diction
   (E) past tense to present tense

7. The Hermit referred to in lines 21–22 may be
   (A) an actual person the poet met
   (B) a symbol of the life the speaker wishes to lead
   (C) God
   (D) a character the speaker imagines
   (E) nature personified

8. In line 16, "sportive" may best be defined as
   (A) unruly
   (B) involved in organized sports
   (C) being a good sport
   (D) wild
   (E) playful

9. The poem is written in
   (A) blank verse
   (B) free verse
   (C) sonnet form
   (D) ballad form
   (E) heroic couplets

10. Which of the following are true? The effect of the repetition in lines 1–2 is to
    I.   emphasize the length of time
    II. stress the speaker's age
    III. indicate wasted time
    (A) I only
    (B) II only
    (C) III only
    (D) I and II
    (E) I and III

11. "Slight" in the context of this poem (line 32) probably means
    (A) thin
    (B) insubstantial
    (C) weak
    (D) insulting
    (E) delicate

12. With which statement would the speaker probably agree?
    (A) Cities are better than rural areas.
    (B) Past experiences cannot be recaptured.
    (C) Memories fade with time.
    (D) Homeless vagrants should be sent to the country.
    (E) Nature has a positive influence.

Go on to next page

> Questions 13–23 are based on the following excerpt from Great Expectations, *by Charles Dickens, which describes a performance of Shakespeare's* Hamlet.

(01)   On our arrival in Denmark, we found the king and queen of that country elevated in two arm-chairs on a kitchen-table, holding a Court. The whole of the Danish nobility were in attendance;
(05) consisting of a noble boy in the wash-leather boots of a gigantic ancestor, a venerable Peer with a dirty face who seemed to have risen from the people late in life, and the Danish chivalry with a comb in its hair and a pair of white silk legs, and
(10) presenting on the whole a feminine appearance. My gifted townsman stood gloomily apart, with folded arms, and I could have wished that his curls and forehead had been more probable.
    Several curious little circumstances tran-
(15) spired as the action proceeded. The late king of the country not only appeared to have been trou-bled with a cough at the time of his decease, but to have taken it with him to the tomb, and to have brought it back. The royal phantom also
(20) carried a ghostly manuscript round its trun-cheon, to which it had the appearance of occa-sionally referring, and that, too, with an air of anxiety and a tendency to lose the place of refer-ence which were suggestive of a state of mortal-
(25) ity. It was this, I conceive, which led to the Shade's being advised by the gallery to "turn over!" — a recommendation which it took extremely ill. It was likewise to be noted of this majestic spirit that whereas it always appeared
(30) with an air of having been out a long time and walked an immense distance, it perceptibly came from a closely contiguous wall. This occasioned its terrors to be received derisively. The Queen of Denmark, a very buxom lady, though no doubt
(35) historically brazen, was considered by the public to have too much brass about her; her chin being attached to her diadem by a broad band of that metal (as if she had a gorgeous toothache), her waist being encircled by another, and each of her
(40) arms by another, so that she was openly men-tioned as "the kettledrum." The noble boy in the ancestral boots, was inconsistent; representing himself, as it were in one breath, as an able seaman, a strolling actor, a grave-digger, a clergy-
(45) man, and a person of the utmost importance at a Court fencing-match, on the authority of whose practised eye and nice discrimination the finest strokes were judged. This gradually led to a want of toleration for him, and even — on his being
(50) detected in holy orders, and declining to perform the funeral service — to the general indignation taking the form of nuts. Lastly, Ophelia was a

prey to such slow musical madness, that when, in course of time, she had taken off her white muslin scarf, folded it up, and bried it, a sulky (55) man who had been long cooling his impatient nose against an iron bar in the front row of the gallery growled, "Now the baby's put to bed let's have supper!" Which, to say the least of it, was out of keeping. (60)
    Upon my unfortunate townsman all these incidents accumulated with playful effect. Whenever that undecided Prince had to ask a question or state a doubt, the public helped him out with it. As for example; on the question (65) whether 'twas nobler in the mind to suffer, some roared yes, and some no, and some inclining to both opinions said "toss up for it;" and quite a Debating Society arose. When he asked what should such fellows as he do crawling between (70) earth and heaven, he was encouraged with loud cries of "Hear, hear!" When he appeared with his stocking disordered (its disorder expressed, according to usage, by one very neat fold in the top, which I suppose to be always got up with a (75) flat iron), a conversation took place in the gallery respecting the paleness of his leg, and whether it was occasioned by the turn the ghost had given him. On his taking the recorders — very like a little black flute that had just been played in the (80) orchestra and handed out at the door — he was called upon unanimously for Rule Britannia. When he recommended the player not to saw the air thus, the sulky man said, "And don't you do it, neither; you're a deal worse than him!" (85)

13. The reader may infer that the "I" in the passage

   (A) would like to be an actor in the play

   (B) did not see the performance

   (C) is a member of the Danish court

   (D) does not understand Shakespeare

   (E) is a member of the audience

14. The best interpretation of the character "who seemed to have risen from the people late in life" (lines 7–8) is that the character

   (A) retains customs of a lower-class upbringing

   (B) woke up late

   (C) is elderly

   (D) stands throughout the scene

   (E) is a man of the people

15. The narrator's statement in lines 12–13, "I could have wished that his curls and forehead had been more probable," most likely means that

    (A) the narrator believes that curls are appropriate for the character

    (B) the actor probably has an interesting facial expression

    (C) the actor's hair and makeup are unrealistic

    (D) the narrator does not wish to change anything about the actor's appearance

    (E) makeup is essential to achieve a good theatrical performance

16. The tone of the passage may best be described as

    (A) mocking

    (B) contemptuous

    (C) nonjudgmental

    (D) ironic

    (E) appreciative

17. The passage includes all of the following EXCEPT

    (A) hyperbole

    (B) symbolism

    (C) action

    (D) dialogue

    (E) imagery

18. In the context of line 47, "nice" may be defined as

    (A) friendly

    (B) precise

    (C) good

    (D) enjoyable

    (E) admirable

19. The passage moves gradually from

    (A) irony to realism

    (B) third to first person

    (C) description to dialogue

    (D) comedy to tragedy

    (E) a description of the actors to a focus on the audience

20. The "ancestral boots" (line 42) are probably

    (A) a bequest of a noble family

    (B) valuable antiques

    (C) Danish in origin

    (D) another actor's

    (E) a cost-saving measure

21. Which of the following statements are true? The audience calls the queen "the kettle-drum" (line 41) because

    I. the actor playing the queen can't be heard over the background music

    II. the actor playing the queen is fat

    III. the queen's costume resembles the brass rings on that type of musical instrument

    (A) all of the above reasons

    (B) none of the above reasons

    (C) II and III

    (D) II only

    (E) III only

22. The audience for the play may be described by all of the following EXCEPT

    (A) involved

    (B) well educated

    (C) vocal

    (D) disorderly

    (E) argumentative

23. It may be inferred that the narrator attends the play because

    (A) he knows one of the actors

    (B) there is little else to do

    (C) he wants to write a review

    (D) he loves Shakespeare

    (E) he's an aspiring actor

Go on to next page

> Questions 24–33 are based on the following poem, entitled "Elegy Before Death," by Edna St. Vincent Millay.

(01) There will be rose and rhododendron
 When you are dead and under ground;
 Still will be heard from white syringas
 Heavy with bees, a sunny sound;

(05) Still will the tamaracks be raining
 After the rain has ceased, and still
 Will there be robins in the stubble,
 Brown sheep upon the warm green hill.

 Spring will not ail nor autumn falter;
(10) Nothing will know that you are gone,
 Saving alone some sullen plough-land
 None but yourself sets foot upon;

 Saving the may-weed and the pig-weed
 Nothing will know that you are dead,–
(15) These, and perhaps a useless wagon
 Standing beside some tumbled shed.

 Oh, there will pass with your great passing
 Little of beauty not your own,–
 Only the light from common water,
(20) Only the grace from simple stone!

24. What is the subject of the verb phrase, "will be heard," in line 3?

 (A) Still

 (B) syringas

 (C) bees

 (D) you

 (E) sound

25. The poetic device that does NOT appear in the poem is

 (A) enjambment

 (B) allusion

 (C) personification

 (D) assonance

 (E) alliteration

26. The repetition of "still" in stanzas one and two serves to do which of the following?

 I. emphasize what remains after death

 II. add to the impression of the silence of death

 III. give a feeling of finality

 (A) all of the above

 (B) none of the above

 (C) I only

 (D) II only

 (E) III only

27. The expression "your great passing" (line 17) is best interpreted as

 (A) a slight movement

 (B) success

 (C) a journey

 (D) death

 (E) decay

28. The references to plants ("rose," "rhodo-dendron," and "syringas") in the first stanza

 (A) glorify nature

 (B) imply that death is a natural part of life

 (C) portray nature as fragile

 (D) appeal to gardeners

 (E) give a sense of permanence

29. The main point of stanza four (lines 13–16) is that

 (A) "the may-weed and the pig-weed" (line 13) must be saved

 (B) no one or nothing will know you are gone

 (C) nature is uncaring

 (D) "you" lived alone

 (E) only that which is undervalued will be affected by your death

30. The word "tumbled" (line 16) in this context may best be defined as

    (A) turned head over heels

    (B) tripped

    (C) ruined

    (D) rustic

    (E) natural

31. Between the fourth and fifth stanza, the meaning of the death shifts from

    (A) unimportant to important

    (B) important to trivial

    (C) far in the future to imminent

    (D) natural to unnatural

    (E) natural to supernatural

32. The references to "common water" (line 19) and "simple stone" (line 20) imply that

    (A) water and stone have no beauty

    (B) only water and stone endure

    (C) the death will take place in a rural area

    (D) the person who will die is a peasant

    (E) the death being discussed will remove the beauty of essential elements

33. This poem may be classified as

    (A) a ballad

    (B) a dramatic monologue

    (C) an elegy

    (D) a sonnet

    (E) free verse

Go on to next page

Questions 34–43 are based on the following excerpt from The Promised Land, by Mary Antin.

(01) I was born, I have lived, and I have been made over. Is it not time to write my life's story? I am just as much out of the way as if I were dead, for I am absolutely other than the person whose (05) story I have to tell. Physical continuity with my earlier self is no disadvantage. I could speak in the third person and not feel that I was masquerading. I can analyze my subject, I can reveal everything; for *she*, and not *I*, is my real heroine. (10) My life I have still to live; her life ended when mine began.

A generation is sometimes a more satisfactory unit for the study of humanity than a lifetime; and spiritual generations are as easy to (15) demark as physical ones. Now I am the spiritual offspring of the marriage within my conscious experience of the Past and the Present. My second birth was no less a birth because there was no distinct incarnation. Surely it has hap- (20) pened before that one body served more than one spiritual organization. Nor am I disowning my father and mother of the flesh, for they were also partners in the generation of my second self; copartners with my entire line of ancestors. They (25) gave me body, so that I have eyes like my father's and hair like my mother's. The spirit also they gave me, so that I reason like my father and endure like my mother. But did they set me down in a sheltered garden, where the sun should (30) warm me, and no winter should hurt, while they fed me from their hands? No; they early let me run in the fields — perhaps because I would not be held — and eat of the wild fruits and drink of the dew. Did they teach me from books, and tell (35) me what to believe? I soon chose my own books, and built me a world of my own.

In these discriminations *I* emerged, a new being, something that had not been before. And when I discovered my own friends, and ran home (40) with them to convert my parents to a belief in their excellence, did I not begin to make my father and mother, as truly as they had ever made me? Did I not become the parent and they the children, in those relations of teacher and (45) learner? And so I can say that there has been more than one birth of myself, and I can regard my earlier self as a separate being, and make it a subject of study.

A proper autobiography is a death-bed con- (50) fession. A true man finds so much work to do that he has no time to contemplate his yesterdays; for to-day and to-morrow are here, with their impatient tasks. The world is so busy, too, that it cannot afford to study any man's unfinished work;

for the end may prove it a failure, and the world (55) needs masterpieces. Still there are circumstances by which a man is justified in pausing in the middle of his life to contemplate the years already passed. One who has completed early in life a distinct task may stop to give an account of it. One (60) who has encountered unusual adventures under vanishing conditions may pause to describe them before passing into the stable world. And perhaps he also might be given an early hearing, who, without having ventured out of the familiar paths, (65) without having achieved any signal triumph, has lived his simple life so intensely, so thoughtfully, as to have discovered in his own experience an interpretation of the universal life.

I am not yet thirty, counting in years, and I (70) am writing my life history. Under which of the above categories do I find my justification? I have not accomplished anything, I have not discovered anything, not even by accident, as Columbus discovered America. My life has been (75) unusual, but by no means unique. And this is the very core of the matter. It is because I understand my history, in its larger outlines, to be typical of many, that I consider it worth recording. My life is a concrete illustration of a multitude of statistical (80) facts. Although I have written a genuine personal memoir, I believe that its chief interest lies in the fact that it is illustrative of scores of unwritten lives. I am only one of many whose fate it has been to live a page of modern history. We are the (85) strands of the cable that binds the Old World to the New. As the ships that brought us link the shores of Europe and America, so our lives span the bitter sea of racial differences and misunderstandings. Before we came, the New World knew (90) not the Old; but since we have begun to come, the Young World has taken the Old by the hand, and the two are learning to march side by side, seeking a common destiny.

34. All of the following techniques are employed in paragraph one (lines 1–11) EXCEPT

(A) first person

(B) figurative language

(C) rhetorical question

(D) inverted sentence

(E) parallel structure

35. The writer's statement that she is "absolutely other than the person whose story I have to tell" (lines 4–5) implies that she

    (A) will be objective in her approach

    (B) is writing about a person who has died

    (C) does not know what to write about

    (D) is writing about someone else

    (E) has changed in a significant way

36. Which of the following are true? The narrator is grateful to her parents because they

    I.   gave her life

    II. helped her become the person she is

    III. sheltered her from life's hardships

    (A) all of the above

    (B) none of the above

    (C) I and II

    (D) II and III

    (E) I and III

37. To "eat of the wild fruits and drink of the dew" (lines 33–34) most likely symbolizes

    (A) a total lack of family structure

    (B) a challenge to society's rules

    (C) an inadequate diet

    (D) exploration without supervision and restriction

    (E) poverty

38. In the context of line 37, "discriminations" means

    (A) choices

    (B) prejudices

    (C) unjustices

    (D) perceptions

    (E) differences

39. According to the writer, which of the following is true?

    (A) Her parents should have been stricter.

    (B) She regrets not waiting until she was older to write a proper autobiography.

    (C) She has accomplished great things in her lifetime.

    (D) She had as much influence on her parents as her parents did on her.

    (E) She is completely different from her parents.

40. The shift between paragraphs three and four may be characterized as

    (A) metaphorical to literal

    (B) reminiscence to speculation

    (C) theoretical to concrete

    (D) personal to universal

    (E) general to specific

41. The pronoun "many" in line 79 refers to

    (A) "facts" (line 81)

    (B) "outlines" (line 78)

    (C) the events of the author's life

    (D) all who write autobiographies

    (E) histories

42. The "strands of the cable" (line 86) is an example of

    (A) a simile

    (B) a metaphor

    (C) a symbol

    (D) personification

    (E) hyperbole

43. The author's purpose in this passage is to

    (A) justify the writing of her autobiography

    (B) illustrate how her life is typical of many other lives

    (C) explore the ways in which children mature

    (D) explain why people write about their lives

    (E) make the reader aware that the Old and New Worlds are connected

Go on to next page ➡

Questions 44–50 are based on the following poem called "Words," by Hettie Jones (reprinted from Drive, ©1998, by Hettie Jones, by permission of Hanging Loose Press)

Words

(01)   are keys
     or stanchions
          or stones

     I give you my word
(05) You pocket it
     and keep the change

     Here is a word on
     the tip of my tongue: love

     I hold it close
(10) though it dreams of leaving

44. Which of the following poetic techniques is NOT used in this poem?

(A) personification

(B) alliteration

(C) metaphor

(D) onomatopoeia

(E) enjambment

45. The scarcity of punctuation in this poem

(A) implies that words flow without meaning

(B) forces the reader to read the poem with his or her own pauses

(C) implies that all the statements about "words" in the poem are related

(D) implies that the speaker is uninhibited

(E) removes all barriers for the reader

46. To "keep the change" (line 6)

(A) refers only to coins

(B) implies that the listener will not "change" after receiving "my word" (line 4)

(C) means that the speaker is reluctant to make a promise

(D) states that the speaker owes money to "you" (line 5)

(E) reveals that the listener will be affected when given "my word" (line 4)

47. In line 9, the pronoun "it" most likely refers to

(A) love

(B) one of the "keys" (line 1)

(C) the "tongue" (line 8)

(D) one of the "stones" (line 3)

(E) the person being addressed ("you" in line 5)

48. With which statement would the speaker probably agree?

I. Words may reveal mysteries.

II. Words may confine as well as liberate.

III. Words may be a burden.

(A) I only

(B) II only

(C) III only

(D) I, II, and III

(E) None of the statements

49. The phrase "dreams of leaving" in line 10 may be interpreted as

(A) a yearning for escape

(B) the realization that love is impossible to define

(C) the speaker's desire to say that he or she is in love

(D) the inability of the poet to communicate

(E) the poet's wish to declare love

50. Lines 3 and 4 may be characterized as a shift from

(A) literal to interpretive

(B) conflict to resolution

(C) definition to situation

(D) analysis to argument

(E) metaphor to simile

Questions 51–55 are based on the following poem entitled "Mother Night," by James Weldon Johnson.

(01) Eternities before the first-born day,
Or ere the first sun fledged his wings of flame,
Calm Night, the everlasting and the same,
A brooding mother over chaos lay.

(05) And whirling suns shall blaze and then decay,
Shall run their fiery courses and then claim
The haven of the darkness whence they came;
Back to Nirvanic peace shall grope their way.

So when my feeble sun of life burns out,
(10) And sounded is the hour for my long sleep,
I shall, full weary of the feverish light,
Welcome the darkness without fear or doubt,
And heavy-lidded, I shall softly creep
Into the quiet bosom of the Night.

51. What is personified in this poem?

(A) wings

(B) night

(C) light

(D) darkness

(E) fear

52. The form of this poem is

(A) an elegy

(B) a haiku

(C) a ballad

(D) an ode

(E) a sonnet

53. Line 9 may be described as a shift from

(A) the universal to the individual

(B) figurative to literal language

(C) pessimism to optimism

(D) formal to informal diction

(E) auditory to visual imagery

54. The speaker's attitude toward death is

(A) ecstatic

(B) joyful

(C) apprehensive

(D) dread

(E) welcoming

55. With which statement would the speaker in "Mother Night" most likely agree?

(A) Death is unnatural.

(B) The death of a sun is more important than the death of an individual person.

(C) Death is similar to a peaceful sleep.

(D) The world will end in a blaze of fire.

(E) Night is the calmest time of the day.

STOP DO NOT TURN THE PAGE UNTIL TOLD TO DO SO.
DO NOT RETURN TO A PREVIOUS TEST.

Section 2: Essays

Time: 2 hours

3 essays

Two of the three essays in this section are based on a literature selection supplied here; the other is based on a literary work of your own choice. You may annotate the selections in this booklet, but only what is written on your loose-leaf paper will be graded.

Essay 1

The following passage is excerpted from George Bernard Shaw's play *Major Barbara*. In a well-developed essay, discuss how Shaw establishes the family relationships and conflicts in this, the opening scene between Lady Britomart and her son Stephen.

Suggested time you should devote to this essay: 40 minutes.

(01) STEPHEN. What's the matter?
LADY BRITOMART. Presently, Stephen.
[Stephen submissively walks to the settee and sits down. He takes up *The Speaker*.]
LADY BRITOMART. Don't begin to read, Stephen. I shall require all your attention.
(05) STEPHEN. It was only while I was waiting —
LADY BRITOMART. Don't make excuses, Stephen. [He puts down *The Speaker*.] Now! [She
    finishes her writing; rises; and comes to the settee.] I have not kept you waiting very long,
I think.
STEPHEN. Not at all, mother.
(10) LADY BRITOMART. Bring me my cushion. [He takes the cushion from the chair at the desk and
    arranges it for her as she sits down on the settee.] Sit down. [He sits down and fingers his tie
    nervously.] Don't fiddle with your tie, Stephen: there is nothing the matter with it.
STEPHEN. I beg your pardon. [He fiddles with his watch chain instead.]
LADY BRITOMART. Now are you attending to me, Stephen?
(15) STEPHEN. Of course, mother.
LADY BRITOMART. No: it's not of course. I want something much more than your
    everyday matter-of-course attention. I am going to speak to you very seriously, Stephen. I
    wish you would let that chain alone.
STEPHEN [hastily relinquishing the chain]. Have I done anything to annoy you, mother? If so,
(20)   it was quite unintentional.
LADY BRITOMART [astonished]. Nonsense! [with some remorse] My poor boy, did you think
    I was angry with you?
STEPHEN. What is it, then, mother? You are making me very uneasy.
LADY BRITOMART [squaring herself at him rather aggressively]. Stephen: may I ask how
(25)   soon you intend to realize that you are a grown-up man, and that I am only a woman?
STEPHEN [amazed]. Only a —
LADY BRITOMART. Don't repeat my words, please: It is a most aggravating habit. You
    must learn to face life seriously, Stephen. I really cannot bear the whole burden
    of our family affairs any longer. You must advise me: you must assume the
(30)   responsibility.

STEPHEN. I!

LADY BRITOMART. Yes, you, of course. You were 24 last June. You've been at Harrow and Cambridge. You've been to India and Japan. You must know a lot of things now; unless you have wasted your time most scandalously. Well, advise me.

(35) STEPHEN [much perplexed]. You know I have never interfered in the household —

LADY BRITOMART. No: I should think not. I don't want you to order the dinner.

STEPHEN. I mean in our family affairs.

LADY BRITOMART. Well, you must interfere now; for they are getting quite beyond me.

STEPHEN [troubled]. I have thought sometimes that perhaps I ought; but really, mother, I know
(40) so little about them; and what I do know is so painful — it is so impossible to mention some things to you — [he stops, ashamed].

LADY BRITOMART. I suppose you mean your father.

STEPHEN [almost inaudibly]. Yes.

LADY BRITOMART. My dear: we can't go on all our lives not mentioning him. Of course
(45) you were quite right not to open the subject until I asked you to; but you are old enough now to be taken into my confidence, and to help me to deal with him about the girls.

Essay 2

Following these instructions are two poems, "Success," by Emily Dickinson and "Not They Who Soar," by Paul Laurence Dunbar. Read both poems carefully. Then, in a well-organized essay, discuss the attitude of each poet to success and the techniques the poet employs to convey that attitude.

Suggested time you should devote to this essay: 40 minutes.

Success

(01) Success is counted sweetest
By those who ne'er succeed.
To comprehend a nectar
Requires sorest need.

(05) Not one of all the purple host
Who took the flag to-day
Can tell the definition,
So clear, of victory,

As he, defeated, dying,
(10) On whose forbidden ear
The distant strains of triumph
Break, agonized and clear!

Not They Who Soar

Not they who soar, but they who plod (01)
Their rugged way, unhelped, to God
Are heroes; they who higher fare,
And flying, fan the upper air,
Miss all the toil that hugs the sod. (05)
'Tis they whose backs have felt the rod,
Whose feet have pressed the path unshod,
May smile upon defeated care,
Not they who soar.
High up there are no thorns to prod, (10)
Nor boulders lurking 'neath the clod
To turn the keenness of the share,
For flight is ever free and rare;
But heroes they the soil who've trod,
Not they who soar! (15)

Go on to next page

Essay 3

An author frequently develops a character by showing the character in conflict with or in contrast to another character. In a well-developed essay, discuss two characters from a literary work and explain how one helps to define the other. Do not limit your comments to plot summary. You may choose a work from the following list or discuss another work of comparable literary merit.

Suggested time you should devote to this essay: 40 minutes.

Anna Christie	*Lord of the Flies*
Beloved	*Macbeth*
David Copperfield	*Mrs. Dalloway*
Death of a Salesman	*Oedipus Rex*
A Doll's House	*Of Mice and Men*
Emma	*Obasan*
Ethan Frome	*The Piano Lesson*
Fences	*Tess of the D'Urbervilles*
Hamlet	*Their Eyes Were Watching God*
The Hours	*Things Fall Apart*
The House of Seven Gables	*White Noise*

STOP DO NOT TURN THE PAGE UNTIL TOLD TO DO SO.
DO NOT RETURN TO A PREVIOUS TEST.

Chapter 17

The Moment of Truth: Scoring Practice Exam 1

*E*verything's filled in and correct on your Practice Exam 1, right? Good. Close the book and pull out the scuba gear. Take a swim and refresh your mind. Now you're ready to read the answers and explanations for Practice Exam 1.

Resist the temptation to cut corners when you check your answers. Read all the explanations, even for the questions that you answered correctly. I've tucked some great information into this chapter that will help you with the real AP exam.

First go through the exam, marking the multiple choice questions you answered wrong. Once you've scored (stop snickering — I'm talking about the multiple-choice questions), use the formula at the end of this chapter to convert your raw score into an AP grade. Take a good look at the multiple-choice questions that you answered wrong. See if you can figure out what types of questions trip you up (inference, vocabulary, tone, or literary terminology, for example). Then go back to Parts II or III for extra practice in those areas. Next, read the instructions for evaluating AP essays, and take a look at the sample answers and scores. Now grade your own.

After you have a score for the multiple-choice section as well as for each of the three essays, enter the scores on the conversion chart in the last section of this chapter to get your final AP exam score.

Almost Like Drawing Lines in the Sand: Scoring the Multiple-Choice Questions

This section has 55 questions. Check your answers, tallying the total you got right and the total you got wrong (ignore the ones you left blank), and follow the steps for calculating your multiple-choice score at the end of this section. (You should of course read the answer and explanation for anything you left blank.) Then record your multiple-choice score in the section "Putting It All Together: Calculating Your Composite Score" at the end of this chapter.

Individual answers

1. **(B).** Check out the meaning and the language of the poem (the *diction*) to figure out the tone. The scene is "wild" (line 16) and the speaker refers to "deep seclusion" (line 7). Not exactly Friday night at the local bowling alley, so choice (A) bites the dust. Nor is the speaker making a case against a vacation at Disneyland in favor of a camping trip; therefore, no opposing point of view leads you to choice (C). Choice (D) is out because even though the speaker is

thinking about quality of life, no detached, analytical point of view emerges. What's left? Nostalgic and regretful. The speaker tells you in lines 27–28 that "sensations sweet" have been "felt in the blood." Regretful is now out the door. Nostalgic, however, fits nicely with the looking-back feel of the opening lines, "Five years have past . . . five long winters . . ." (lines 1–2).

Note: This excerpt from William Wordsworth's poem "Tintern Abbey" is officially (and long-windedly) called "Composed a Few Miles Above Tintern Abbey, on Revisiting the Banks of the Wye During a Tour." You don't have to know the poet, the poem, or the artistic period during which the poem was written (Romanticism) to answer an AP question. All the evidence you need is in the poem.

2. **(D).** Here you're looking for something that isn't in the poem, and that something is apostrophe. In grammar, an apostrophe is the little hook that shows possession or fills in for missing letters. In poetry, however, *apostrophe* indicates words directed at someone who isn't in the poem ("O, Georgina, why did you dump me?") or to an idea ("Loyalty, you never met Georgina!"). Apostrophe, when used for an idea, overlaps with another poetic device, personification, when a nonhuman takes on human qualities. However, choice (D) wins out over (B) because although the "plots of cottage-ground" (line 11) are "clad" (line 13) or dressed, as people are dressed, the plots aren't spoken to directly. Hence you have personification but *not* apostrophe.

To find the correct answer, you can also eliminate the two sound choices, (A) and (E). The "murmur" in line 4 gives you onomatopoeia, the term for a word that sounds like its meaning, and "little lines" (line 15) is one of many instances in the poem of *alliteration,* or repetition of consonant sounds. *Metaphor,* a description created when one thing is equated with another, appears in line 15 when the "hedge-rows" are called "little lines."

3. **(D).** Lines 28–29 refer to the speaker's feelings. The feelings are "unremembered," implying that the literal memories are absent. Choices (A) and (E) are out because nowhere does the poem mention the willingness to remember or explain. Choices (B) and (C) are close, but because neither mentions feelings, choice (D) is best.

4. **(E).** The syntax in the second stanza begins with a statement, that the "beauteous forms" (line 22) haven't been away from the speaker, as a landscape may be to "a blind man's eye" (line 24). The speaker has felt "sensations sweet" (line 27) because of the memory of those forms. The long introductory statement in lines 25–26 ("But oft, in lonely rooms, and 'mid the din / Of towns and cities") simply clues you in to the time and place but tells you nothing about "them." Choice (C), nature, is too general.

5. **(A).** You can dump choices (B), (D), and (E) because the nature described in the poem is ideal. You're not going to swat a fly or step into a patch of poison ivy in this poem. Instead, you're watching "orchard-tufts" (line 11) and hearing "the quiet of the sky" (line 8). No criticism anywhere! And choice (C) is out because an elegy memorializes something dead and gone — not the case in this poem.

6. **(C).** Check out the first stanza. The whole thing takes you into a description of nature, minus the mosquitoes that always seem to find me whenever I leave Manhattan. The second stanza hits a high note: What the speaker saw in the natural setting helps when "weariness" (line 27) hits in "lonely rooms" (line 25) in the noise ("din," line 25) of urban areas. Furthermore, nature influences the "best portion of a good man's life" (line 33). The shift is clearly from description to interpretation. Choice (A) is out because the first stanza isn't melancholy, and you can dump choice (B) because the whole poem is in first person. The diction doesn't shift, and the past and present tenses appear in both stanzas.

7. **(D).** The setting of the first stanza is a "wild secluded scene" (line 6). So who lives there? The speaker mentions the possibility of "some Hermit's cave" (line 21) where the imagined character of the Hermit "sits alone" (line 22). Backtrack to the verb in this sentence ("might seem" in line 19) and choice (D) becomes the best choice. Choice (A) fails because of that verb, "seems," and because you have no way of knowing anything about the poet's experience. Choice (C) is out because the poet says nothing about God, and choice (E) is eliminated because the hermit is *in* nature, not a stand-in for nature. The most difficult answer to

eliminate is choice (B). The speaker clearly admires the rural setting and credits it with improving human nature, but making the Hermit a symbol of the speaker's desire is stretching the point a little too far.

8. **(E).** Leave baseball bats and good sportsmanship alone here; in other words, drop choices (B) and (C). Choices (A) and (D) are tempting, because the "sportive wood" (line 16) does "run wild" (line 16). But if you choose (A) or (D), you're saying that the "wild wood runs wild." Poets do repeat themselves at times, but in this case, "playful" gives a sense of child-like innocence that's more than justified by the idealized natural setting the poet presents.

9. **(A).** *Blank verse* isn't, as its name implies, a series of empty spaces. Rather it's the form of unrhymed poetry that has ten syllables per line in an unstressed-stressed pattern known as *iambic pentameter*. Here are the reasons why choices (B) through (E) don't make the grade: *Free verse* lacks regular rhythm, and this poem has ten syllables per line. A sonnet has 14 lines and all sorts of other features, including snow tires, which this poem doesn't have. (Check out Chapter 4 if you want to know the characteristics of a sonnet.) *Ballads* have rhyme, and *heroic couplets* are rhymed pairs of iambic pentameter lines. Because this poem isn't rhymed, you can immediately rule out choices (D) and (E).

10. **(A).** Repetition always emphasizes an idea. The words "length" (line 1) and "long" (line 2) add to the emphasis and also steer you toward statement I. How do you know how old the speaker is? You don't, so drop statement II. Statement III is tempting, but wrong because there's no indication of what the speaker has been doing in those five years that may have caused regret or frustration about lost time. So you're left with (A) as the best answer.

11. **(B).** All five answers are definitions of "slight." In context, however, the word means insubstantial or "unimportant." The word "trivial" (line 32) is a clue; you're looking for a synonym. Something "trivial" has little substance and is therefore "insubstantial."

12. **(E).** The idealized natural setting rules out choice (A). The speaker *does* remember the past and even reexperiences it in line 2 ("And again I hear . . ."). Therefore, choices (B) and (C) are out. The poem refers to "vagrant dwellers in the houseless woods" (line 20) only to make a point about the isolation of the area, not to press a social agenda.

13. **(E).** The "I" in the passage can be identified as the lucky ticket holder by the narrator's close observation of the actors' performances. Choice (B) is a dud for exactly that reason. After all, no one could quote the audience (line 26) without having attended the performance. The Danish Court is clearly *in* the play, not *at* the play, so (C) bites the dust. The justified criticism reveals that the narrator does understand Shakespeare and how the play should (and should not) be performed. That leaves (A), but because the narrator says nothing about wanting a role, (A) isn't a good choice.

14. **(A).** Those born into the upper class, a category that includes Peers (nobles), aren't likely to have dirty faces unless they've just hopped off a polo pony after a particularly muddy afternoon. "Risen from the people" (lines 7–8) means that the character gained nobility, instead of being born in the right place at the right time. The other choices aren't supported by the passage, though I'm always willing to vote for a man (or a woman) "of the people."

15. **(C).** I'm not sure what this actor did to his hair and face, but the narrator sees the effect as unnatural (not "probable") and wishes that the "curls and forehead" were more realistic ("probable"). The unusual verbs in this sentence (lines 11–13) may have fooled you; the second ("could have wished") is a way of toning down the narrator's criticism, and the third ("had been") expresses a condition that's contrary to fact. Three answers — (A), (B), and (D) — are wrong because they say the opposite, that the hair and forehead are good. Choice (E) is far too general and isn't supported in the passage.

16. **(A).** Process of elimination helps you with this question. Choices (C) and (E) aren't in the running because the narrator doesn't like the performance. Choice (D) is out because the passage doesn't present you with a disconnect. (With irony you're expecting one thing and the opposite happens, such as when a letter carrier bites a dog.) Choice (B) is a possibility, but the gentle criticisms of the narrator ("a noble boy in the wash-leather boots of a gigantic ancestor," for example) make (A) the better answer.

17. **(B).** To succeed here you need to know some literary terms. You know that you're in the territory of *symbolism* when something in the story represents more than itself. *Hyperbole* is exaggeration, as in "I spent a million hours studying for this dumb test." Lines 3–4 claim that "the whole of Danish nobility were in attendance," which is clearly an overstatement. In this passage, several things happen, including the spectators' debate on Hamlet's famous question, "To be or not to be." Choice (C) is voted off the island. *Dialogue* quotes what people say, as in lines 58–59 ("Now the baby's put to bed let's have supper!"). *Imagery* appeals to the senses. When authors describe information that you pick up through the senses (sight, hearing, touch, and so on), they're using imagery. This passage is filled with such details.

18. **(B).** A favorite trick of those who write the AP English exam is to ask for the meaning of a word in context and then supply lots of other legitimate meanings of the same word as camouflage. This question is a great example of this type of trickery. Everyone knows that "nice" (line 47) may mean "friendly" ("she's nice because she didn't tell the teacher that I ate her homework") or "good," "enjoyable," or "admirable" ("nice to hear about your nuclear fusion experiment"). However, few people these days know that "nice" may also mean "neat or precise," exactly the definition called for in this passage.

19. **(E).** The first paragraph of the passage describes the people on stage. The second includes details about the actors, such as the late king's cough (line 17), and comments about the audience, such as the fact that they threw nuts at the stage (line 52). (These must have been the same people who saw the latest James Bond movie with me.) The last paragraph refers to one actor, but the concentration is on the audience's reaction to his performance.

20. **(E).** This production relies on "two arm-chairs on a kitchen-table" (lines 2–3) to represent the thrones of the King and Queen of Denmark. Not exactly Hollywood or even Indie-film quality! Go for (E), the cheapest answer, and stay away from (A) and (B) because they suggest good financing. The boots appear to have belonged to an "ancestor" (line 6), so (E) wins out over (D).

21. **(C).** The queen is described as "a very buxom lady" (line 34), indicating that the actor shops in the XXL department. The broad metal bands of the queen's costume also appear in the passage (lines 37–39) and are directly linked to the musical instrument. True, music shows up in line 82, but it's not directly related to the queen. The best answer is (C), which selects statements II and III.

22. **(B).** The fact that the audience obviously isn't very polite knocks out choice (D). Because they're throwing nuts at the stage and yelling at the actors, you can eliminate choices (C) and (D). They're debating with each other and with Hamlet, so there goes choice (E). Granted, they are certainly involved — referring to choice (A). The one thing the audience can't be called is well educated, as witnessed by their speech in lines 84–85 ("And don't you do it, neither.")

23. **(A).** The narrator refers to "my gifted townsman" (line 11) and "my unfortunate townsman" (line 61), so (A) is your best choice. No evidence for the other answers appears in the passage.

24. **(E).** Grammarians can have fun with this one (if they ever actually have any fun). They get the correct answer by asking, "What or who will be heard?" The answer: "Sound" will be heard. Yes, the subject here is after the verb — not the usual order of an English sentence, but poets (who definitely have fun) like to play around with word order.

25. **(B).** All of the devices show up to the party except *allusion,* which is a reference to a work of art, popular culture, or history that's outside the poem. See Chapter 4 for more on allusion. *Enjambment,* running lines of poetry together without punctuation, occurs at the end of lines 1 and 3, among many other spots. *Personification,* giving human qualities to a nonhuman, shows up in the third stanza when "Spring will not ail nor autumn falter" (line 9). *Assonance* is the repetition of vowel sounds ("S<u>a</u>ving the m<u>a</u>y-weed" in line 13, for example). *Alliteration* is the repetition of consonants ("<u>r</u>ose and <u>r</u>hododendron" in line 1).

26. **(A).** The word "still" in this poem means, in a literal sense, remaining or continuing. But "still" also means "silent," and death is the ultimate silence. Finally, "still" means "not moving," again a characteristic of death. The poem is about death, so all three meanings apply. Don't you love poetry? One little word does so much work!

27. **(D).** The whole poem — a real jolly experience, isn't it? — deals with death. The poem addresses someone ("you" in line 2) and, in line 17, contemplates "your" death. Yup. Real jolly.

28. **(B).** The poem deals with what happens "when you are dead" (line 2). Placing natural images before and after those words emphasizes the naturalness of death. Choice (A) is out because the plants are simply mentioned, not glorified. This fact also rules out choice (D), because gardeners would want to hear something about how beautiful the flowers are. Choice (C) is out because although plants are, by definition, fragile, the poem states that the "rose and rhododendron" will still be around. (Clearly this poet hasn't seen my house-plants!) Choice (E) is out for the opposite reason: True, the plants endure, but their names surround a statement of loss, so a sense of permanence isn't what the poet is going for here.

29. **(E).** The fourth stanza says that when you're outta here, only weeds, a "useless wagon" (line 15), and a ruined shed will know. What do these items have in common? They're all undervalued. This stanza isn't about ecology — choice (A) — or personal problems — choice (D). The stanza contradicts (B) and (C) because the weeds *will* know you're gone, and if they know, nature is somehow affected by your death, so "uncaring" is wrong.

30. **(C).** The shed has "tumbled," meaning that it's in ruins. Choices (A) and (B) are alternate meanings of "tumbled," but in this context those definitions don't fit. Choices (D) and (E) make sense in the context of the poem, but unfortunately "rustic" and "natural" aren't definitions of "tumbled."

31. **(A).** The first four stanzas set up a number of situations in which the death being discussed sounds like no big deal — it will still rain, the roses will still bloom, and only some weeds will notice. Then whammo, the fifth stanza hits with the knockout punch: The death will take "little of beauty" (line 18) away except "your own" (line 18), just "the light from common water" (line 19) and the "grace from simple stone" (line 20). These references are to pretty important stuff. After all, no one can live without water, and stone makes up the earth itself. Both of these are natural, so stay away from choices (D) and (E). And time, or choice (C), isn't a factor.

32. **(E).** To answer this question you have to untangle the sentence in the last stanza. To state the meaning simply: Little will pass when you die except the beauty of light from "common water" (line 19) and "the grace from simple stone" (line 20). Water and stone, as explained in the preceding question, are essential elements.

33. **(C).** Edna St. Vincent Millay, the author of this poem, called it "Elegy Before Death." An *elegy* is a lament for the dead, which this poem clearly is, even though the death hasn't occurred yet. A *ballad* has short stanzas with regular rhythm and rhyme, but a ballad needs a story, and this poem doesn't have one. A *dramatic monologue* presents a character — not the case here. *Sonnets* have 14 lines and follow all sorts of strange rules — also not true of this poem. *Free verse* has no regular pattern of rhythm and rhyme, and this poem does.

34. **(B).** This question gives you another chance to show off your knowledge of the fancy terms English teachers (and AP exam writers) love. *Figurative language* departs from what's real or literal ("Helena was barefoot") and moves into interpretation territory ("Helena's feet wore their birth shoes"). The first paragraph stays on the literal level, with straightforward statements about the narrator. *First person* is the "I" voice, as in "I was born" (line 1). A *rhetorical question,* one that no one is supposed to answer, shows up in line 2 ("Is it not time to write my life's story?"). A sentence with *inverted structure* flips the usual subject-verb-object order, as in "My life I have still to live" (line 10). *Parallel structure* presents a series of sentences or clauses with a repeated pattern. The first sentence in this passage ("I was born, I have lived, and I have been made over") is an example of parallel structure.

35. **(E).** The second sentence makes it clear that you're getting "my life's story" (line 2), so choices (B) and (D) don't make the cut. Nor does choice (C), because the subject — the author's life — is given. Choice (A) is a good one because the writer says she could speak "in the third person" (lines 6–7), *about* the subject instead of *as* the subject, implying some degree of objectivity. However, the winner is choice (E) because "her life ended when mine began" (line 10–11), indicating that the writer has changed totally.

36. **(C).** The writer says her parents "gave me body" (line 25), a much more positive statement than the I-didn't-ask-to-be-born statement kids sometimes scream when their parental units are being particularly annoying. Therefore, statement I is correct. The writer also claims that her parents were "partners in the generation of my second self" (line 23), so statement II stays in the game as well. Statement III is a dud, however, because lines 28–29 declare that they didn't set her down "in a sheltered garden."

37. **(D).** Lines 34–37 show that the writer was given a great deal of freedom to explore and choose her own path. Choice (A) isn't supported by the passage; the writer may have had more freedom than the kid whose parents sign up for a GPS tracking system, but a family structure, even an unconventional one, may still exist. Similarly, you can't assume that the writer is challenging society. In fact, the "wild fruit" line implies that she's ignoring society, because "wild" is associated with untamed and uncivilized territory. Diet and poverty, choices (C) and (E), are literal readings, and a symbol extends way beyond the literal into imagination territory.

38. **(A).** At the end of the second paragraph, the narrator claims to have "built me a world of my own" (line 36) after choosing "her own books" (line 35). In other contexts, "discriminations" may refer to prejudices, injustices, perceptions, and differences. Here "choices" fits best.

39. **(D).** In lines 43–45, the narrator asks, "Did I not become the parent and they the children, in those relations of teacher and learner?" This is a *rhetorical question,* one that has an implied answer embedded within it, as in "Do you have time to take out the garbage?" In both cases, *yes* is the only possible reply. Rather than criticizing her parents (choice A), the narrator makes several positive statements, such as "The spirit also they gave me" (lines 26–27). The same line rules out choice (E). Choice (B) bites the dust because the fifth paragraph (lines 70–94) justifies writing an autobiography before the major part of one's life is over. The same paragraph also declares that the narrator hasn't done anything particularly remarkable, so you can cross out choice (C).

40. **(D).** In the third paragraph, the author speaks almost exclusively about herself. In the fourth paragraph, the author considers what constitutes a "proper autobiography" (line 49), a much more universal concept. Incidentally, the author is a woman (Mary Antin, who wrote about her life as an immigrant in the early 20th century). True to the customs of that time period, she uses "man" and "he" to represent everyone, including females.

41. **(E).** Ah, grammar. Everyone hates it, including me (and I write grammar books!). But it does come in handy from time to time. This question asks you to name the *antecedent,* a grammatical term for the word replaced by a pronoun. Read lines 76–79 and fill in the implied word, and you'll immediately see the antecedent: the author's "history" is typical of "many" *histories.* Bingo, choice (E) wins the prize.

42. **(B).** A *metaphor* is an implied comparison. It describes something by equating it with another. The author states that "We are the strands of the cable" (lines 85–86) because "we" link the Old and New Worlds. Choice (A) would have been okay if the comparison had contained "like" or "as." A *symbol* occurs within a piece of literature and adds meaning from *outside* the work. Had the author been discussing an actual cable between, say, Europe and North America, the cable might have been a symbol of unity. In this case, however, the cable isn't real. *Personification* occurs when something nonhuman is given human qualities. *Hyperbole* is exaggeration.

43. **(A).** To figure out the purpose, you have to look at the entire passage, not just one section. Most of this passage explains how the author views herself — as a person with two distinct lives and as someone linked to her parents and to two worlds. The fourth paragraph discusses why someone may write an autobiography at a young age, but the fifth paragraph comes back with a reason not stated in the fourth — that one life may represent the experiences of many. The whole passage is clearly trying to tell the reader why the author is justified in writing about herself.

44. **(D).** This short but beautiful poem by Hettie Jones has *personification,* which is lit-speak for giving human qualities to an inanimate object or any nonhuman entity. The "word," which is not a person, "dreams of leaving" (line 10). Hit the sound button for *alliteration,* the repetition of consonant sounds ("tip" and "tongue" in line 8). The whole first stanza (lines 1–3) employs *metaphor,* an implied comparison. Equating "words" (the title) with "stones" (line 3) creates a metaphor. Choice (E) refers to the end of a line in which no punctuation appears. The line break implies a pause, but the meaning runs into the next line or stanza. Enjambment is everywhere. The only thing missing in this poem is onomatopoeia, the literary term for a word that sounds like its meaning.

45. **(C).** Here's the thing about writing poetry: You get to break all sorts of grammar and punctuation rules without penalty. In fact, poets often do so on purpose to create a specific effect. In this poem the poet makes several distinct statements about words, but the lack of punctuation causes the reader to run those ideas together and to ponder the connection between them. Choice (A) is wrong because nothing in the poem denies meaning. Choice (B) is a flop because the line breaks and the stanza separations tell the reader where a pause is appropriate. Choice (D) drops out of the running because in line 9 the speaker *does* acknowledge an inhibition, or self-censoring ("I hold it close"). Finally, choice (E) is tempting, but the line breaks, the stanza breaks, and even the hidden meanings of the poem may all be seen as "barriers."

46. **(E).** In this poem "change" (line 6) is a play on words, as in "here's a dollar; you can keep the change." However, the poet isn't really talking about money; therefore, choices (A) and (D) aren't appropriate. Nor does the poet refer to promises, so choice (C) is out as well. The poet implies that giving "my word" (line 4) creates a change in the listener, a change that the listener may "keep" (line 6). Choice (B) gets voted off the island and choice (E) wins.

47. **(A).** The third stanza (lines 7–8) talks about "a word" (line 7). The colon clearly identifies the word as "love" (line 8). Therefore the "it" (line 9) that the speaker "holds close" (line 9) is love.

48. **(D).** One of the many wonderful things I love about poetry is its economy. A single word may have several meanings, all of which add to the overall effect of the poem. In "Words," author Hettie Jones says that words "are keys" (line 1). Keys unlock or open, so you don't have to stretch too far to say that words may unlock or reveal mysteries. Therefore, statement I is true. A "stanchion" (line 2) is an upright post, as in a fence, so words may confine. In the second stanza (lines 4–6) a word is given away — a liberating act. That means statement II is correct. Because words may be "stones" (line 3) and because at least one — love — may be difficult to say, words may be a burden. Therefore statement III is fine. Choice (D) deems all three statements correct.

49. **(C).** An important issue in the poem is the identity of "I" (lines 4 and 9 in this poem). The "I" isn't necessarily the poet. Lots of poets create a fictional *persona,* a character bearing the pronoun "I" but distinct from the author. You can therefore immediately dump choices (D) and (E). Choice (A) is tempting, because in a sense the "I" in the poem wants a change, and change may certainly be an escape from a particular situation. However, choice (C) is more directly supported by evidence in the poem. The speaker, for instance, keeps the word "love" on "the tip of my tongue" (line 8). The love "dreams of leaving." It has a desire to declare "yes, yes, you're the one I love." Choice (B) has no support in the poem at all.

50. **(C).** Using metaphor, the first three lines of the poem define "words" (the title). The next stanza (lines 4–6) cites a situation, as do the last two stanzas (lines 7–10).

51. **(B).** The "Calm Night" (line 3) is a "brooding mother" (line 4) and has a "bosom" (line 14), which is a fancy word for chest. Thus night is personified, or given traits usually associated with people.

52. **(E).** It's yet again time to dust off your knowledge of poetic terminology, and this time, the term is *sonnet.* A sonnet has 14 lines, an intricate rhyme scheme, and ten syllables per line (though poets sometimes cheat a bit with the syllable count). If you take a close look at James Weldon Johnson's "Mother Night," you notice 14 lines, an intricate rhyme scheme (ABBA ABBA CDE CDE), and ten syllables per line. Sounds like a match!

53. **(A).** The first eight lines of this poem take place on a big stage, with "eternities" (line 1) and "whirling suns" (line 5). You're in the territory of the universe. The last six lines of the poem are more personal, speaking of "my feeble sun of life" (line 9) and "I" (lines 11 and 13). Choice (A) is the clear winner here. Choice (B) is bad because the whole poem uses figurative language. Choice (C) doesn't cut it either, because both parts of the poem deal with death with more or less the same attitude. The poem's *diction,* or word choice, is formal throughout — ruling out choice (D). The first stanza contains visual imagery ("whirling suns" in line 5), so choice (E) is out.

54. **(E).** Check out lines 11–12. The darkness in this poem is a stand-in for death. Choices (A) and (B) are too extreme. The speaker doesn't fear death, and so choices (C) and (D) aren't correct either.

55. **(C).** Did you notice all the positive references to death and all the equations between death and sleep? In line 7, for example, death is a "haven," and in line 8 it's considered "peace." And, the speaker says he will "Welcome the darkness without fear or doubt" (line 12) and hang out in the "quiet bosom of the Night" (line 14) when he dies. Maybe Johnson pulled an all-nighter before writing this poem!

Multiple-choice conversion chart

To go from your raw multiple-choice score to a converted score, you have to subtract ¼ of the number of wrong answers from the number of correct answers. This process sounds complicated, but it really isn't that bad. Follow these steps to get it right:

1. **Multiply the number of answers you got wrong by ¼.**

   For example, if you got 8 answers wrong, your result for this step would be 2.

2. **Subtract the result from Step 1 from the total number of answers you got right.**

   The answer is your converted multiple-choice score.

   Continuing the example from Step 1, if you got 47 answers correct, your converted multiple-choice score would be 45.

Now that you have the converted multiple-choice score, enter it in the later section "Putting It All Together: Calculating Your Composite Score."

Clear as Mud: How to Score an Essay

The essays are trickier to score than the multiple-choice questions because you have to make some judgment calls. But I know you're up to the task, and in this section I give you plenty of guidelines and samples to help you through the maze of AP-essay scoring. So sharpen your pencil — and your brain — and get to work.

Before you score your essay, I recommend that you read the sample answers I provide in the next sections — along with the explanations of the good and bad points of each — so that you can have a clear path to follow when assessing the quality of your own work according to AP standards.

When scoring the essays, use the following checklist to rate yourself according to AP standards:

✔ Does the essay address the question?

✔ How in-depth is the literary analysis?

✔ Does the writer offer sufficient support for his/her analysis?

✔ What is the level of writing fluency shown in the essay?

Each item in the checklist has a range of scores. You have to pick one of the three numbers. Here's what to do:

✔ **Give yourself the highest number in a scoring range if the answer almost, but not quite, fits into the next higher category.** In other words, if an essay just brushes the 7–9 slot, give yourself a 6.

✔ **Likewise, award yourself the lowest number in a scoring range if an answer just barely escapes the next lower category.** Therefore, if you decide that one area deserves a place in the 7–9 slot after toying with the 4–6 rung of the ladder, give yourself a score of 7.

✔ **If an essay appears to sit squarely in one category, go for the middle score.** A solid 7–9 essay, in other words, gets an 8.

After assessing each aspect of an essay, add the scores for the four assessment questions together and divide by four to calculate the raw score. An essay scores a zero only if it doesn't address the question or if it's left blank.

Only the lowest category (1–3) of the checklist for writing skills mentions what English teachers call *mechanics,* or grammar and spelling errors. Dedicated grammarians (and I am one) hate to admit that the College Board tells its exam graders to count grammar and spelling errors only when the mistakes slap the reader in the face. (But of course, AP readers are high school or college English teachers, so they're going to notice when you make "missteaks.") The bottom line is this: Be careful with grammar and spelling. One more thing: Every English teacher I've ever met gets grumpy when the characters' names are misspelled. Check the passage and your essay to be sure that you aren't writing about Lady Britmart, Kmart, Walmart, or any other mart. I guarantee that you don't want a grouchy exam grader.

Essay 1: Family Relationships and Conflicts in Shaw's "Major Barbara"

George Bernard Shaw, a British writer, was famous for dry wit and artful pokes at society's conventions. In this excerpt from *Major Barbara,* a family conflict is established in just a few lines. Because this is a drama passage, you don't have much beyond dialogue to work from — just a couple of stage directions. However, the content and diction of each character's remarks offers a great deal of information.

Scoring grid for essay 1

Before you hit the following scoring grid, reread your essay. Underline spots where you might have done better, and give yourself a star for sections where you excelled. Then work your way through the categories in this scoring section, assigning yourself a number in each one.

Addresses the question: _____

The most important factor an AP grader looks for is, sadly, all too easy to overlook: addressing the question from the prompt. This prompt has three parts: the family relationships, the conflict, and *how* Shaw reveals them to the reader. Choose the number from the following list that best describes your essay:

0   The essay doesn't answer the question or is left blank.

1–3   The essay merely summarizes the plot or meaning and contains only one or two points that relate to family relationships and conflict or to Shaw's writing style.

4–6   The essay contains some unnecessary plot summary but makes a few points that relate to family relationships and conflict. The essay discusses one or two techniques that Shaw uses to reveal the family dynamic. The essay may occasionally stray from the topic.

7–9   The essay focuses on the relationship between Lady Britomart and her son and the implied relationship of each to the father. The essay explores the conflict between the mother and son and the implied problems with the father and the girls. The essay analyzes Shaw's writing style and avoids unnecessary plot summary and off-topic statements.

Literary analysis: _____

The College Board is testing your ability to pick apart a literary work and analyze its contents. Scan your essay and then choose the number from this list that best represents your analysis of *Major Barbara:*

1–3   The essay stays solely on the literal level, with no interpretation of the characters' statements or actions. One or more statements about relationships and conflict may be wrong.

4–6   The essay offers an interpretation of the characters' statements or actions but doesn't go into depth. The family conflict is explained in simple terms.

7–9   The essay digs into the text, unearthing and exploring the interchange between mother and son and their relationship to the father. The implied conflict with the father and the problem with the girls are both included. The essay interprets the dialogue and stage directions and also addresses what the characters don't say, as well as such elements of style as diction, syntax, punctuation, and so on.

Evidence/support: _____

No evidence, no case. That fact applies to the justice system and also to AP essay scores. How much evidence have you supplied? Evaluate your response by choosing a number from this list:

1–3   The writer makes only general statements with no or very few specific references to the text.

4–6   The writer's interpretation is supported by some references to the text. The references may not be the best or most sophisticated choices. Some quotations may be overly long, too short, or not supportive of the writer's point.

7–9   The writer provides strong support for his or her interpretations by choosing specific and relevant evidence from the text. Quotations are excerpted and analyzed so that the idea the quotation communicates is made clearly and concisely.

Writing skills: _____

The second half of the exam title — the part informing you that you're taking a "composition" test — is important to your score. Grade your essay according to the criteria listed here:

1–3   The essay is disorganized or filled with distracting grammar and spelling errors. Transitions between one point and another are awkward or missing entirely.

4–6 The essay has a logical structure. The writer's thesis (main idea) and supporting points are easily defined. The writing doesn't always flow smoothly or may contain repetitive or wordy statements. Quotations are inserted awkwardly.

7–9 The essay demonstrates clear, fluid style with a good command of language. The essay moves from a clear thesis through supporting points, each accompanied by evidence, to a logical conclusion.

Overall score: _____

Fill in each of the following blanks with the appropriate score, and then add your scores to determine the total:

Addresses the question _____

Literary analysis _____

Evidence/support _____

Writing skills _____

Raw score total _____

To figure out your overall score, divide your raw score by 4. Insert that number here: _____

Sample answer 1

Many playwrights show family conflicts and have various family members in several types of relationships. George Bernard Shaw's play "Major Barbara" is one play that reveals family relationships. The family relationships and conflict between the two characters in this scene, Lady Britomart and her son, are important.

Lady Britomart in this scene talks to her son Stephen. She tells him that it is time for him to take a more active role in the family. She says that he must help her because she is a woman and he is a man. Stephen is nervous during this conversation, which is shown when he plays with his tie and then with his watch. Stephen doesn't want to help his mother with the housework, showing that he is in conflict with her. "You know I have never interfered in the household —" Stephen is a man, and years ago men did not get involved with housework. However, Stephen does not use this to argue with his mother. He seems willing to try, if she wants him to, but that's not what <u>he</u> wants. Although Lady Britomart says that she is only a woman, she seems more powerful than Stephen, a man.

Lady Britomart is worried about her relationship with her husband. She asks Stephen to help her with him. "My dear, we can't go on all our lives not mentioning him. Of course you were quite right not to open the subject until I asked you to; but you are old enough now to be taken into my confidence, and to help me to deal with him about the girls." She never says what is wrong with the girls, but she wants Stephen's help in some specific way. This is another conflict in the story. Stephen, in the part on the exam, doesn't ask how he is supposed to help. The audience senses that Stephen will probably not know how to help.

George Bernard Shaw uses dialogue and stage directions to show the relationship between Stephen and Lady Britomart. Stephen's lines of dialogue are much shorter than Lady Britomart's. He says less because she is in control of him. Lady Britomart appears to be a woman used to getting her way. She dominates Stephen by talking a lot. Lady Britomart orders Stephen around when she tells him to put down <u>The Speaker</u> and listen to her. She tells him to stop playing with his tie. She also says he has to interfere. "Stephen: may I ask how soon you intend to realize that you are a grown-up man, and that I am only a woman?" Stephen also walks "submissively" to a settee and sits down, showing that she is the boss of him, even though the characters seem traditional, and the tradition is that the male character will have more power than the female character.

Family conflicts are in every family, and the Britomarts are no exception. In the play George Bernard Shaw uses dialogue and stage directions to show how the mother and the son are in conflict and to show how they are worried about the father.

Analysis of sample answer 1

In this section, I explain how I would score the preceding essay in each of four categories.

Addresses the question: 5

This essay does address the question; it stays mostly on topic, but it also includes some repetitive or general statements. The introductory paragraph wastes a whole sentence on a vague comment about literature: "Many playwrights show family conflicts and have various family members in several types of relationships." A better essay gets to the point about Lady Britomart and her son and husband. Also, the sentences about male and female roles aren't tied to the question of family conflict and only vaguely show the relationship between Lady Britomart and her son.

Literary analysis: 4

This essay makes a couple of good points: Lady Britomart is in control of the conversation, and her son is nervous around her. (Can you blame him? As I read this dialogue, even I find myself feeling guilty about fiddling with my tie — and I don't even have a tie!) The writer also notes that both characters are worried about the father. However, the writer stays on a fairly basic level, mentioning these ideas without exploring deeper levels. Shaw's writing technique is mentioned, but the writer doesn't dig into diction, pauses, or other details.

Evidence/support: 5

The essay pulls in some evidence in the form of quotations, but they're simply plopped into the paragraphs without any link to the preceding or following sentences. The quotations also aren't excerpted well. Unnecessary words such as "My dear" should be cut. The writer correctly makes some concrete references to the text, such as the tie and the watch and the fact that Lady Britomart orders her son to sit down.

Writing skills: 5

A couple of mechanical errors show up in this essay. For example, the title of the play should be underlined, not enclosed in quotation marks, and the quotations from the play aren't cited by line number. However, these mechanical problems don't inhibit the reader. A more important problem is the structure of the essay. Ideas discussed in the second paragraph show up again in the fourth paragraph. These ideas should be combined. Also, the essay has a summary, not a real conclusion.

Overall score: 5

Here's how you calculate the overall score for sample 1:

5 + 4 + 5 + 5 = 19

19÷4 = 4.75 (which rounds up to 5)

Sample answer 2

George Bernard Shaw's <u>Major Barbara</u> begins with a conversation between Lady Britomart and her son, who is afraid of her. This point is emphasized when the stage directions say that Stephen walks "submissively" (line 3) to the settee. He also stops reading when his mother asks him to and plays with his tie and watch chain, which also shows his fear of her. He even asks, "Have I done anything to annoy you, mother?" and tells her that if he did, it was "quite unintentional" (line 20). Some of his lines end with dashes, showing that he is afraid to say things to her. It is interesting that the magazine Stephen is reading is called The Speaker. It is almost as if Stephen has to read about speaking because he doesn't know how to speak for himself with any confidence.

Although Lady Britomart says that she is "only a woman" (lines 25–26) and that Stephen is a "grown-up man" (line 25), she doesn't act as if she felt that Stephen has more power than she does. Lady Britomart's first line, "Presently, Stephen" (line 2) shows that she is in control, not Stephen. Many of her lines are commands: "Bring me my cushion" (line 10), "Don't repeat my words" (line 27) and "Don't make excuses" (line 6). Her stage directions say that she is "squaring herself at him rather aggressively" (line 24). Her speeches are also longer than Stephen's, again showing that she dominates the relationship they have between them. Also, Stephen's answer when Lady Britomart asks for his help is just one word: "I!" and the exclamation point says it all. He can't believe that his mother needs anything from him.

The family has some conflicts besides the tension that Stephen feels when he is with his mother and the exasperation she feels when she is with him. As soon as Lady Britomart explains that she doesn't want help to "order the dinner" (line 36), Stephen thinks of his father, but he has trouble talking about it. (And he has stopped reading The Speaker!) His lines are "troubled" (line 39) and he is "ashamed" (line 41). He can't even say what the problem is, simply referring to "it" (lines 25 and 45). Yet Lady Britomart knows right away what he means, saying, "I suppose you mean your father" (line 42). Though the problem with the father is never specified in this excerpt, the last line says that Lady Britomart wants Stephen to "help me to deal with him about the girls" (line 46). So another relationship in the Britomart family is in trouble in some way.

Shaw's characterization sets up first a triangle (mother-son-father) and then a more complicated relationship (mother-son-father-girls). The fact that the dialogue doesn't give all the answers keeps the audience interested, and the stage directions help the actors realize what sort of people they are playing.

Analysis of sample answer 2

If you read the first sample answer and then this one, you immediately see that this one is superior. It digs more deeply into Shaw's scene, working from nuances that the first writer didn't notice. The following sections show how I would grade this essay.

Addresses the question: 8

This essay does address the question; it stays on topic and goes right to the point about Lady Britomart and her son and husband. The writer discusses three family relationships and mentions a fourth (the girls), explains the conflicts, and takes a pretty good shot at the crucial part of the question — how Shaw establishes these relationships and conflict.

Literary analysis: 7

This essay crams in quite a few good points: Lady Britomart does dominate her son, and her son is nervous around her. After a false start in thinking about the dinner order (takeout tonight or pizza?), Stephen's thoughts go directly to his father, and his mother is keenly aware of that fact. A few aspects of Shaw's writing technique are explored, including the length of lines, the dashes at the end of Stephen's comments, and the commands that Lady Britomart gives to her son. The writer makes a nice point about The Speaker but doesn't deal with diction. And wouldn't you say that the words in the excerpt are quite formal for a family argument? Nor does the writer address anything that these characters don't say, such as all that Stephen leaves out in lines 39–41. Still, in a 40-minute essay, this writer achieved a great deal.

Evidence/support: 8

The essay uses quotations effectively, choosing just the right sections to make the point and leaving out irrelevant words. Every statement about the play ("Many of her lines are commands," for example), is backed up with a quotation. This writer (like the writer of sample 1) also makes references to the tie and the watch.

Writing skills: 7

This writer created a logical structure and shows a good, though not excellent, command of language. The introductory paragraph gets right to the point, but no overall statement indicates what the essay is about. In other words, the writer didn't include a thesis. The conclusion isn't very sophisticated, but it *is* a real conclusion, not a summary. The essay has very few mechanical problems.

Overall score: 8

Here's how you calculate the overall score for sample 2:

8 + 7 + 8 + 7 = 30

30÷4 = 7.5 (which rounds up to 8)

Essay 2: Dickinson's and Dunbar's Attitudes toward Success

Paired poems appear fairly often on the AP English exam, and these two are a typical match because each author has a distinct style and view of a common subject, in this case, the meaning of success.

Scoring grid for essay 2

As real AP graders do, review the poems and your essay about them before hitting the following scoring grid. If you're starting the essay-grading process with this essay, read the general instructions earlier in this chapter before evaluating essay 2.

Addresses the question: _____

The prompt calls for a comparison of two elements: the poets' attitude toward success and the poetic techniques each uses to convey those attitudes to the reader. Use these numbers to measure your skill in addressing the question:

0   The essay doesn't answer the question or is left blank.

1–3   The essay merely summarizes the literal meaning of each poem and contains only one or two points relating to the poets' attitudes toward success. The essay makes very few references to the poets' writing styles. No attempt is made to link writing style to meaning.

4–6   The essay focuses on the poets' attitudes toward success, both stated and implied. The essay discusses three or four techniques the poets use to reveal the poets' attitudes toward success. However, the essay doesn't always link the ideas about success to comments about the poets' techniques.

7–9   The essay explores the literal and underlying meaning of each poem, clearly defining each poet's attitude toward success. The essay analyzes each poet's writing style and relates those techniques to the poet's attitude toward success.

Literary analysis: _____

Especially in this essay, digging under the surface level of the texts is important, because in poetry, the deeper level is where all the action is. Examine the literary analysis in your essay with the following standards, choosing the number that best represents your essay:

1–3   The essay stays solely on the literal level, with no interpretation of the figurative language, diction, or imagery. One or more statements about meaning of the poems may be wrong.

4–6   The essay offers an interpretation of the poets' attitudes toward success but doesn't go into depth. The link between what the poem says about success and how the poem is written is explained in simple terms.

7–9   The essay digs into the text, unearthing and exploring the subtleties of each poet's attitude toward success. The relationship between the poet's technique and meaning is clearly established. The essay addresses such elements of style as diction, syntax, punctuation, figurative language, imagery, and so on.

Evidence/support: _____

Quotations from the poems are essential in this essay, because you can't refer to events in the poems as you can when you're writing about a story or a dramatic scene. How well did you do? Check your essay and give yourself one of these scores:

1–3   The writer makes only general statements with no or very few specific references to the text.

4–6   The writer's interpretation is supported by some references to the text. The references may not be the best or most sophisticated choices. Some quotations may be overly long, too short, or not supportive of the writer's point.

7–9   The writer provides strong support for his or her interpretations by choosing specific and relevant evidence from the text. Quotations are excerpted so that the point is made clearly and concisely.

Writing skills: _____

You don't have to be a poet to write about poetry, but you do have to present your analysis of these poems clearly and logically. Evaluate your writing style and pick a number that fits:

1–3   The essay is disorganized or filled with distracting grammar and spelling errors. Transitions between one point and another are awkward or missing entirely.

4–6   The essay has a logical structure. The writer's thesis (main idea) and supporting points are easily defined. The writing doesn't always flow smoothly or may contain repetitive or wordy statements. Quotations are inserted awkwardly.

7–9   The essay demonstrates clear, fluid style with a good command of language. The essay moves from a clear thesis through supporting points, each accompanied by evidence, to a logical conclusion.

Overall score: _____

Fill in each of the following blanks with the appropriate score, and then add your scores to determine the total:

Addresses the question _____

Literary analysis _____

Evidence/support _____

Writing skills _____

Raw score total _____

To figure out your overall score, divide your raw score by 4. Insert that number here: _____

Sample answer 1

In "Not They Who Soar" Paul Lawrence Dunbar says that people who aren't successful but who work very hard are "heroes." The ones who "soar" are usually the people we think are the best, but Dunbar doesn't see it that way. He sees the people who suffer as better off. They can smile on "defeated care" even though they aren't successful. The ones who are "high up", the successful people, haven't learned very much. The people who plod are probably farmers because the poem mentions "sod" and "thorns." They may be slaves, too, because the "backs have felt the rod." Dunbar rhymes every two lines, creating rhyming couplets. So the ideas in the two lines are closely related. Dunbar also makes an allusion to thorns, which makes the reader think about thorns in the bible. He also uses a metaphor when he talks about "boulders."

Emily Dickenson, on the other hand, thinks that the sweetest victory comes when you think you haven't won anything. If you have lost, you are agonized and clear about what victory or success means. She probably lived during a war or had soldiers in her family. Dickinsen has a lot of alliteration in the first stanza, which has many words beginning with the letter s. She uses a metaphor when she calls success a "nectar."

In a way both poets agree with each other. Defeat is not such a bad idea because you learn from your mistakes. Successful people haven't learned much about life and don't appreciate what they have. The way each poem is written helps give this message.

Analysis of sample answer 1

This writer tried, but the results fall short of perfection. In this section, I explain what's good and bad about sample 1 and show you the grades I would have awarded in each category.

Addresses the question: 3

This essay does address the question; it stays mostly on topic (attitude toward success) but includes some off-topic statements about farmers and slavery in the first paragraph and about war in the second. The poetic techniques are mentioned, but the essay doesn't make any connection between the way the poem is written and the attitude of the poet toward success.

Literary analysis: 3

This essay gets the main idea: People who succeed don't appreciate their victory as much as those who go down in defeat. However, the writer includes very little analysis beyond this main idea of each poem. The literary techniques that the writer mentions are simply dropped in the essay almost like a shopping list. The writer doesn't consider how those techniques work in the poem or how they affect the reader.

One clue that the writer of this sample is in trouble is the length of the essay — 265 words, in case you're interested. A good AP essay averages 450 to 500 words. This writer has come up short in words and, more importantly, in ideas.

Evidence/support: 2

The essay pulls in some evidence in the form of quotations, but they're just single words. The writer misses a couple of great opportunities to quote whole lines and explore their relationship to the idea of success. Also, quite a few more literary techniques and examples could be mentioned.

Writing skills: 3

A couple of mechanical errors show up in this essay. For example, the comma in the fifth line of the first paragraph should be inside the closing quotation, not outside. The quotations from the poems aren't cited by line number. However, the mechanical problems don't inhibit the reader. The essay doesn't flow smoothly, but it isn't bad either.

This essay contains a big no-no: The authors' names are misspelled, and, in the case of Emily Dickinson, in two different ways! Remember that your essay will be graded by an English teacher or professor, and we tend to get very possessive about authors. So be sure to spell their names correctly!

Overall score: 3

Here's how to calculate the overall score for sample 1:

3 + 3 + 2 + 3 = 11

11÷4 = 2.75 (which rounds up to 3)

Sample answer 2

Emily Dickinson and Paul Laurence Dunbar both explore success and the meaning attached to it by contrasting those who experience success with those who taste defeat. Both poets agree that you have to experience defeat to know the meaning of success.

In Dickinson's poem <u>Success</u> it is described as a "nectar" (3) that you can "comprehend" (3) only when you have "sorest need" (4). Success is taking "the flag" (6), but the ones who most appreciate success hear the "distant strains of triumph" (11) and are "agonized" (12). Dickinson's metaphors make success sound wonderful, because nectar is sweet, a flag is usually respected, and triumph is enjoyable. By contrast, the "defeated" (9) person who hears the "distant strains" (11) is nearly dead. Success is so far away and so closed to this person that they hear the success with a "forbidden ear" (10). Dickinson's word choice in this poem is very simple. Most of the words are easy to understand, implying that the main idea is a simple, natural concept — you appreciate success when you have been defeated. Two four-line stanzas with the second and fourth line rhyming also create a simple pattern, reinforcing the idea of naturalness. The "purple host" in line 5 makes the reader think of bruises or wounds, so Dickinson is telling the reader that success has its price. The "host" is also a religious image, making the experience of success or defeat an almost holy quest.

Paul Laurence Dunbar compares success with soaring in the air and defeat with working on the land below. Dunbar doesn't think that soaring is a big accomplishment. The "flight is ever free" (13) for someone who succeeds, and they don't have to face "thorns" (10) and "boulders" (11). Dunbar makes allusions to the Bible, the "thorns" (10) and "the rod" (6) make you think of the death of Christ, who has to wear a crown of thorns and who is beaten by Roman soldiers. The rod also brings slavery to mind, another allusion. Dunbar's last two lines make the point: real "heroes [are] they the soil who've trod, / Not they who soar! (14–15). Dunbar uses formal words, and his sentences are complicated. By making his sentences complicated, he shows that the two ideas, success and defeat, are not as simple as they first appear.

Dunbar's poem is also about freedom and slavery, but freedom is a kind of success. Dickinson and Dunbar both understand that pain and suffering is worth something, that you can learn from your sorrows and tragedies. Those "who soar," as Dunbar says, may miss an essential part of life because they never taste defeat or even face obstacles.

Analysis of sample answer 2

The writer of sample essay 2 was on a roll the day he or she tackled it. It's a fine effort, one I'd be happy to see from any AP student. The following sections go into the details.

Addresses the question: 8

This essay does address the question; it mostly stays on the idea of success, and the poetic techniques cited are related to the idea of success. The writer of this sample makes a correct point in the last sentence: the poem *is* also about freedom and slavery. However, the question asks for an alternate reading of the poem — success and, by implication, defeat. Thus the essay would be better without that last line.

Literary analysis: 8

This essay makes quite a few good points. The general idea of the two poems is easy to grasp. The essay writer digs into the text, unearthing deeper meanings, such as the significance of "purple" (5) and the "forbidden ear" (10), the Biblical allusions in Dunbar's poem, and Dickinson's word choice.

Evidence/support: 8

The essay uses quotations from the poem effectively, giving examples for nearly every point made. The quotations are cited by line number in proper MLA format.

Writing skills: 7

This sample shows an effective and fluid style. The introductory paragraph states the thesis and names the authors. A few grammar problems show up (for example, in the last paragraph "someone who succeeds" is referred to as "they" instead of "he or she"), but the reader will have little difficulty sailing through this essay. The writer had a good structure. He or she included an introduction, body paragraphs, and a conclusion.

Overall score: 8

Here's how to calculate the overall score for sample 2:

8 + 8 + 8 + 7 = 31

31÷4 = 7.75 (which rounds up to 8)

Essay 3: The Open-Ended Essay

By now you're probably tired of grading — a sentiment your teachers often feel. But muster up a little more energy to evaluate your third essay. Reread your response and settle in for a grading session according to the categories in the following sections.

Scoring grid for essay 3

The open-ended essay is probably the easiest to write because you can work from a piece of literature that you've studied in school and are ready to write about. (See Chapter 14 for information on preparing for the open-ended essay.) However, because you may select any of thousands of novels or plays, I can't be very specific in this scoring guide. So here's the deal: I give you the general standards, and I provide two graded essays and explanations. Apply the general scoring principles to your own work.

Three situations give you a zero for the third, open-ended essay. The first is not addressing the question. The second is omitting the essay. The third is writing about a work that isn't of good literary quality. A few (misguided) exam-takers have composed essays on children's books or songs. Dr. Seuss is great, but not in this context. And stay away from Bob Dylan, no matter how many votes you'd give him for Artist of the Century. Films and popular literature (bestsellers) are also off-limits.

Addresses the question: _____

Even though the AP exam writers don't tell you which work to write about, they do ask a question. In this case, they want to know how one character in a literary work helps to define another. Grade your essay's response to this question according to the following categories:

0   The essay doesn't answer the question or is left blank. The subject of the essay isn't a work of literary quality.

1–3   The essay merely summarizes the plot or meaning and contains only one or two points about how one character defines another.

4–6   The essay contains some unnecessary plot summary but makes a few points that relate to the way one character is in conflict with or in contrast to another. The essay may occasionally stray from the topic.

7–9   The essay focuses on the relationship between two characters, showing how the reader's view of one character is shaped by the other. The essay avoids unnecessary plot summary and off-topic statements.

Literary analysis: _____

I hope you chose a work that's like sandy soil: easy to dig into. Review your essay's literary analysis and assign it one of the numbers listed here:

1–3   The essay stays solely on the literal level, with no interpretation of the characters' statements or actions. One or more statements about the characters may be wrong.

4–6   The essay offers an interpretation of the characters but doesn't go into depth. The comparison, contrast, or interaction between the characters is explained in simple terms.

7–9   The essay digs into the text, unearthing and exploring the interchange between the two characters or, if the characters don't interact, the essay explores the juxtaposition of the characters.

Evidence/support: _____

The case you're making for character definition depends on references to both characters — the one being defined and the one doing the defining. Grade yourself according to the standards listed here:

1–3   The writer makes only general statements with no or very few specific references to the text.

4–6   The writer's interpretation is supported by some references to the text. The references may not be the best or most sophisticated choices. Some references may not support the writer's point.

7–9   The writer provides strong support for his or her interpretations by choosing specific and relevant evidence from the text.

Because you aren't writing about a selection that's provided on the test, you can't easily quote from the work you're discussing. However, if you do remember some important quotations (lines from a *Hamlet* soliloquy, for example), you'll impress the exam grader. Don't risk a mistake, however. Quote only if you're sure that you know the words.

Writing skills: _____

How does your essay sound? Does it flow smoothly, or do you stumble through a set of choppy, half-baked sentences? Score your work by assigning it one of the following numbers:

1–3   The essay is disorganized or filled with distracting grammar and spelling errors. Transitions between one point and another are awkward or missing entirely.

4–6   The essay has a logical structure. The writer's thesis (main idea) and supporting points are easily defined. The writing doesn't always flow smoothly or may contain repetitive or wordy statements. Evidence is inserted awkwardly.

7–9   The essay demonstrates clear, fluid style with a good command of language. The essay moves from a clear thesis through supporting points, each accompanied by evidence, to a logical conclusion.

Overall score: _____

Fill in each of the following blanks with the appropriate score, and then add your scores to determine the total:

Addresses the question   _____

Literary analysis   _____

Evidence/support   _____

Writing skills   _____

Raw score total   _____

To find your overall score, divide your raw score by 4. Insert that number here: _____

Sample answer 1

Virginia Woolf's <u>Mrs. Dalloway</u> transverses two worlds in post WWI England — that of Clarissa Dalloway and Septimus Warren Smith. Both present a disillusioned unsatisfied view of the world, and yet Clarissa chooses to live in the society whose worth she is unsure of, and Septimus chooses to commit suicide. Though Clarissa and Septimus are not directly linked, Septimus's suffering and ultimate death cause her to reevaluate her own situation and choose life. In this way, Septimus defines Clarissa Dalloway.

Septimus was an idealistic young poet who enlisted in the army as a symbol of poetic patriotism. He married a beautiful Italian woman named Lucrezia and was a lively soul. He suffered from shell shock and returned from the war unable to function as a normal human being. He was not sad or angry — he was numb. He watched his best friend Evan die and claimed to not have felt much sadness because he was already numb. Back in England, he hears and sees Evans. His wife is forced to deal with his mental instability alone, and her dream of a perfect family is ruined. She and Septimus are sitting in a park one day and she comments on how they must appear — like a happy couple, when in reality, they can barely communicate, and she has to hold him back from screaming random phrases about "human nature."

Lucrezia tries to help Septimus and take him to see two doctors: Dr. Holmes and Sir William — both of whom cannot help him and represent to Septimus all that is wrong with English society and, perhaps, humankind. He refers to Dr. Holmes as "human nature" and jumps out of a window when Holmes tries to take him to an asylum. Sir William says that Septimus suffers from a "lack of proportion" and tells Lucrezia, the only person who truly cares for Septimus, that Septimus must be away from her as if she were the problem. Right after Septimus kills himself — in hopes of saving his soul and not having to live in the society he abhors — the doctors give Lucrezia drugs to effectively numb her. The doctors have replaced what the war did to Septimus. One doctor then attends Clarissa's party immediately afterward, which is when the two stories cross and Clarissa hears of Septimus's death. The two doctors represent the uncaring position-obsessed English society and do not think another moment of Septimus's death except when it seems an interesting piece of gossip.

Upon hearing of Septimus's death, Clarissa leaves her party and retreats into a room of her own. There she contemplates why Septimus killed himself and how she feels similarly to what he must have felt when he made that choice. Like Septimus, she struggles with the balance of privacy and outside communication. She also dislikes society but has, thus far, conformed to it and chosen to live in it. She looks through her window and sees an old woman living her life. Clarissa ultimately chooses to continue living — to continue communicating, unlike Septimus, in addition to having her own private room, her own private life. Septimus could not. Clarissa returns to her party.

Though Septimus is only one man, he represented many of the returning soldiers and disillusioned men and women who lived during the war. Society had no place for them; it did not know how to handle them and chose to ignore their problems. Woolf contrasts this disillusionment with the money-obsessed society of the rich elite, where wanton luxury has replaced feelings and emotions. Though Clarissa chooses life, Septimus is the most moral character at Clarissa's party, and he defines the compromises Clarissa has made.

Analysis of sample answer 1

I love this essay. It isn't perfect, but it's a very fine discussion of one of my all-time favorite novels. Here's how the essay rates, according to AP (and my) standards.

Addresses the question: 8

This essay does address the question; it stays on topic and shows how the juxtaposition of Septimus and Clarissa serves to define Clarissa's character. The information about Lucrezia may be omitted as it does not directly relate to the two characters being discussed, Septimus and Clarissa.

Literary analysis: 9

The writer understands *Mrs. Dalloway,* and her observations about the two main characters are insightful. The second paragraph nails the characterization of Septimus, mentioning his relationship with his wife and the appearance of a happy family that's belied by Septimus's inner turmoil. The third paragraph explains the symbolic meanings of the doctors' treatment of Septimus. The fourth paragraph turns to Clarissa Dalloway, analyzing her in light of Septimus's suicide. The last paragraph beautifully explains that Clarissa's choice of life is made in the context of Septimus's death.

Evidence/support: 8

Because the text isn't available to the writer, the exam graders won't expect quotations. They will, however, expect specifics, and this essay includes quite a few, such as the condition of Septimus after the war, his random statements, the values of society, the doctors' treatment of Septimus, the reaction of Clarissa to the death, the old woman that Clarissa sees, and Clarissa's eventual return to the party. These examples come from various spots in the novel, not just one place. Thus the writer has demonstrated an understanding of the whole work, a plus on the AP exam.

Writing skills: 8

This writer has a strong command of language, with very few mechanical errors. The essay gets to the point, moves smoothly from one idea to another, and comes to a logical conclusion.

Overall score: 8

Here's how to calculate the overall score for sample 1:

8 + 9 + 8 + 8 = 33

33÷4 = 8.25 (which rounds up to 8)

Sample answer 2

In the play, <u>Hamlet</u>, written by William Shakespeare, Hamlet is contrasted with Fortinbras and Laertes. The people who see <u>Hamlet</u> understand that the character of Hamlet is different than the other two sons in the play. All three lose fathers. Hamlet finds out in the beginning of the play that his father was murdered by Claudius. Fortinbras, the guards and Horatio explain, lost his father in a war. He was killed by the old king, also named Hamlet. Laertes's father is Polonius, and Hamlet stabs him.

The three characters react very differently to the deaths of their fathers. Hamlet spends most of his time worrying about revenge and his mother's marriage to Claudius, but he doesn't do anything until his mother dies. Fortinbras begins to invade Denmark, but his uncle (another parallel to Hamlet, because Denmark is ruled by Hamlet's uncle) tells him to stop, and he does. Laertes is the most active character. After his father is killed by Hamlet, Laertes tries to kill Hamlet at the grave of Ophelia. Then, when he is stopped, he agrees to kill Hamlet in a sneaky way, in a duel that Claudius sets up. The only character who goes right to revenge and is not stopped is Laertes. Hamlet stops all the time, whenever he thinks of an excuse. Laertes and Fortinbras define Hamlet by showing that a real man, who is sad because of an unjust death, will act and Hamlet doesn't.

The other two characters also contrast with Hamlet by the way they deal with power. Laertes is respectful to Claudius and to his father, early in the play. After his father dies, Laertes is willing to kill whoever did it, even if it was Claudius, and he speaks to Claudius angrily. Fortinbras is only on stage for a little while, at the end, but he respects the dead prince, Hamlet, and says that Hamlet would have been a good king. Hamlet, on the other hand, is disrespectful to Claudius throughout the play. Hamlet looks more disrespectful because the other two characters contrast with him.

Analysis of sample answer 2

Hamlet is a great work of literature, but sample 2 isn't a great essay. The writer certainly read the play, but he or she appears to have rested comfortably on the surface, following the plot but not the essence of Shakespeare's drama. Following are specifics on the essay's merits and weaknesses.

Addresses the question: 4

The writer of this sample makes a crucial and fairly common mistake. Instead of dealing with two characters, as the question specifies, the writer can't resist throwing in a third. Yes, the essay discusses how Hamlet is defined by another character, but instead of sticking with Laertes, the best foil for Hamlet, the writer plops Fortinbras into the mix. Bad idea. First of all, exam writers — and exam graders — tell you what to do and then expect you to obey. Not fair, perhaps, but true. Second, the writer's points about Fortinbras aren't great. How can they be when the character shows up only in the last scene? Fortinbras *is* discussed by other characters, but the limited time given for this essay would have been better spent analyzing Laertes and Hamlet.

Literary analysis: 4

Sample 2 makes a couple of good points about Hamlet — his lack of action in comparison to Laertes's rush to vengeance and Hamlet's disrespect for authority. However, this essay conveniently ignores the fact that the authority in question, Claudius, got there by murdering the previous authority, Hamlet's father. The information about Fortinbras, while not called for, is accurate. The reader definitely won't drown in the literary depth of this essay, even if he or she wears lead weights and has no idea how to swim.

Evidence/support: 3

This essay has no quotations (not even "To be or not to be"!), but you can't expect quotations without a text to work from. However, the graders do expect some specific facts from the work. Everything in sample 2 is general. The writer doesn't speak about Laertes's fight at Ophelia's grave, Hamlet's chance to kill Claudius when Claudius is praying, or any other events. The details just aren't there.

Writing skills: 4

This writer hasn't created a fluent, graceful sentence. Not even one! Just read the first sentence aloud. Hear the choppiness? The essay is readable, but there are several grammar mistakes.

Overall score: 4

Here's how to calculate the overall score for sample 2:

4 + 4 + 3 + 4 = 15

15 ÷ 4 = 3.75 (which rounds up to 4)

Putting It All Together: Calculating Your Composite Score

The AP exam is weighted: 45 percent of your score comes from the multiple-choice questions and 55 percent from the three essays. The AP statistics experts take the overall scores from each section and fiddle with them a bit more until they come up with five categories, which are called (drum roll, please!) 1, 2, 3, 4, and 5. Plug your numbers into the following formula. Then add up the right-hand column to see how you rate:

Multiple-choice overall score _____ × 1.25 = _____

Essay 1 score _____ × 3.1 = _____

Essay 2 score _____ × 3.1 = _____

Essay 3 score _____ × 3.1 = _____

Total _____

After you get your total from the four different categories, compare it to the following table to get your final overall AP exam score.

Overall Score from the Four Categories	Equivalent AP Exam Score
Above 119	5
90–118	4
70–89	3
45–88	2
Below 45	1

If you score a 4 or a 5, take a moment to celebrate. You've demonstrated college-level ability. A grade of 3 means you can pat your back, but just once. Some colleges recognize a 3 as credit-worthy, but many don't. Scores of 1 or 2 mean that you have some work to do. Turn back to chapters reviewing topics that stumped you, and then try again.

Answer Sheet

1. Ⓐ Ⓑ Ⓒ Ⓓ Ⓔ   31. Ⓐ Ⓑ Ⓒ Ⓓ Ⓔ
2. Ⓐ Ⓑ Ⓒ Ⓓ Ⓔ   32. Ⓐ Ⓑ Ⓒ Ⓓ Ⓔ
3. Ⓐ Ⓑ Ⓒ Ⓓ Ⓔ   33. Ⓐ Ⓑ Ⓒ Ⓓ Ⓔ
4. Ⓐ Ⓑ Ⓒ Ⓓ Ⓔ   34. Ⓐ Ⓑ Ⓒ Ⓓ Ⓔ
5. Ⓐ Ⓑ Ⓒ Ⓓ Ⓔ   35. Ⓐ Ⓑ Ⓒ Ⓓ Ⓔ
6. Ⓐ Ⓑ Ⓒ Ⓓ Ⓔ   36. Ⓐ Ⓑ Ⓒ Ⓓ Ⓔ
7. Ⓐ Ⓑ Ⓒ Ⓓ Ⓔ   37. Ⓐ Ⓑ Ⓒ Ⓓ Ⓔ
8. Ⓐ Ⓑ Ⓒ Ⓓ Ⓔ   38. Ⓐ Ⓑ Ⓒ Ⓓ Ⓔ
9. Ⓐ Ⓑ Ⓒ Ⓓ Ⓔ   39. Ⓐ Ⓑ Ⓒ Ⓓ Ⓔ
10. Ⓐ Ⓑ Ⓒ Ⓓ Ⓔ   40. Ⓐ Ⓑ Ⓒ Ⓓ Ⓔ
11. Ⓐ Ⓑ Ⓒ Ⓓ Ⓔ   41. Ⓐ Ⓑ Ⓒ Ⓓ Ⓔ
12. Ⓐ Ⓑ Ⓒ Ⓓ Ⓔ   42. Ⓐ Ⓑ Ⓒ Ⓓ Ⓔ
13. Ⓐ Ⓑ Ⓒ Ⓓ Ⓔ   43. Ⓐ Ⓑ Ⓒ Ⓓ Ⓔ
14. Ⓐ Ⓑ Ⓒ Ⓓ Ⓔ   44. Ⓐ Ⓑ Ⓒ Ⓓ Ⓔ
15. Ⓐ Ⓑ Ⓒ Ⓓ Ⓔ   45. Ⓐ Ⓑ Ⓒ Ⓓ Ⓔ
16. Ⓐ Ⓑ Ⓒ Ⓓ Ⓔ   46. Ⓐ Ⓑ Ⓒ Ⓓ Ⓔ
17. Ⓐ Ⓑ Ⓒ Ⓓ Ⓔ   47. Ⓐ Ⓑ Ⓒ Ⓓ Ⓔ
18. Ⓐ Ⓑ Ⓒ Ⓓ Ⓔ   48. Ⓐ Ⓑ Ⓒ Ⓓ Ⓔ
19. Ⓐ Ⓑ Ⓒ Ⓓ Ⓔ   49. Ⓐ Ⓑ Ⓒ Ⓓ Ⓔ
20. Ⓐ Ⓑ Ⓒ Ⓓ Ⓔ   50. Ⓐ Ⓑ Ⓒ Ⓓ Ⓔ
21. Ⓐ Ⓑ Ⓒ Ⓓ Ⓔ   51. Ⓐ Ⓑ Ⓒ Ⓓ Ⓔ
22. Ⓐ Ⓑ Ⓒ Ⓓ Ⓔ   52. Ⓐ Ⓑ Ⓒ Ⓓ Ⓔ
23. Ⓐ Ⓑ Ⓒ Ⓓ Ⓔ   53. Ⓐ Ⓑ Ⓒ Ⓓ Ⓔ
24. Ⓐ Ⓑ Ⓒ Ⓓ Ⓔ   54. Ⓐ Ⓑ Ⓒ Ⓓ Ⓔ
25. Ⓐ Ⓑ Ⓒ Ⓓ Ⓔ   55. Ⓐ Ⓑ Ⓒ Ⓓ Ⓔ
26. Ⓐ Ⓑ Ⓒ Ⓓ Ⓔ   56. Ⓐ Ⓑ Ⓒ Ⓓ Ⓔ
27. Ⓐ Ⓑ Ⓒ Ⓓ Ⓔ
28. Ⓐ Ⓑ Ⓒ Ⓓ Ⓔ
29. Ⓐ Ⓑ Ⓒ Ⓓ Ⓔ
30. Ⓐ Ⓑ Ⓒ Ⓓ Ⓔ

Chapter 18

Spoiling Three More Hours: Practice Exam 2

. . . .

*B*ecause most people count up from one, I'm assuming that you've already taken the practice exam in Chapter 16 and checked your results in Chapter 17. If you're the unconventional type, no worries. The practice exam in this chapter is equivalent to the one in Chapter 16. It doesn't matter which one you do first. Though if you count down from two to one, I think I'll pass on your offer to balance my checkbook.

If you *have* taken the first practice exam, you know the drill: simulate real test conditions and follow the timing carefully. Also, be sure to look over the corrected first exam before starting the second one. Figure out where you need improvement. As you work through this exam, devote extra attention to those areas.

If this is your first attempt to take the AP exam, Chapter 16 begins with a list of pretest preparations. Check it out before you start this exam.

Section 1: Multiple Choice

Time: 1 hour

56 questions

This section contains six selections, each of which is followed by a set of questions. Read each selection and answer the questions following it, choosing the best possible answer. Fill in the corresponding oval, being sure to darken the entire oval. Do not select more than one answer. If you erase an answer, take care to do so completely. Questions with more than one oval darkened are automatically scored as wrong. Blank answers receive no credit; one quarter of a point is deducted for each wrong answer.

Questions 1–12 are based on the following poem, "Ellic Camel Gets a Hit," by Dave Johnson (from Marble Shoot, *published by Hummingbird Press in 1996). The poem describes a baseball game played by a team of convicts, watched over by prison guards with rifles. The spectators are townspeople. Read the poem carefully before answering the questions.*

(01) On day three forty-seven of Ellic Camel's sentence,
Miss Allie took me to see the opener at Camp Field.
Four guards lined the outfield; one behind the umpire, one by
the foul pole, one in the bird's eye, one just over the mound.

(05) On the first base side was the Gibson drive-in, where we got
hot dogs and cotton candy for a quarter. Free colas
were given out after every home run. And just behind
the backstop Roy Jowers sold corn liquor[1] in Ball fruit jars.[2]

The place was packed, kids and old folks. Adults cost a dollar,
(10) kids fifty cent. And if you wanted a spot in the shade,
under the tin roof, it was two dollars. Most time we sat
outside. Sometimes that hot silver tin would just bake your head.

That day Ellic Camel got a big hit and everyone cheered him on. He was barreling around second, headed
(15) for third, a standing triple, but he just kept on running,
out of the base path, by the dugout, and through the entrance.

Somebody left the gate open and Ellic just took off.
The umpire called him out, but he just kept on. And when he
was about ten yards outside the fence, the fans all sucked air, (20)
it sounded like the whole stadium was left on one wing.

No one said anything and all the guards just watched him go.
Like a match dropped in dry woods, the fans rose up, one by one,
cheering till the whole place went up in flames. Jack "the runner"
began taking bets and almost everyone took him up.

We were glad. We forgot what he did and we did (25) not care.

From nowhere rang a hammer.[3] He went down wriggling, plucked
in half. His hands gripped dirt. The crowd was dead. He was dead. I
died. And Jack "the runner" jingled change in a coffee can.

1. An alcoholic beverage.

2. Jars used for home-canning.

3. The mechanism that causes a gun to fire.

Go on to next page

1. The primary purpose of the first three stanzas (lines 1–12) is to

   (A) introduce the character of Ellic Camel

   (B) create an atmosphere of menace

   (C) set the scene for a unique event

   (D) contrast rural and urban baseball

   (E) establish the conflict in the poem

2. The first line of the poem

   (A) shows that Ellic Camel has been counting the days until his jail term is over

   (B) focuses the reader's attention on one convict

   (C) indicates that Ellic Camel is a career criminal

   (D) reveals that Ellic Camel has nearly finished his jail term

   (E) criticizes the justice system

3. Given that selling corn liquor is illegal, line 8

   (A) creates a link between the crowd and the players

   (B) emphasizes the theme of unfair punishment

   (C) shows that the townspeople have no respect for the law

   (D) adds a simple, descriptive detail

   (E) condemns Roy Jowers

4. The "big hit" referred to in line 13

   (A) is not enough to win the game

   (B) foreshadows the shooting

   (C) elevates Ellic Camel to hero status

   (D) quotes Ellic Camel's view of his actions

   (E) asks the reader to consider the nature of success

5. "The umpire called him out" (line 18) may be seen as

   (A) arbitrary

   (B) coincidental

   (C) critical

   (D) unfair

   (E) ironic

6. With the shift in line 20, the townspeople move from

   (A) spectators to participants

   (B) uninvolved to involved

   (C) supportive to critical

   (D) casual to serious

   (E) despair to hope

7. Line 20, "The whole stadium was left on one wing," may be interpreted as

   (A) the crowd ran to one side of the stadium

   (B) the fans had mixed feelings about Ellic Camel's actions

   (C) Ellic Camel's run is doomed

   (D) the fans were caught off-balance by Ellic Camel's actions

   (E) freedom is an illusion

8. "Like a match dropped in dry woods" (line 22) illustrates which of the following?

   I. the readiness of the fans to cheer for the underdog

   II. the feelings of the fans as they stand up

   III. the swiftness with which the fans become emotionally involved in Ellic Camel's escape

   (A) all of the above

   (B) none of the above

   (C) I only

   (D) I and II

   (E) I and III

9. One interpretation of the statements about death in lines 26–28 is that

   (A) the fans identify strongly with Ellic Camel

   (B) the cycle of life must be completed

   (C) the guards fired indiscriminately

   (D) the speaker cannot relate to Ellic Camel

   (E) the fans are indifferent to Ellic Camel's death

Go on to next page

10. All of the following statements about Jack "the runner" are true EXCEPT

    (A) He runs a gambling operation.

    (B) He is a convict.

    (C) He represents the only winner in the situation depicted in the poem.

    (D) He shows that one man's life-and-death struggle is another's advantage.

    (E) He adds to the small-town atmosphere of the poem.

11. In the context of the poem, which of the following statements may be made about the "change" (line 28)?

    I. "Change" is difficult or impossible to achieve.

    II. The coins represent the hopes of the crowd.

    III. Change is tempting but comes at a price.

    (A) all of the above

    (B) none of the above

    (C) I and II

    (D) II and III

    (E) I and III

12. The title of this poem may be described as

    (A) a simplistic account of the events in the poem

    (B) an erudite introduction to country baseball

    (C) a sophisticated comment on life

    (D) a pun illustrating the main events of the poem

    (E) a formal introduction to the game of baseball

Questions 13–22 are based on the following excerpt from The Age of Innocence, *by Edith Wharton.*

---

(01) There was no better match in New York than May Welland, look at the question from whatever point you chose. Of course such a marriage was only what Newland was entitled to; but young (05) men are so foolish and incalculable — and some women so ensnaring and unscrupulous — that it was nothing short of a miracle to see one's only son safe past the Siren Isle and in the haven of a blameless domesticity.

All this Mrs. Archer felt, and her son knew (10) she felt; but he knew also that she had been perturbed by the premature announcement of his engagement, or rather by its cause; and it was for that reason — because on the whole he was a tender and indulgent master — that he had (15) stayed at home that evening. "It's not that I don't approve of the Mingotts' esprit de corps; but why Newland's engagement should be mixed up with that Olenska woman's comings and goings I don't see," Mrs. Archer grumbled to Janey, the only wit- (20) ness of her slight lapses from perfect sweetness.

She had behaved beautifully — and in beautiful behaviour she was unsurpassed — during the call on Mrs. Welland; but Newland knew (and his betrothed doubtless guessed) that all through (25) the visit she and Janey were nervously on the watch for Madame Olenska's possible intrusion; and when they left the house together she had permitted herself to say to her son: "I'm thankful that Augusta Welland received us alone." (30)

These indications of inward disturbance moved Archer the more that he too felt that the Mingotts had gone a little too far. But, as it was against all the rules of their code that the mother and son should ever allude to what was upper- (35) most in their thoughts, he simply replied: "Oh, well, there's always a phase of family parties to be gone through when one gets engaged, and the sooner it's over the better." At which his mother merely pursed her lips under the lace veil that (40) hung down from her grey velvet bonnet trimmed with frosted grapes.

Her revenge, he felt — her lawful revenge — would be to "draw" Mr. Jackson that evening on the Countess Olenska; and, having publicly done (45) his duty as a future member of the Mingott clan, the young man had no objection to hearing the lady discussed in private — except that the subject was already beginning to bore him.

Mr. Jackson had helped himself to a slice of (50) the tepid filet which the mournful butler had handed him with a look as skeptical as his own, and had rejected the mushroom sauce after a scarcely perceptible sniff. He looked baffled and hungry, and Archer reflected that he would prob- (55) ably finish his meal on Ellen Olenska.

Mr. Jackson leaned back in his chair, and glanced up at the candlelit Archers, Newlands and Van der Luydens hanging in dark frames on the dark walls. (60)

"Ah, how your grandfather Archer loved a good dinner, my dear Newland!" he said, his eyes

Go on to next page ⟶

on the portrait of a plump full-chested young man
in a stock and a blue coat, with a view of a white-
(65) columned country-house behind him. "Well —
well — well . . . I wonder what he would have said
to all these foreign marriages!"

Mrs. Archer ignored the allusion to the
ancestral cuisine and Mr. Jackson continued with
(70) deliberation: "No, she was NOT at the ball."

"Ah —" Mrs. Archer murmured, in a tone that
implied: "She had that decency."

"Perhaps the Beauforts don't know her,"
Janey suggested, with her artless malice.

(75) Mr. Jackson gave a faint sip, as if he had
been tasting invisible Madeira. "Mrs. Beaufort
may not — but Beaufort certainly does, for she
was seen walking up Fifth Avenue this afternoon
with him by the whole of New York."

(80) "Mercy —" moaned Mrs. Archer, evidently
perceiving the uselessness of trying to ascribe
the actions of foreigners to a sense of delicacy.

"I wonder if she wears a round hat or a
bonnet in the afternoon," Janey speculated. "At
(85) the Opera I know she had on dark blue velvet,
perfectly plain and flat — like a night-gown."

"Janey!" said her mother; and Miss Archer
blushed and tried to look audacious.

"It was, at any rate, in better taste not to go
(90) to the ball," Mrs. Archer continued.

A spirit of perversity moved her son to rejoin:
"I don't think it was a question of taste with her.
May said she meant to go, and then decided that
the dress in question wasn't smart enough."

(95) Mrs. Archer smiled at this confirmation of
her inference. "Poor Ellen," she simply remarked;
adding compassionately: "We must always bear
in mind what an eccentric bringing-up Medora
Manson gave her. What can you expect of a girl
(100) who was allowed to wear black satin at her
coming-out ball?"

"Ah — don't I remember her in it!" said
Mr. Jackson; adding: "Poor girl!" in the tone of
one who, while enjoying the memory, had fully
(105) understood at the time what the sight portended.

13. In line 8, "Siren Isle" is
(A) an illusion
(B) a symbol
(C) a metaphor
(D) an allusion
(E) hyperbole

14. The word "master" in line 15 implies that
Mrs. Archer's son
(A) makes his own decisions
(B) is in charge of the family's social calendar
(C) keeps household servants
(D) is engaged to be married
(E) never does what his mother asks

15. The tone of the passage may be described as
(A) ironic
(B) mocking
(C) contemptuous
(D) critical
(E) sarcastic

16. Line 34 refers to a "code." Which statement
does NOT belong to the social code implied
in the passage?
(A) One's most important thoughts should remain secret.
(B) Best behavior is expected on social occasions.
(C) Sincerity is more important than manners.
(D) Family loyalty is paramount.
(E) How one dresses is a matter of public concern.

17. The word "draw" (line 44) in this context
means to
(A) sketch the character of
(B) describe the appearance of
(C) delineate the faults of
(D) remove from discussion
(E) encourage a discussion of

Go on to next page

18. The statement that Mr. Jackson "would probably finish his meal on Ellen Olenska" (lines 55–56) may best be paraphrased as

    (A) Ellen Olenska will be Mr. Jackson's dinner partner for the remainder of the meal.

    (B) Mr. Jackson blames the poor choice of food on Ellen Olenska.

    (C) Mr. Jackson thinks of nothing else but Ellen Olenska.

    (D) Mr. Jackson will tear into Ellen Olenska and destroy her reputation.

    (E) Mr. Jackson will talk of Ellen Olenska throughout the rest of the meal.

19. The description of the dining room decorations (lines 57–65) serves to

    (A) show the family's wealth and status

    (B) establish an atmosphere of comfort

    (C) symbolize the world Mrs. Archer aspires to

    (D) reveal the decline of the Archer family

    (E) characterize Mr. Jackson as a social climber

20. Which of the following most aptly describes the comments of Mrs. Archer and her daughter Janey (lines 72–90)?

    (A) They agree with Mr. Archer's opinion of the Countess.

    (B) They make excuses for Countess Olenska's behavior.

    (C) They approve of Countess Olenska's behavior.

    (D) They criticize Countess Olenska's behavior indirectly.

    (E) They admire the Countess's fashion sense.

21. What is the implication of the last few words of the passage, which state that Mr. Jackson "had fully understood at the time what the sight portended"?

    (A) Deviating from social norms means life as a social outcast.

    (B) Anyone who wears a black satin dress will come to no good.

    (C) Youthful rebellion may be overcome by maturity.

    (D) Breaking one social rule leads to additional transgressions.

    (E) Luxurious clothing should be avoided.

22. A theme of this passage is

    (A) love in the face of adversity

    (B) the rigidity of social norms

    (C) the conflict between generations

    (D) appearance in contradiction of reality

    (E) freedom from traditional gender roles

Questions 23–30 are based on the following poem, entitled "Good Hours," by Robert Frost.

I had for my winter evening walk —   (01)
No one at all with whom to talk,
But I had the cottages in a row
Up to their shining eyes in snow.
And I thought I had the folk within: (05)
I had the sound of a violin;
I had a glimpse through curtain laces
Of youthful forms and youthful faces.
I had such company outward bound.
I went till there were no cottages found.   (10)
I turned and repented, but coming back
I saw no window but that was black.
Over the snow my creaking feet
Disturbed the slumbering village street
Like profanation, by your leave,   (15)
At ten o'clock of a winter eve.

Go on to next page

23. The poem implies all of the following EXCEPT that the speaker

    (A) lives in a cold climate

    (B) has little contact with other people

    (C) thinks that he or she understands the villagers

    (D) is young

    (E) is the only one awake

24. The word "had" (lines 1, 3, 5, 6, 7, 9)

    (A) emphasizes what the speaker owns

    (B) illustrates what the speaker wants

    (C) shows the relationship of the speaker to various people and things

    (D) implies that the speaker's life is over

    (E) shows the speaker's greed

25. Which of the following statements is true?

    (A) The poem is written in rhyming couplets.

    (B) The poem is a sonnet.

    (C) The poem is written in third person.

    (D) The rhythm of the poem is iambic pentameter.

    (E) The turning point of the poem occurs in line 13.

26. The speaker's journey may represent

    (A) his or her dreams

    (B) the consequences of not conforming to an established norm

    (C) the cycle of life

    (D) the importance of nature

    (E) the essential solitude of all people

27. Which of the following is the best interpretation of "by your leave" (line 15) in the context of this poem?

    (A) The speaker will not return to town.

    (B) The reader should accept the extreme term "profanation" (line 15).

    (C) The townspeople have left.

    (D) The townspeople leave the speaker alone.

    (E) No one ever really leaves this town.

28. All of the following poetic techniques appear in the poem EXCEPT

    (A) alliteration

    (B) enjambment

    (C) hyperbole

    (D) assonance

    (E) personification

29. The attitude of the speaker may best be described as

    (A) detached

    (B) apprehensive

    (C) ironic

    (D) argumentative

    (E) overly emotional

30. Line 12 may be restated in which way?

    (A) Every window I saw was bright.

    (B) The windows appeared brighter because of the darkness.

    (C) I did not see any windows because it was too dark.

    (D) I did not see any black windows.

    (E) All the windows were dark.

Go on to next page

> Questions 31–35 are based on the poem "Aphasia" by Abby Wender. **Note:** "Aphasia" is a condition in which a person is unable to speak.

(01)   Like a worm in a robin's beak,
        today a word in my mouth squiggled away.

        My student's eyes were brown
        with gold and green flecks
(05)   and the lashes

        precise strokes of black paint,
        like a portrait in a quiet, empty gallery.

        I stood before her face
        and the word would not come back,
(10)   it seemed to spiral

        the way a twig does
        when you throw it off a little bridge,

        the gulf between us growing faster and faster,
        the twig rushing away from me.

31. The juxtaposition of "worm" (line 1) and the description of the student's eyes (lines 3–7)

    (A) emphasizes the student's vulnerability

    (B) shows the speaker's contempt for the student

    (C) indicates that the speaker knows what to say

    (D) reveals the student's deceptiveness

    (E) conveys a sense of natural behavior

32. The "twig" (line 11) primarily serves to

    (A) indicate that the speaker does not want to recall the word

    (B) show that the relationship is broken irreparably

    (C) reveal the growing inability of the teacher to communicate with the student

    (D) emphasize that the speaker is in control of the situation

    (E) portray the speaker as unfeeling

33. The speaker's feelings are conveyed by all of the following EXCEPT

    (A) simile

    (B) narrative

    (C) metaphor

    (D) imagery

    (E) personification

34. The tone of the poem is best described as

    (A) nostalgic

    (B) sympathetic

    (C) regretful

    (D) argumentative

    (E) ironic

35. In the context of this poem, which statement best expresses the effect of "like a portrait in a quiet, empty gallery" (line 7) on the meaning of the poem?

    (A) The student waits silently for the teacher's instruction.

    (B) The student is too stubborn to show feelings.

    (C) The student does not like the teacher.

    (D) The teacher interprets the student's silence as ignorance.

    (E) The student has no feelings or thoughts.

> Questions 36-46 are based on the following excerpt from Jacob's Room by Virginia Woolf.

(01)   Mrs. Jarvis walked on the moor when she was unhappy, going as far as a certain saucer-shaped hollow, though she always meant to go to a more distant ridge; and there she sat down, and took out the little book hidden beneath her cloak (05) and read a few lines of poetry, and looked about her. She was not very unhappy, and, seeing that she was forty-five, never perhaps would be very unhappy, desperately unhappy that is, and leave her husband, and ruin a good man's career, as (10) she sometimes threatened.

Go on to next page

Still there is no need to say what risks a clergyman's wife runs when she walks on the moor.
Short, dark, with kindling eyes, a pheasant's
(15) feather in her hat, Mrs. Jarvis was just the sort of
woman to lose her faith upon the moors — to
confound her God with the universal that is —
but she did not lose her faith, did not leave her
husband, never read her poem through, and went
(20) on walking the moors, looking at the moon
behind the elm trees, and feeling as she sat on
the grass high above Scarborough . . . Yes, yes,
when the lark soars; when the sheep, moving a
step or two onwards, crop the turf, and at the
(25) same time set their bells tinkling; when the
breeze first blows, then dies down, leaving the
cheek kissed; when the ships on the sea below
seem to cross each other and pass on as if drawn
by an invisible hand; when there are distant con-
(30) cussions in the air and phantom horsemen gal-
loping, ceasing; when the horizon swims blue,
green, emotional — then Mrs. Jarvis, heaving a
sigh, thinks to herself, "If only some one could
give me . . . if I could give some one . . . " But she
(35) does not know what she wants to give, nor who
could give it her.

36. What may the reader infer from the fact that
Mrs. Jarvis walked to a "hollow" instead of
to a "more distant ridge" (line 4)?

(A) Her health is not good.

(B) She has made many compromises in
her life.

(C) She does not know what she really
wants to do.

(D) Her husband's wishes are paramount.

(E) She finds consolation in nature.

37. According to the passage, who thinks that
Mrs. Jarvis might "ruin a good man's
career" (line 10)?

(A) Mr. Jarvis

(B) a clergyman

(C) Mrs. Jarvis

(D) Mrs. Jarvis's friends

(E) no one

38. Mrs. Jarvis's "kindling eyes" (line 14) may
be interpreted as

(A) a sign that she has untapped passion

(B) an unusual color

(C) revealing her generous and loving
nature

(D) an indication that she has lost her good
looks

(E) a symptom of a physical ailment

39. The word "confound" (line 17), in the context of the passage, means

(A) interchange

(B) deny

(C) amaze

(D) obstruct

(E) confuse

40. If Mrs. Jarvis had "read her poem through"
(line 19), she would probably

(A) understand more about her life

(B) stay out after dark

(C) be more religious

(D) leave her husband and fulfill her own
potential

(E) adhere more closely to society's rules

41. The shift between paragraphs one and two
may be categorized largely as

(A) descriptive to narrative

(B) first to third person

(C) descriptive to figurative language

(D) thoughts to action

(E) summary to fantasy

42. The "risks" (line 12) that Mrs. Jarvis runs
include all of the following EXCEPT

(A) leaving her husband

(B) losing her faith

(C) understanding that her life is not
fulfilling

(D) realizing that she loves her husband

(E) feeling temptation

Go on to next page

43. Who or what kisses "the cheek" (line 27)?

    (A) Mr. Jarvis

    (B) the breeze

    (C) the lark

    (D) the sheep

    (E) the phantom horseman

44. The purpose of lines 22–32 ("Yes, yes . . . emotional") is to

    (A) symbolize the lifting of restrictions

    (B) describe the setting of Mrs. Jarvis's walks

    (C) explain what Mrs. Jarvis is thinking

    (D) reveal Mrs. Jarvis's worries

    (E) depict the limitations of Mrs. Jarvis's imagination

45. The ellipses in Mrs. Jarvis's thoughts (line 34) indicate that she

    (A) needs someone else to complete her thoughts

    (B) regrets her choices in life

    (C) is open to possibility

    (D) feels vague longings that she cannot articulate

    (E) has been interrupted

46. In this passage Mrs. Jarvis is NOT characterized by

    (A) her thoughts

    (B) her actions

    (C) others' reactions to her

    (D) the setting

    (E) description

Questions 47–56 are based on the following excerpt from Gulliver's Travels, *by Jonathan Swift. In this selection the narrator, Gulliver, is marooned in the land of the Houyhnhnms, intelligent horses.*

My principal endeavour was to learn the language, which my master (for so I shall henceforth call him), and his children, and every servant of his house, were desirous to teach me; for they looked upon it as a prodigy, that a brute animal (05) should discover such marks of a rational creature. I pointed to every thing, and inquired the name of it, which I wrote down in my journal-book when I was alone, and corrected my bad accent by desiring those of the family to pro- (10) nounce it often. In this employment, a sorrel nag, one of the under-servants, was very ready to assist me.

In speaking, they pronounced through the nose and throat, and their language approaches (15) nearest to the High-Dutch, or German, of any I know in Europe; but is much more graceful and significant. The emperor Charles V made almost the same observation, when he said "that if he were to speak to his horse, it should be in (20) High-Dutch."

The curiosity and impatience of my master were so great, that he spent many hours of his leisure to instruct me. He was convinced (as he afterwards told me) that I must be a Yahoo; but (25) my teachableness, civility, and cleanliness, astonished him; which were qualities altogether opposite to those animals. He was most perplexed about my clothes, reasoning sometimes with himself, whether they were a part of my body: for I (30) never pulled them off till the family were asleep, and got them on before they waked in the morning. My master was eager to learn "whence I came; how I acquired those appearances of reason, which I discovered in all my actions; and (35) to know my story from my own mouth, which he hoped he should soon do by the great proficiency I made in learning and pronouncing their words and sentences." To help my memory, I formed all I learned into the English alphabet, and writ the (40) words down, with the translations. This last, after some time, I ventured to do in my master's presence. It cost me much trouble to explain to him what I was doing; for the inhabitants have not the least idea of books or literature. (45)

In about ten weeks' time, I was able to understand most of his questions; and in three months, could give him some tolerable answers. He was extremely curious to know "from what part of the country I came, and how I was taught to imitate a (50) rational creature; because the Yahoos (whom he saw I exactly resembled in my head, hands, and face, that were only visible), with some appearance of cunning, and the strongest disposition to mischief, were observed to be the most unteach- (55) able of all brutes." I answered, "that I came over

Go on to next page

the sea, from a far place, with many others of my own kind, in a great hollow vessel made of the bodies of trees: that my companions forced me to (60) land on this coast, and then left me to shift for myself." It was with some difficulty, and by the help of many signs, that I brought him to understand me. He replied, "that I must needs be mistaken, or that I said the thing which was not;" for (65) they have no word in their language to express lying or falsehood. "He knew it was impossible that there could be a country beyond the sea, or that a parcel of brutes could move a wooden vessel whither they pleased upon water. He was (70) sure no Houyhnhnm alive could make such a vessel, nor would trust Yahoos to manage it."

The word Houyhnhnm, in their tongue, signifies a horse, and, in its etymology, the perfection of nature. I told my master, "that I was at a loss (75) for expression, but would improve as fast as I could; and hoped, in a short time, I should be able to tell him wonders." He was pleased to direct his own mare, his colt, and foal, and the servants of the family, to take all opportunities of (80) instructing me; and every day, for two or three hours, he was at the same pains himself. Several horses and mares of quality in the neighbourhood came often to our house, upon the report spread of "a wonderful Yahoo, that could speak (85) like a Houyhnhnm, and seemed, in his words and actions, to discover some glimmerings of reason." These delighted to converse with me: they put many questions, and received such answers as I was able to return. By all these (90) advantages I made so great a progress, that, in five months from my arrival I understood whatever was spoken, and could express myself tolerably well.

47. The "brute animal" referred to in line 5 is

   (A) a sorrel nag

   (B) the author

   (C) a horse

   (D) the narrator

   (E) a Houyhnhnm

48. How does paragraph two (lines 14–21) differ from the paragraphs immediately before and after it?

   (A) Paragraph two is out of chronological order.

   (B) Paragraphs one and three explain the interactions between the narrator and the Houyhnhnms, but paragraph two describes language.

   (C) Paragraph two contains more figurative language.

   (D) Paragraphs one and three are more analytical than paragraph two.

   (E) Paragraph two concerns Europe, not the land of the Houyhnhnms.

49. The passage implies that a Yahoo

   (A) has difficulty learning and keeping clean

   (B) is a wild horse

   (C) cannot be compared to the narrator

   (D) looks very different from the narrator

   (E) is a rational creature

50. The expression "This last" in line 41 refers to

   (A) the author's story

   (B) the appearances of reason

   (C) books or literature

   (D) the English alphabet

   (E) writing Houyhnhnm words and their translations

51. Which of the following are true of Houyhnhnms, as may be inferred from this passage?

   I.   They do not lie.

   II. They see themselves as perfect creatures.

   III. They have never left their own land.

   (A) all of the above

   (B) none of the above

   (C) I and II

   (D) II and III

   (E) I and III

Go on to next page

52. As depicted in this passage, Houyhnhnms
    (A) assume that strangers mean to harm them
    (B) place great value on individual achievement
    (C) do not have personal names
    (D) live in harmony with Yahoos
    (E) have a literate society

53. The tone of this passage may be described as
    (A) critical
    (B) analytical
    (C) passionate
    (D) playful
    (E) satirical

54. All of the following are used to characterize the narrator EXCEPT
    (A) actions
    (B) reactions of others
    (C) appearance
    (D) thoughts
    (E) dialogue

55. The comment by Charles V (lines 19–21) serves to
    (A) remind the reader of Gulliver's homeland
    (B) mock European rulers
    (C) illustrate a common human view of animals
    (D) insult the Dutch
    (E) describe the sound of the Houyhnhnm language

56. Overall, the purpose of this passage is probably to
    (A) describe an ideal society
    (B) make the reader reconsider the qualities of animals
    (C) depict a perfectly rational family
    (D) parody a travel narrative
    (E) criticize the tendency of humans to feel superior to others

STOP DO NOT TURN THE PAGE UNTIL TOLD TO DO SO. DO NOT RETURN TO A PREVIOUS TEST.

Section 2: Essays

Time: 2 hours

3 essays

Two of the three essays in this section are based on a literature selection supplied here; the other is based on a literary work of your own choice. You may annotate the selections in this booklet, but only what is written on your loose-leaf paper.

Essay 1

The following passage is taken from Harriet Jacobs's autobiography, *Incidents in the Life of a Slave Girl, Written by Herself.* This excerpt takes place just after Jacobs was compelled to flee from her owner, Dr. Flint. In it Jacobs describes her hiding place, a crawl-space in an attic, where she lived for seven years before escaping to the North. In a well-developed essay, explain the techniques Jacobs employs to further her cause, the abolition of slavery. In your answer, consider the intended audience for this autobiography.

Suggested time you should devote to this essay: 40 minutes.

(01)   A small shed had been added to my grandmother's house years ago. Some boards were laid across the joists at the top, and between these boards and the roof was a very small garret, never occupied by any thing but rats and mice. It was a pent roof, covered with nothing but shingles, according to the southern custom for such buildings. The garret was only nine feet long and seven
(05) wide. The highest part was three feet high, and sloped down abruptly to the loose board floor. There was no admission for either light or air. My uncle Phillip, who was a carpenter, had very skillfully made a concealed trap-door, which communicated with the storeroom. He had been doing this while I was waiting in the swamp. The storeroom opened upon a piazza. To this hole I was conveyed as soon as I entered the house. The air was stifling; the darkness total. A bed had
(10) been spread on the floor. I could sleep quite comfortably on one side; but the slope was so sudden that I could not turn on my other without hitting the roof. The rats and mice ran over my bed; but I was weary, and I slept such sleep as the wretched may, when a tempest has passed over them. Morning came. I knew it only by the noises I heard; for in my small den day and night were all the same. I suffered for air even more than for light. But I was not comfortless. I heard the
(15) voices of my children. There was joy and there was sadness in the sound. It made my tears flow. How I longed to speak to them! I was eager to look on their faces; but there was no hole, no crack, through which I could peep. This continued darkness was oppressive. It seemed horrible to sit or lie in a cramped position day after day, without one gleam of light. Yet I would have chosen this, rather than my lot as a slave, though white people considered it an easy one; and it was so com-
(20) pared with the fate of others. I was never cruelly overworked; I was never lacerated with the whip from head to foot; I was never so beaten and bruised that I could not turn from one side to the other; I never had my heel-strings cut to prevent my running away; I was never chained to a log and forced to drag it about, while I toiled in the fields from morning till night; I was never branded with hot iron, or torn by bloodhounds. On the contrary, I had always been kindly treated, and ten-
(25) derly cared for, until I came into the hands of Dr. Flint. I had never wished for freedom till then. But though my life in slavery was comparatively devoid of hardships, God pity the woman who is compelled to lead such a life!
    My food was passed up to me through the trap-door my uncle had contrived; and my grandmother, my uncle Phillip, and aunt Nancy would seize such opportunities as they
(30) could, to mount up there and chat with me at the opening. But of course this was not safe in the daytime. It must all be done in darkness. It was impossible for me to move in an erect position, but I crawled about my den for exercise. One day I hit my head against something, and found it was a gimlet. My uncle had left it sticking there when he made

(35) the trap-door. I was as rejoiced as Robinson Crusoe could have been at finding such a treasure. It put a lucky thought into my head. I said to myself, "Now I will have some light. Now I will see my children." I did not dare to begin my work during the daytime, for fear of attracting attention. But I groped round; and having found the side next the street, where I could frequently see my children, I stuck the gimlet in and waited for evening. I bored three rows of holes, one above another; then I bored out the interstices between. I

(40) thus succeeded in making one hole about an inch long and an inch broad. I sat by it till late into the night, to enjoy the little whiff of air that floated in. In the morning I watched for my children. The first person I saw in the street was Dr. Flint. I had a shuddering, superstitious feeling that it was a bad omen. Several familiar faces passed by. At last I heard the merry laugh of children, and presently two sweet little faces were looking up at

(45) me, as though they knew I was there, and were conscious of the joy they imparted. How I longed to tell them I was there!

My condition was now a little improved. But for weeks I was tormented by hundreds of little red insects, fine as a needle's point, that pierced through my skin, and produced an intolerable burning. The good grandmother gave me herb teas and cooling medicines, and

(50) finally I got rid of them. The heat of my den was intense, for nothing but thin shingles protected me from the scorching summer's sun. But I had my consolations. Through my peeping-hole I could watch the children, and when they were near enough, I could hear their talk. Aunt Nancy brought me all the news she could hear at Dr. Flint's. From her I learned that the doctor had written to New York to a colored woman, who had been born and

(55) raised in our neighborhood, and had breathed his contaminating atmosphere. He offered her a reward if she could find out any thing about me. I know not what was the nature of her reply; but he soon after started for New York in haste, saying to his family that he had business of importance to transact. I peeped at him as he passed on his way to the steamboat. It was a satisfaction to have miles of land and water between us, even for a little

(60) while; and it was a still greater satisfaction to know that he believed me to be in the Free States. My little den seemed less dreary than it had done. He returned, as he did from his former journey to New York, without obtaining any satisfactory information. When he passed our house next morning, Benny was standing at the gate. He had heard them say that he had gone to find me, and he called out, "Dr. Flint, did you bring my mother home? I

(65) want to see her." The doctor stamped his foot at him in a rage, and exclaimed, "Get out of the way, you little damned rascal! If you don't, I'll cut off your head."

Benny ran terrified into the house, saying, "You can't put me in jail again. I don't belong to you now."

Essay 2

Read the following prose poem, "Spraying the Chickens" by John Allman (from *Attractions,* 2River Press, 2006). In a well-organized essay, discuss how the poetic elements Allman employs reveal the poet's attitude toward the two ways of living implied in the poem.

Suggested time you should devote to this essay: 40 minutes.

(01) It wasn't necessary back when the hen kept her chicks close and they pecked at her fecal droppings and they swallowed just the right kind of mother love, a touch of illness, a taste of their own blood, and they trembled in sleep. Those days you could eat them without a care. Maybe even find a dark spot near the pimply shoulder, a piece of quill, the

(05) memory of a certain kind of flapping. The farmer's wife wiped her hands on her apron after she put the naked thing in the oven and she wiped the dirt off potatoes and she cut the bread, and you were so happy and hungry you wanted to kiss her hands that kept layer upon layer of so much world intact. And if something of that got into your mouth, it was proof against the evil to come, the corruption of bodies. The cold touch of strangers.

Essay 3

A betrayal of trust appears often in novels and plays. In a well-developed essay, discuss how a betrayal of trust occurs in a work of literary merit and how this event adds to the reader's understanding of character, plot, or theme. Do not limit your comments to plot summary. You may choose a work from the following list or discuss another work of comparable merit. Do not write about a short story or a poem.

Suggested time you should devote to this essay: 40 minutes.

All the King's Men	*A Raisin in the Sun*
Antigone	*The Piano Lesson*
David Copperfield	*The Remains of the Day*
King Lear	*Rosencrantz and Guildenstern Are Dead*
Macbeth	
Madame Bovary	*The Scarlet Letter*
Medea	*Sense and Sensibility*
Nineteen Eighty-Four	*A Separate Peace*
Of Mice and Men	*The Shipping News*
Orlando	*Their Eyes Were Watching God*
Othello	

Chapter 19

Checking In: Scoring Practice Exam 2

$\boldsymbol{I}$n this chapter, you get to see how truly boring a teacher's life can be. Take out your red pen and get ready to score. Not the fun kind of score, such as in "the Dodgers win the pennant!" but the annoying "is it right or not" kind of score. After you've checked your answers, convert the raw scores into the proper AP form. This number tells you what score you would have received had this been the real test. If you're happy with your score, fine. If you still have a micrometer's room for improvement, turn back to the appropriate chapters for a short, refreshing — okay, refresher — course.

Seeking Straight Answers: Scoring the Multiple-Choice Questions

This section has 56 questions. Check your answers and record the number of correct answers in the "multiple-choice conversion formula" section. If you left any questions blank, simply ignore them for scoring purposes. You should of course read the answer and explanation for anything you left blank. If you answered any questions wrong (of course you didn't!), enter that number in the conversion section as well.

Individual answers

1. **(C).** Lines 1–26 describe the setting, Camp Field, with details such as the refreshments ("hot dogs and cotton candy" in line 12) and the spectators' accommodations ("hot silver tin" roof in line 23). Though Ellic Camel is mentioned in line 1, his character doesn't appear again until the fourth stanza (line 27), so (A) is wrong. Ellic Camel's character clearly isn't the primary purpose of the first three stanzas. Similarly, the guards lining the baseball field are menacing figures, but they occupy only four lines of the first 26 in the poem. Therefore, choice (B) doesn't do the job either. Answers (D) and (E) are off base because urban baseball isn't in the poem, and the conflict shows up a lot later, when the guards shoot the escaping Ellic. Answer (C) is the best because the "unique event" — the shooting of Ellic Camel — is firmly grounded in the setting established in the first three stanzas.

2. **(B).** Line 1 doesn't give a lot away. For instance, you don't know how long Ellic Camel is supposed to be in jail, so answer (D) is out of the running. Nor do you have any idea why Ellic Camel is doing time. Okay, you drop (C) too. Choice (A) is tempting, because *someone* has been counting, but you can't figure out whether Ellic, the spectators, or the speaker ("me" in line 2) is keeping track of the days. Choice (E) strikes out — I know, I know, enough already with the baseball puns — because line 1 gives you nothing but one fact: how long Ellic has been in jail. Therefore, (B) is your answer, because line 1 focuses on Ellic and nothing else.

3. **(A).** The corn-liquor business is illegal. However, (B) bows out because you can't tell whether it's unfair that Jowers breaks the law and remains free while Ellic is imprisoned. Why? Because you don't know what Ellic's crime is. Choice (C) is too extreme. The towns-people may tolerate the corn-liquor trade, but to say that they have "no respect for the law" isn't supported by the poem. Choice (E) comes out of left field. (Sorry, I couldn't resist one more baseball joke. I'll stop now. I promise.) Roy is selling, somebody's probably buying, and who's to say he's condemned? (D) doesn't give credit to the one thing line 16 actually does: show that the crowd is able to tolerate some illegal activity, an attitude that Ellic Camel must share, given that he did *something* to wind up in jail. With this line, Camel and the spectators are linked, and (A) wins.

4. **(B).** When Ellic goes down (line 56), he has been hit. So the "big hit" of line 28 — a double or maybe a triple — foreshadows a fatal gunshot wound in lines 56–61. None of the other answers are supported in the text. For example, you don't know the score, so (A) is a dud, and (C) is a loser because the crowd doesn't cheer for Ellic in the same way until he heads for the fence (lines 35–37). Choices (D) and (E) also aren't supported in the text.

5. **(E).** Irony is easier to illustrate than define. When something turns out differently from what you expect, yet there's an element of "oh, that's perfect" in it, you're in ironic territory. Think of a Web site condemning the Internet. (I actually saw one!) Ellic Camel *is* out — out of the fenced-in field, out of the prison guards' territory, and ultimately, out of his life. However, the umpire's statement refers only to the rules of baseball. How ironic. The other choices aren't a good fit. "Arbitrary" — choice (A) — means "because I said so" or "without justifying reasons." But the umpire *does* have a reason: Camel is out because he left the base path. Nor is the umpire's call "coincidental," because his job is to make judgments about the game. Hence (B) is a bad choice. The umpire also isn't "critical" or "unfair"; he's just accurate in his call. That means choices (C) and (D) get eliminated as well.

6. **(D).** The fans don't jump into the game, so (A) is out. You can't make a case for (B) because the townspeople *were* involved. After all, they've already "cheered him on" (line 29). Line 53 makes it clear that the fans *do* support Camel's escape, so choice (C) strikes out. Nor can you select (E), because no one showed "despair" in the first 42 lines of the poem. Bingo, (D) wins. The phrase "the fans all sucked air" (in line 40) indicates a collective hush and a sudden, serious mood.

7. **(D).** A bird can't fly on only one wing, so the statement implies a handicap or a lack of balance. The fans are shocked by Ellic Camel's run out of the stadium; in other words, they're "off-balance," as (D) states. Choice (A) isn't supported by the text because the fans only "sucked air" (line 40); no one actually moves. Line 53 states that the fans were "glad," so (B) is out. The escape attempt *is* futile, so choice (C) is tempting, but line 41 specifically refers to "the stadium," which in this line is a stand-in for the crowd. Choice (D) is therefore the better answer because it mentions the fans. (E) is from some other universe entirely — or at least from some other poem.

8. **(E).** The "match dropped in dry woods" quickly starts a fire because the "woods" are ready to burn. In other words, the fans are ready — but for what? The poem clearly shows that the fans are on Camel's side ("We were glad," line 53). Statements I and III make the cut, but II is a dud because the "match dropped in dry woods" addresses process, from readiness to full fire, not the feelings themselves.

9. **(A).** In lines 56–58, Camel goes down wriggling, plucked / in half"; obviously he's mortally wounded. The three statements about death place Camel's death between the death of the "crowd" and the death of the speaker ("I / died," lines 59–60). The identification of (A) is supported by the crowd's cheers (line 48).

10. **(B).** Jack's taking bets (line 50), so (A) is A-OK. The fact that Jack *can* take bets in the presence of the guards strongly implies that he isn't a convict, though perhaps he should be, depending on the gambling laws of that particular location. However, because the gambling laws don't appear in the poem (and because no one arrests Jack), (B) is false (and is therefore your answer). Choice (C) comes across in the last line of the poem: Everyone's dead, at

least metaphorically, but Jack is jingling his profits. (D) is also true because while the escape costs Ellic Camel his life, Jack sees a chance to make money. The fans seem to know and tolerate Jack, and he's using a coffee can for his business — not exactly Wall Street or Las Vegas! Therefore, choice (E) also is true.

11. **(A).** The coins, or change, are confined in a coffee can. Also, Ellic Camel dies in a futile attempt to change his life. Put these two statements together and they justify statement I. The crowd bets when Ellic takes off. Yes, some of the people may have bet against Camel, but the fact that the fans cheer him on shows that the crowd ultimately *wants* Ellic Camel to get out, to *change* his circumstances. All these ideas add up to statement II. The jingling (line 60) represents the temptation. Because the "change" is "jingled," and because Camel dies, III makes the cut. Bingo! That means (A) is your answer.

12. **(D).** Ellic Camel gets two hits: one with his bat and one with a bullet. These two events anchor the poem. First, Camel hits the ball and sets the stage for his escape. Then, the guards fire and "hit" him. Thus, (D) is clearly the best answer. Did I catch you on (A)? "Simplistic" means "overly simple." The title is simple, but not simplistic. You can vote (B) off the island because the poem isn't really about "country baseball" (even though it is technically set at a country baseball game). Choice (E) fails for the same reason, and (C) is just way too general.

13. **(D).** Dust off the brain cells that carry your literary definitions, and you'll see that "Siren Isle" (line 8) is an *allusion,* or a reference to something outside the literary work that brings all of its meaning into the work. Here Mrs. Archer is alluding to an episode in Homer's *Odyssey* about the Sirens, magical creatures whose singing entices and entraps men (the ancient version of a pop vocalist whose talent is slightly smaller than the tiny amount of clothing she wears).

14. **(A).** The word "master" appears in a sentence implying that Mrs. Archer's son decided to humor his mother because she was "perturbed by the premature announcement of his engagement" (lines 11–13). The key is that the son had the power to make the decision, not Mrs. Archer.

Question 14 contains a typical AP trick; it includes statements that are true (choice D, for example) but not relevant to the question, which is asking for the meaning of the word "master" in the context of this passage. Be sure you know what question you're answering.

15. **(B).** Mrs. Archer's thoughts, such as her idea that "young men are so foolish and incalculable" (line 5), and the description of her "slight lapses from perfect sweetness" (line 21) immediately establish a mocking tone. Choice (D) is true in the sense that the passage is critical of the society depicted, but mockery better captures the author's gentle humor. Choices (C) and (E) are too harsh. (A) implies an element of surprise, something unexpected. Unless you were raised by wolves, you've met someone resembling Mrs. Archer and Mr. Jackson, so choice (B) is best.

16. **(C).** The characters in this passage emphasize outward appearances and behavior. Mrs. Archer and her son never "allude to what was uppermost in their thoughts" (lines 35–36), so (A) is out. Mrs. Archer "had behaved beautifully" (line 22), clearly part of the social contract as expressed by (B), and she understood the "Mingotts' esprit de corps" (line 17), a reference to family loyalty — choice (D). The conversation about clothes, especially Janey's and Mrs. Archer's comments (lines 83–86 and 96–100), shows that in the world described in this passage, you *are* what you *wear.*

17. **(E).** Mrs. Archer wants the dirt on the Countess, so she sets out to "draw" (line 44) information from Mr. Jackson, to encourage him to give her all the gossip available. The other choices all relate to real meanings of the word "draw." However, the key here is to look for the meaning of the word in context.

18. **(E).** Ellen Olenska isn't around, so you can rule out choices (A) and (B). He gives no indication of being obsessed with her, as in choice (C). She's fair game for the gossip mill, so (D) and (E) are both possible. (D) is a little extreme, and in fact it's the women, not Mr. Jackson, who really eat up Ellen Olenska. The best answer is therefore (E).

19. **(A).** Fancy paintings of wealthy ancestors, including one with a "white-columned country house" in the background, shout "old money," which means that (A) is a good choice. The Archers are part of this social set, as is Mr. Jackson, so choices (C), (D), and (E) don't make the grade. The only choice left is (B). And unless you find stuffy old paintings relaxing and comforting, that answer also bites the dust.

20. **(D).** To decode the remarks of Mrs. Archer and Janey, you need to notice a few details. For instance, Janey speaks with "artless malice" (line 74), a fancy way of saying that her bad intentions come across as natural or unstudied. Mrs. Archer "moaned" (line 80) because she couldn't see a "sense of delicacy" (line 82) as the motivation for the Countess's walking with a man. Even the compliments or excuses are little stabs at the Countess. Mrs. Archer's "Ah" (line 71) is shorthand for "She had that decency" (line 72), which itself is a stand-in for "she's usually indecent." Because most of the comments are in shorthand, the criticism is indirect.

21. **(D).** Ellen Olenska wore a (gasp) black satin dress at her coming-out ball (lines 100–101). Even if you don't know the social rules for debutantes (and I don't either), you can tell that this clothing was a no-no by the reference to "an eccentric upbringing" (line 98). Mrs. Archer says, "What can you expect . . ." implying that anyone who doesn't get the dress code will go on to bigger mistakes. Therefore, (D) is your best answer. Choices (A), (B), and (E) are tempting, but the Countess isn't a total outcast (after all, she *was* seen walking with Mr. Beaufort in lines 77–78). And the point isn't the dress alone, but when and where it was worn. Choice (C) isn't supported anywhere in the passage.

22. **(B).** The rules of this society are quite strict: no black satin at coming-out balls, no walking with other women's husbands, and so forth. No one in this passage is in love, so (A) isn't a good answer. And while Mr. Archer rebels a bit, his sister isn't in conflict with the older generation, represented by her mother. Therefore, (C) is out. Choice (E) is also a loser; the passage doesn't challenge gender roles. (D) is tempting because of the characters' insincerity, but as they're fairly open about their disapproval of the countess, (B) is a better choice.

23. **(D).** The speaker comments on a "glimpse" (line 7) of "youthful forms and youthful faces" (line 8), but the poem gives no information at all about the speaker's age. The fact that the poet contrasts the speaker with the rest of the village may even imply the opposite — that the speaker is older than the other villagers. Clearly, choice (D) is the answer. The snow takes care of choice (A). And the fact that the speaker is walking alone and has not even one person "with whom to talk" (line 2) leads you to dump (B). Line 5, "And I thought I had the folk within," implies choice (C), because one meaning of "had" is "understood." The dark windows (line 12) and the "slumbering" in line 14 take care of choice (E).

24. **(C).** Who would have thought that there were so many nuances of "had"? In lines 1 and 5 "had" is personal, much like the way you "have" or "had" a friend. The other instances of "had" reveal what the speaker heard and saw: the small signs of human life that sustain him or her. The next "had" sums up these things that the speaker latches onto, despite being alone: "I had such company" (line 9). Thus, the simple verb shows the relationship between the speaker and the inhabitants of the village and the homely signs of life. Of the other choices, the most tempting is probably (B), because the speaker's solitude implies a wish for more company. However, the poem is entitled "Good Hours," so that choice is a bit of a stretch. The speaker may be one of those people who like to know that others are around but don't want to interact.

25. **(A).** In this poem, you can pair off the lines by rhymes. "Walk" partners with "talk," "row" with "snow," and so on. These pairs are *couplets*, an easy poetic term to remember because it sounds like "couples." Choice (B) is out for the count because a sonnet has 14 lines. Third person is the point of view of an outsider, talking about someone else (the "he," "she," or "they" point of view), so (C) is wrong. Iambic pentameter, the ten-syllable heartbeat line, doesn't fit here, so (D) also bites the dust. The poem does have a turning point, between the outward and the inbound journey (line 11), but (E) specifies line 13, so you're left with (A).

26. **(B).** The speaker strikes out alone and goes farther and farther until no one else is around, whereupon the speaker "turned and repented" (line 11). This journey, in a metaphorical sense, may represent the speaker's choosing a different path in life from the path of the other villagers. In other words, he doesn't conform to an established norm. Thus, (B) wins out. The other choices aren't supported in the poem. The reader learns nothing about the speaker's dreams. Choice (C) is always a favorite because poets so often write about the cycle of life, but in this poem you don't have any cycles. Choices (D) and (E) sound important and poetic, but they're also irrelevant here.

27. **(B).** "Profanation" (line 15) refers to the desecration of something sacred. The speaker says that the sound of his or her "creaking feet" (line 13) came across as "profanation." Choice (A) wipes out because the speaker *does* return to town. (C) is wrong because the townspeople are "slumbering" (line 14), not gone. Because the townspeople are asleep, you can't tell whether they've chosen to leave the speaker alone. After all, you can't socialize when you sleep! Therefore, choice (D) is out. Can anyone leave the town? Who knows? And because you don't know, (E) isn't the correct choice.

28. **(C).** *Hyperbole* is exaggeration, and this poem sticks to the facts of a walk through the snow. As you see, choice (C) is the correct answer. Choice (A) appears in line 1, among other places, when the consonant "w" repeats ("winter evening walk"), giving you *alliteration*. Choice (B), *enjambment,* is a fancy term for a line that wraps around the line break, continuing the meaning. You can find enjambment in lines 3, 7, 11, 13, and 14. *Assonance,* the repetition of vowel sounds, is shown in line 4 with "shining eyes." Those same eyes, the house windows, create *personification,* which is lit-speak for giving nonhuman items human characteristics.

29. **(A).** The tone of this poem is so detached that you might think the speaker is on a witness stand, telling the reader the truth, the whole truth, and nothing but the truth. Granted, a little emotion leaks in by way of words such as "repented" (line 11), but mostly you get a sense of uninvolvement, a synonym for "detachment."

30. **(E).** The *syntax* (a fancy term for the way words fit together grammatically) is odd here, but decipherable. The lighted windows the speaker saw on the way out of town are all dark now.

31. **(A).** The worm is relatively powerless. True, it may have "squiggled away" like the word in line 2. However, a worm's life can be severed in an instant by the sharp beak of a robin. In the same way, the student is less powerful than the teacher. The student's eyes watch the teacher, as prey watches a predator. Nowhere does the speaker show contempt (B), nor does the student behave in a sneaky way (D). Choices (C) and (E) aren't correct because aphasia means the speaker *can't* express himself or herself and, as everyone's cellphone bills prove, speechlessness isn't natural.

32. **(C).** Choice (A) is out because the speaker does want to recall the word but is unable to do so. (B) is tempting, but it's less extreme than (C) and nothing in the poem supports the idea of a permanent break. (D) is flat-out wrong because the speaker isn't in control. Finally, choice (E) might draw you in because the speaker's feelings are implied, not stated. However, the fact that the teacher describes the aphasia so carefully shows that the speaker does have feelings about the situation.

33. **(E).** The first stanza is a *simile* (the worm is compared to a word), and the second and third stanzas contain a *metaphor* (a description created when one thing is equated with another). Therefore you can eliminate choices (A) and (C). The poem narrates a short incident, with the speaker standing in front of a student and losing words. So (B) drops out. The eyes are described in detail, taking care of (D). Personification, choice (E), is the only element left, and it isn't present in the poem.

34. **(C).** The poem describes an incident and also a relationship, one in which two people lose a connection. In other words, they become detached. As a teacher myself, I'd see that situation as regretful.

35. **(A).** The "quiet, empty gallery" (line 7) is a vacuum, waiting for something to fill it. In this poem, the filler might be what the teacher intended to say. Choice (B) is out because nothing in the poem shows stubbornness. And (C), (D), and (E) aren't supported anywhere in the passage.

36. **(B).** The "saucer-shaped hollow" (lines 2–3) is a compromise, a shorter walk than "to a more distant ridge" (line 4). Mrs. Jarvis's walks, therefore, symbolize the compromises she has made in her life. The passage says nothing about her health or her love of nature — choices (A) and (E) — so you can rule out those answers. Ditching (C) and (D) is more difficult because her husband and her wishes *are* in the passage. For instance, the last two lines do imply confusion, as does (C). But the statement about the hollow and the ridge doesn't say that she *can't* decide where she wants to go. She knows; she just doesn't go there. Choice (D) is wrong because although line 10 tells you that she doesn't want to "ruin a good man's career," not killing his job prospects and making his wishes a priority aren't equivalent.

37. **(C).** This answer is easy after you invert the unusual word order of the last sentence of the first paragraph. With this flip-flopping, for example, line 11 states that "she sometimes threatened" to "leave her husband, and ruin a good man's career." "She" has to be Mrs. Jarvis, the only female in the passage.

38. **(A).** Did I catch you with this question? The word "kind" is embedded in "kindling," but the two are quite different. "Kindling" is the term for small pieces of wood that are used to start a fire, and fire is a symbol of passion. Mrs. Jarvis doesn't have "blazing" eyes, so her passion is still waiting to ignite or, as choice (A) puts it, her passion is "untapped." None of the other choices are supported by the passage.

39. **(E).** Mrs. Jarvis would "lose her faith" (line 16) during her walk if she confused God with the "universal" (line 17). The only other answer remotely close is (A), but she isn't swapping; she muddling the two together.

40. **(D).** Virginia Woolf, who wrote the novel from which this passage is taken, loved to throw symbols into her work for you to interpret. *Symbols* are things or events in the literary work that represent larger ideas. In this passage, Mrs. Jarvis "read a few lines of poetry" (line 6) and "never read her poem through" (line 19). She's "not very unhappy" (line 7) and thinks "if only . . ." (line 33). All of these lines indicate that she wants more than she has. Throw in the reference to leaving her husband in lines 9–10 and you're there: finishing the poem symbolizes completing a task, such as leaving her husband, and changing that "if only" to "Yes!"

41. **(C).** The first paragraph mostly describes what Mrs. Jarvis does and how she feels. It has a symbol. (See the preceding answer, which explains how Mrs. Jarvis's poetry reading is symbolic.) However, most of the paragraph is straightforward. The second paragraph moves into *figurative language,* in which words or phrases have more than a literal level of meaning. The second paragraph is full of symbols — the "kindling eyes" (line 14), the soaring lark (line 23), and so forth. Choice (A) doesn't work because the second paragraph isn't *narrative*; in other words, it doesn't tell a story. You can vote the other choices off the island because the whole passage is in third person. Not much action happens in the second paragraph, and the first paragraph isn't a summary.

42. **(D).** Mrs. Jarvis doesn't love her husband. The big sigh in line 33 and the clues at the end of first paragraph make this fact perfectly clear.

43. **(B).** Simple decoding snags the correct answer for this question. The "breeze" is a subject matched with three actions: "blows," "dies," and "leaving the cheek kissed" (lines 26–27). Also, Mr. Jarvis does *not* sound like the kind of fellow who would trek over a moor just to kiss his wife. And I don't even want to think about those sheep smacking their lips!

44. **(A).** These lines contain many images of freedom, from a soaring lark (line 23) to the movement of sheep "onwards" (lines 23–24) to the "ships on the sea" (line 27). The images become increasingly more fanciful with the "distant concussions in the air" (lines 29–30) and the "phantom horsemen" (line 30) until the "horizon" (line 31) is reached. Symbolically, Mrs. Jarvis can *see* freedom; she just can't figure out how to achieve it.

45. **(D).** The half sentences of lines 33–34 end with *ellipses,* a handy punctuation mark indicating omission. The last sentence of the passage is the clue as to what Mrs. Jarvis is omitting and why. The only other answer that comes close is (B), because Mrs. Jarvis clearly does have regrets. However, those regrets aren't revealed by the ellipses.

46. **(C).** You hear Mrs. Jarvis's thoughts (line 33), see her actions (lines 1–4), and learn about the places that she goes (lines 1–4). She's described in lines 14 and 15. The only thing missing is other people. We know what she says to her husband, but we don't how he or anyone else reacts to her.

47. **(D).** The Houyhnhnms are shocked that the narrator can learn a language. Throughout the first paragraph, the narrator is seen as a "brute animal" (line 5) and a "prodigy" (line 5) who has "marks of a rational creature" (line 6). Imagine your dog politely asking you to play a Beethoven sonata, and then you'll be in the same mood as the Houyhnhnms.

Did you choose (B)? If so, you made a common error. The author isn't the same as the narrator. The author may certainly choose elements of his or her own life, but the great thing about fiction is that you have license to lie. In fact, you're expected to do so. Makes you wonder why politicians don't write more novels.

48. **(B).** The first and third paragraphs describe both the narrator's efforts to learn the language and the way the horses react to the narrator. The second paragraph is a comment on the language itself; it compares the language to "High Dutch" (line 16). You may have been snagged by choice (A). True, the chronology is broken by the second paragraph, but that paragraph isn't a narrative, so chronology is irrelevant. Thus, you should go with choice (B).

49. **(A).** Take a look at line 26, in which the narrator's "teachableness, civility, and cleanliness" surprise the master, who has been sure that the narrator is a Yahoo. These qualities, furthermore, are "altogether opposite to those animals" (lines 27–28). Choice (B) bombs because Yahoos aren't horses. Choices (C), (D), and (E) lose because the passage compares the narrator to a Yahoo several times, such as in lines 51–56. In these lines, the narrator is said to share a physical resemblance with a Yahoo but not to behave like one, because the narrator imitates a rational creature (lines 50–51).

50. **(E).** The activity described just before "This last" (line 41) is turning "all I learned into the English alphabet, and writ[ing] the words down, with the translations" (lines 40–41). Therefore, you need an answer that includes those activities, and (E) wins the prize.

51. **(A).** The Houyhnhnms have no word for lying; they can only say of the narrator that he "must needs be mistaken, or that I said the thing which was not" (lines 63–64). The word Houyhnhnm is derived from "perfection of nature" (lines 73–74). Because they're shocked that "there could be country beyond the sea" (line 67), you know that Houyhnhnms stay put. (You would too if you had to spell that name on a hotel registration slip.) All three statements are true, so (A) is the answer you want.

52. **(C).** The passage mentions a master, a foal, a nag, a mare, and a couple of other words for horses, but no names. Without names, you can assume that individuality isn't important to these horses, so (B) drops out. Choice (A) is wrong because the Houyhnhnms are puzzled, but not threatened, by the narrator. The passage contains numerous comments showing that Houyhnhnms see themselves as superior to Yahoos but no information about harmony or conflict, so you can eliminate (D). Line 45 specifically states that Houyhnhnms have "not the least idea of books or literature." This statement means they aren't likely to have a literate society as (E) suggests. Clearly, (C) is the best choice.

53. **(E).** The passage is an extended joke, poking fun at human notions of superiority. In this society, the horses are in charge and the humans — or Yahoos — are irrational, dirty, stupid, and, well, you get the point. When a text pokes fun at something in this way, it's considered a *satire.* Besides (E), the only other choice remotely possible is (A), because Swift criticizes human society by showing a better crowd (the horses). Choice (E), however, is more specific to literature, so it's the better answer.

54. **(D).** The narrator tells you what he does, what he says, and how the Houyhnhnms react. He's also described in general terms (he looks like a Yahoo), but in this passage, he has no inner life. Thus, thoughts aren't in the passage.

55. **(B).** Humans tend to see themselves as superior to animals, and emperors imagine that they're superior to other humans. The idea of Charles V figuring out how to talk to a horse in a different language should bring a smile to your face. (I know, during an AP test even the funniest comedy routine falls flat.) Here Swift is mocking the feeling of superiority — of human beings and of their rulers.

56. **(E).** Like most satires, *Gulliver's Travels* depicts an extreme — in this case, a land of intelligent horses — in order to show the silliness of human nature. By flipping the usual horse/human relationship and by showing how the Houyhnhnms feel about Yahoos (human beings), Swift criticizes the usual "we're number one" attitude that many people have (except, of course, those who live with a pet cat). Were you tempted by (B)? That choice is wrong because the passage isn't describing real animals. The Houyhnhnms aren't horses, with equine behavior. They're people with fur and hooves.

Multiple-choice conversion formula

To go from your raw multiple-choice score to a converted score, you have to subtract ¼ of the number of wrong answers from the number of correct answers. This process sounds complicated, but it really isn't that bad. Follow these steps to get it right:

1. **Multiply the number of answers you got wrong by ¼.**

   For example, if you got 8 answers wrong, your result for this step would be 2.

2. **Subtract the result from Step 1 from the total number of answers you got right.**

   This answer is your converted multiple-choice score.

   Continuing the example from Step 1, if you got 47 answers correct, your converted multiple-choice score would be 45.

Now that you have the converted multiple-choice score, enter it in the later section "Putting It all Together: Calculating Your Overall AP Exam Score."

A Challenge for the Indecisive: Scoring the Essays

Scoring essays isn't much fun. I know, because I regularly take home stacks of papers to wade through. Okay, I'm lying. I do take home stacks of papers, but I mostly enjoy reading them, because I get a chance to see how my students' writing abilities and insights into literature have developed. Now you get a chance to do the same for your own work. If this is the second practice exam you've graded, you know what to do. If it's the first, here's the drill:

1. **Read through the instructions on how to score an essay, which I provide in Chapter 17.**

2. **Read the sample essays for each question.**

   I provide two samples per question, and I explain what's good and bad about each.

3. **Reread your own essay.**

4. **Go over the general checklist, evaluating your essay and entering a score for each category.**

Each category contains three possibilities (4, 5, 6 or 7, 8, 9, for example). If you can't decide between two numbers, ask yourself whether your essay is closer to the next higher or next lower category. If it misses a higher category by a hair, take the highest number of the three. If it narrowly escapes the lower category, choose the lowest number of the three. Can't decide? Go for the middle.

5. **Use the formula at the end of the checklist to convert your score.**

Two errors draw a zero for an essay. These two errors include an essay that's left blank or an essay that doesn't answer the question. If one of these situations applies to you, check out Chapters 7 or 12 for help with essay writing.

Essay 1: Harriet Jacobs and the Abolition of Slavery

Harriet Jacobs's justly famous autobiography communicated the horrors of slavery by means of her own experience. The passage in the exam prompt clearly conveys her terrible living conditions while in hiding. After the AP exam is out of your hair, I recommend that you read the entire, amazing story. But first, score your essay.

Scoring grid for essay 1

Before you fill in the following scoring grid, reread your essay. Underline spots where you might have done better, and indicate areas in which you excelled. Then work your way through the categories in this scoring section, assigning yourself a number in each one.

Addresses the question: _____

The prompt requires you to consider three things: the intended audience for Harriet Jacobs's writing, her cause (the abolition of slavery), and the literary techniques she employs to win over her audience. Choose a number from the following list that reflects how well your essay addresses the question:

0   The essay doesn't answer the question or is left blank.

1–3   The essay summarizes what Harriet Jacobs went through and mentions one or two elements of her style. The issue of the intended audience isn't addressed in any detail. The essay doesn't explain how Jacobs's passage furthers the abolitionist cause.

4–6   The essay contains some summary of Jacobs's experience but makes several points about literary techniques and their possible effect on the intended audience. The essay doesn't explore in depth how the passage furthers the abolitionist cause. The essay may stray from the question and include some irrelevant material.

7–9   The essay identifies the intended audience for this book and explains why that particular audience would read it. The essay explains the literary techniques used in this passage and discusses how each may affect the intended audience, linking those effects to abolition. Few, if any, off-topic and summary statements appear in the essay.

Literary analysis: _____

The AP English exam evaluates your ability to analyze a literary work and the author's writing technique. Scan your essay and then choose the number from this list that best represents your analysis of _Incidents in the Life of a Slave Girl:_

1–3   The essay simply lists the hardships that Jacobs endured and defines the intended audience without discussing why or how the definition was made. Little or no analysis of literary techniques is included. No interpretation or analysis links the passage to the abolitionist cause.

4–6   The essay explains how Jacobs and others lived as slaves, and it also mentions one or two other literary devices and explains their effect on the reader on a simple level. An intended audience is identified and briefly explored. Some link is made between the passage and the abolitionist cause.

7–9   The essay describes the formal diction, syntax, allusion, imagery, and figurative language of the passage and their effect on the reader. The intended audience is inferred from the technique and content of the passage. The link between the passage and the abolitionist cause is clearly made.

Evidence/support: _____

How much evidence have you supplied? Have you made a strong case to persuade the jury (the exam graders) that your ideas are correct? Evaluate your response by choosing a number from this list:

1–3   The writer makes only general statements with very few or no specific references to the passage.

4–6   The writer's interpretation is supported by some references to the text. The references may not be the best or most sophisticated choices. Some quotations may be overly long, too short, or not supportive of the writer's point.

7–9   The writer provides strong support for his or her interpretations by choosing specific and relevant facts from the text. Quotations are excerpted so that the point is made clearly and concisely.

Writing skills: _____

To grade your writing skills, step back a bit and pretend that you're reading someone else's essay. Does the writing sound smooth? Can you detect a logical path from start to finish? Evaluate your work and assign a number from one of these categories:

1–3   The essay is disorganized or filled with distracting grammar and spelling errors. Transitions between one point and another are awkward or missing entirely.

4–6   The essay has a logical structure. The writer's thesis (main idea) and supporting points are easily defined. The writing doesn't always flow smoothly, or it may contain repetitive or wordy statements. Quotations are inserted awkwardly.

7–9   The essay demonstrates clear, fluid style with a good command of language. The essay moves from a clear thesis through supporting points, each accompanied by evidence, to a logical conclusion.

Overall score: _____

Fill in each of the following blanks with the appropriate score, and then add your scores to determine the total:

    Addresses the question   _____

    Literary analysis   _____

    Evidence/support   _____

    Writing skills   _____

    Raw score total   _____

To figure out your overall score, divide your raw score by 4. Insert that number here: _____

Sample answer 1

Harriet Jacobs's <u>Incidents in the Life of a Slave Girl</u> is an account of her "escape" from slavery. Jacobs hid in an attic for seven years under terrible conditions, yet she still believed that anything was better than being owned by another human being. Jacobs was probably writing for an audience that was already opposed to slavery because it is not likely that pro-slavery people would buy her book. Her audience was probably white and free, perhaps living in the North or in other countries. Jacobs wants her readers to work for the abolition of slavery and her book was probably meant to inspire readers to take action.

Right from the start Jacobs shows the bad conditions she lived in after her escape. First she was in a swamp and then in a "very small garret" (line 2) where she can't stand up straight or even roll over without hitting her head. She says that "the air was stifling; the darkness total" (line 9). She couldn't exercise, and until she bored a hole in the wall, she couldn't see her children. She was bitten by insects and burned by "the scorching summer's sun" (line 51). In spite of all these hardships, she finds it better than to be a slave.

Jacobs also talks about what other slaves went through, even worse than her own situation. In lines 20–24, she says that she wasn't overworked, wasn't whipped or cut or tortured by a branding iron or bit by dogs. Even though these things didn't happen to her, Jacobs still says that God should "pity the woman who is compelled to lead such a life" (lines 26–27) as hers. Jacobs goes on to explain how her "owner" Dr. Flint searched for her. He questioned her children, so she couldn't tell them where she was, couldn't speak to them or have anything to do with them except see them through the hole in the wall. She puts up with this because slavery is so awful.

Jacobs's literary techniques include quoting dialogue from Dr. Flint and her children and detailed description of her living conditions. The sadness of her children's comments would make anyone work to end slavery. She writes in very formal diction with good grammar to show that former slaves are capable of being educated. She makes an allusion to Robinson Crusoe, a fictional character who lived mostly alone on a desert island, to show the loneliness she had to suffer, again attempting to inspire action. What could be the excuse for not working against slavery, compared to Harriet Jacobs's sacrifices and sufferings?

Analysis of sample answer 1

The AP student who wrote sample 1 did a good but not great job on the first essay. Check out the following categories to see how this essay was evaluated.

Addresses the question: 8

The writer addresses all the key elements of the question: the intended audience, the literary techniques used, and the furthering of the cause of abolition. The essay stays on topic.

Literary analysis: 6

Most, but not all of the literary techniques are included. The writer doesn't mention imagery (the sensory details in the first and second paragraphs of the passage) or figurative language (the "tempest" in line 12). The writer's fourth paragraph lists the literary techniques without much sophisticated analysis. The writer says that the audience is probably "white and free" but doesn't explore that concept except to say that pro-slavery people wouldn't buy the book.

Evidence/support: 6

The writer includes some general statements about the audience without using some of the supportive evidence available, such as the reference to "white people" in line 19 of the passage. The essay includes a fair amount of detail about living conditions and some good quotations to show that slavery imposed a terrible burden on slaves. Formal diction is mentioned, but no examples are supplied.

Writing skills: 7

This sample doesn't have too many grammar errors, and the spelling is great. Some of the quotations don't have line numbers in parentheses, but otherwise, the writing is technically sound and the quotations are inserted smoothly. The vocabulary and style are adequate, though not sophisticated, and the command of language is only fair. The essay comes to an abrupt conclusion. To the writer's credit, however, the last paragraph actually is a conclusion, not a summary.

Overall score: 7

Here's how you calculate the converted score for sample 1:

$8 + 6 + 6 + 7 = 29$

$29 \div 4 = 7.25$ (which rounds down to 7)

Sample answer 2

Harriet Jacobs lived a terrible life as a slave. She had to hide in an attic, like Anne Frank did during World War II, and she was not allowed to speak to anyone or see anyone for many years. In this essay I will prove that Harriet was writing to people who thought slavery was good. She wanted to change their minds.

Harriet tells all about the barn and its attic. It was hot and there were bugs. Her chidren were outside, but she could see them sometimes. She could also see her owner and that made her scared. She did not try to run away more, she stayed near her children. The list of things she put up with is a good technique to convince people that slavery is wrong. She also tells about other things that slaves put up with, like branding and cuting their legs. She writes about Benny to show that he can't stand up to a white man, the white man doesn't own Benny but it is still dangerous.

Analysis of sample answer 2

Oh my, sample essay 2 needs help! Even before you read it, you notice that the writer hasn't made much of a case. There simply isn't enough text! After you read the essay, you see what's missing. Check out the following scores.

Addresses the question: 3

The writer addresses some parts of the question, including the intended audience, and indirectly refers to furthering the cause of abolition (in the first paragraph, where he or she writes "She wanted to change their minds."). The essay doesn't deal with literary techniques except for a quick list of details of the attic. Even though the writer lists the details, that technique — imagery — isn't named.

Literary analysis: 2

The essay includes no real interpretation of Jacobs's techniques or their effect on the reader.

Evidence/support: 2

Some of the information or interpretation is just plain wrong in this essay. For example, Harriet Jacobs (who shouldn't be called "Harriet" in a literary essay) *did* speak to the adults who were helping her, and she *did* see her children and others through the holes that she bored in the wall. Other details are correct but sparse. And quotations aren't anywhere to be found.

Writing skills: 2

This writer won't win any prizes, but the grammar and spelling errors (for example, "cuting" instead of "cutting" and "chidren" instead of "children") don't rise to a level that impedes the reader. Therefore, these mistakes aren't counted heavily against the writer's score. However, the essay has no real structure and no logical flow from introduction to conclusion. The vocabulary is elementary, and some of the statements (such as, "In this essay I will prove . . .") are the equivalent of scratching a fingernail on the chalkboard for an AP exam grader.

Overall score: 2

Here's how you calculate the converted score for sample 2:

3 + 2 + 2 + 2 = 9

9÷4 = 2.25 (which rounds down to 2)

Essay 2: John Allman on Ways of Life

John Allman's poem, "Spraying the Chickens," is from *Attractions* (2River Press, 2006). It is a *prose poem,* a hybrid that has the form of a paragraph but the poetic devices that you expect to find in a poem that has a more conventional appearance. The beauty of Allman's poem is in its simple, direct language and concrete sensory detail.

Scoring grid for essay 2

This section explains how to score your essay on "Spraying the Chickens."

Addresses the question: _____

The prompt asks you to determine the poet's attitude toward two ways of life implied in the poem. You also have to explain the poetic elements that Allman employs to convey his attitude. Score your essay according to the following criteria:

0   The essay doesn't answer the question or is left blank.

1–3   The essay doesn't clearly state the two ways of living or the poet's attitude toward these lifestyles. Little mention is made of poetic technique, and only a weak link is made between technique and meaning.

4–6   The essay contains a simple statement about the two ways of living and the poet's attitude toward them. The essay may stray from the question and may include some irrelevant material. Some explanation of the poetic techniques is included, and these techniques are linked at least in part to the meaning of the poem.

7–9   The essay clearly explains the two ways of living discussed in the poem. It also fully explains the literary techniques that are used in this poem and discusses how each reveals more about the poet's view. Few, if any, off-topic and summary statements appear in the essay.

Literary analysis: _____

How well have you understood the levels of meaning in this poem? The following scoring categories help you decide which number is appropriate for your essay:

1–3   The essay decodes the meaning of the poem incorrectly or simplistically, contrasting earlier times, when human beings were more closely connected to nature, with the modern era, when sterile practices mandate that chickens must be sprayed. Literary techniques are merely listed, and no interpretation or analysis relates these techniques to the poet's attitude.

4–6   The essay delves into the implications of the practices of the earlier era, mentioning death and linking the preparation of the chicken and potatoes to human mortality. The essay mentions several literary techniques and explores one or two deeply. Some link is made between literary technique and the poet's view.

7–9   The essay explores the meaning of the poem in depth, considering the lack of perfection implied by the "dark spot near the pimply shoulder" (line 4). The theme of human mortality is discussed at length. The poet's view is presented with some complexity, and the link between literary technique and attitude is clearly made.

Evidence/support: _____

Though the poem is short, it's packed with possible evidence for your case — establishing the poet's attitude toward two ways of life. Evaluate your essay with help from these standards:

1–3   The writer makes only general statements with very few or no specific references to the poem.

4–6   The writer's interpretation is supported by some references to the text. The references may not be the best or most sophisticated choices. Some quotations may be overly long, too short, or not supportive of the writer's point.

7–9   The writer provides strong support for his or her interpretations by choosing specific and relevant words or phrases from the text. Quotations are excerpted so that the point is made concisely.

Writing skills: _____

The graders love to read good prose. Does your essay make the grade? Score it using these criteria:

1–3   The essay is disorganized or filled with distracting grammar and spelling errors. Transitions between one point and another are awkward or missing entirely.

4–6   The essay has a logical structure. The writer's thesis (main idea) and supporting points are easily defined. The writing doesn't always flow smoothly or may contain repetitive or wordy statements. Quotations are inserted awkwardly or incorrectly.

7–9   The essay demonstrates clear, fluid style with a good command of language. The essay moves from a clear thesis through supporting points, each accompanied by evidence, to a logical conclusion.

Overall score: _____

Fill in each of the following blanks with the appropriate score, and then add your scores to determine the total:

Addresses the question   _____

Literary analysis   _____

Evidence/support   _____

Writing skills   _____

Raw score total   _____

To figure out your overall score, divide your raw score by 4. Insert that number here: _____

Sample answer 1

"Spraying the Chickens" is a poem by John Allman. In the poem it talks about a farm, and the hen and her chicks. The hen is a good mother but she dies anyway. People eat her. The hen is not perfect and she can't protect her chicks. They "tremble" in sleep, showing that somehow they know that they are in danger. They also taste "their own blood" which shows that death is coming in spite of the hen's efforts. The farmer's wife doesn't care about the chicken. It says that the chicken is a "naked thing" not a real animal. The chickens represent the older time. They are not perfect. Some have a "pimply shoulder," which symbolizes a fault. The potatoes are dirty. The person the poem talks to, the "you," is very hungry and accepts the imperfect meal anyway.

The modern world is different. Chickens are sprayed, so they are more sanitary. The "proof" in the last line means that we now have ways of being safe and of showing when something is wrong. In the old days there was "corruption of bodies." The modern world has better hygiene, but the chicken feels "the cold touch of strangers." The cold touch is a symbol of the disconnection of modern life. So the modern world isn't much better than the older one.

Overall the poet likes the old world better. He probably grew up on a farm and liked having fresh food, even though it wasn't always clean. The last part of a poem sticks with the reader, and this poem ends with the "cold touch of strangers." So the poet rejects the modern world with this line.

Analysis of sample answer 1

This is a middling essay. It won't win any prizes, but it isn't completely terrible either. Check out the evaluation in this section to see where it falls short.

Addresses the question: 4

This essay does address the question; the writer attempts to define the two ways of living and mentions one or two poetic techniques, though not always accurately. The writer also tries to link the techniques to the poet's attitude. The essay includes some irrelevant statements about the hunger of the speaker and an incorrect statement about the writer's childhood.

Literary analysis: 4

This writer gets some things right and some things wrong. The older way of life does have imperfections, but those imperfections are seen as positive because they, in the form of the hands of the farmer's wife, "kept layer upon layer of so much world intact." This writer recognizes that the poet sees the closeness of nature in its reality as "proof" or evidence (and therefore forewarning) of death to come. The warmer, older world is contrasted with the coldness and alienation of the modern world. The writer also mentions some literary devices and ties some (but not all) of them to meaning.

Evidence/support: 5

The writer includes quite a few quotations from the poem to back up his or her ideas. These quotations aren't always the best choices, but there are a fair number of them.

Writing skills: 4

This writer has a fair command of language, but the essay isn't well structured. The first paragraph hops around. Each paragraph in the essay makes several points, but the writer provides few transitions from one point to another.

Overall score: 4

Here's how to calculate the converted score for sample 1:

4 + 4 + 5 + 4 = 17

17÷4 = 4.25 (which rounds down to 4)

Sample answer 2

John Allman's "Spraying the Chickens" compares the modern, clean world in which mankind is alienated from nature to another era, which allowed people to be closer to nature and therefore closer to reality. Allman's choice of words, the images he presents, and the symbolism of the "cold touch of stranger" add up to a clear choice. He prefers the earlier time when "so much world [was] intact." The poem also talks about death, a part of reality we cannot escape even now, despite the fact that we are always "spraying the chickens" against disease.

The first part of the poem talks about "back then" when things were simple. The world is dirty — "fecal droppings" and "a dark spot near a pimply shoulder" show that. But some things were better. The hen gives "just the right kind of mother love." Surprisingly, the right kind includes "a touch of illness" and "a taste of their own blood." The hen's sons and daughters are eating mortality, a sign that they will die. The farmer's wife "wiped the dirt off potatoes" but not completely, because "something of that got into your mouth" sometimes, or at least possibly.

The last part of the poem talks about death more directly. The dirt on the potatoes is a symbol of the dirt that we will all be buried in. The last two sentences talk about "the corruption of bodies" and the "cold touch of strangers." When we die, we will be buried and we will decay. The strangers may be the funeral workers who prepare the body for burial and in a way hide reality from us; we don't have to deal with death face to face. The farmer, on the other hand, raises, kills, and eats animals. Death is a fact of life, and even though it is unpleasant, it is better than pretending that death doesn't exist. No matter what we do now — spraying chickens to kill germs and hiding their deaths from our sight — we die. To know that fact is to face reality, which the poet prefers.

Apart from the symbols the poet uses, his word choice also helps get the message across. Most of the language is very simple. Many words have only one syllable, and all are very direct. Even if you don't know anything about farming, you can understand the simple life Allman describes. Some of the sentences are fragments, not complete sentences. This kind of writing implies that we don't really ever understand death completely, only parts of it.

Analysis of sample answer 2

Okay, my English-teacher heart is singing! Here I see a good essay by a student who understands the literature and writes with some skill. I go into the specifics in the following sections.

Addresses the question: 8

This essay addresses the question; it defines the way of living "back then" and today. The writer mentions a couple of poetic techniques, and explores others without specifying the name of the literary device. The writer links techniques to the poet's attitude fairly well.

Literary analysis: 7

The writer does a reasonably good job of exploring the underlying meaning of the poem, discussing, for example, the idea of death and human mortality as well as the comparison between the older and more modern ways of life. The writer makes some fine points about literary technique, including the simple language and sentence fragments. These techniques are also linked to the poet's attitude.

Evidence/support: 8

The writer includes quite a few quotations from the poem to back up his or her ideas. These quotations are well chosen.

Writing skills: 7

This writer has a fairly strong command of language, and his or her essay is well structured. The quotations are inserted neatly into the text, and the introduction gets right down to business. The last paragraph, however, seems to be a dead end, not a real conclusion.

Overall score: 8

Here's how to calculate the converted score for sample 2:

8 + 7 + 8 + 7 = 30

30÷4 = 7.5 (which rounds up to 8)

Essay 3: The Open-Ended Essay

Finally you get some choice in the matter. (However, you may have too much choice! Take care not to sit around for an hour deciding between *Hamlet* and *Antigone,* for example.) This section takes you through the third, open-ended essay.

Scoring grid for essay 3

I can't give you an exact scoring grid for the open-ended essay because I don't know what work you've chosen to write about. However, I do provide guidelines and two graded essays with explanations. Read the guidelines, check out the samples, and then digest the explanations before you fill in the scoring checklist for your own work.

Each category on the checklist has three sets of numbers, with the exception of the "addresses the question" category, which has four because that's the only category in which you can score a zero. If you leave this essay blank, if you haven't chosen a work of literary quality, or if you don't answer the question, give yourself zero points. (Chapter 14 helps you out if you aren't sure what fits the definition of "literary quality" or if you need general help with the open-ended question.) The formula at the end of the checklist converts your score.

Addresses the question: _____

This prompt mentions a "betrayal of trust" that adds to your understanding of character, plot, or theme. In other words, you have to figure out a time when someone betrayed someone else and then place that betrayal in the context of one of the three literary elements cited in the prompt. Score your essay using the following list:

0   The essay doesn't answer the question or is left blank. The subject of the essay isn't a work of literary quality.

1–3 The essay merely summarizes the plot or makes only one or two points about betrayal of trust. The essay barely touches on the relationship between the betrayal and the reader's understanding of character, plot, or theme.

4–6 The essay contains some unnecessary plot summary, but it makes several points that relate to the relationship between the betrayal and the reader's understanding of character, plot, or theme. The essay may occasionally stray from the topic.

7–9 The essay focuses on the relationship between betrayal and the reader's understanding of character, plot, or theme. The essay avoids unnecessary plot summary and off-topic statements.

Literary analysis: _____

The prompt tells you that plot summary isn't enough. You have to dig into the story and analyze it. Score your essay according to the criteria listed here:

1–3 The essay stays solely on the literal level, with no interpretation of the betrayal or of one of the three elements (plot, character, and theme) cited in the question. One or more statements about the characters may be wrong.

4–6 The essay offers an interpretation of the betrayal but doesn't go into depth. The analysis of the betrayal in terms of plot, character, or theme is explained in simple terms.

7–9 The essay digs into the text, unearthing and exploring the interplay between one of the literary elements and the act of betrayal.

Evidence/support: _____

No matter which work you choose, you can't create a good essay without citing specific events that support the case that you're trying to make. Rate your essay according to these standards:

1–3   The writer makes only general statements with no or very few specific references to the text.

4–6   The writer's interpretation is supported by some references to the text. The references may not be the best or most sophisticated choices. Some references may not support the writer's point.

7–9   The writer provides strong support for his or her interpretations by choosing specific and relevant evidence from the text.

You don't have a passage to work from for this essay, but you can still be specific. Don't say, for example, that Hamlet argues with his mother. Instead, say that Hamlet is furious with his mother for remarrying so soon after her husband's death and that he wants his mother to refrain from sleeping with Claudius. Directly quote only if you're sure that you know the exact words.

Writing skills: _____

The graders are looking for clear, mature prose. Does the quality of writing in your essay make the grade? Take a look at these standards and choose a score for your work:

1–3   The essay is disorganized or filled with distracting grammar and spelling errors. Transitions between one point and another are awkward or missing entirely.

4–6   The essay has a logical structure. The writer's thesis (main idea) and supporting points are easily defined. The writing doesn't always flow smoothly or may contain repetitive or wordy statements. Evidence is inserted awkwardly.

7–9   The essay demonstrates clear, fluid style with a good command of language. The essay moves from a clear thesis through supporting points, each accompanied by evidence, to a logical conclusion.

Overall score: _____

Fill in each of the following blanks with the appropriate score, and then add your scores to determine the total:

Addresses the question   _____

Literary analysis   _____

Evidence/support   _____

Writing skills   _____

Raw score total   _____

To find your overall score, divide your raw score by 4. Insert that number here: _____

Sample answer 1

Macbeth, the tragic hero of vaulting ambitions, slowly ascends to the throne of Scotland through a series of world-class treacheries. A master of manipulation accompanied by the equally-proficient and deceptive Lady Macbeth, Macbeth betrays those who most desperately seek allegiance, specifically King Duncan.

King Duncan is deeply disturbed by the betrayal of the Thane of Cawdor. Duncan suffers from the new-found knowledge that those one trusts most can become traitors. In some sense, Duncan places all his hopes in Macbeth, the military hero who will now become Thane. Duncan may believe that Macbeth can reclaim his lost confidence in allies and friends. And in an almost comical tragic twist, Duncan has made one of the worst character assessments in literary history. Macbeth will have his face "hide what the false heart doth know" and lure the king into a trap, at which point Macbeth transcends mere ambition and becomes an executioner. This betrayal, made possible by Duncan's thirst for loyalty, contributes to the tragic vision of the play: that those he trusts as friends can be the basest of all enemies.

But Macbeth is far from a two-dimensional character. It seems unlikely that his ambitions would be made manifest without the diabolical support of Lady Macbeth. Lady Macbeth suffers from frustration, frustration that her husband cannot climb higher on the social ladder. She pressures and nurtures Macbeth's dark desires and teaches him the art of deceitfulness. Also, she gives Macbeth really bad advice, since he should have been satisfied with Thane. Thus she betrays him as well.

Macbeth betrays Duncan's thirst for loyalty, and is betrayed by his wife's manipulation. Macbeth's actions lead King Duncan to the afterlife and Lady Macbeth into madness.

Analysis of sample answer 1

This writer wins a prize — not the gold stars they give out in kindergarten, but a fairly high score on the AP open-ended essay. Read on for specifics about the strengths and weaknesses of this essay.

Addresses the question: 8

This essay addresses the question; it stays on topic and shows how the Thane of Cawdor's betrayal defines Duncan's character because Duncan needs to prove that he can have at least some faith in humanity. This point leads directly to Duncan's death at the hands of Macbeth. The information about Lady Macbeth also helps to define Macbeth's character.

Literary analysis: 7

The writer of this essay proves that he or she understands *Macbeth* well. His or her observations about Duncan and Macbeth are good. The writer understands that Duncan needs loyalty from his subjects and that Macbeth's ambition ultimately trumps loyalty.

Evidence/support: 6

Here's the place for the most improvement in this essay. The writer is correct in his or her interpretation of the play but doesn't really provide evidence for the idea that Duncan needs to have faith and thus deems Macbeth trustworthy. A few more specifics on both Duncan and Lady Macbeth would have been helpful.

Writing skills: 8

This writer has a strong command of language. The essay gets to the point, moves smoothly from one idea to another, and comes to a logical conclusion.

Overall score: 7

Here's how to calculate the converted score for sample 1:

$8 + 7 + 6 + 8 = 29$

$29 \div 4 = 7.25$ (which rounds down to 7)

Sample answer 2

<u>Antigone</u> by Sophocles is a play in which betrayal plays an important part. Because Creon betrays the trust of the city of Thebes, the plot moves forward. Without Creon's betrayal, which is to choose his own law over the ancient rules set by the gods about burial, there would be no story because Antigone would have no reason to rebel. She would marry Haemon, Creon's son, and live happily ever after, or at least as happy as Oedipus's children can be.

The story begins when Antigone's brothers fight over who should rule Thebes. One hires foreign soldiers to attack his brother's army, which is all Thebans. In the fight the brothers die. Creon becomes the only ruler of Thebes and says that the traitorous brother, the one who betrayed Thebes, may not be buried. The body is supposed to be left out in the open where animals can eat it. Antigone buries her brother's body and is killed by Creon because of it. Antigone goes to her death willingly because she thinks that the rules the gods made are more important than the ones that Creon made. Also, Antigone feels that she has to do this because it is her brother.

Creon's duty is to the city. The citizens of Thebes need someone to rule them, and Creon has their trust. He doesn't deserve that trust because he makes a bad decision. You could say that no one is perfect in decisions, but Creon keeps going, even after the blind prophet Tiresias and the citizens, who are in the chorus, and his own son tell him that he is wrong. To be stubborn and to put yourself above the laws of the gods is betrayal of the city's trust.

In the end Creon realizes that he is wrong. He tries to undo his actions, ordering the burial of the traitorous brother and running to save Antigone from death. But it is too late. The betrayal is permanent. Antigone is dead, his son is dead, his wife is dead (she commits suicide), and Creon is left alone.

Analysis of sample answer 2

This essay isn't exactly in critical condition, but it's definitely in the literary intensive care unit. A few aspects of the essay are fair, but there's plenty of room for improvement. Take a look at the details in each category.

Addresses the question: 4

The essay addresses *parts* of the question, but the writer makes a fairly common mistake: He or she spends far too much time retelling the events of Sophocles' play. The writer does mention that the betrayal of the city's trust — an interesting and justifiable idea — drives the plot. However, the writer never discusses how the betrayal adds to the reader's understanding of plot, character, or theme.

Literary analysis: 3

The writer identifies Creon's betrayal of the citizens' trust. After that idea, however, the writer has only one other valuable thing to say: that Creon's stubborn refusal to listen to others' advice adds to the betrayal. These two points could certainly form the basis of a sophisticated literary analysis, but the writer doesn't develop them. The only other point the writer makes is the far-too-simple statement that "the plot moves forward" because of Creon's betrayal.

Evidence/support: 3

The writer includes a fair number of details about the plot. However, he or she doesn't do much with the details. In other words, the details don't serve as evidence for the essay's thesis — that Creon has betrayed the public's trust.

Writing skills: 4

This writer has some style. The essay flows in vaguely chronological order, and it has an introduction and a conclusion. However, there are also several grammar mistakes.

Overall score: 4

Here's how to calculate the converted score for sample 2:

$$4 + 3 + 3 + 4 = 14$$

$$14 \div 4 = 3.5 \text{ (which rounds up to 4)}$$

Putting It All Together: Calculating Your Overall AP Exam Score

The AP exam is weighted: 45 percent of your score comes from the multiple-choice questions and 55 percent from the three essays. The AP statistics experts take the overall scores from each section and fiddle with them a bit more until they come up with five categories, which are called (drum roll, please!) 1, 2, 3, 4, and 5. Plug your numbers into the following formulas, and then add up the right-hand column to see how you rate:

Multiple-choice overall score _____ × 1.25 = _____

Essay 1 score _____ × 3.1 = _____

Essay 2 score _____ × 3.1 = _____

Essay 3 score _____ × 3.1 = _____

Total _____

After you get your total from the four different categories, compare it to the following table to get your final overall AP exam score.

Overall Score from the Four Categories	Equivalent AP Exam Score
Above 119	5
90–118	4
70–89	3
45–88	2
Below 45	1

If you score a 4 or a 5, hooray! You've demonstrated college-level ability. A grade of 3 means you can jump in the air to celebrate, but just once. Some colleges give credit for a 3, but many don't. Scores of 1 or 2 mean that you have some work to do. Turn back to chapters reviewing topics that stumped you, and then try again.

Part VI
The Part of Tens

The 5th Wave   By Rich Tennant

"Yeah, I think I can fix this. Look in that toolbox and hand me a 3/16 dactylic hexameter."

In this part . . .

Got your fingers ready? Good, because you'll need them to count Dummies-style in this part, which is the traditional part of tens. Here you find "avoid-no-matter-what" traps for your essays and ten ways to score higher without adding extra study time to your life. So flex those digits and start counting to ten.

Chapter 20

Ten Mistakes That Kill
Your Essay Score

• •

In This Chapter
▶ Identifying common mistakes
▶ Avoiding unnecessary errors

• •

*O*kay, maybe "kill" is too strong a word. English teachers are decent people. (I make this claim without any bias whatsoever, despite the fact that I'm an English teacher.) In fact, if the graders can find a way to give your essay an extra point, they most certainly will. But they'll also knock off points if you make mistakes. This chapter describes ten ways that you can mess up, big time, when you write an AP essay. I show you these common mistakes so you can avoid them like the plagues that they are.

Not Answering the Question

Think of AP essay questions as armed robbers on a deserted street in the middle of the night. In the interests of self-defense, give them whatever they want. Don't argue, don't reconfigure the prompt, and don't write whatever pops into your head. Just answer the question, the whole question, and nothing but the question.

Sounds simple and obvious, right? But in the heat of battle, when you're watching the clock with one eye and reading a literary selection with the other, it's fairly easy to lose sight of the basics — a category that includes decoding the prompt. (For detailed instructions on prompt-decoding, turn to Chapter 3.)

Furthermore, lots of AP test takers tend to respond to part of the prompt, but not to all of it. For example, suppose the prompt asks you to consider the conflict between two characters and their responses to the conflict. You have to do three things:

✔ Define the conflict

✔ Explain how character A responds

✔ Explain how character B responds

Two out of three isn't acceptable, though you will receive some points for your efforts.

One more pitfall: the clock. The AP English Literature and Composition exam allots two hours for three essays. You can't spend one hour on the first essay and another hour on the second, because then you hit the third essay with . . . oops, no time left at all (meaning, obviously, that you won't answer the question and will receive a zero on the essay).

Summarizing the Plot or Meaning

The mistake of summarizing the plot or meaning of a work shows up most frequently when the literary passage is especially difficult to comprehend, perhaps because the language or syntax is old or obscure. I think I know why test takers limit themselves to plot summary or, in the case of a poem, to restatement of meaning. After cracking a tough selection, the feeling of triumph — "I got it! I know what it says!" — takes over. In the first flash of relief, the essay writer records what he or she understood. It seems like enough, given how difficult it was to figure the thing out. But summarizing the plot or meaning generally isn't a great idea. Yes, the graders want to see that you comprehend the excerpt or poem, but you display that comprehension by using plot or meaning to make a point. Remember, the graders want to know whether you can analyze a text and select relevant sections to support a thesis.

I should mention that in one particular case, a small amount of plot summary is a good idea (say, three or four sentences). If you're writing about a lesser-known literary work for the open-ended essay, you probably should take a moment to orient the grader by reviewing the basic events of the work that you're discussing. (Turn to Chapter 14 for more information on the open-ended essay.)

Writing about Yourself

Consider this sample excerpt from an AP essay:

> When I first read T. S. Eliot's poem "The Love Song of J. Alfred Prufrock," I started to cry. I remember having trouble making friends when I moved from Chicago to Albany, and the speaker's immense loneliness echoed what I felt on prom night, when everyone but me had a date, a limousine, and great clothes, not to mention the pictures for the senior album, while I was wandering around like a pair of "ragged claws."

What's wrong with this excerpt? As my students say when I'm blathering, "Too much information!" And this is besides the fact that the necessary info isn't present. I'm glad to see that someone relates to Eliot's masterpiece (though just for the record, he wasn't writing about prom night). One of the major benefits of great literature is its ability to hook into our souls and express otherwise incoherent emotions and thoughts. But the above excerpt belongs in a diary, not in the pink AP answer-booklet. The message is simple: Stay out of the essay. The literature is the star, not you.

The sample essay excerpt is exaggerated to make a point, but injecting even a *little* of yourself into a literary essay can be a problem. Avoid "in my opinion," "I think," and other similar expressions. You don't need them because the information they convey is obvious. Of course you think that Hamlet is too emotional, otherwise why would you say it?

Another common mistake is to write about your experience when your were reading the work, saying something like "At first I was on Sethe's side, but as Beloved became more and more monstrous, I began to sympathize with Denver and to oppose Sethe's intense relationship with Beloved. Then I realized that. . . ." Unless the prompt asks for your reactions (and once, years ago, one unusual prompt did just that), keep them to yourself.

Writing about the Author's Life

When I introduce a book or a poem to my class, I always waste a couple of minutes on literary gossip. I give a capsule biography of the author, including the juicy scandals that would rate a story in the tabloids if the subject were a movie star instead of a 19th-century writer. Why? I guess because I'm a sucker for that kind of information — even though I read only quality literature. Honest. Okay, an occasional mystery and some sci-fi make it to my bookshelf too. And sometimes a trashy magazine. But that's it.

Those minutes of lit-gossip come back to haunt me when I give a test. Invariably, someone in my class "analyzes" the literary work by connecting it to the life story of the author, writing something like "Because Dylan Thomas was an alcoholic, he missed the innocent days of his childhood, as seen in his poem 'Fern Hill.'" Uh-oh. That essay's in trouble! Yes, Dylan Thomas drank too much, and yes, the poem is about the end of childhood innocence, among other things. However, Dylan Thomas's adult life isn't in the poem. Neither is his bar bill. An essay about "Fern Hill" should be about "Fern Hill," and not about the poet's substance abuse problem.

Here's the bottom line: If you happen to know something about the author of the literary selection you're writing about, don't put that information in the essay.

Writing about the Time Period

I often read essay paragraphs resembling this excerpt:

> Ophelia obeys her father, Polonius, because in this time and place (Denmark, in ancient times), women couldn't control their own destinies. Unlike a modern Ophelia, who can move out of the palace and get a job if her father and brother reject her, Ophelia is bound to do whatever the men in her family want her to do.

Even though I enjoy learning about history, that subject shouldn't intrude on your AP English essay for the following very good reasons:

- ✔ The essay is supposed to discuss the literary work, not the social or historical context. Unless the prompt specifically asks you to relate the selection to something in reality, stay inside the imaginary world the author created.

- ✔ Without an opportunity to do some research, most test takers don't know enough history to write a good essay about a particular era. In the sample essay excerpt, for instance, notice the phrase "in ancient times." The writer is wrong!

- ✔ It's easy to confuse two time periods — when the literary work was written and when the story takes place.

Getting Sloppy with Grammar and Spelling

By the time you sit down in front of an AP test booklet, you've suffered through more than a decade of instruction in grammar and spelling. You've learned how to distinguish between who and whom, you've discovered when apostrophes are called for, and you know why double negatives are no-nos. (Sorry about the lame joke. I couldn't resist the pun.)

While all this education was taking place, however, you maintained your fluency in casual, conversational English. You never asked your friends, "Would you care to see the new James Bond movie?" Of course not! You said, "Wanna catch the 10 p.m. Bond?" Or you may have sent an instant message: "Bond 10PM C U L8R?"

Fine. I advocate bilingualism because I think that formal, grammatically perfect English is too stilted for friend-to-friend chats. However, the reverse is also true: Friend-to-friend-style comments are completely out of place in a literary essay. You must use formal writing rather than informal, conversational prose. After all, the AP English Literature and Composition exam tests your ability to write correctly. So ditch slang and abbreviations — including & (and), b/c (because), and s/b (should be). Polish up your sentences, and write it right.

You may be the next Superstar Comedian and everyone's favorite class clown. Good for you. However, assume that the graders have no sense of humor whatsoever. (They do, but they lock it in the closet for the duration of the grading period.) Silly jokes detract from your essay and lower your score.

If grammar drives you nuts, you may want to consult *English Grammar For Dummies* (Wiley, 2001) or practice in the *English Grammar Workbook For Dummies* (Wiley, 2006). I wrote both of them, and I'd love to see my royalties increase.

Especially when answering the third, open-ended essay (see Chapter 14 for more information), take care to spell the characters' names correctly. If you prepare plot and character summaries in advance, give yourself a short spelling test before test day. Reading an essay about McBath or Mac Bethe or (my personal favorite) Shakespeare Williams puts graders in a very bad mood. And if you put your grader in a bad mood, say goodbye to a high score.

Forgetting to Support Your Claims

When I'm grading homework papers, my teeth grind loudly when I see a paragraph like this one:

> Guy, the father in Edwidge Danticat's short story "A Wall of Fire Rising," is desperate. He feels that he has no future, and he sees no upward mobility for his son. He is tied to his family by the love he feels for them, but that love isn't enough for him. Guy goes up in the balloon because all his dreams have died already, and his own death is almost an afterthought.

Nicely written paragraph, don't you think? Everything in it is correct (according to my interpretation of Danticat's story). The sentences are complete, and the spelling and grammar are impeccable. So why am I making more work for my dentist? Because (drum roll, please!) the writer has included no supporting evidence!

Here are some points the essay writer could have made:

- Guy's desperation is revealed by his suicide, which occurs when he jumps out of a hot-air balloon. Guy steals the balloon, symbolically attempting to escape his own life, but dies when he realizes that no escape is possible.

- Guy tells his wife that he has secured work cleaning lavatories at the factory. However, he is still far down on the list for a permanent job. His comments about this situation show that he sees no potential for a better life.

- Guy and his wife discuss their son's future. Guy wants to put his son on a waiting list for a factory job, but his wife opposes the plan. She thinks that her son may achieve more; Guy does not. This conversation supports the assertion that Guy "sees no upward mobility for his son."

I could go on, listing more events from the story, but you get the point. The sample excerpt asks the reader to accept all its assertions on faith. But in an AP English essay, faith isn't what you need. Evidence and analysis are essential.

Leaving Out Specifics

Take a look at this lovely excerpt:

> Great poets write about issues that matter to everyone. Ted Hughes is no exception. In his poem "The Thought-Fox," Hughes considers many important themes and ideas. His topic is creativity, an issue of importance to poets and non-poets alike. In this poem Hughes discusses how creativity occurs. He tells a story about creativity, illustrating the process. Because creativity varies from person to person and artistic accomplishment is difficult, the reader understands more about how a poem is written after reading "The Thought-Fox."

Excuse me while I gag. The writer of the preceding clunker has managed to place 82 words on the page and explain absolutely nothing about Hughes' poem — except for the fact that he wrote it and that it has a story in it. With that information, Hughes and his work remain a mystery.

The writer's problem here is generality. So Hughes "considers many important themes and ideas." Great. Which ones? And which writer doesn't consider important themes and ideas? Rather, which writer *suitable for the AP* doesn't? (See why general statements are problematic?)

The alternative to a general essay, as you have already guessed, is an essay filled with specifics. Quotations, of course, are always great. But even without quoting, you can go into detail, as in this sample excerpt:

> Hughes' poem imagines a writer in the calm of midnight. The writer in the poem, in turn, imagines a fox. First to be described is the fox's dark nose, which contrasts with the snow. Next the animal's eyes appear; they flicker back and forth, checking the surroundings. The footprints, closely followed by legs and a body, arrive in stanza four. By the sixth and last stanza the poet can smell the fox, which has become real to both the reader and to the poet-in-the-poem. The poem has also become real, as the poet finishes his job of imagining a "thought-fox" and prints out the page on which he has described the animal.

Repeating Yourself

Forty minutes doesn't give you much time to write an essay because you have only forty minutes, which means you're pressed for time, given the fact that you have less than an hour and that's not enough time to write everything you can think of.

Snoring yet? I am. The preceding paragraph says everything, and then says everything, and then says everything again. I got the point the first time, and I'm sure you did too. When you repeat yourself, you

- ✔ Waste precious time
- ✔ Make the graders feel that your essay is a waste of time

Repetition, I've often noticed, often arises from a lack of confidence. Perhaps you're afraid that you haven't been clear, so you repeat yourself just in case the reader didn't get it. You don't trust yourself, or you don't trust the reader. Either way, you blow the essay when you go over the same ground again and again.

Writing concisely is a skill you can master. Before test day, take out some old papers or reports. Go through them with a scalpel, cutting every unnecessary word you can find. Choose a couple of fat sentences and put them on a diet. See if you can slim each from, say, 14 words to 10.

Writing Ideas in Random Order

Hopping around is good — if you're a rabbit. If you're an AP-exam writer, however, hopping around is poison. Consider this example:

> Nathaniel Hawthorne's classic novel, The Scarlet Letter, is set in colonial New England. The Puritans, an extremely strict religious group, condemn adultery. A single mother is sentenced to jail. When she is released, she must wear a scarlet "A" on her clothing. The mother never reveals the name of the baby's father. The A is ornate; the embroidery makes a decoration of what was meant to be a condemnation. The mother was actually married, but the Puritans are unaware of that fact. The baby's name is Pearl. The A becomes a badge of honor. The Puritans at one point try to remove Pearl from her mother's care. The father doesn't reveal his identity until late in the story, when his guilt is overwhelming. Pearl stays with her mother.

The preceding sample essay excerpt skips from the scarlet letter A to the baby to the father and back so many times that the grader will get whiplash from reading it. The moral of the story? Be sure that your essay contains a logical thread that the reader can follow. (Check out Chapter 3 for tips on structuring an essay.)

Chapter 21

Ten Ways to Increase Your Know-How Without Studying

In This Chapter

▶ Developing literary skills while having fun

▶ Enjoying English-related activities that improve your skill

*J*ust for the record: despite what the title of this chapter might imply, I heartily recommend that you study for the AP English Literature and Composition exam. As a matter of fact, only geniuses have a shot at passing the exam cold. And not even all geniuses! However, while you're prepping for test day (see Chapter 2 for a good schedule), you may want to participate in a few, nonacademic activities that pump up the literary area of your brain. This chapter describes those activities.

Attend Poetry Readings

It's Friday night. What do you do? Go to a movie, attend a skateboard tournament, or maybe boogie the night away at a school dance? Sometimes those are the best choices. As the old saying goes, "All work and no play makes Jack a dull boy." And Jacqueline, I should point out, doesn't do very well on a 24/7 study regimen either. However, sometimes you may want to dip your toe into a more unusual (and perhaps more productive) leisure activity: poetry readings.

Most major book chains, as well as many local stores, sponsor free poetry readings from time to time. Some even serve food. And not all are on Friday night; check your local newspaper or the Internet for listings of nearby events. When you find one, pencil it into your calendar. Not only will you have fun, but you'll learn a lot too.

 I suggest poetry readings because they're the ones that give you the most additional information about literature. However, readings from fiction and nonfiction works are also beneficial. Either way, the authors' comments and reactions from the audience may add to your understanding of the work.

At readings, imaginative people who spin words into beauty stand behind a podium and offer their latest poems for your appreciation. Most poets comment on the inspiration for their work. Be sure to listen when they divulge this information, because it gives you insights into poetry and the creative process that you can't get any other way. Just hearing poetry changes the way you think about this genre; after all, poetry used to be nothing more than an auditory experience.

Here's a real-life example of the value of poetry readings: Dave Johnson, whose work appears in this book, once visited my class to read his work. Dave comes from a long line of Southern preachers, and their voices echo in his reading style. I've studied many of his poems (they're really good), but until I heard him read, I didn't fully appreciate the sense of place and the characterization that enriches his writing.

Besides, even if you don't learn much about poetry, at a reading you may meet someone who also likes movies, skateboard tournaments, and school dances. Then you'll have a companion for the nights when you don't want to exercise your poetic-appreciation muscles.

Write for School Publications

Writing for school publications can give you plenty of practice for the dreaded AP exam essays. Don't have any school publications? Start one. Fancy printing is nice, but all you really need is a copier, a dream, and, depending on the rules of your school, a faculty advisor. If your school does sponsor publications, submit your work. Consider these possibilities:

- **Articles for the school newspaper:** Because you're on deadline with newspaper writing, you learn how to organize information and create a coherent structure quickly.

- **Poems and stories for the school literary magazine:** Writing poetry helps you understand what goes into the creation of a poem. If you have to work out a rhyme scheme, for instance, you know what it adds to the meaning. Similarly, creating characters or tucking exposition into a prose scene helps you decode what other writers have done.

- **Topical research for themed publications:** My school has a feminist magazine, a social science journal, a health publication, and about a dozen other publications. Writers for these publications discover how to state a thesis and prove it — exactly what you have to do in an AP essay.

It doesn't really matter what you write or where your work appears (though a list of publications is an asset on your college application). In my opinion, writing ability is a muscle, and if you exercise your muscles, they get stronger. So write something — anything — and do so as often as you can.

Solve Crossword Puzzles

AP-level work relies on mature vocabulary, and a painless (okay, mostly painless) way to increase your fund of words is to solve a daily or weekly puzzle from a local or national newspaper. Bookstores also sell compilations of puzzles on various levels. Aim for puzzles with difficult vocabulary (such as the one in the *New York Times*). And don't forget to keep a dictionary nearby so you can look up unfamiliar words. The first few puzzles you try may be challenging, because it takes a while to get into the puzzle maker's mindset. But stick with it, and the puzzles will get easier. Your vocabulary will thank you, and your AP scores (not to mention your SAT and ACT scores) will rise.

All those new words you come across in crosswords can help you decode AP passages, but be wary of introducing newly acquired vocabulary into your essays. Graders grumble when they encounter an essay packed with ten-syllable words. When I plow through an essay that's dense with obscure language, I often assume that the writer ate a vocabulary book for breakfast and was determined to cough up every last word. Needless to say, I'm glad the writer has learned vocabulary, but moderation is a virtue.

Give Your Library Card a Workout

When I say that you should give your library card a workout, I'm not talking about using it as a minifan on hot, humid, pre–AP test days. I'm talking about using the card to borrow books . . . and then actually reading them. Yes, I'm aware that the title of this chapter contains the phrase "without studying." But, honestly, reading doesn't have to be homework or punishment. (Imagine: *I sentence you to 20 years in the classic-novel penitentiary, with time off for good behavior . . . .*) Reading is a way to escape the real world — the one in which you have to fill out college apps or feed your pet tarantula. If you find a book that grabs you, everything else fades away.

However — you were waiting for that one loophole that ruined your plans to check out an easy read, weren't you? — you get the most benefit from reading quality literature. Check out Appendix A for some great suggestions. Then settle down with a book that transports you, entertains you, and as a side effect, raises your AP score.

Talk about Literature at Lunch

Okay, so lunching with literature may sound like a one-way ticket to Nerds Anonymous, but it doesn't have to be. Think of it this way: Everyone in your English class is probably reading the same book or the same poems. Everyone has homework to do and tests to take. So if you happen to bring up an argument that started in class and continued until the closing bell, you're actually helping yourself and your friends.

Not convinced? I don't blame you. I probably wouldn't have believed me either when I was AP age. But now, as a teacher, I have lunch duty, the absolute most boring activity on the planet, except perhaps for faculty meetings. Once a week, as I patrol for errant pickle slices and airborne cole slaw, I listen. Sometimes — quite often, actually — I hear an interesting conversation based on homework reading or classroom discussion.

Before you burn this page, try one thing. Come up with a single, debatable idea — something catchy. Sit with your friends and unwrap that mystery-meat sandwich the cafeteria lady calls "ham and cheese." Before you take a bite, say something like "Hamlet has a lot in common with Spiderman, you know? He doesn't want to be special, but he doesn't have much choice. Neither does Spidey. Plus, they both lost father figures." If no one throws a french fry at you, you're fine, and the discussion may actually take off. If you get hit with a french fry, experiment at another table. Teachers teach, but so can students. And you can learn from both.

A lunch- or dinner-table conversation about literature can give you a great idea for a class assignment or a test essay. However, if you use someone else's idea without crediting the source, you risk a plagiarism charge. Yes, even for a non-written, we-were-just-talking source. So tell your teacher where that great analysis of Hamlet's relationship with Gertrude came from. Ask him or her the preferred way to cite — footnotes, endnotes, parentheticals, or just a little personal note at the end of the essay (for example, "For the analysis of Hamlet's relationship with Gertrude, I credit Peter Smith, my classmate").

Listen to Debates and Arguments

The AP essay section checks whether you can assert an idea and defend it with solid evidence. And not surprisingly, the AP English Literature and Composition exam concerns literature. But arguing effectively is a skill that can carry over from one subject area to another. (Think about what would happen if you said something like this: "You want me to dry the dishes? Let me explain why you will benefit from taking care of this chore yourself . . .")

If your school has a debate team, a Model UN or similar organization, or a student government, join in the fun. Or, if you have enough activities in your schedule to fill 32 hours a day, simply attend a debate from time to time. At the event, listen carefully. Who made a good case? Why? What did that particular debater do to convince you? What you learn by listening to a sophisticated argument will improve your own ability to state your position regarding a literary work, dish-drying, global warming, car-borrowing, curfews, and tons of other important issues.

School isn't the only place to master the art of debate and argument. You can easily debate with your family at home about all sorts of fun issues. My son is a litigator, the type of attorney that steps in when something is in dispute. In other words, he gets paid very well to argue. I often remind him that he learned this skill at home, as we discussed everything from which New York team had the better shortstop to the likely outcome of an election. If your family is quieter than mine and debating isn't a habit, you can also listen to debates on television. As you listen, consider the relative effectiveness of each speaker and analyze how an argument is presented. Adapt the same techniques as needed when you're writing.

Go to the Theater (A Live One, That Is)

Drama exists in written form, but don't forget that all those plays you've read and dissected in English class were originally intended for performance. When you see actors inhabit the roles, hear the words spoken aloud, and watch the interactions live, the play changes. Plus, theater — from amateur productions in the school cafeteria to professional presentations on Broadway — is an amazing experience for anyone.

Seeing a play that you've read affects your understanding of the work. Even better, if you have the opportunity, is to see two productions of the same play. The directors' and actors' contributions become clear when you compare their interpretations.

I can hear you now: "What about films? Does going to see a movie based on a play count as an AP grade-raising experience?" The answer is a definite maybe. If the film is well made, you may learn just as much from it as you do from a staged performance. However, because the two media have different requirements and conventions, film directors often change a lot when they convert a theater script to a screenplay.

Use the live theater or film experience for "deep background" only. If you write about a work you've been fortunate enough to watch on stage or at the movies, be sure to discuss the text, not the little touches that the director, designers, and actors add (for example, movement on stage, lighting design, costumes, facial expressions, or tone of voice). The AP exam is oriented to the written word, not to performance.

Participate in English Class

The horror! I actually want you to stop doodling, ogling, gargling, burping, and all the other things you enjoy doing while the teacher is babbling away about some ancient poem. (Not that you'd ever do any such thing during class.) But in case you're tempted, resist. Take full advantage of the 45 or 50 minutes you have in the presence of an English teacher and other students who are focused on literature. (Chapter 3 explains how to get the most mileage from a high school English class, whether it carries the official AP designation or not.) Even if your teacher speaks in a monotone so boring that the chalk tries to sneak out the door, you can still learn something. And if you're paying attention, you can participate by asking meaningful questions. Then you can learn even more.

Consider this fact: The largest slice of every school's budget is devoted to teachers' salaries. Therefore, the most valuable item in the school budget is teacher time (even though you may beg to differ). So when you ask a question or make a comment, you have a chance to receive feedback on your analysis of the work, to clarify misconceptions, and to liven up the discussion. (Maybe then the chalk will even try to sneak back in . . . .)

Analyze Your Strengths and Make the Most of Them

As you probably know by now, this book prepares you for the AP English Literature and Composition exam. If you're like most test-prep readers, you're probably dipping into the book to bolster your skills in areas of weakness. (Not that you have any!) However, you can also benefit from thinking about your strong points. Here's why: Suppose you're very good at interpreting poetry. For instance, perhaps you can latch onto a poem and draw meaning from it the way aliens in sci-fi films inhale the flight crew's essence as green glowing clouds waft around the cabin. If you know you're good at poetry, during the AP exam you can attach yourself to the poetry multiple-choice or essay prompts first. Go with your strength, extract maximum points, and then move on to things that are tougher for you — perhaps questions on prose or drama.

You get the same number of points for any question you answer correctly. Go for the easy ones, and return to the difficult questions later. And even then, be sure to answer only those for which you can make an educated guess.

Sleep

Yes, I'm serious: I want you to sleep to increase your know-how. During the school year, you may be tempted to burn the candle at both ends, while toasting the middle over a roaring campfire. And guess what will happen if you do? You'll burn out. Need I mention that cinders and piles of ashes have very little brain power? Students who have to prop their eyes open with toothpicks during the AP exam probably won't produce their best work. And I'm not just talking about AP week or even test day; I'm talking about the whole school year. Yes, you have to get your homework done if it's humanly possible. (And if it isn't, you're overcommitted and need to cut back on your academic or extracurricular load.) However, staying up all night to study for an exam or to instant message the entire senior class is counterproductive. The moral of the story: When you're tired, go to sleep. Wake up and hit the books as needed, but don't deprive yourself of sack-time.

Part VII
Appendixes

The 5th Wave   By Rich Tennant

"In preparation for the AP English Literature
test, I've focused my reading on books
reflecting a common idea: that they end
in fewer than 200 pages."

In this part . . .

To fill the spare slots that gape in your daily planner (.0009 seconds a day, right?), you may want to read some great literature. Appendix A describes novels, plays, and poems that have graced the "suggested works" list provided by the AP exam writers for the open-ended essay. You've probably read some, but you may find more that interest you. Appendix B is a quick review of grammar. Like the one in your body, this appendix isn't really necessary. You can ignore it unless something goes wrong. However, If grammar ails you, I suggest that you spend some quality time with Appendix B.

Appendix A

Literary Works

Can I interest you in a good book? How about a hundred? Maybe a play or a slab of poetry? Whatever your taste, something in this appendix should interest you. At one time or another, the College Board has listed all these works (and more) as possible choices for the third, open-ended essay on the AP English Literature and Composition exam. (For more information on preparing for the open-ended essay, turn to Chapter 14.) You don't have to read all or even any of these works. Personally, though, I believe that every book here merits your time and attention because each features beautiful writing, wisdom and insight, and interesting and timeless subject matter. (In case you were wondering why I became an English teacher . . . .)

The list in this appendix is divided by genre and includes novels, plays (written in both prose and verse), and poetry. The titles are alphabetized, though I ignored "a," "an," and "the" when I put them in order. I include the author, date of publication or performance, and a sentence or two about each.

I assume that you've developed your own standards for quality literature. Not every work on this list may meet those standards. For example, words that you can't use in polite company appear in some of these books. Others may describe situations that make you uncomfortable. I decline the role of censor, so consider yourself warned that you should proceed at your own risk. Check my description, ask a trusted teacher or librarian, or thumb through a work before you decide to read it. However, you will find that this list contains enough variety to suit everyone.

Poetry

***Iliad* (Homer, 7th–8th century BCE):** One of the oldest poems, Homer's *Iliad* describes the war — in exquisite and excruciating detail — between the Greeks and the Trojans. If you've read any Greek mythology, you'll recognize these characters: Achilles, Paris, Hector, Agamemnon, Odysseus, and many others.

"The Love Song of J. Alfred Prufrock" (T.S. Eliot, 1915): A dramatic monologue, this poem portrays the restlessness and disconnection that many see as a key facet of modern life. The speaker invites the reader: "Let us go then, you and I." Then the speaker takes the reader through rooms where people "come and go / talking of Michelangelo" but never really communicate.

***Odyssey* (Homer, 7th–8th century BCE):** Odysseus has many adventures as he travels home from the Trojan War. Meanwhile, his loyal wife Penelope and his son Telemachus gamely fend off the suitors who are trying to steal Odysseus's wife and kingdom.

***The Rape of the Lock* (Alexander Pope, 1612):** A mock epic, this poem details how a lovesick young man cuts a lock of hair from the head of his beloved; the poem also describes the ensuing feud between the families of the pair. Based on a real incident, the poem was written as an attempt to reconcile the families.

Novels

***The Adventures of Huckleberry Finn* (Mark Twain, 1884):** This is the classic American road trip novel: Huck and escaped slave Jim travel by raft down the Mississippi. Woven through Huck and Jim's adventures are serious themes: coming of age, Huck's maturation, and race relations.

***All the King's Men* (Robert Penn Warren, 1946):** This novel describes a Southern politician's rise from poverty to the governor's mansion. The story is told by a staff member who's willing to cheat and blackmail to consolidate his boss's power. The moral landscape is complicated by the fact that the politician genuinely tries to help the poor.

***As I Lay Dying* (William Faulkner, 1930):** The Bundren family takes a horrific journey to bury a deceased relative. During their journey, the family questions family ties, tradition, the nature of existence, and the impossibility of human communication. The novel has many narrators, so keep a scorecard handy as you read.

***The Autobiography of an Ex-Colored Man* (James Weldon Johnson, 1912):** The son of a white man and a black woman, who's also known as the "ex-colored man," narrates his path from a little boy unaware of race to his decision as an adult to "pass" as white. Johnson criticizes race relations and addresses issues of identity and justice.

***The Awakening* (Kate Chopin, 1899):** *The Awakening* is an early feminist classic: The wife of a staid businessman leaves her home, family, and marriage for an affair. Later she drowns — perhaps a suicide. Women's roles, the nature of marriage, individual desires, destiny versus obligation, and the role of art are all themes.

***Beloved* (Toni Morrison, 1987):** An escaped slave kills her child rather than see the baby live in slavery. Elements of magical realism (the child returns) illuminate the process by which people recover from traumatic events. Themes include the power one should or shouldn't have over others, racial identity, and the role of community.

***Catch 22* (Joseph Heller, 1961):** If you're sane enough to want out of the army, you're too sane for a discharge by reason of insanity — the "Catch 22" of the title. Set during World War II, the novel criticizes the military, war, bureaucracy, and pretty much everything else.

***The Catcher in the Rye* (J.D. Salinger, 1951):** Holden Caulfield narrates his odyssey in New York City after he's expelled from school. Searching for innocence and hating "phonies," Holden gradually disintegrates as he parties, visits his little sister, and realizes that everything changes over time.

***The Color Purple* (Alice Walker, 1982):** Celie, a woman raised by an abusive father and married off to an abusive husband, writes letters to God and to her sister, Nettie. Even though Celie suffers, she becomes stronger through her relationship with Shug, her husband's mistress, and other friends. Gender roles and the power of friendship are key.

***A Farewell to Arms* (Ernest Hemingway, 1929):** Set in Italy during World War II, this novel follows the relationship between an ambulance driver and his lover. War, love during wartime, and gender roles are all important themes.

***Frankenstein* (Mary Shelley, 1817):** *Frankenstein* isn't just a monster story! Shelley's famous tale of a scientist who fabricates life considers the responsibility of the creator for the created, the effect of society on an innocent individual, the nature of learning, and a host of other ideas. You'll be left wondering who the real monster is.

***Great Expectations* (Charles Dickens, 1860–1861):** Working-class orphan Pip meets an eccentric rich lady and the beautiful Estella. His expectations change, especially after he hears that a mysterious benefactor will fund his transformation into a gentleman.

***The Great Gatsby* (F. Scott Fitzgerald, 1925):** In this "Roaring Twenties" tale, Jay Gatsby yearns for the love of his youth. When she reappears — married — the relationship between Jay and his beloved becomes complicated and tragic. The nature of the American Dream, the role of wealth, and the ability of people to reinvent themselves are central to this story.

***Gulliver's Travels* (Jonathan Swift, 1626):** Gulliver visits four fantastic lands — one populated by tiny creatures, one by giants, one by philosophers living on a floating island, and one ruled by intelligent horses. These strange creatures are vehicles for criticism of human nature, culture, and society. The tone is harshly satiric.

***Heart of Darkness* (Joseph Conrad, 1899):** Set in London and the Congo during the era of colonization, this novel explores the nature of "civilization" as a European company exploits Africans. One employee, Kurtz, lives in the interior of Africa and abandons European customs. Themes include colonialism and the definition of civilization.

***Invisible Man* (Richard Wright, 1952):** The title character, an African American man, tells the story of his life, beginning in a Southern college and moving through his experiences in a Northern factory, a protest movement, and finally as an "invisible" man living underground. Alienation, racism, and the risks of rigid belief systems are all themes here.

***Jane Eyre* (Charlotte Brönte, 1847):** Orphan Jane, after a difficult childhood, becomes governess to the ward of Mr. Rochester. And then there's that strange noise in the attic . . . Though this is a serious coming-of-age story, it's also an intriguing mystery and romance.

***The Joy Luck Club* (Amy Tan, 1989):** Tan's novel follows four pairs of mothers and daughters, all Chinese American. The pairs see things differently (what else is new?), but some resolve their conflicts and grow closer to each other. Immigrants' struggles, family relationships, the importance of culture, and the effect of assimilation are key.

***The Lord of the Flies* (William Golding, 1954):** A plane crashes after an unexplained global disaster, and two bands of boys find that they're alone on a mysterious island. Their efforts to form a society, the gradual dissolution of civilized behavior, and a killer ending make this one worth your time.

***The Metamorphosis* (Franz Kafka, 1915):** Gregor wakes up one morning and finds that he has become a giant bug. His family isn't happy, his boss fires him, and he struggles to survive. Symbols abound in this novella.

***Moby-Dick* (Herman Melville, 1851):** Captain Ahab has a wooden leg; his flesh-and-blood limb was lost fighting Moby-Dick, a legendary white whale. Now Ahab wants revenge. The nature of obsession is Topic A here. This book is great for "man-against-nature" essays.

***Mrs. Dalloway* (Virginia Woolf, 1925):** A society woman throws a party while a shell-shocked veteran disintegrates. These characters don't know each other and never meet, but their stories entwine as Woolf considers memory, choices, war and its aftermath, and other all-important themes.

***A Portrait of the Artist as a Young Man* (James Joyce, 1916):** Stephen Daedalus grows up and is faced with a decision between religion and art. Given the title, guess which one he chooses? However, the point of this book is the forces that shape one's destiny, creativity, and outlook on life. The novel attempts an answer.

***Pride and Prejudice* (Jane Austen, 1813):** The five Bennet daughters have little dowry, an unconcerned father, and an idiotic mother who schemes to find marriage partners for all of them. This comedy of manners is serious about female power, hypocrisy and sincerity, and the human tendency to, well, pride and prejudice.

***The Scarlet Letter* (Nathaniel Hawthorne, 1850):** Hester Prynne has a baby out of wedlock. Who's the father? She's not talking, but as she wears a scarlet letter A embroidered on her clothes, she gradually achieves redemption. The father, on the other hand . . . Read it and see.

***Their Eyes Were Watching God* (Zora Neale Hurston, 1937):** Janie has three husbands in this novel, and each relationship teaches her something about life. Hurston, an anthropologist as well as a novelist, paints a realistic portrait of an African American community in the early 20th century. This novel is also a classic coming-of-age story.

***Things Fall Apart* (Chinua Achebe, 1959):** The main character lives in a pre-colonial African village. His family's disgrace and redemption are described as well as the European colonizers' clueless view of African customs. Colonialism, father-son relationships, gender roles, and the definition of civilization are important in this book.

***Wuthering Heights* (Emily Brönte, 1847):** Heathcliff, a foundling child, falls hard for Cathy, but this novel isn't a love story. Instead, the novel traces a history of obsession and revenge through several generations. The brooding setting adds atmosphere.

Plays

***Antigone* (Sophocles, 5th century BCE):** A classic Greek drama, this play centers on the conflicts between God and the state and nation and family. The title character buries her traitorous brother despite the ruler's prohibition. Her "crime" is justified, she believes, because the gods mandate burial of the dead and because she has a familial obligation.

***The Crucible* (Arthur Miller, 1952):** Set during the Salem witch hunt, this play actually attacks the Red Scare of 1950s America. Miller's hero, John Proctor, is asked to sign a false confession in order to save his life, but Proctor refuses to compromise his name. The power of the state, individual conscience, and husband-wife conflict are key.

***Dancing at Lughnasa* (Brian Friel, 1990):** The narrator of this play is Michael Munday, an adult reflecting on the summer when he was seven years old. The relationships between the five Munday daughters and one son are explored. Themes include tradition/change, Irish identity, and family conflict.

***A Doll's House* (Henrik Ibsen, 1879):** In *A Doll's House,* Nora, a devoted wife, forges a signature to obtain a loan that will pay for the lifesaving cure her husband needs. When someone threatens to expose the fraud, the strains in Nora's marriage, the shallowness of her life, and two opposing views of morality are revealed.

***The Glass Menagerie* (Tennessee Williams, 1944):** Imagine it: You've got a Southern Belle mother, a shy daughter, and a new guy who visits. Sounds like trouble, and it is. Important issues: the nature of memory, idealized vision of the past, parental expectations, and family relationships.

***Hamlet* (Shakespeare, 1600–1602):** *Hamlet,* the greatest Shakespearean tragedy, takes you into the mind of the title character, who's charged with avenging his father's murder.

Appearance/reality, mortality, human will, emotion/intellect/action, justice, and a host of other important ideas show up in this play.

***Joe Turner's Come and Gone* (August Wilson, 1988):** This play details the so-called "Great Migration" of African Americans from the South to Northern cities at the beginning of the 20th century. The protagonist, Harold, is searching for his wife but also for his own identity. Themes considered include memory, identity, and one's relation to the past.

***A Long Day's Journey into Night* (Eugene O'Neill, 1957):** This play is a family party that you'd rather not attend: the Tyrone family includes a morphine addict, an alcoholic, and a tuberculosis victim, as well as a strong tendency to fight the same battles over and over again. They're all imprisoned in the past.

***Macbeth* (Shakespeare, 1603–1606):** A war hero who's the title character of this play is tempted by predictions from three witches that he will become king. Initially against the idea, Macbeth bows to his wife's pressure and murders King Duncan. It's all downhill from there as the Macbeths descend into madness and evil.

***Man and Superman* (G.B. Shaw, 1903):** Based loosely on the Don Juan legend, Shaw's play concerns John Tanner, a confirmed bachelor and, well, a Don Juan. As in *Pygmalion* (another tirade against marriage), this play considers the effect of societal norms on male and female behavior.

***Medea* (Euripides, 5th century BCE):** When abandoned by her husband, Jason, Medea plots revenge. In fact, she isn't above killing her children just to make Jason suffer more. This play proves that the ancient Greeks understood obsessive love, jealousy, and vengeance every bit as much as Hollywood does.

***Murder in the Cathedral* (T.S. Eliot, 1935):** The real-life murder of Archbishop Thomas Becket is the source for Eliot's drama, which details the struggle between individual conscience and secular power. Becket is visited by three tempters who try to lure him away from his convictions. They fail and he dies, poetically.

***Oedipus Rex* (Sophocles, 5th century BCE):** The drama by which all other dramas are measured, this play illustrates the downfall of Oedipus, once the savior and now the ruler of Thebes, who unwittingly killed his own father and married his mother. The themes of fate, free will, the will of the gods, and human ignorance have never been better explained.

***The Piano Lesson* (August Wilson, 1987):** Should you sell an heirloom piano? Not if it's haunted. In this play, a family argues about whether to get rid of the piano, which is decorated with carvings representing the faces of their enslaved ancestors. African American identity and heritage top the list of important themes here.

***A Raisin in the Sun* (Lorraine Hansberry, 1959):** An African American family buys a home, and their neighbors try to bribe them into moving out of the white neighborhood. Issues include the importance of dreams and the need to combat prejudice.

***Rosencrantz and Guildenstern Are Dead* (Tom Stoppard, 1967):** Stoppard reinvents *Hamlet* by focusing on two minor characters from Shakespeare's play who are killed by Hamlet almost as an afterthought. Their lives, however, are not an afterthought to Rosencrantz and Guildenstern, who are puppets of forces beyond their control.

***Trifles* (Susan Glaspell, 1916):** In this short play that packs a punch, two women wait in the kitchen of a farmhouse where a man has been murdered by his wife. While the sheriff investigates upstairs, the women discover the small, domestic items that identify the woman's motive for the crime.

***Twelfth Night* (Shakespeare, 1600–1602):** A woman pretending to be a man falls in love with a man (Orsino) who sends her as his love emissary to another woman, Viola, who falls in love with the woman messenger that she thinks is a man. Confused yet?

***Waiting for Godot* (Samuel Beckett, 1949):** Two tramps sit on a bare stage and wait for Godot (a stand-in for God) and illustrate existentialist philosophy while trading hugely entertaining wisecracks. They discuss religion, the meaning of existence, and lots of other stuff. Interpretations abound.

***Who's Afraid of Virginia Woolf* (Edward Albee, 1962):** A drunken foursome — two married couples — spend the evening quarreling. Eventually the tragedy at the heart of the older couple's life is revealed. (No, I won't tell you what it is.) Dreams, the lies people tell themselves, and spousal relationships are all illustrated by this play.

Appendix B

Quick Grammar Review

Grammar. It's a little word, but it's a big headache. Don't worry, though. This appendix is the aspirin. If you're a little rusty on any topic, check out the examples and the rules I include here. Just don't forget to apply them when you write your AP English essay.

Grammar rules and examples could fill a whole book. (As a matter of fact, I've personally filled two whole books: *English Grammar For Dummies* and *English Grammar Workbook For Dummies,* both published by Wiley.) But here I have only a few pages, so I concentrate on the essentials that often trip up AP exam takers.

Complete Sentences versus Fragments and Run-Ons

When you're writing a novel or a poem or anything informal, you're allowed to write *fragments* (incomplete sentences) or *run ons* (more than one sentence improperly joined). In a proper AP English essay, however, you should stick to complete sentences, which need the following:

- ✔ A *verb* (a word expressing action or state of being)
- ✔ A *subject* (whoever or whatever is doing the action or is in the state of being)
- ✔ A complete thought

Here's what I mean:

> **Fragment:** Because I painted each toe a different color.
>
> **Why it's a fragment:** You have a subject ("I") and a verb ("painted"), but the word "because" implies cause and effect, and no effect is stated.
>
> **Sentence:** Because I painted each toe a different color, my feet attracted attention.
>
> **Run-on:** I painted each toe a different color, my feet attracted attention.
>
> **Why it's a run-on:** Two complete thoughts are linked only by a comma. Penalty box! A comma isn't allowed to join sentences.
>
> **Sentence:** I painted each toe a different color; my feet attracted attention.
>
> **Another sentence:** I painted each toe a different color, and my feet attracted attention.

These words are often mistakenly used to link two complete thoughts: "nevertheless," "consequently," "however," "then," and "furthermore." Feel free to employ these perfectly good words in your writing, though. Just insert a semicolon as an officially approved link:

> My pink pinky broke when I stubbed it; however, my turquoise big toe was fine.

Noun-Verb and Noun-Pronoun Agreement

"Agreement" is the English teacher term for the rule that singular goes with singular and plural goes with plural. They don't mix, ever. Agreement problems crop up when you're choosing a verb or a pronoun. I explain both situations in the following sections.

Subject-verb agreement

When subjects and verbs pair off, the mating may be smooth or disastrous. (Quite a few parallels to human pairing, don't you think?) Here are some examples of correct matches:

> My feet are drying under the sun lamp. ("Feet" is a plural subject and "are drying" is a plural verb.)

> My left foot is burning. ("Foot" is a singular subject and "is burning" is a singular verb.)

Agreement problems often appear when something intrudes between the subject and the verb:

> **Incorrect pairing:** My right foot, as well as Oscar's and Melinda's feet, are toasty.

> **Why it's incorrect:** The expression "as well as Oscar's and Melinda's feet" interrupts the true subject-verb pair. Grammatically, it isn't a factor when you match a verb to "foot."

> **Correction:** My right foot, as well as Oscar's and Melinda's feet, is toasty. ("Foot" is a singular subject and "is" is a singular verb.)

Mistakes abound when these interrupters appear: "as well as," "along with," "in addition to," "not including," and "except." Ignore the intruders, no matter what form they take. Simply match the subject and the verb, singular to singular and plural to plural.

Sentences with "either/or" and "neither/nor" have two subjects. They're simple, if you have a ruler or even a finger handy. Simply match the verb to the closest subject. Check out these examples:

> Neither Ella nor her parents were happy with the new apartment. (The plural subject "parents" matches the plural verb "were.")

> Either her parents or Ella is planning major renovations. (The singular subject "Ella" matches the singular verb "is planning.")

Pronoun agreement

Pronouns can also create agreement problems. These pronouns are always singular and, when they're subjects, always take singular verbs: "either," "neither," "each," "every," "one," "anyone," "no one," "someone," "everyone," "anything," "nothing," "something," "everything," "anybody," "nobody," "somebody," "everybody." To make your life even more miserable, any pronoun referring to one of these singular pronouns must also be singular. Here are some examples:

> Each of the shoes is covered with mud, especially on its toe. ("Each" is a singular pronoun, "is" is a singular verb, and "its" is a singular pronoun referring to "each.")

Everybody is required to bring his or her cheat sheet to the exam. ("Everybody" is a singular pronoun, "is required" is a singular verb, and "his or her" is a singular pronoun expression.)

A very common mistake is to pair "everybody" with "their." I sympathize. "Everybody" sounds like a plural word, but it's actually singular. Think for a moment; you don't say "everybody are here." You say "everybody is here." Singular all the way!

A real pronoun-agreement headache strikes when you're talking about "one of the" or "the only one." (This type of sentence is a pronoun issue, though the problem comes when you select a matching verb.) Scan this sentence:

George is one of the boys who (think/thinks) the Yankees are unbeatable.

The key to solving this sort of puzzle is to figure out the meaning of "who." After you know whether "who" is singular or plural, the verb choice is a cinch. Use logic. For instance, according to the sentence, who thinks the Yankees are unbeatable? Some boys do. "Boys" is a plural, so "who" is plural, as is the verb:

George is one of the boys who think the Yankees are unbeatable.

Contrast the preceding example with this sentence:

George is the only one of the boys who (think/thinks) Jeter is a great shortstop.

Apply logic again. Who thinks Jeter is a great shortstop? According to the sentence, only George. Therefore "who" must refer to George and must be singular, paired with a singular verb:

George is the only one of the boys who thinks Jeter is a great shortstop.

By the way, I also think Derek Jeter is a great shortstop. Sadly, I realize that the Yanks sometimes lose.

Pronoun Case

Case is the term English teachers apply to the quality that distinguishes between "who," "whom," and "whose," "he," "him," and "his," and "they," "them," and "their." The pronouns divide into these three sets:

Subject pronouns: I, you, he, she, it, we, they, who, whoever

Object pronouns: me, you, him, her, it, us, them, whom, whomever

Possessive pronouns: my, mine, your, yours, his, her, hers, its, our, ours, their, theirs, whose

The rules governing these pronouns are fairly simple: Use subject pronouns as subjects, possessive pronouns to indicate ownership, and object pronouns for everything else. Objects show up in many different situations; don't waste your time learning all of them. The process of elimination works fine. If you don't need a subject or a possessive, go for an object.

In simple sentences, the proper pronoun nearly always leaps naturally from your pen. Errors occur in complicated sentences. So uncomplicate your life by untangling a difficult sentence into its component thoughts. Then you generally "hear" the right answer, as in this example:

Complicated sentence: Jenny, (who/whom) I think is the best candidate, will never win the election.

Untangled: (1) Jenny will never win the election (2) I think (3) who/whom is the best candidate

Right choice: who

After you compare "who is the best candidate" with "whom is the best candidate" the choice is a no-brainer.

Pronoun Clarity

Earlier in this appendix, I explain how to choose a singular or plural pronoun and how to stay in the correct case. In this section, I tackle clarity, which is arguably more important in an AP essay than any other factor. Why? Because if the graders can't figure out what you're saying, you're in trouble.

One problem shows up when the sentence refers to two males or two females, as in the following sentence:

Gertrude and Ophelia discuss her relationship with Hamlet.

Whose relationship are we talking about? The Gertrude-Hamlet relationship or the Ophelia-Hamlet one? Beats me. The sentence gives no clue. Corrections for this error may be simple-but-clunky or they may call for a complete rewrite:

Simple but clunky: Gertrude and Ophelia discuss Ophelia's relationship with Hamlet.

Why it's clunky: Placing *Ophelia* and *Ophelia's* next to each other is repetitious.

Smoother rewrite: Gertrude and Ophelia discuss the girl's relationship with Hamlet. (Gertrude, Hamlet's mother, is too old to be a girl.)

The pronouns "this," "that," and "which" also tend to muddle your essay. Check out this example:

Muddled sentence: The king kneels to pray, and Hamlet decides not to kill him, which is a problem.

Why it's muddled: What's the problem? That the king is praying, or that Hamlet decides not to kill him?

Correction: The problem is that Hamlet decides not to kill the kneeling, prayerful king.

The preceding "muddled" sentence is illegal for another reason too. According to the laws of grammar (which are enforced by legions of English teachers), a pronoun may replace a noun (a person, place, or thing) or another pronoun. A pronoun isn't allowed to replace a subject-verb pair, a sentence, or anything else. In the "muddled" sentence, "which" refers to "The king kneels to pray," to "Hamlet decides not to kill him," or to both. Verdict: two years of hard labor in the grammar penitentiary.

Verb Tense

This topic isn't a discussion of how you feel when you enter the exam room. In the context of grammar, *tense* means time, as in when the action happened, is happening, or will happen. You have very few tense decisions to make in an AP English essay because by tradition, literature is discussed in present tense. If you're writing an essay centered on one event in a novel, play, or poetic narrative, opt for present tense when you're talking about that event:

> Hamlet fights Laertes, who wounds Hamlet, and in turn is wounded by Hamlet. Gertrude, unaware of Claudius's schemes, drinks from the poisoned cup.

Here's one exception to the present-tense-for-literature rule: Anything earlier than the key event you're discussing may be in past tense. For example:

> Before the duel, Hamlet enraged Laertes by killing Polonius. Laertes also blames Hamlet for his sister's madness. Earlier, Laertes was so angry that he fought Hamlet at his sister's grave.

If your essay ranges over several events, stay with present tense, as in the following lines:

> Hamlet feigns madness when he confronts Ophelia in her private room and later when he spars with Polonius. His behavior during the play-within-a-play scene also borders on madness, as he interrupts the actors.

Two words, "has" and "have," may indicate action begun in the past and continuing in the present:

> Hamlet has agonized about his inaction, and in this soliloquy he berates himself again.

> Rosencrantz and Guildenstern have attempted to win Hamlet's trust several times, and Hamlet is bitter about their betrayal.

Adjective and Adverb Placement

Descriptive words or expressions belong near the words they describe so that the meaning is crystal clear. Take a look at these examples:

> Refined sugar works best in this recipe. ("Refined" describes "recipe.")

> A cup of sugar, refined or raw, should be added to the batter. ("Refined or raw" describes "sugar.")

> Stir the batter thoroughly. ("Thoroughly" describes "stir.")

> When the batter is smooth, pour it into the pan. ("When the batter is smooth" describes "pour.")

> The baseball, which had been caught by a Red Sox fan, was displayed in the museum. (The phrase "which had been caught by a Red Sox fan" describes "baseball.")

The general rule is easy to remember, but a couple of situations may trip you up:

Common mistake: Heating the sauce, the pan may tip.

Why it's a mistake: Who's heating the sauce? No one.

Correction: Heating the sauce, the cook should avoid tipping the pan.

Common mistake: Stirring the gravy frequently ruins the taste.

Why it's a mistake: What does "frequently" describe — how often the gravy is stirred or how often the taste is ruined? Because "frequently" is right in the middle of two, the sentence is unclear.

One possible correction: Stirring the gravy tends to ruin the taste. (Sometimes the best way to fix this sort of error is to change the descriptive word.)

Another possible correction: Frequent stirring of the gravy ruins the taste.

Common mistake: I paid for the fender I dented with a cashier's check.

Why it's a mistake: No matter what kind of check it is, a piece of paper can't dent a fender.

Correction: With a cashier's check, I paid for the fender I dented.

The word "only" should come with a warning label because it's misplaced so often. These sentences have different meanings, which I've placed in parentheses:

Only Ellen ate supper at home. (Her friends went to a restaurant.)

Ellen only ate supper at home. (She was in the house just for a few minutes, enough to scarf down a plate of spaghetti. Then she went out.)

Ellen ate only supper at home. (She dined out for breakfast and lunch.)

Ellen ate supper only at home. (She refused to eat supper at her friends' houses or in restaurants.)

Parallelism

Math fans and art majors, rejoice! Everything you know about parallel lines helps you avoid errors in parallelism when you're writing. Here's the deal: When you list ideas in a sentence, their formats need to be the same. Sounds simple, but in practice, parallel errors abound. For example, consider these:

Not parallel: Edward learns to speak softly, to carry a big stick, and how to communicate with wild animals.

Why it isn't parallel: Edward learns three things, all listed in the sentence. One has the word "how" tacked on, and the other two don't.

Parallel: Edward learns to speak softly, to carry a big stick, and to communicate with wild animals.

Another common parallelism problem stems from paired conjunctions. (A *conjunction* is a word that joins, such as "and," "but," "because," "since," and so on.) The pairs I'm talking about are "not only/but," "either/or," and "neither/nor." The rule is that anything these pairs join must have the same grammatical identity. You can link two sentences, two nouns, two adjectives, or two anythings, as long as you don't mix the pairs. Check these out:

Not parallel: Elizabeth not only danced all night, but she also sang the blues.

Why it isn't parallel: After "not only" you have "danced all night" — just a verb without a subject. After "but" you have a subject-verb pair: "she . . . sang."

Correction: Elizabeth not only danced all night but also sang the blues.

Why it's parallel: After "not only" comes a verb, "danced." After "but" comes a verb, "sang." Two verbs indicate parallelism.

Not parallel: Either I will go to the movies or to the mall.

Why it isn't parallel: After "either" comes a complete sentence: "I will go to the mall." After "or" you have only "to the mall," which isn't a complete sentence.

Correction: I will go either to the movies or to the mall.

Differentiating between Confusing Words

A few word pairs that frequent AP English essays come with built-in sand traps; they're just waiting for you to fall in. Be careful to use them correctly.

Affect / Effect The first is usually a verb, the second a noun:

Ahab's quest for the whale affects the sailors' lives.

Ahab's quest for the whale has an effect on the sailors' lives.

Uninterested / Disinterested The first means you don't care, the second means you're fair:

Ahab was relatively uninterested in the blue whale.

The disinterested narrator reports all sides of the story.

Its / It's The first is a possessive pronoun, and the second is a contraction of "it is":

Her plan is simple, but its execution is not.

It's obvious that her plan will fail.

Allusion / Illusion The first is a literary term, a reference to something outside the literary work. The second is a fantasy:

The allusion to the Declaration of Independence emphasizes the speaker's patriotism.

Willy clings to the illusion that he will again become a great salesman.

Speaker / Narrator The first is the "I" voice in poetry. The second is the "I" voice in prose:

In Dylan Thomas's poem "Fern Hill," the speaker is an older man reflecting on his childhood.

Melville's famous novel begins with the narrator's command: "Call me Ishmael."

Paragraph / Stanza The first is a division of prose (a novel, a story, or a nonfiction account), and the second is a division of a poem:

The first paragraph of the essay establishes the author's argument.

The third stanza marks a shift in poetic technique.

Index

subject-verb-complement, establishing, 68
subplots, 125
subtext, excavating, 35–36
subtopics
choosing, 46
creating for a poetry essay, 91
defined, 46
one paragraph for each, 174
in paired-passage essays, 222
placing in order, 29
"Success" (Dickinson), 251, 266–270
summarizing, the plot or meaning, 320
summary, in a memoir or biography, 149
summer reading, planning quality, 22
"Sunset in the Tropics" (Johnson, James Weldon), 226, 230–231
Swift, Jonathan
"A Modest Proposal", 159–160
Gulliver's Travels, 288–290, 335
symbolism
defined, 256
examples, 59
symbols
defined, 258, 300
described, 58
obviousness of, 59
quotations essential on, 172
revealing, 35–36
synecdoche
defined, 57
examples, 58
syntax
checking in a poem, 68
defined, 60, 68, 80, 163
in drama, 140
of a passage, 145
in a poem, 69–70
quotations essential on, 172
rhetorical techniques related to, 144
singling out grammatical structure in poetry, 80–82
in Sonnet 56, 119
untangling, 11
in "You Get What You Pay For", 115

syntax questions
described, 163–164
focus of, 81–82

● T ●

Tan, Amy
The Joy Luck Club, 335
technique, role of, 160–164
The Tenant of Wildfell Hall (Bronte, Anne), excerpt from, 162–163
ten-minute break, during the exam, 19
Tennyson, Alfred, Lord
"In Memorium A.H.H.", 65
tense
defined, 343
past, 48
present, 48, 195, 343
test center, time required at, 10
test day, showing up, 18–19
test preparation. *See* preparation
test site, finding an alternate route to, 25
text, analyzing in relation to the prompt, 174
textual knowledge, showing for the entire work, 214
theater
as a collaborative art, 138
going to, 328
Their Eyes Were Watching God (Hurston), 336
thematic approach, to paired-passage essays, 222–223
themed publications, topical research for, 326
themes
defined, 35
in dramatic works, 139
in fiction and drama, 137–138
identifying in a literary work, 137–138
imagery reinforcing, 82
in plays, 138
in a poem, 72
thesis
defined, 45
of an essay, 43

thesis statement(s)
constructing for an essay on a prose or drama passage, 168–169
creating, 29, 45–46
creating for a paired-passage essay, 221
creating for a poetry essay, 91
creating for an open-ended essay, 213
examples of good, 46
Things Fall Apart (Achebe), 336
third-person limited, 137
third-person omniscient, 137
third-person point of view, 137
"Thirteen Ways of Looking at a Blackbird" (Stevens), shifting reality of, 209
"This Living Hand" (Keats), poetic fragment, 60
Thoreau, Henry David, essay by, 179–180
time period, writing about, 321
timeline
constructing, 147
determining in a plot, 125
time-saving techniques, for the multiple-choice questions, 26–27
titles
of full-length works, 206
imagining for main-idea questions, 157
To Kill a Mockingbird (Lee), point of view in, 136
"To Lucasta, Going to the Wars" (Lovelace), 61–62
analyzing, 69–70
To the Lighthouse (Woolf)
important events placed in brackets, 36
issues in, 206
"To the Right Honourable William" (Wheatley), excerpt from, 65
tone
assessing in a story or novel, 134
checking diction to figure out, 253
defined, 60, 85
detached, 299

Notes

BUSINESS, CAREERS & PERSONAL FINANCE

0-7645-9847-3

0-7645-2431-3

Also available:
- Business Plans Kit For Dummies
  0-7645-9794-9
- Economics For Dummies
  0-7645-5726-2
- Grant Writing For Dummies
  0-7645-8416-2
- Home Buying For Dummies
  0-7645-5331-3
- Managing For Dummies
  0-7645-1771-6
- Marketing For Dummies
  0-7645-5600-2

- Personal Finance For Dummies
  0-7645-2590-5*
- Resumes For Dummies
  0-7645-5471-9
- Selling For Dummies
  0-7645-5363-1
- Six Sigma For Dummies
  0-7645-6798-5
- Small Business Kit For Dummies
  0-7645-5984-2
- Starting an eBay Business For Dummies
  0-7645-6924-4
- Your Dream Career For Dummies
  0-7645-9795-7

HOME & BUSINESS COMPUTER BASICS

0-470-05432-8

0-471-75421-8

Also available:
- Cleaning Windows Vista For Dummies
  0-471-78293-9
- Excel 2007 For Dummies
  0-470-03737-7
- Mac OS X Tiger For Dummies
  0-7645-7675-5
- MacBook For Dummies
  0-470-04859-X
- Macs For Dummies
  0-470-04849-2
- Office 2007 For Dummies
  0-470-00923-3

- Outlook 2007 For Dummies
  0-470-03830-6
- PCs For Dummies
  0-7645-8958-X
- Salesforce.com For Dummies
  0-470-04893-X
- Upgrading & Fixing Laptops For Dummies
  0-7645-8959-8
- Word 2007 For Dummies
  0-470-03658-3
- Quicken 2007 For Dummies
  0-470-04600-7

FOOD, HOME, GARDEN, HOBBIES, MUSIC & PETS

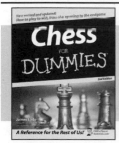

0-7645-8404-9

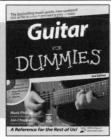

0-7645-9904-6

Also available:
- Candy Making For Dummies
  0-7645-9734-5
- Card Games For Dummies
  0-7645-9910-0
- Crocheting For Dummies
  0-7645-4151-X
- Dog Training For Dummies
  0-7645-8418-9
- Healthy Carb Cookbook For Dummies
  0-7645-8476-6
- Home Maintenance For Dummies
  0-7645-5215-5

- Horses For Dummies
  0-7645-9797-3
- Jewelry Making & Beading For Dummies
  0-7645-2571-9
- Orchids For Dummies
  0-7645-6759-4
- Puppies For Dummies
  0-7645-5255-4
- Rock Guitar For Dummies
  0-7645-5356-9
- Sewing For Dummies
  0-7645-6847-7
- Singing For Dummies
  0-7645-2475-5

INTERNET & DIGITAL MEDIA

0-470-04529-9

0-470-04894-8

Also available:
- Blogging For Dummies
  0-471-77084-1
- Digital Photography For Dummies
  0-7645-9802-3
- Digital Photography All-in-One Desk Reference For Dummies
  0-470-03743-1
- Digital SLR Cameras and Photography For Dummies
  0-7645-9803-1
- eBay Business All-in-One Desk Reference For Dummies
  0-7645-8438-3
- HDTV For Dummies
  0-470-09673-X

- Home Entertainment PCs For Dummies
  0-470-05523-5
- MySpace For Dummies
  0-470-09529-6
- Search Engine Optimization For Dummies
  0-471-97998-8
- Skype For Dummies
  0-470-04891-3
- The Internet For Dummies
  0-7645-8996-2
- Wiring Your Digital Home For Dummies
  0-471-91830-X

* Separate Canadian edition also available
† Separate U.K. edition also available

Available wherever books are sold. For more information or to order direct: U.S. customers visit www.dummies.com or call 1-877-762-2974.
U.K. customers visit www.wileyeurope.com or call 0800 243407. Canadian customers visit www.wiley.ca or call 1-800-567-4797.

WILEY

SPORTS, FITNESS, PARENTING, RELIGION & SPIRITUALITY

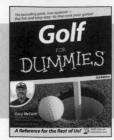

0-471-76871-5

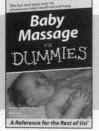

0-7645-7841-3

Also available:

- Catholicism For Dummies
  0-7645-5391-7
- Exercise Balls For Dummies
  0-7645-5623-1
- Fitness For Dummies
  0-7645-7851-0
- Football For Dummies
  0-7645-3936-1
- Judaism For Dummies
  0-7645-5299-6
- Potty Training For Dummies
  0-7645-5417-4
- Buddhism For Dummies
  0-7645-5359-3

- Pregnancy For Dummies
  0-7645-4483-7 †
- Ten Minute Tone-Ups For Dummies
  0-7645-7207-5
- NASCAR For Dummies
  0-7645-7681-X
- Religion For Dummies
  0-7645-5264-3
- Soccer For Dummies
  0-7645-5229-5
- Women in the Bible For Dummies
  0-7645-8475-8

TRAVEL

0-7645-7749-2

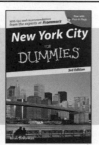

0-7645-6945-7

Also available:

- Alaska For Dummies
  0-7645-7746-8
- Cruise Vacations For Dummies
  0-7645-6941-4
- England For Dummies
  0-7645-4276-1
- Europe For Dummies
  0-7645-7529-5
- Germany For Dummies
  0-7645-7823-5
- Hawaii For Dummies
  0-7645-7402-7

- Italy For Dummies
  0-7645-7386-1
- Las Vegas For Dummies
  0-7645-7382-9
- London For Dummies
  0-7645-4277-X
- Paris For Dummies
  0-7645-7630-5
- RV Vacations For Dummies
  0-7645-4442-X
- Walt Disney World & Orlando
  For Dummies
  0-7645-9660-8

GRAPHICS, DESIGN & WEB DEVELOPMENT

0-7645-8815-X

0-7645-9571-7

Also available:

- 3D Game Animation For Dummies
  0-7645-8789-7
- AutoCAD 2006 For Dummies
  0-7645-8925-3
- Building a Web Site For Dummies
  0-7645-7144-3
- Creating Web Pages For Dummies
  0-470-08030-2
- Creating Web Pages All-in-One Desk
  Reference For Dummies
  0-7645-4345-8
- Dreamweaver 8 For Dummies
  0-7645-9649-7

- InDesign CS2 For Dummies
  0-7645-9572-5
- Macromedia Flash 8 For Dummies
  0-7645-9691-8
- Photoshop CS2 and Digital
  Photography For Dummies
  0-7645-9580-6
- Photoshop Elements 4 For Dummies
  0-471-77483-9
- Syndicating Web Sites with RSS Feeds
  For Dummies
  0-7645-8848-6
- Yahoo! SiteBuilder For Dummies
  0-7645-9800-7

NETWORKING, SECURITY, PROGRAMMING & DATABASES

0-7645-7728-X

0-471-74940-0

Also available:

- Access 2007 For Dummies
  0-470-04612-0
- ASP.NET 2 For Dummies
  0-7645-7907-X
- C# 2005 For Dummies
  0-7645-9704-3
- Hacking For Dummies
  0-470-05235-X
- Hacking Wireless Networks
  For Dummies
  0-7645-9730-2
- Java For Dummies
  0-470-08716-1

- Microsoft SQL Server 2005 For Dummies
  0-7645-7755-7
- Networking All-in-One Desk Reference
  For Dummies
  0-7645-9939-9
- Preventing Identity Theft For Dummies
  0-7645-7336-5
- Telecom For Dummies
  0-471-77085-X
- Visual Studio 2005 All-in-One Desk
  Reference For Dummies
  0-7645-9775-2
- XML For Dummies
  0-7645-8845-1

HEALTH & SELF-HELP

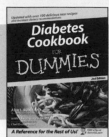

0-7645-8450-2

0-7645-4149-8

Also available:

- Bipolar Disorder For Dummies
  0-7645-8451-0
- Chemotherapy and Radiation
  For Dummies
  0-7645-7832-4
- Controlling Cholesterol For Dummies
  0-7645-5440-9
- Diabetes For Dummies
  0-7645-6820-5* †
- Divorce For Dummies
  0-7645-8417-0 †

- Fibromyalgia For Dummies
  0-7645-5441-7
- Low-Calorie Dieting For Dummies
  0-7645-9905-4
- Meditation For Dummies
  0-471-77774-9
- Osteoporosis For Dummies
  0-7645-7621-6
- Overcoming Anxiety For Dummies
  0-7645-5447-6
- Reiki For Dummies
  0-7645-9907-0
- Stress Management For Dummies
  0-7645-5144-2

EDUCATION, HISTORY, REFERENCE & TEST PREPARATION

0-7645-8381-6

0-7645-9554-7

Also available:

- The ACT For Dummies
  0-7645-9652-7
- Algebra For Dummies
  0-7645-5325-9
- Algebra Workbook For Dummies
  0-7645-8467-7
- Astronomy For Dummies
  0-7645-8465-0
- Calculus For Dummies
  0-7645-2498-4
- Chemistry For Dummies
  0-7645-5430-1
- Forensics For Dummies
  0-7645-5580-4

- Freemasons For Dummies
  0-7645-9796-5
- French For Dummies
  0-7645-5193-0
- Geometry For Dummies
  0-7645-5324-0
- Organic Chemistry I For Dummies
  0-7645-6902-3
- The SAT I For Dummies
  0-7645-7193-1
- Spanish For Dummies
  0-7645-5194-9
- Statistics For Dummies
  0-7645-5423-9

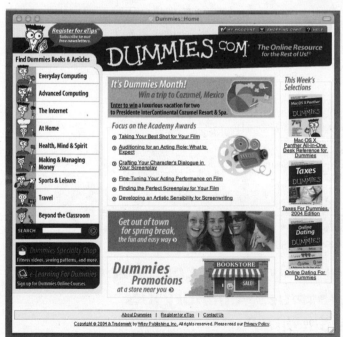

Get smart @ dummies.com®

- **Find a full list of Dummies titles**
- **Look into loads of FREE on-site articles**
- **Sign up for FREE eTips e-mailed to you weekly**
- **See what other products carry the Dummies name**
- **Shop directly from the Dummies bookstore**
- **Enter to win new prizes every month!**

* **Separate Canadian edition also available**
† **Separate U.K. edition also available**

Available wherever books are sold. For more information or to order direct: U.S. customers visit www.dummies.com or call 1-877-762-2974.
U.K. customers visit www.wileyeurope.com or call 0800 243407. Canadian customers visit www.wiley.ca or call 1-800-567-4797.